ARCHIVE WARS

Stanford Studies *in* Middle Eastern
and Islamic Societies *and* Cultures

ARCHIVE WARS

The Politics of History in Saudi Arabia

Rosie Bsheer

STANFORD UNIVERSITY PRESS
Stanford, California

STANFORD UNIVERSITY PRESS
Stanford, California

© 2020 by Rosie Bsheer. All rights reserved.

No part of this book may be reproduced or transmitted in any form or by any means, electronic or mechanical, including photocopying and recording, or in any information storage or retrieval system without the prior written permission of Stanford University Press.

Printed in the United States of America on acid-free, archival-quality paper

Library of Congress Cataloging-in-Publication Data

Names: Bsheer, Rosie, author.

Title: Archive wars : the politics of history in Saudi Arabia / Rosie Bsheer.

Other titles: Stanford studies in Middle Eastern and Islamic societies and cultures.

Description: Stanford, California : Stanford University Press, 2020. | Series: Stanford studies in Middle Eastern and Islamic societies and cultures | Includes bibliographical references and index.

Identifiers: LCCN 2019051739 (print) | LCCN 2019051740 (ebook) | ISBN 9781503605183 (cloth) | ISBN 9781503612570 (paperback) | ISBN 9781503612587 (ebook)

Subjects: LCSH: Archives—Saudi Arabia—History. | Historic preservation—Saudi Arabia. | Urban renewal—Saudi Arabia. | Saudi Arabia—History—Study and teaching. | Saudi Arabia—Historiography.

Classification: LCC DS222.92 .B74 2020 (print) | LCC DS222.92 (ebook) | DDC 026/.9538—dc23

LC record available at https://lccn.loc.gov/2019051739

LC ebook record available at https://lccn.loc.gov/2019051740

Cover art: Nasser Al Salem, *They Will Be Seen Competing In Constructing Lofty Buildings*, 2014, 58 x 90 x 35 cm

Cover design: Rob Ehle

Typeset by Newgen in Brill 10/14.4

In loving memory of Khalil Bsheer
(1949–1987)

Selection is a necessary feature of *any* historical story, and there can be no such thing as definitive or exhaustive history, however much space the historian takes to write about any passage of the past. What we select inevitably represents our interests, even if we aim all the while to "tell it like it really was." That is to say, there is inevitably something of "us" in the stories we tell about the past. This is the historian's predicament, and it is foolish to think there is some method, however well intentioned, that can extricate us from this predicament.

Steven Shapin, *The Scientific Revolution* (1996)

Contents

Preface xi
Acknowledgments xix
Note on Transliteration xxiii
List of Frequently Mentioned Institutions, Organizations, and Movements xxv

INTRODUCTION
The Archive Question 1

1 OCCLUDED PASTS 30

2 A STATE WITH NO ARCHIVE 60

3 ASSEMBLING HISTORY 89

4 HERITAGE AS WAR 127

5 BULLDOZING THE PAST 165

CONCLUSION
The Violence of History 208

Notes 233
Bibliography 323
Index 357

Preface

On September 6, 2004, Saudi Arabia's defense minister Sultan ibn Abdulaziz responded to media pundits with a most peculiar comment: "The Saudi government is committed to cooperating with the United States in the global war on terrorism. We have altered 7 percent of the content of our religious textbooks and removed all the objectionable material deemed offensive to other religions. We will continue to cooperate with the international community, but be advised . . . *we will never touch our history textbooks*. The consequences of doing so are too grave."[1] In the years following the September 11, 2001, al-Qaeda attacks on the United States, the US, European, and Israeli governments, and several of their think tanks, pressured the Saudi rulers to reform the country's religious education.[2] Religious textbooks, they charged, had produced violent subjects capable of committing heinous crimes. While they demanded the removal of the "bigoted content" from the religious textbooks, they made no mention of the country's official history; it remained outside the purview of international scrutiny. Yet the late Prince Sultan (d. 2011) felt the need to publicly draw a red line at disciplinary history, warning of the gravity of altering the historical narrative and not the ostensibly more salient religious one.

Even though the relationship between secular and religious powers in Saudi Arabia was often contentious, dissonance between the two was rarely publicized in such a manner, let alone to the detriment of religious discourse. I wondered what had compelled one of the most powerful rulers of the self-proclaimed Islamic

Saudi state—a religious conservative by all measures—to pronounce the regime's willingness to negotiate the official religious discourse—regardless of whether it eventually did or not—and not the historical one. Why was *history* suddenly so important? Surely the decision to make the Saudi Arabian national day, celebrated on September 23, an official public holiday a mere three months after Sultan's comments was no coincidence.[3] In the past, state clerics had opposed the move, as well as the official recognition of nonreligious events. This time, the royal order passed without incident, despite the unfamiliar fanfare and street celebrations that marked the event's first official commemoration in 2005. The order was one of many that subsequently countered conventional religious sensibilities in Saudi Arabia. Coupled with the defense minister's statement, the measures were striking. They privileged secular history and curbed the authority of the religious establishment. The measures also came on the heels of a major expansion project in the holy city of Mecca that saw the mass destruction of Islamic heritage. If history came to publicly matter in the opening years of the twenty-first century, clearly some histories mattered more than others.

I came across the defense minister's statement in 2005, while conducting research on the politics of historical production in Saudi Arabia. Initially, I traced shifts and elisions in the state-sanctioned historical discourse by exploring the different editions of Saudi Arabian history textbooks that the Ministry of Education had issued since the centralization of education in 1970. These shifts largely reflected developments in the political economy and the attendant requirements of Saudi Arabian subject formation. They also spoke to the protracted power struggles over the Ministry of Education, which state clerics had largely commanded. While oil, remarkably, is barely mentioned in history textbooks, and then only in the context of being a sign of God's blessing (*ni'ma*) on Al Saud, religion appeared to be a central unifying force. This remained the case throughout the 1980s and into the 1990s. In subsequent decades, however, the importance of religion to the making of the Saudi state and its citizens became less and less important. This challenged most of what I had read about Saudi Arabia until then, which prepared me even less for the realities I encountered on the ground when I moved there a few years later.

Navigating an unfamiliar research terrain as I traveled from the capital, Riyadh, to Mecca and Medina in the west and Qatif and Dhahran in the east impressed upon me just how present the past was in people's everyday lives. This was most visible in Riyadh, where a heritage industry—museums, archives, and historical sites—was well on its way, if still in the making, by the late 2000s. But it was also palpable in the hours-long discussions I had with the hundreds of Saudi Arabians who readily welcomed me into their homes and offices. No matter the topic or the interlocutor's political dispositions, the conversation always involved some discussion of the politics of the past. History, it seemed, was on everybody's minds, and many were eager to talk about it. My discussions with ordinary Saudi Arabians, intellectuals, activists, and journalists featured two interrelated issues that stood out as especially odd.

The first was a refrain that recurred regardless of one's class, profession, or political persuasion: "They," referring to Al Saud, "have no history." Even a high-ranking Saudi diplomat, surprised at my desire to conduct research in Saudi Arabia, asked: "What is there to study in Saudi Arabia?" Not waiting for an answer, he remarked, "We have no history." He was alluding to the idea that with one sanctioned historical narrative, there was nothing else to research. It was a futile endeavor. More often than not, the tone and intended meaning of the statement varied according to one's politics and view of the past. At times, the claim served to rationalize the state's grandiose investments in the production of historical artifacts and spaces in Riyadh. Accordingly, doing so necessitated and thus justified demolishing historical sites elsewhere. At other times, the charge was critical and disparaging of the violent politics of erasure that aimed to enshrine a singular history out of many.

If the politics surrounding Al Saud's history was the first issue, violence was the second. Indeed, violence was inseparable from any talk of history. Those who supported the regime and the state-sanctioned historical narrative regularly acknowledged the violence of forcing all Saudi Arabians to submit to one historical narrative. But after all, as those advocates were prone to point out, history is written by the victors, Al Saud, who were responsible for building a nation. Others were not as sympathetic to the project of constructing, let alone enshrining, a singular national history based solely on that of the monarchy. They framed their experiences of belonging to the Saudi nation, or lack thereof, through the lens of both history and violence. Jarring was the ease and regularity with which conversations about history slipped into testimonials about state violence, in its myriad forms. Muhammad, an eighty-year-old intellectual and longtime resident of Riyadh, gave me a tour of Medina, where he was born and came of age. His family was displaced twice as a result of the expansion of the Prophet's Mosque. Stories of dispossession such as that of Muhammad abound in the holy cities of Mecca and Medina, where space was limited and proximity to the main mosques was in high demand. But they were also common in once sparsely populated cities such as Riyadh and Jeddah.

Describing a life of struggle, Muhammad pointed to two hotel buildings across from the mosque, not far from each other, where the small apartments he lived in once stood: "They have taken away everything: our land, our livelihoods, our history. But we will never forget. At least they cannot take our memories away from us. Talk to families here and you will see. Our history is preserved right here," pointing to his head. Although oral traditions persisted throughout Arabia, people still attempted to safeguard their memories in more material ways. Muhammad, in fact, introduced me to two private archives where families had actually safeguarded their parents' and grandparents' records and artifacts. To preserve forbidden memories and occluded pasts, individuals and community neighborhoods elsewhere in the country also formed their own private archives. Most remained secret, indexing as they did unsanctioned histories of Arabia.

Encountering stories of loss and injustice became part of my research landscape on the making of history. Unsurprisingly, such stories dominated my conversations with over a few dozen former political prisoners I spoke with over the years. Without exception, they moved seamlessly between discussing history, historicity, and the preservation and destruction of historical sites, on the one hand, and political struggle and violence, on the other. Nassir recounted how, after sessions of electric shock and before daily interrogations started, his jailers made him say, "Al Saud are the crown of my head" (*Al Saud taj rasi*), followed by "I am garbage" (*ana huthala*). He once pointed out to them the irony of the combined phrases, which earned him a punch in the face. Nassir and his immediate family members were placed under house arrest and forbidden to leave the country years after his release. Two of his cousins were not as lucky; they remained in prison for joining a protest, their sentences extended more than once over the years. Nassir, bitter but hopeful, was invested in distancing himself from the regime. He retorted: "We are civilized people. We are not terrorists like the perpetrators of September 11, and we are not savages like those who rule the country. We have history. We do not need to spend millions on building historical spaces to prove to the world that we do." Maha's story ran along similar lines: "In prison, they tortured me. They humiliated me. They did everything but rape me, thank God for that. That's the only thing that got me through this ordeal. They call themselves Muslim! They are nothing. At least we have history. What do they have?"

It was impossible for many activists and intellectuals to disentangle the politics of historical production from sociopolitical struggle, past and present, and the violence they had endured. Where the physical violence had ceased, it was the symbolic violence they had to contend with, that of being in a place they increasingly felt alienated from. To be sure, understandings of history and its politics varied. But Saudi Arabians who dared fight for a different future largely agreed that historical production was one front in the broader war with those in power. They invariably found that not only were their presents devastated but also their pasts, their political struggles erased from the pages of history and the archives that contained them. During moments of great despair, when all was either lost or broken, the past was the only thing that many could still hold on to. But even in times of peace, it was their lifeline and their pride, what differentiated them from a regime that, in their eyes, had no history and had to pay in order to create one.

Even the most ardent regime supporters concurred, noting that Al Saud's was a "young monarchy" that needed to invest in mechanisms of historical legitimation. Little did they all know, at least then, the extent to which the regime went to commemorate, monumentalize, and commercialize the historical narrative the regime sanctioned. *Archive Wars* narrates the state's top-down material efforts to do exactly that while examining the role of material politics in both statecraft and the nature of power. Understanding the symbolic politics of writing official Saudi history as well as counternarratives to that history is necessary and important, and scholars have compellingly done that.[4] Yet archival, ethnographic, and oral history research in Saudi Arabia foregrounded the centrality of materiality—of documents, artifacts, buildings, and spaces—to the state's history-making project. Surely there was more to an Islamic state that actively destroyed ancient Islamic history and yet preserved that of a ruling family.

For three years, I followed the lifeworlds of historical documents. I traced the processes through which they were discovered; how they ended up in basements in several of Riyadh's archives, never to see the light of day; and how some were slated for preservation, digitization, and cataloging. I also conducted research in these very same archives, spending months at a time at the King Abdulaziz Foundation for Research and Archives (Darah), the Institute of Public Administration, and the King Fahd National Library. I mapped the collections at these institutions as well as the logic of how they were organized and made accessible to researchers, regularly interviewing archivists, historians, and those in charge of digitizing these collections. I perused the collections at the King Faisal Center for Research and Islamic Studies, the Arriyadh Development Authority, the Saudi Commission for Tourism and Antiquities (now the Saudi Commission for Tourism and National Heritage), the Mecca Development Authority, and the Custodian of Holy Shrines Institute for Hajj Research at Umm al-Qura University in Mecca. Through oral history interviews, I became closely acquainted with employees of these institutions and their storied careers.

In addition to tracking the evolution of historical records, I traced the making and unmaking of some of the most renowned spaces in Saudi Arabia. Concurrent with my research on archives, I shadowed planners, architects, engineers, and archeologists who worked on the redevelopment of historical sites in Riyadh as well as those who oversaw the complete overhaul of the Central District of Mecca. At the same time, I spent some time following community organizers and the struggles they fought with the state to renovate historical sites in their towns or cities, all of which had ended in failure. The ethnographies and oral histories I did were crucial for supplementing the official view and written documentation. They provided unique and critical insights into social, cultural, urban, and popular political life outside the purview of the state and its institutions. Combined, these methodologies have allowed me to pose new questions about Arabian history and politics since the late nineteenth century. They made it possible to critically probe the symbolic and material production of the state-sanctioned historical narrative and how it was being enshrined in the urban built environment.

I arrived in Saudi Arabia in the fall of 2009, a period of relative openness often referred to as *infitah*. As part of the Saudi state's attempt to improve its image abroad, some foreign researchers were permitted to enter the country. Saudi Arabian researchers continued to face the same severe limitations to conducting their research and accessing local archives—both of which were already circumscribed by academic advisers as per university rules. To my surprise, the institutions I worked with were more welcoming and supportive than many of those I had dealt with elsewhere in the world. I understood much later on that they had assumed I was a US citizen, indeed one with the "right" Ivy League credentials. In a country with a circumspect national, racial, gender, and class hierarchy, being a particular kind of "North American" was a privileged category. This is what many still refer to colloquially as the foreigner complex, or *'iqdat al-ajnabi*, which benefited certain non–Saudi Arabians over everyone else, citizens included. For a time, it seemed that this exclusionary system applied to archival access.

I also arrived in the country at a time when the struggle over the collection of archival documents was at its height. As a result, and because I was not affiliated as a researcher with a local institution, I found myself witness to a bidding war in which archivists reluctantly but competitively allowed me to observe the processes of collection, preservation, digitization, and, rarely, categorization. Along the way, I read uncategorized documents from the personal archives of former Saudi kings, crown princes, other ruling members of Al Saud, and state dignitaries. The records being digitized also included newspapers and a plethora of nonstate sources: pamphlets, letters, photographs, diaries, and other documents. In mid-2011, the challenges to accessing state archives reemerged. The Arab uprisings, and their local reverberations, had put state institutions on alert. Many archive employees became defensive and, in many cases, rightfully scared. They worried that they would be implicated in facilitating the work of researchers who might be critical of the regime. My sense at the time was that archival research would be foreclosed for the near future.

Archive Wars began as an exploration of questions of historical production and memorialization. In the final outcome, it is a window into the nature of power in Saudi Arabia and the continual practices of state formation. The sociopolitical mobilizations that Saudi Arabians have organized since the mid-twentieth century have informed the writing of the book, even if they do not factor in systematically. In many ways, *Archive Wars* is a history of the present, one that is all the more urgent given the heightened state of oppression that the country has experienced since Salman ibn Abdulaziz assumed the throne in 2015. While the research herein spans the nineteenth and twentieth centuries and the opening decade of the twenty-first, it only touches on developments in the archival and urban planning industries after 2015. Yet without intending to do so, the book explains Salman's rise to power and historicizes the vision he has long held for the country.

The Saudi state is authoritarian. But with each regime, the boundaries of what is permissible and what is not—what one can say or do, and not—shift and change. Under Salman's reign, restrictions on speech have reached levels not experienced since the 1960s. Saudi Arabian intellectuals, journalists, clerics, and activists are punished not simply for being critical of the regime but also for not actively showing support for the rulers. Silence itself has been criminalized. I have therefore anonymized the names of many interlocutors when discussing topics that may jeopardize their safety, even when the discussions we had were on the record. I have not done so where the gist of what is being said is already in the public domain and/or when those involved are in powerful positions in the current regime. Now more than ever, in the face of heightened repression coupled with historical revisionism, the imperative to remember, record, and document is urgent. Historicizing Saudi Arabia's archive wars is an effort to do exactly that.

Acknowledgments

In the past ten years, I accrued more debts than I can possibly repay. I am most grateful to the many Saudi Arabians who took me in and trusted my scholarly capabilities and curiosities despite my critical political convictions. Many of them opened their homes to me in al-ʿUlayya (in Riyadh), in al-Nahda (in Jeddah), in Tarout (in the Eastern Province), and in al-ʿAwali (in Mecca) as though to preemptively scuttle the feelings of isolation and vulnerability typical of any fieldwork experience. The company, camaraderie, and sense of humor of my hosts, interlocutors, and friends saw me through my time in Saudi Arabia. This could not have been truer or more necessary after the doom of the Saudi-led counterrevolution cast its shadow over the country when Saudi Arabia invaded Bahrain to crush the national uprising there on March 14, 2011. While their influence is evident throughout this book, I must keep their identities confidential and am thus unable to publicly express my gratitude and appreciation for all that they have taught me. M, in particular, first inspired my academic interest in Saudi Arabia without even knowing it. He remained supportive, inspiring, and intellectually curious until the very end.

I joined the editorial team of *Jadaliyya* in summer 2010 while doing research in Saudi Arabia. The many hours I spent working with authors and colleagues after long days at the archives and in meetings sustained me through the thick and thin of conducting primary research. Ziad Abu-Rish was doing his own research in

Lebanon, and together, we escaped our respective fieldworks' frustrations into the online world of *Jadaliyya*. Ziad has seen me through the many trials of academic life with the poise of a mentor, the empathy of a peer, and the commitment of a teammate. His integrity, generosity, and historian's craft are inspirational. From New York, John Warner was my night-light over video chat night after long night, when insomnia got the best of me as the 2011 uprisings brought much-needed but short-lived hope and excitement to the region. His boys, Idris and Zidan, are maintaining our tradition of regular long-distance communication and bring wonder and laughter to my life, even from afar. My brother and unwitting guardian, Hadi, whose time in Riyadh coincided with mine, gave our life much-needed levity and our diets excessive servings of steak, even as he managed not to spend a single weekend in the country. Sherene Seikaly has accompanied this manuscript from its infancy, and I have benefited immensely from her friendship, fierce intellect, and unfailing support. She is a true exemplar of intellectual rigor and political commitment, a historian's historian.

I was fortunate enough to receive the mentorship, wisdom, and unrivaled compassion of Anupama Rao, Rashid Khalidi, and Timothy Mitchell at Columbia University. I am reminded daily of their generosity, diligence, and engaged scholarship, which I can only hope to impart to students and colleagues. Lila Abu Lughod, Madawi Al-Rasheed, Peter Awn, Janaki Bakhle, Orit Bashkin, Richard Bulliet, Toby C. Jones, Daniel Magaziner, Mahmood Mamdani, Gwenn Okruhlik, Christine Philliou, Zainab Saleh, Fawwaz Traboulsi, and Robert Vitalis each influenced me, and this work, in crucial ways. For reading the whole manuscript and providing insightful feedback, I thank Ziad Abu-Rish, Sultan Alamer, Abbas Amanat, Fadi Bardawil, Fabian Drixler, Marwa Elshakry, Inderpal Grewal, Cemal Kafadar, Laleh Khalili, Ilham Khuri-Makdisi, Mary Lewis, Joanne Meyerowitz, Alan Mikhail, Derek Penslar, Nisreen Salti, Sherene Seikaly, Anders Stephanson, John Warner, John Willis, and the editors and anonymous reviewers at Stanford University Press. For commenting on specific chapters I presented at various institutions over the years, I thank Myriam Amri, Beth Baron, Aslı Bâli, Beshara Doumani, Arang Keshavarzian, Mandana Limbert, Zachary Lockman, Mohit Mandal, Afsaneh Najmabadi, Eve Troutt Powell, Deen Sharp, Susan Slyomovics, and Elizabeth Thompson. Chris Toensing moved this work forward with his nimble pencraft.

I received generous support for the research and writing of this book from several institutions and funding agencies: Swarthmore College's History Department, where I spent an exciting semester as a visiting professor; the Faculty Development Research Grant, Griswold Faculty Research Fund, MacMillan Center Faculty Research Grant, and the Frederick W. Hilles Publication Fund at Yale University; and the History Department at Harvard University, where I have already made lasting friendships and exciting intellectual connections. In Cemal Kafadar, I have found a most supportive colleague and mentor, a model of a politically committed intellectual. The conference that William Granara and Gareth Doherty organized, *Mecca: The Lived City*, was inspiring and connected me with an exciting group committed to documenting the city and the grave losses it has incurred.

Thanks are also due to other friends (some of whose last names I must conceal): Seth Anziska, Ashraf, Tareq Baconi, Bandar, Lama Bashour, Ahmed Dailami, Mona Damluji, Rohit De, Carolyn J. Dean, Fadel, Fawwaz, Ulrike Freitag, Hala, Ameen Hannoun, Hussam, Mustapha Jundi, Khalid, Mona Khalidi, Muna (née) Khalidi, Maha, Carol Mansour, Masha, May, Durba Mitra, Laura Poitras, Rasha, all the Saras, Francesca Trivelato, and Jeannette and Jim Zaza. I am especially grateful to the many strong women in Saudi Arabia who taught me how to navigate and thrive in a fraught, gender-segregated space. I could not have completed this book without them. Writing about Saudi Arabia, particularly during charged times such as these that are punctured with toxic hypernationalism, facile polemicism, and extensive surveillance, has cost me dear friendships. I am hopeful that this shall pass.

My mother was the first avid book lover in my life. Today, I add a volume to the shelves that she stocked so tenaciously, and against all odds, in my childhood. She and my sister have, in the face of the many blows that life has dealt them, treaded lithe and tall where most would have barely managed to trudge. They are the models of perseverance that have towed me through life's swamps. My childhood house would not have been a home without Nabiha. And while my family never got around to understanding the demanding nature of academic life, they accepted it nonetheless. They supported me through long absences as well as difficult temperaments when I did eventually join them. My three nephews and one niece were especially unfazed by it all. They kept me in check and dragged me away from my laptop whenever they could. Through it all, Nis has been my best critic and my rock, enduring several in- and out-of-state relocations with me, the challenges of adjusting to new academic institutions, and the missing out on life's many joys. It is one history I will certainly revise.

Note on Transliteration

This book follows a simplified version of the transliteration system of the *International Journal of Middle East Studies*, with modifications intended to keep the narrative accessible to all readers. I do not use diacritics or long vowel markers, with the exception of the glottal stop hamza (') and the pharyngeal fricative ayn ('). I nonetheless try to minimize these where possible (Ali not 'Ali, Abdullah not 'Abdullah). In the same vein, I use Abdulaziz and Abdulrahman, not 'Abd al-'Aziz or 'Abd al-Rahman, with the exception of Muhammad ibn Abd al-Wahhab (not Abdulwahhab). For common Arabic words that have entered the English lexicon, I use the conventional English spelling as recommended by *Merriam-Webster* (Quran, hajj). I also use the names of institutions or organizations as they would spell them and as they appear on the documents I perused, even if the names or the spelling have been altered or amended since I concluded my research (Saudi Binladin Group, Arriyadh Development Authority). Finally, I use "Al" to refer to "House of," as in Al Saud (House of Saud) and Al al-Shaykh (House of al-Shaykh).

Frequently Mentioned Institutions, Organizations, and Movements

Arabian American Oil Company (Aramco)
Arriyadh Development Authority (ADA)
Consultative Council (Majlis al-Shura)
Development of King Abdul Aziz Endowment Project (DOKAAE)
Hajj Research Center (HRC)
High Commission for the Development of Arriyadh (HCDA)
High Commission for the Development of Dir'iyya (HCDD)
High Commission for the Development of Mecca (HCDM)
Institute of Public Administration (IPA)
Islamic Awakening Movement (al-Sahwa al-Islamiyya)
King Abdulaziz Foundation for Research and Archives (KAFRA, better known as the Darah)
King Abdulaziz Historical Center (KAHC)
King Fahd National Library (KFNL)
King Faisal Center for Research and Islamic Studies (KFCRIS)
Mecca Development Authority (MDA)
Metropolitan Development Strategy for the Arriyadh Region (MEDSTAR)
Ministry of Municipal and Rural Affairs (MOMRA)
Muhammad Binladin Organization (MBO)
National Center for Documents and Archives (NCDA)

Public Investment Fund (PIF)
Saudi Arabian Oil Company (Aramco)
Saudi Binladin Group (SBG)
Saudi Commission for Tourism and Antiquities (SCTA)
Saudi Commission for Tourism and National Heritage (SCTH)
Supreme Commission for Tourism (SCT)
Two Holy Mosques Institute for Hajj Research

ARCHIVE WARS

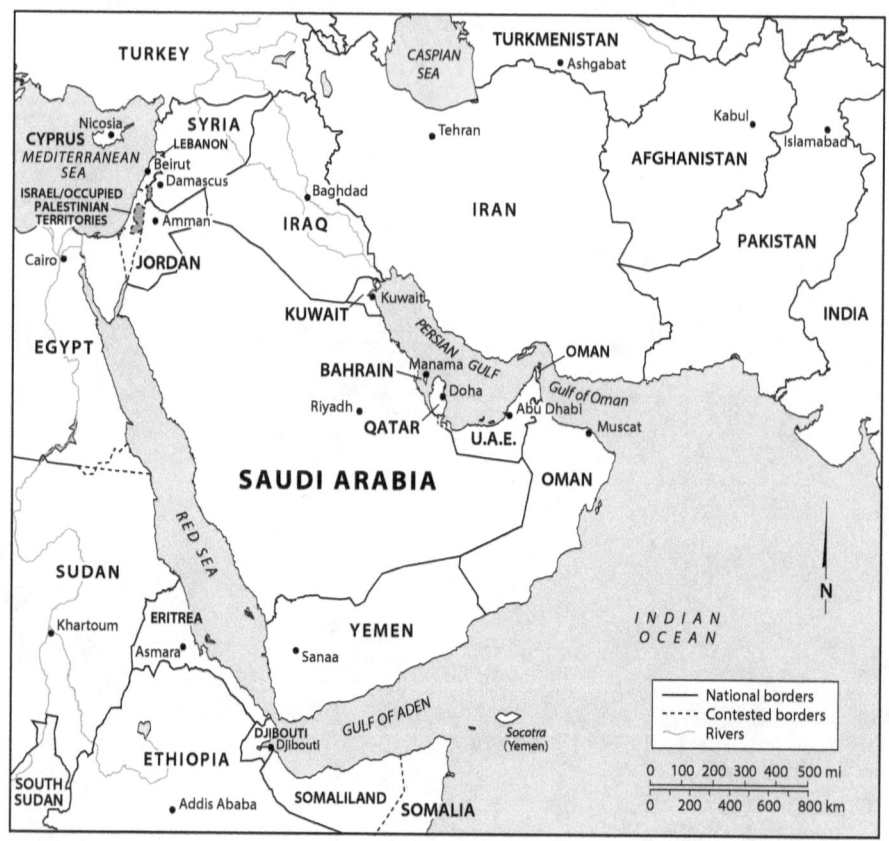

MAP 1. Saudi Arabia and its surrounding areas.

Introduction

THE ARCHIVE QUESTION

IN LATE 2010, BULLDOZERS WERE DEMOLISHING CENTURIES-OLD Ottoman-era architectural structures on the edges of the Grand Mosque in Mecca when the deafening scrape of metal on metal brought everything to a sudden halt. The South Asian laborers operating the heavy machinery were clearing ground as part of a multibillion-dollar mosque expansion. To the workers' surprise, they had unearthed twelve metal boxes holding sheaves of old documents and manuscripts.[1] The laborers scrambled to grab as many of the dusty records as they could. Within days, some of the rare materials turned up in the old markets of Jeddah, where a local collector purchased them. Many more appeared months later in the Cairo offices of a well-known document trader, who then traveled to Riyadh to sell the papers to state and private archives with which he had conducted business for more than ten years.

The highest bidders, who secured the bulk of the treasure trove, were the King Abdulaziz Foundation for Research and Archives—better known as the Darah—and the King Faisal Center for Research and Islamic Studies.[2] A few records made it to the King Fahd National Library. Competition between these and other state and private archives, coupled with a thriving black market in historical documents, authentic and forged, inflated the price of the documents and manuscripts. Each institution acquired what it could afford, often discovering several forgeries after the fact.³ What these repositories did not purchase ended up in smaller private collections across Saudi Arabia.

The initial inspection of the recovered materials revealed a random assortment of documents mostly related to Egyptian pilgrimage caravans to Mecca. Mixed into the collection, however, were documents concerning Muhammad ibn Abd al-Wahhab, the founder of the eighteenth-century Islamic movement that, along with the Al Saud clan, first conquered parts of the Arabian Peninsula in 1744.⁴ The Wahhabi movement was the progenitor of the Muslim clergy who have backed Al Saud since the clan established its rule across the peninsula again in 1932.⁵ It also inspired some of the Sunni Islamists who have been the ruling family's most caustic domestic critics. The Wahhabi movement's role in state formation is incontrovertible. Official pronouncements, school curricula, and state-sanctioned history acknowledge as much. Yet the collection about Ibn Abd al-Wahhab soon became a bone of contention. The Darah was holding an exhibition titled *Rare Manuscript Exhibition on Saudi Arabia*. The curators decided to showcase some of the newly purchased items but to exclude those about the original Wahhabi.⁶ Word of this suppression circulated among visitors at the exhibition. The Darah, some suggested, was up to its old tricks: deliberately concealing manuscripts that shed light on Ibn Abd al-Wahhab's role in the making of Al Saud's eighteenth-century emirate. They accused the Darah of rewriting history to the benefit of the ruling family alone. A brawl ensued at the exhibition between followers of Ibn Abd al-Wahhab who wanted his role shown prominently and Darah employees and supporters. Security personnel intervened to end it.

The embarrassment of this fracas notwithstanding, the documents' exhibition was an ironic success for the Darah. Under the tutelage of its chairman, Prince Salman ibn Abdulaziz, who was governor of Riyadh from 1954 to 2015, when he became king, the Darah had been consolidating its archival power. It capitalized on the rivalries between Riyadh's main archiving institutions to expedite the centralization of historical records on Saudi Arabia, scattered as they were across the country and the world. It had sponsored several countrywide marketing campaigns in the first decade of the twenty-first century to raise awareness of the importance of historical documents. This awareness had obviously filtered down from Saudi Arabia's political and intellectual elites to the construction workers in Mecca. As South Asians lacking citizenship, these workers were some of the kingdom's poorest and most vulnerable residents. They risked their livelihoods and deportation to sell the historical documents. Indeed, when news of the confrontation at the exhibition reached the contractor responsible for the expansion of the Grand Mosque, the company fired or disciplined everyone who had been working at the site that day.

As news of the incident spread, the politics of making Saudi Arabian history became a topic of debate in Riyadh's intellectual salons. A few conversations touched on the fledgling National Museum and other newly developed historical sites that were gradually becoming part of Riyadh's urban landscape. The state was spending millions to rehabilitate sites that were little more than ruins in order to bolster Al Saud's past. Many thought it was offensive, not to mention a waste of money. Yet the concomitant destruction of historical and religious spaces in and around Mecca's Grand Mosque did not elicit as much public condemnation as the Darah incident. The material life of Islamic heritage was hardly ever the main topic of discussion and debate in these salons.

The demolition at the mosque—disguised as expansion—was part of an enormous remaking of the city's built environment. Ancient markets and coffee houses, Ottoman-era forts, Shi'i and Sufi shrines, houses said to have belonged to descendants of the Prophet Muhammad—all would crumble beneath the bulldozers' blades. Historic Mecca would become a thing of the past. King Fahd and, after him, King Abdullah commissioned the Saudi Binladin Group—the global contracting company of their main local allies, the Binladin family—with overseeing redevelopment works in Mecca. Together, they claimed that the destruction of neighborhoods in Central Mecca was necessary to accommodate a ballooning Muslim population. The destruction, they said, would also prevent sites that were significant to Islam's early beginnings from becoming shrines for visitation, which Wahhabis consider heretical and an innovation in Islamic belief and practice (bid'a). Despite the wholesale destruction of the city's historical districts, there was little talk of Mecca's urban transformations beyond those immediately affected by it. The scale of destruction in Mecca remained largely visible only to those who had lived in or visited the holy city.[7] As late as 2010, media coverage was still scant. When local media covered the urban redevelopment, they did so in a positive light and hailed the state's modernizing accomplishments. The global mainstream media did not emphasize the topic for another three years. Saudi Arabians—experts and nonexperts alike—who were critical of the nature of urban redevelopment simply did not connect what was happening in the Darah and other archives to the reordering of the built environment, whether in Riyadh, Mecca, or elsewhere in the country.

REDEFINING THE ARCHIVE

This book shows how the battles to erase and remake history through archives and the built environment, and the commodification of historical artifacts and space, were part of the same state project to erase and remake the country's discursive and material history. Rooted in Riyadh and Mecca, the project was in turn part of the regime's battle to reconfigure Saudi state power following the Gulf War (August 2, 1990–February 28, 1991) and the political, social, religious, and economic crises the war created.[8] As the underpinnings of history writing, documents and artifacts hold great value for historians as well as rulers, even when they are marginal to people's daily experiences and how they relate to the past. The built environment, in contrast, reveals centuries, if not millennia, of human history and is ever present in everyday lived experience. It structures people's lives, the ways they inhabit or challenge their surroundings, and how they view the past.[9] The built environment, and space more generally, also reflects the ideological, affective, and material tendencies of those in power and how they aim to use the past to shape the future.

Historical documents, archives, commemorative spaces, and the built environment are types of archives designed to tell a certain story about the past as well as about futures that are in the making. As forms of political communication that knit across state and society, such technologies of knowledge production are evidentiary networks through which official historical knowledge moves and becomes visible, "set[ting] the stage for future historical narratives."[10] But they are more than just spectacles whose salience lies in the symbolic power they hold.[11] The very materiality of these archives—the overabundance of records, limitations on space, deteriorated sites of heritage, private property ownership, and financial constraints—sets the conditions of possibility for these spaces of memory making. It brings historical narratives to life and makes them into monuments in their own right.[12] These monuments are also sites of capital accumulation that, in postwar Saudi Arabia, responded to looming economic and financial crises. They are central to the state's material politics and are constitutive of the political economy of state making.

Importantly, archives and built environments structure what is preserved and what is not. The production of history as well as the state is in fact premised on and necessitates the selective erasure of some pasts and these records, objects, and spaces that stand witness to them. The singling out of Riyadh and Mecca for the state's post–Gulf War cultural, economic, and political reengineering projects indeed reflects that.[13] To pay attention to the lifeworlds of the built urban environment—the production and destruction of cities as archives—is to read physical geographies along and against the grain and how they lend themselves to state power.[14] It is to understand the truths that erasure mobilizes, materializes, and normalizes in the service of state formation.[15] Erasure is not simply a countermeasure to the making of history: it is History. From the hiding or purging of documents and artifacts to the demolition of monuments and buildings, destruction is a requisite for the making of History and, as we will see, of the state.

Understanding this fact is key to understanding history and modern state making everywhere. Contrary to popular and academic belief, the elision and destruction of historical artifacts and spaces are not particular to certain types of states: authoritarian, religious, "nonmodern." These bureaucratized, everyday forms of violence, which Chiara De Cesari describes as "cultural governmentality," are pillars of modern statecraft and sovereignty.[16] They are structural even to those states hailed as the most modern, secular, and liberal, such as France, the United Kingdom, and the United States.[17] What varies from place to place is the precise political-economic stakes in the struggle over knowledge production and state form. In late twentieth-century Saudi Arabia, the struggle—what I call archive wars—revolved around the production of history, the reordering of space, and the repurposing of valuable real estate as a means to diversify the petroleum economy. It aimed to reshape modern Saudi power, society, culture, and economy. Historicizing these practices helps us rethink the nature of modern archival formation and statecraft and call into question scholarly assumptions about the cohesiveness of authoritarian states and of states in general. From the mundane lifeworlds of historical documents and the spaces that house them in Riyadh to the spectacular commercial megaprojects that dot the once-familiar landscape in Mecca, such infrastructural sites of power are rarely folded into discussions of the state because we tend to think of archiving, memorializing, and urban planning as distinct and separate. The domains of history making and urban planning are, in fact, mutually constitutive; to make history is to (re)make space, and like all archival formations, both are ongoing and contested material practices of state formation.

In Saudi Arabia, as elsewhere, these struggles were (and are) complex, multisited, and ridden with tensions, contradictions, and contingencies. They involved intraregime rivalries in which high-ranking members of the ruling family and of the government competed with one another over power, capital, and the Saudi state form. Historically, power has been diffused among regional and institutional fiefdoms, each dominated by a different member of Al Saud.[18] The king himself could not act unilaterally and had to account for the different power centers. The archive wars mapped onto these competing zones of political authority, which one can think of as islands of sovereignty. They also entailed battles between ruling elites—both secular and religious—and the nonruling classes, which included low-ranking government employees, nonstate clerics, document dealers, archivists, historians, urban planners, and contractors. Motivated by different material and ideological interests, these figures and the organizations they oversaw or worked in—the Darah, in Salman's case—inadvertently heightened existing rivalries in Saudi Arabia's archiving and other state institutions.

At times of heightened crisis, Saudi rulers relied on religion as the first resort to (re)shape the national idea and confront threats to their rule. A case in point is the ways they instrumentalized religion to pacify post–Gulf War popular contestation and shifted the basis of state legitimation to secular historical memorialization, political commemoration, and urban redevelopment.[19] *Archive Wars* centers on these top-down yet understudied material practices to explore the nature of state power and its imbrication with archive formation. It does so with the understanding that statecraft, even in authoritarian regimes, evolves diachronically in response to a multiplicity of challenges, not least of which is popular opposition.[20] The extent to which such strategies were successful, if at all, is beyond the purview of this study. Suffice it to say that the diversity of religious and political views among decision makers, religious institutions, and society writ large casts doubt on the efficacy of these approaches. This rings truer in the aftermath of the Gulf War, when Saudis lost what trust they had in state institutions and sought political, economic, and religious sources of authority outside of state structures. The state's response to these developments is instructive. That the project of archival centralization in Saudi Arabia is ongoing makes it a good example from which to study statecraft, in its messiness, contradictions, and flexibilities. Using the challenges that the Gulf War posed as the "problem space"—to borrow from David Scott—*Archive Wars* ultimately shows how the state's postwar response centered at once on historicizing a national space, territorializing a national history, and refracting both of those through new modes of capital accumulation.[21]

ORIENTALISM AND THE MAKING OF HISTORY

Saudi Arabia is often regarded as a country without history. Mecca and nearby Medina are of course the birthplace of Islam and the first Muslim community, respectively. But the great Islamic centers of the past were never in the Arabian Peninsula. They were headquartered in Damascus, Baghdad, Cairo, Istanbul, Mashhad, and Lahore. The consolidation of major Muslim dynasties under the Abbasids, Ottomans, Safavids, Mughals, and others likewise took place far from Arabia. In the eyes of many scholars of the Middle East, not to mention Arabs and Muslims more generally, the contemporary Saudi state is a parvenu; it has no cultural or "civilizational" pedigree; it owes not just its founding but also its continued existence to a geographical lottery that placed it atop the world's largest known reserves of oil.[22] The Saudi ruling family's claim to religious legitimacy—that it is the protector of the two holy cities in the Hijaz—does not resonate outside the kingdom and is resented by many within its borders as well.

Saudi Arabia is certainly regarded as a country with a present. It is virtually synonymous with the global oil economy. As the world's only "swing producer," at least until 2016, it is the country that can most easily withstand cutting or ramping up its production to affect oil prices. In this capacity, it shapes world politics; it is one of the United States' strongest allies; and it is the periodic subject of intense scrutiny. And yet as an authoritarian monarchy that severely restricts travel to and within the country, it remains something of a mystery: even the best-informed students of the Saudi ruling family's inner workings are wont to quip, "Those who know don't talk, and those who talk don't know." Even less is known about the huge expanse of the country outside the palaces—its cities and rural areas, the diverse populations that call the region home, and the social movements they have organized.

As little is known about the country, the focus on the present has masked Saudi Arabia's history almost completely. Despite recent advances in scholarship,[23] Saudi Arabia, and indeed the Arabian Peninsula, with the possible exception of Yemen, is largely absent from Middle East studies.[24] The dearth of scholarship is partly due to limitations on access to the country (and region) and challenges to conducting research there. It is doubtless partly due as well to persistent Orientalism that sees the entire Middle East as static in comparison to a dynamic "West." But it also reflects popular and scholarly perceptions—especially in the Arab world—of the kingdom as a vast desert, a place particularly lacking not only history but also politics and culture, ruled by profligate princes and thinly peopled by well-paid bureaucrats with no desire to bite the hand that feeds them. This "secondary Orientalism" that dominates knowledge production on Saudi Arabia is common across the political spectrum in the Arab world, from the most ardent leftists and Arab nationalists to liberals and those on the extreme right.[25] The typical popular and scholarly depiction of Saudi Arabia is flat and two-dimensional: an image of special stasis that, if anything, has been reinforced by the kingdom's association in recent decades with extremist variants of political Islam.

The Saudi regime appears in popular discourse and in the scholarship as a curious exception and, at times, as an object of derision (perhaps tinged with jealousy) because of its oil riches. But the Saudi state is not all that exceptional and is, of course, far from being devoid of history. Indeed, controlling the Saudi Arabian past and its material sites has been central to the forging of state institutions. Yet it is not just the persistent prejudice of outsiders that is at stake here. The institutionalized version of national history has also gone far to feed the flattening of Saudi life and history. On the one hand, the state claims a divine mandate to protect the so-called (Wahhabi) religious awakening that first brought together the Al Saud clan with the religious reform movement in 1744. According to the state's narrative, it was this mandate that spared Saudi Arabia the fate of secular states in the region, which succumbed to the forces of colonialism and imperialism following World War I. On the other hand, the state alleges that ordinary Saudi Arabians are deficient as historical subjects. Successive Saudi rulers regularly claim that Saudi Arabians are either perennially quiescent (and thus suspended in time) or so reactionary as to require perpetual autocratic rule and slow social, cultural, and political change.[26] In both cases, state representations of the kingdom are anchored in a set of absences: a place without social divisions, without conflict, without the warp and weft of historical change.

Such an exceptionalist depiction has been possible because successive Saudi regimes have invested heavily in crushing the domestic social mobilizations—secular and religious—that emerged since the Saudi state's inception and subsequently removing them from the historical and archival record.[27] At the same time, the regimes have tried to purchase and polish their preferred image abroad by hiring public relations firms and lobbyists and by donating to US universities and think tanks.[28] Together, these practices have elevated the state-sponsored narrative above all others, placing the ruling family firmly at the center while rendering Saudi Arabians' labor, sacrifices, and diverse intellectual lifeworlds largely invisible. Wahhabism's rich tradition of debate was also relegated, and a particular strand became the singular state ideology, one that elided other forms of belief and belonging. This one-dimensional view animated Saudi Arabia's official historical narrative. At the turn of the twenty-first century, it would be revised and subsequently enshrined in the built environment.

DISCIPLINARY HISTORIOGRAPHY

For most of the twentieth century, the religious establishment played an instrumental role in the production of school curricula and textbooks. Its historians overemphasized religion's role in state formation at least until the 1990s, when a belated revision of official history saw a gradual shift from "religious time" to "scientific time." To understand the transition, we must first understand the central role of religion in the making of the Saudi state, both discursively and materially.[29] Until the 1990s, Saudi Arabian official historiography did not convey the liberal notion of historical progress, which equates secularization and emergent conceptions of human agency with the unfolding of history.[30] Such an ideologically permeated concept of history is also often marked by the introduction of a scientific measurement of time.[31] State-sanctioned history did not replicate the transformations of social life associated with secular modernity so much as it enacted a set of novel associations between religion and nation.[32] Indeed, "religious time," and the unfolding of Wahhabi religious truth that it exemplified, was the hallmark of official historiography. In the absence of preserved or accessible local archival records and historical artifacts and sites, many historians and scholars, even those outside the pay of the regime, replicated the state-sanctioned narrative.

Until the 1990s, official history centered on Shaykh Muhammad ibn Abd al-Wahhab and the eponymous Wahhabi movement he inspired. It was this eighteenth-century reformer, and the religious awakening his movement supposedly heralded, that enabled a so-called divinely appointed Al Saud clan to conquer much of the peninsula and establish a hereditary monarchy almost two centuries later. Historians at the Arabian American Oil Company, or Aramco, first produced this Wahhabi-centered narrative in the 1940s.[33] It was their way of legitimizing the twentieth-century rule of the Al Saud based on Wahhabi Unitarianism, which foregrounded the need to cleanse the peninsula of unorthodox Islamic practices.[34]

The so-called founding father of Saudi Arabia, Abdulaziz ibn Saud, increasingly adopted Aramco's narrative, especially as opposition to the idea of the regime, the nation, and/or the state intensified by the early 1950s. His son and first heir to the throne, Saud (r. 1953–1964), did the same. As anti-imperialist Arab nationalist and secular leftist movements flourished during his reign, Saud began to strategically adopt more progressive policies. In so doing, Saud also sought to counter conservative forces emerging from within the ruling family in opposition to his rule. As we will see, this firmly pitted him against Faisal, his powerful brother and the crown prince. Faisal overthrew Saud in 1964 and purged the regime. Fearing secular nationalism in its mid-twentieth-century, revolutionary manifestation, Faisal's regime intensified links between state and mosque as an effective way to oppose and contain local and regional secular opposition movements. Political religion thereafter came to color all aspects of life in Saudi Arabia, including the state's historiographical self-representation. In this, Faisal had the support of his maternal uncle, the popular and influential Shaykh Muhammad ibn Ibrahim Al al-Shaykh—Saudi Arabia's first grand mufti (1953–1969) and a descendant of Ibn Abd al-Wahhab. The shaykh had an unrivaled grip on religious institutions. He ensured the success of Faisal's coup against Saud even when his vision for a post-Saud state differed. The shaykh sought a Saudi Arabia that was far more austere than that of Faisal, and the two struggled over the nature of politics until the shaykh's death in 1969. With the shaykh gone, Faisal was able to bureaucratize the religious establishment—a term I use not to gloss over this institution's rich ideological diversity but to denote those Islamic scholars (ulama) and "religious ritual specialists" (*mutawwa'a*) in the pay of the state who at least publicly support and endorse its policies.[35] Faisal replaced the Office of the Grand Mufti with that of the Ministry of Justice and further weakened religious institutions by incorporating them under the state's authority.[36] He also began sidelining the Al al-Shaykh family from positions of power in the government. Throughout the 1960s, Faisal's regime had actively offered refuge in Arabia to Islamists from other Arab states, especially members of Egypt's Muslim Brotherhood who were escaping Nasser's persecution. It used them to serve government purposes, particularly in the field of education and media. On the one hand, the influx of Arab Islamists was meant to counter the growing trend of secular popular politics of the 1950s and 1960s. On the other hand, the regime hoped that the presence of non-Wahhabi Islamists who worked within the bureaucracy would balance the power of hard-line Wahhabi clerics.[37]

To produce an official historical narrative that promoted the Saudi state under Al Saud's rule as the only legitimate and permissible form of political organization, Faisal sought to centralize education and unify school curricula. For this purpose, his regime established the Supreme Commission on Educational Policies, which brought the Ministry of Education under the king's jurisdiction.[38] Although the religious scholars continued to shape the state's educational policies and curricula, they did so under the centralized auspices of the state. The regime institutionalized a form of nationalism in which religion was the bond that was to unite people living in Saudi Arabia.[39] Disciplinary historiography was premised on a distinct reading of past Islamic civilizations, one that projected an ideal Muslim identity based on the tenets of Wahhabism that Al Saud and the Wahhabi movement enabled and protected. Unlike nationalism in neighboring states, the founding ideology in Saudi Arabia was rooted in strict obedience to the official Wahhabi interpretation of Islam and loyalty to the monarch as the enforcer of religious piety. Obedience to the rulers was equated with obedience to God, and resistance to the monarchy was a crime. Together with the descendants of Muhammad ibn Abd al-Wahhab, the story went, the ruling family suffered the pain of descent into war, ignorance, and a debased form of Islam before rising up to "reunite" an imagined nation.[40] The ascent of Al Saud to political power was meant to mirror the ascent of the nascent Saudi citizen-subject to higher stages of Islamic civilization and, hence, modernity.[41] This conception of the past animated the first set of centralized history textbooks, which was largely written by a network of non-Saudi historians, poets, and writers and published in 1972.[42]

The consolidation of the oil economy in the early 1970s caused a sense of alienation generated by the fast-paced economic, social, cultural, and spatial transformations, or "petromodernity." This further incentivized linking the Saudi state with religion, thereby claiming legitimacy for political sovereignty through Islamic genealogy. In so doing, Faisal was able to consolidate a politically reactionary, religiously conservative, authoritarian monarchy. The Saudi state form with which we are familiar, and that we associate with Islamic fundamentalism, was not always an inevitability. As in other Arab states like Egypt and Iraq, it was a calculated response to opposition movements that threatened the status quo in the mid-twentieth century.

As Faisal continued building the institutional capacity of the state, including the centralization of education and, with it, a state-sanctioned historical narrative, some citizens attempted to document and preserve the history of a diverse Arabian past. It so happened that many graduates in history, archeology, and museology, who had studied in Egypt, Lebanon, France, Great Britain, or the United States—such as librarian Yahya ibn Junayd and historian Ali al-Mughannam—returned home in the early 1970s. They initiated public and private endeavors to construct museums and document repositories for nongovernmental records. The Darah was one of them, inaugurated in 1972, as was the Museum of Archeology and Ethnography that opened six years later and was the first museum of its kind in Saudi Arabia.[43] Other, even smaller museums and archives also emerged at the neighborhood level in various parts of the kingdom, such as in Jeddah, Medina, and Qatif.[44] The new graduates also sponsored archeological excavations around the country. King Faisal had issued the country's first archiving law in 1966, which heralded official attempts at establishing state archives and maintaining government records. But state policy was not the main force behind any of these other projects. Instead, the projects were largely individual responses to state centralization and to the ravages of a fledgling petromodernity that, especially following the 1973 oil boom, upended everyday life and the familiarity that came with it.

The nonstate conservation efforts failed to effect change in the national cultural policies or to secure the necessary state support to ensure their success. They therefore remained underfunded and largely ignored by the secular branches of the state. The rulers were indifferent to the potential of these historical remnants but also to the danger that they could pose. Under Faisal, the regime even rejected several fully funded proposals it received from architects and urban planners for preserving Al Saud's own material heritage in Riyadh, seeing such projects as futile and frivolous.[45] The same disinterest marked the reign of King Khalid (r. 1975–1982). The individual projects of historical recovery that did take off in the 1970s aimed to uncover and document the diverse histories of the peninsula. The construction of archives and museums, which some political elites feigned interest in, represented efforts to safeguard that which was familiar: history in its multiple forms. They were the material out of which contested collective memories were taking shape. These memories decentered or challenged Al Saud's role in the nation's history and tapped into popular desires for an alternative future. They were inserted into the narratives that people ascribed to material remnants littering their cities, written into their cognitive maps of the urban space. They fit as historical fragments into the multiple, incomplete pasts that exceeded, and often subverted, the boundaries of the Saudi national project.[46] The regime, therefore, was not particularly interested in supporting these efforts. It was also simply not committed to material politics and cultural engineering in general. This attitude explains the alarming plea of archeologist Abdullah Masri in 1980: "Unless our cultural heritage is carefully preserved, 20 years from now Saudis may be walking around like zombies with only a veneer of modern life to call civilization."[47]

Some of those overseeing the museums and archeological sites in the 1970s and 1980s even described having to operate under circumstances of great caution, lest they attract the attention of vandals.[48] On the one hand, they regularly encountered raids by religious ritual specialists who accused them of contravening the monotheistic teachings of Islam by memorializing objects and spaces. Equating such actions with polytheism, these specialists often vandalized some of the artifacts they saw during their raids, which some scholars view as acts of iconoclasm.[49] On the other hand, regular citizens who adhered to this interpretation also regularly attacked sites of commemoration, and with great impunity. While the religious establishment had been weakened, the regime was simply not willing to confront those in the religious establishment who saw the monumentalization of symbolic material structures as a mediated form of worship and an association with God, for the sake of projects it considered marginal to its political operation.[50] The regime had shared the judicial branch and the arena of cultural production, which included education, with the religious elites in exchange for sole control over political and economic offices of state.[51] It was an olive branch of power sharing intended above all to pacify contestation.

The high hopes for pacification, however, would not last long. In the shadow of the religious establishment that was incorporated into the state grew diverse popular Islamist groups that would constitute the politico-religious opposition parties in the decades to come. In 1979, several hundred armed Saudi Arabian men who once adhered to the official Wahhabi interpretation of Sunni Islam took over Mecca's Grand Mosque for two weeks.[52] They were disgruntled with the official religious establishment, especially with how its clerics had become quiescent with what they saw as the irreligious rule of Al Saud.[53] They sought to purify Wahhabism. In a separate incident mere days later, the state security apparatus clamped down on Shi'i citizens in the Eastern Province who were celebrating

'Ashura—the annual mourning of the martyrdom of Imam Hussein.[54] In so doing, they turned a peaceful religious procession into a weeklong uprising that King Khalid's regime countered with great violence. Both opposition movements, though quite different from one another, were a response to the state's increasing authoritarianism and strengthening ties to the US government, matched only by the ruling family's corruption.[55] Proponents of both movements tried to discredit Al Saud's claims to religious legitimacy and to challenge the ruling family's monopoly on power and resources.[56] The regime imposed a media blackout and allowed only the state-owned channel to broadcast news about the event. It prevented any other mention of either movement in the oral and written record, during the events as well as after their suppression.[57] The regime went on to score military and symbolic victories over both movements, painting all the oppositionists as Shi'i terrorists and Iranian fifth columnists.[58] It mattered little that the predominantly peaceful protestors in the Eastern Province had been subjected to decades of structural violence and exclusion, or that the Sunni Islamists who took over the Grand Mosque had once adhered to the Wahhabi school of thought and had legitimate political and religious grievances.

The religious insurgents who took over the Grand Mosque especially threatened the state, whose institutions had been preoccupied with leftists and Arab nationalist mobilizations at least until the early 1970s. The regime was caught off guard by an Islamist group challenging its religious and political underpinnings, let alone doing so through violent means almost concomitantly with the Iranian Revolution and the war in Afghanistan. The religious establishment became once again a site of power and contestation as the ruling elites needed the support of religious leaders.[59] In return for that renewed backing, Khalid's regime expanded even further the religious establishment's control over social and cultural life.[60] Clerics at the Ministry of Education were given almost free rein to shape the state's educational policies.

BELATED HISTORIOGRAPHIES: HOW HISTORY CAME TO MATTER

Until the early 1990s, state-sanctioned history correlated heavily with the developing salience of political religion in Arabia. This trend served to define the Saudi state form and to align practices of state formation and nation building with the religious tradition of Wahhabism as the basis of state sovereignty.[61] Then came the 1991 Gulf War, whose events and aftermath forced King Fahd's regime to reevaluate the economic, sociocultural, and political underpinnings of the state and to instrumentalize the past in unprecedented ways.

When the war began, the country suffered from the global recession and the constriction of investment opportunities abroad, where the lion's share of Saudi oil revenues was invested.[62] From 1970 through 1979, the regime had accrued extraordinary oil revenues, a windfall that allowed for large-scale alteration of the country's structural and infrastructural landscapes. But the following two decades were less remunerative. Not only did oil prices collapse in the 1980s, but that decade also saw the Saudi state binge on military spending. Such spending was part of the petrodollar recycling that the US government had compelled the Saudi regime to undertake, to the great material benefit of Defense Minister Prince Sultan.[63] In 1979, Saudi Arabia's rulers became partners, along with the main Pakistani intelligence agency, in US support for the anti-Soviet jihad in Afghanistan.[64] The Saudis were also the largest financiers of Saddam Hussein's regime during the 1980–1988 Iran-Iraq War as well as the subsequent coalition that went to war with Hussein in 1991.[65] Saudi Arabia compensated for the loss of Iraqi and Kuwaiti oil production during the fighting by increasing its own output. Although doing so stabilized the price of oil, it did little to ease the recession.[66] Yet in this period of economic and political turmoil, and perhaps because of it, the Saudi regime agreed to buy another $20 billion in weapons from the United States. At that point, it was the single largest arms sale in history.[67] The war thus exacerbated the extreme fluctuations in oil revenue streams of previous decades and increased the urgency of realizing other, regular (and more stable) sources of income. The regime identified these other sources in local real estate and development schemes, which at the time it limited to Riyadh and Mecca. Investment in real estate became part of a concerted regime policy whereby only the top members of the monarchy and their allies made decisions on, and benefited from, urban redevelopment plans in Riyadh and Mecca. The property market in these cities had become subject to new terms and forms of regulation and control that conformed to broader trends that marked late capitalism: accelerated urbanization, a return to a form of primitive accumulation, the dismantling of the welfare state, and gentrification and the displacement of the poor.[68]

The Gulf War deeply affected social life in Saudi Arabia. The regime's extraordinary military spending, its ever-closer ties to the United States, and its inability to generate the oil revenue levels of the 1970s strained its developmental capabilities. Importantly, these developments alienated Saudi Arabians of all political stripes. Many began to mobilize, along with existing political groupings, to make constitutional demands and to condemn the regime for permitting the US military to station its troops on Saudi Arabian soil. King Fahd rushed to find clerics who would give religious legitimacy to his political stance and the presence of US troops during the war.[69] He found some, but more than a hundred clerics from within the official religious establishment had also signed a memorandum of advice addressed to the king in which they recommended political, economic, and religious reforms.[70] Other political opponents also framed their demands and condemnations in Islamic terms. And unlike previous expressions of dissent against the state, "representatives of business, the Sunni religious community, women, the Shiʻa community, and the opposition abroad" converged in their demands, even if they espoused different political agendas.[71] They publicly revealed the contradictions of a self-proclaimed Islamic state that was authoritarian, economically unjust, and militarily reliant on foreign powers. They called on Al Saud to sever ties with the United States, curb military spending, and implement a constitutional monarchy. The equal distribution of social and economic rights was at the forefront of their demands.

The regime was unable to immediately use its tried-and-true method of presenting itself as a neutral and necessary arbiter between supposedly warring factions. It had to adjust, especially as the mass Sunni Islamist opposition—known as Islamic Awakening (al-Sahwa al-Islamiyya)—intensified during the war. Mass mobilizations—peaceful and armed, secular and religious—had challenged Al Saud's rule in the past. The Sahwa was different. It was a mass movement that emerged from within the Wahhabi milieu sometime in the 1980s and whose followers were first influenced by members of the Egyptian Muslim Brotherhood who started arriving in Saudi Arabia in the late 1950s and took up positions in the Ministry of Education and in the media industry.[72] Through their positions, they were able to reach the Saudi Arabian masses. Within two decades, the hybrid Islamist ideology became part of mainstream religious culture in Saudi Arabia.

The Sahwa, with its socioeconomically and ideologically diverse factions and nonviolent reformist agenda, managed the unprecedented task of peacefully exposing Al Saud on religious grounds. The movement threw into question the ruling family's political writ and its religious legitimacy.[73] The monarchy had theretofore claimed that its right to hereditary rule was based on divine will and a commitment to protecting the "religious awakening." The Sahwa maintained that the rulers had violated these commitments by allowing US troops to deploy in Arabia to fight another Arab and Muslim country, Iraq. It used the very version of Islam propagated by the state as a site of mass opposition. The regime understood this popular backlash to be a result of a lack of a secular national sense of belonging, the type of consciousness they had actively suppressed in previous decades. Where the regime had instrumentalized religion to counter secular and religious movements throughout the Cold War period, it was religion that, in the post–Cold War period, constituted the major threat to the longevity of the regime. Indeed, the intersection of modern bureaucratic practice with political theology, in this case Wahhabism, produced an instability at the heart of the regime and state institutions, one that forces us to question precisely that which is taken for granted: the history of religion in Saudi Arabia. This instability was occurring at a time of remarkable division among Arab governments over the war with Iraq. It made local and regional threats that much more pressing for a regime facing immense social, financial, and military pressure.[74] These developments scarred the ruling elites in Saudi Arabia and shaped their political views and decisions in subsequent years.

With the war over in February 1991, the regime began to rethink the traditional relationship of politics, economics, and religion. The aim was to confront the twin threats of opposition movements and the global recession. It implemented various strategies of coercion, incarceration, and co-optation to pacify its opponents.[75] Beyond imprisoning the main leaders of these movements, such as Salman al-Odah and Safar al-Hawali, and firing some of the official state clerics, the regime appeased establishment and nonestablishment Islamists and gave in to some of their demands in order to bolster the rulers' religious legitimacy.[76] It also brought many of them into the regime's fold through employment and financial rewards, relying on them years later to counter the emerging threat that al-Qaeda posed in Saudi Arabia.[77] To further appease its critics and respond to popular demands, the regime adopted three legal measures in 1992: the Basic Law of Government, the Law of the Consultative Council, and the Law of the Provinces. The first broadly resembles a constitution that regulates rules of governance in Saudi Arabia in accordance with the Wahhabi interpretation of sharia. The second and third respectively introduced the appointed Consultative Council (Majlis al-Shura) and new administrative laws that led to the emergence of provincial councils.

Scholars have differed in explaining the political and legal mechanisms undergirding these laws. Some argue that the measures were first steps toward liberalization, political participation, and government transparency.[78] Others view them as mere rhetorical maneuvers meant to reaffirm the hereditary monarchical system and legitimate its authoritarian structure.[79] Archival and ethnographic research inside Saudi Arabia complicates such readings, which are largely based on the regime's public statements during and after the war. In an attempt to address Islamists' concerns, regime proclamations emphasized the Islamic nature of the state and continuity in state policies.[80] In practice, however, and out of the public eye, the top decision makers began to view religion as the main threat. This was so even if disagreements over policy matters were rife between King Fahd and Prince Sultan on the one hand and Crown Prince Abdullah on the other.[81] Salman emerged as the middle ground. They nonetheless collectively pushed for major educational, cultural, and spatial policy changes that decentered religion and revised mechanisms of consent generation and subject formation, even if they were not always in agreement about what form the national idea or body politic should take.

To this effect, King Fahd's regime began a long-term policy of limiting the official religious establishment's influence and decision-making power in the kingdom, especially over the realm of cultural production and social policing. In a move that further bureaucratized and incorporated the religious establishment into the state, the regime reinstated the Office of the Grand Mufti under Shaykh Abdulaziz ibn Baz in 1993. Debate and disagreements among the state clerics persisted, and some continued to voice their opposition against state policies and the marginalization of the clerics. But by and large, the gains that the religious establishment had achieved since the 1970s began to erode. Even the judicial branch lost much of its independence. The religious institution writ large came to play a rubber-stamping role, with clerics acquiescing to state policies to unprecedented degrees. In resolving the challenges that political religion played during the war, the regime created its own, if outwardly compliant, internal religious opposition. The decades-long contentious interdependence of the religious and secular branches of the state nevertheless began to recede.[82] Although the effects of these policies would not be felt for another decade, if not longer, it is there that one should look to understand the profound transformations that beset Saudi Arabia in the opening decades of the twenty-first century.

The Postwar Plan

Once the dust of the Gulf War settled, the top ruling elites—Salman prime among them—began to overhaul the grounds for political legitimation and social engineering. They embarked on a secular project of historical memorialization and political commemoration. As governor of Riyadh, Salman was the main architect of the postwar political economy. A close ally and confidant of then king Fahd, he significantly increased his political and economic power after the war through privatization efforts, tightening links with economic elites, and remaking the capital city. Salman, who had become the feared guardian of discipline and order among the ruling family, also had the full support of the religious establishment. He empowered and mobilized its leaders against the women's movement in the 1990s and the increasingly threatening Sahwa, even as he ensured the marginalization of religion in the hegemonic historical narrative and political life. Salman was thus able to begin implementing the postwar plan, at least in Riyadh, where he had the most control.

The plan entailed revising the official historical narrative, with secular nationalism replacing political religion as the driving force of history. Crucially, the plan centered on rendering the revised narrative permanent and visible in the archives and the built environment. The revisions did not overhaul the state-sanctioned narrative. Rather, they maintained many of its central tenets, such as the vilification of the Ottoman past and of tribalism, both of which had long been written into history as obstacles to modern state formation.[83] The revised discourse would, however, sideline the focus on Muhammad ibn Abd al-Wahhab and the Wahhabi movement. It would relegate the role of religious forces to the footnotes of state formation, beginning with the built environment in Dirʿiyya, the movement's birthplace, but also throughout Riyadh.[84] Instead, the revised narrative would rest largely on Al Saud's patrilineal genealogy, incorporating the country's symbolic and material history into that of Al Saud. The story of Arabia became the story of Al Saud alone. All other actors sat on the periphery. The new ideal Saudi Arabian subject was a person who unquestioningly acquiesced solely to the secular state's political, economic, and religious doctrines and civic duties, and performed them inside and outside the borders of the state. The revised narrative would guide the work of museologists, archivists, archeologists, and city planners.

The Gulf War was a pivotal moment in the shift from "religious time" to "historical time" in Saudi Arabia.[85] The transition accelerated with the terrorist attacks inside the country in 1995 and 1996, which targeted US personnel stationed inside Saudi Arabia. Although both temporalities share "conceits about teleology and progress," the latter traces "the evolution of some political formation," in this case the Al Saud monarchy, foregrounding it at the cost of all other social actors.[86] In effect, the regime was redefining cosmological space as state space. Where the regime's postwar public statements and legal maneuvering emphasized the continued importance of religion and the propagation of the Wahhabi call (*al-daʿwa al-Wahhabiyya*), in practice, they concealed the hitherto-unexplored shift to historical memorialization and urban redevelopment. Space, and sites of heritage in particular, like archives, became the regime's preferred battlegrounds. These battlegrounds constituted one register of violence upon which the regime operated. The regular erasure of historical voices, the enclosure of primary source records, and the destruction and reconstruction of spaces became the field for forging a collective identity, one that shapes and is constantly shaped by dynamics and various forms of profit and speculation in Saudi Arabia.

The state thus replaced its basis for political legitimacy: instead of the prior religious foundations, it focused on a secular national mythology built around the selective history of Al Saud. This was the narrative that the regime sought to assemble through state archives and museums as well as the built environment. What this meant was that novel practices of making and memorializing space and time became essential for reproducing state sovereignty and legitimacy, at a time of socioeconomic crisis. Distinct from ongoing scholarly claims, I argue that a form of secularization began to take shape after the 1991 Gulf War through new ideas of historical time, progress, and capital accumulation.[87] Mobilizing and materializing the past in unprecedented ways to privilege Al Saud's secular history, Salman became the face of this new historicism, the pronounced "gatekeeper of Al Saud's history."[88]

ARCHIVE AS WAR

In 1996, a royal decree inaugurated the material production of Saudi Arabia's revised history. It declared that January 16, 1999, would mark the beginning of a yearlong celebration of the passage of one hundred Hijri years since Abdulaziz ibn Saud conquered Riyadh.[89] That the country's first official nonreligious national celebration in the kingdom's history did not mark the 1744 union between Al Saud and Al Abd al-Wahhab or the creation of the Saudi state in 1932 speaks to the centrality of the capital city in the regime's attempts to shape historical consciousness in Saudi Arabia.[90] The memorialization of the revised official history involved several processes: the production of that history's source materials and the archives that would house them, and the territorialization of the revised narrative in the built environment.[91]

The regime commissioned the Darah, with Prince Salman as its new president, to oversee the centralization of the country's primary source documents. Of particular interest were those records that countered the official narrative. The goal was nothing short of controlling processes of knowledge production and the official economy of memory. The regime invited some of its political critics into the history- and heritage-making projects. It did so not to bring them into the revised national story but precisely to legitimate the postwar project through their inclusion while pacifying and co-opting them through institutional engagement. At the same time, many of the archivists, museologists, and architects who partook in the project hailed from marginalized communities (religious minorities, certain tribes) and geographies across Arabia (east, south, north, rural areas). None of them supported the official historical project. They nonetheless saw their participation as attempts to force their own occluded histories and ideologies into the state-sanctioned narrative and Saudi Arabia's commemorative landscape. Instead of challenging the official history and its materiality, however, these cultural producers as well as opposition members gave this narrative legitimacy and failed to "shed positive light" on their communities' economic and cultural contributions to the "nation." Despite their best efforts, they simply could not challenge the state-sanctioned narrative or operate "outside the orbit of official taxonomies."[92]

The regime's push to collect historical documents and manuscripts on Saudi Arabia provoked opposition to its project of memorializing a uniform historical narrative centered on Al Saud. Many owners of private archives in Riyadh, Medina, Jeddah, and elsewhere refused to "surrender" their own collections despite the promise of lucrative financial returns. It was their way of preserving what little was left of their personal histories. This is how they resisted what they regarded as an authoritarian regime intent on excluding them from a national heritage with which, in any case, they did not identify. The regime's centralization efforts especially caused inter- and intrainstitutional opposition and rivalries among Riyadh's state archives. Archivists and preservationists in state institutions subverted the process of collection, preservation, and cataloging to further their own ideological beliefs. At times, they resorted to sabotage—hiding or destroying certain documents and leaking others—as a way to disrupt the official heritage-making project. Decision makers in the archiving regime, such as Fahd al-Semmari, Darah's secretary general, were so wary of their own employees that they outsourced ordinary functions—screening and cataloging historical records, for instance—to minimize sabotage.[93] The external contractors worked in relative isolation and had to sign the equivalent of nondisclosure or confidentiality agreements.

The result was that few employees had knowledge of the historical records in their own institution's possession. This especially applied to those documents purchased since archive fever gripped the industry in the 1990s. The crafting of a national vision that does not trust the crafters was further indication of a regime at odds with itself, lacking the hegemony it regularly claims to have.[94] The onerous and costly archiving process, coupled with the rapid increase in acquisition, meant that the majority of historical documents remained locked in boxes, their contents unknown to anyone. It was possession of the records, and not simply the knowledge they contained, that gave the papers value as artifactual weapons in a broader war over political and economic power.

The belated turn to historiography was being instantiated, monumentalized, and circulated in everyday material life also through the production of memorial spaces. Because Al Saud's past and the genealogical view of history were inscribed in Riyadh's landscape, the city was the target of cultural and urban redevelopment.[95] The Arriyadh Development Authority (ADA), which, like the Darah, was under Salman's leadership, was chosen to micromanage the transformation of the capital's built environment.[96] According to the capital's postwar comprehensive strategic plan, known as the Metropolitan Development Strategy for the Arriyadh Region (MEDSTAR), Riyadh would become the administrative, cultural, economic, and historical center of Saudi Arabia.[97] The ADA worked with the Darah in managing the construction and renovation of museums and memorial spaces in Riyadh's "old city" and in Dir'iyya. It relied on historians, developers, and urban planners to ensure that the built environment itself conformed to the revised official history.

The new sites of historical knowledge production and circulation—archives, monuments, museums, and historical sites, what Pierre Nora has called "realms of memory"—were also new sources of economic production.[98] They became the bedrock of a fledgling national tourism plan that enabled capital investment within and around memorial spaces.[99] Before the Supreme Commission for Tourism (SCT) was established in 2000, the Department of Antiquities at the Ministry of Education worked closely with the ADA to transform the capital into a prime destination for the fledgling domestic tourism industry.[100] Riyadh would become "history's new home."[101] After decades of downplaying such practices and castigating them as unorthodox, state institutions highlighted Riyadh's significance for (a singular) national identity as well as to heritage, modernity, and civilization. They marketed the city accordingly in the brochures that they produced.[102]

The enduring significance of this long-term project was not lost on planners at these institutions: exploiting domestic tourism would materially circulate the regime's newfound legitimation narrative, consolidate Riyadh as the capital, and centralize political power in Najd, long considered the heart of Al Saud loyalism. It would also eventually capture the disposable income of Saudi Arabian tourists, known to be some of the world's biggest tourism spenders.[103] In this vein, the Saudi state has invested hundreds of billions of dollars since the late 1990s on the cultural production of Riyadh, which has guided the city's urban development. Domestic tourists were the tourism strategy's primary targets.[104] Only after a domestic tourism infrastructure was well on its way in subsequent decades would the kingdom open its borders to international visitors and liberalize its highly restrictive visa policies.[105] As the president of the Saudi Commission for Tourism and Antiquities Prince Sultan ibn Salman noted when speaking about heritage preservation and its economic dimensions in 2010, "This is a new sector, and previously there were no opportunities like this in KSA [Kingdom of Saudi Arabia], but now a lot of great opportunities and future developments are available in regards to heritage villages, maintenance, and the development of heritage hotels which we have recently started to license."[106]

The belated turn to material history was circulated in the built environment and in everyday material life. It was also anchored in the erasure of sites that recalled or made possible alternative social imaginaries antagonistic to the regime's legitimating mythos. These are everyday geographies in which people live, dwell, move, and die. If geography and history are locked in an intimate embrace, they are also inseparable from state power and capital (private or otherwise), both of which necessitate a particular ordering of space in order to reproduce themselves. The sites that facilitated the new history were therefore targets of a "development" that sought above all else to enhance the country's "economic, cultural, and touristic" dimensions.[107] Those that did not met a different fate, at least in the first decade of the twenty-first century. With a few exceptions, the state initially prevented the renovation of countrywide historical sites that did not conform to the official history. In Mecca, however, the state took a different approach. As described earlier, it embarked on the wholesale destruction and redevelopment of the central district, where most religious and historical sites evinced competing temporal and spatial orders.[108] There, the regime capitalized on the rhetoric of iconoclasm, coupled with modernization, to justify the violent erasure of these spaces. It did so even when many clerics within the religious establishment did not oppose the preservation of historical artifacts and sites but rather the preservation only of those religious ones that could encourage shrine visitation, as is further discussed in Chapter 5.

The project of history and heritage making was subsumed under urban redevelopment plans that highlighted the importance of the "old" and historic in Riyadh—which referred only to Al Saud's political history—and the "new" and hypermodern in the much older city of Mecca.[109] The ordering of urban space outside of Riyadh, and in Mecca in particular, before the Gulf War already bespoke the limits of Saudi hegemony. On an ideological level, this space was the material out of which alternative histories could be constructed. Ottoman-era forts and mosques hinted at imperial remnants of other political geographies in the peninsula. The houses of the Hashemite Ashraf—a tribal Arab dynasty said to be descendants of the Prophet Muhammad and who governed the Hijaz from the tenth century until the collapse of the Ottoman Empire in 1924—stood as monuments to the historical possibility of an Arabian present absent Al Saud.[110] Religious shrines lurked as permanent reminders of the heterogeneity of Islam's many manifestations and of the Saudi Arabian nation's social body. Schools, coffee shops, and cultural institutions spoke to intellectually diverse and cosmopolitan pasts that troubled the state's insular and homogeneous narration of the past. On a material level, the arrangement of the urban landscape represented the declining profitability and stability of the national economy, with capitalist exploitation hindered by noncapitalist property arrangements and strong communal sentiments connecting people to land.[111] Erasure, then, became a fundamentally important mechanism for the state's new project to remake Saudi Arabia's cities—both in the sense of cleansing the archeological and architectural record of those edificial fragments of subversive histories and in the sense of sweeping away those materially tethered social relations that resist the march of commoditized progress.[112]

In Mecca, as in Riyadh, the regime could simultaneously attend to its territorialization of history—through demolition and reconstruction, respectively—as well as its diversification of the economy away from oil. Doing so allowed the regime to engage in new strategies of capital accumulation and strengthen ties with the economic elites by developing, investing in, and underwriting land and real estate markets. Manipulating and managing the built environment, political and economic elites accumulated wealth while territorializing and spatially circulating the official version of the past.[113] Ruling family members and their contracting allies—the Saudi Binladin Group, Saudi Oger, Al-Rajhi Holding Group, Dallah Albarakah, among others—received priority in contract bidding, favorable terms for bank loans, and insider trading on private property targeted for expropriation or adjacent to development sites. Once the redevelopment vision in Riyadh and Mecca was well under way and planners broke ground in most of the targeted sites there, the regime, then under King Abdullah ibn Abdulaziz (r. 2005–2015), began to selectively develop historical sites outside of these two cities.[114] Al-Hofuf Historical City Center in the east, the Historical City in Jeddah in the west, and Jubba Heritage Town in the northwest received state support in the second decade of the twenty-first century, after rejecting local applications to do exactly that for at least two decades.[115] But planners from the Saudi Commission for Tourism and Antiquities (SCTA) and the Ministry of Municipal and Rural Affairs (MOMRA) were instructed to mute any material evidence in these sites that contradicted the official history.[116] Instead, they focused solely on the sites' economic potential, for which the "traditional souk" assumed a primary place. As a matter of fact, the souk was so central to the future Saudi tourism industry that SCTA and MOMRA embarked on a "program of development and rehabilitation of existing public souks."[117] Outside Riyadh, then, the financialization and commodification of historical value dictated the nature and scope of heritage development.

In territorializing its version of the past following the Gulf War, the regime aimed to neutralize some of the biggest threats to its rule by centralizing many of the dispersed postwar political battles around sites and practices of memory formation. It simultaneously created new realms of investment and profit as well as opportunities for capital accumulation and job creation. These privileged the economic elites who supported Al Saud, politically and financially. In other words, the regime used its bureaucratic power to shift the political battleground from the streets to state institutions. Engaging different communities in the production of the past, without ever intending to include them in the state-sanctioned history, would detract from the more threatening struggles for economic redistribution and political equity. It is on the historical terrain that the regime commanded stronger forces, such as capital, manpower, and real estate, even if the institutions that manage these had multiple and competing interests. These were all sites of political and economic power where Saudi Arabians, especially those in the opposition, could barely compete.

The archive was thus a strategic battleground for realizing the rulers' aims for political legitimation and economic diversification.[118] The archive lies at the intersection of past and present, private and public, the visible and invisible.[119] It structures subjectivity, temporality, and spatiality in ways that engender accumulation and the illusion of unhindered access. It does so while setting boundaries, exclusions, and the "enclosure" of documents and spaces.[120] For all these reasons, archive formation is a violent act, one that triggered new battles and confrontations. Those who ran the archives, museums, contracting companies, and urban development agencies were central figures in the archive war. As directors, secretaries-general, and chairpersons, they competed with one another to secure historical documents, artifacts, real estate, and contracts. These would increase their access to power, profit, and prestige according to who their patron in the ruling family was. Political interests dictated the decisions they made and reflected alliances as well as fissures within the regime. Owners of properties located in Saudi Arabia's fledgling commemorative landscape similarly tried to push back against regime attempts to take over their homes or lands. Some did so for personal and financial reasons. For others, it was to either safeguard or prevent the commodification of historical or religious spaces. Architects, planners, historians, and religious figures joined them in opposing many of the regime's documental and spatial politics. The archive war was thus nestled inside a larger war pitting ruling elites and their proxies against each other and against other citizens, and the alternative histories they might choose to remember and pass down. As we will see, resisting the centralization of movable objects such as documents and artifacts proved easier than fighting the takeover of private property and the wholesale redevelopment of private and public spaces.

READING THE STATE

The post–Gulf War project of national revisionism and reordering, which instrumentalized history in new ways, depended on the passage of time for its own success. Its effects began to materialize only later in the decade, and increasingly so in the early years of the twenty-first century. This should not be surprising. Projects of state making are always ongoing; they require time in order to become "truth," to thread the symbolic and material together, and to form "the architecture of historical knowledge."[121] In the process, new obstacles arose, such as the terrorist attacks in the United States in September 2001 and in Riyadh in May 2003. Strategies and goals had to be altered and different regimes with new agendas and spatial conceptions came to power.[122] Ultimately, once the "facts on the ground" were set in stone, both in the archives and in the built environment, archival meaning would crystallize and the state would be able to further mobilize its own historical truths.[123] The archiving regime is perpetually authoring and authorizing the future. As Jacques Derrida stresses: "The question of the archive is not, we repeat, a question of the past.... It is a question of the future, the question of the future itself, the question of a response, of a promise and of a responsibility for tomorrow. The archive: if we want to know what that would have meant, we will only know in times to come. Perhaps. Not tomorrow, but in times to come, later on or perhaps never."[124]

For Derrida, the archive is, on the one hand, a technology for moving into the future and, on the other hand, the need to recall the past in order to get there. But the form that these projects of state making embody are ever changing. The ways in which certain episodes of the past, as well as the varying visions of the future, are recalled and memorialized while others are silenced and destroyed, reflect and conform to the will of those in power but also to the logic of capital and the political economic exigencies of the time. History making, urban memorialization, and land marketization practices were thus processually inextricable from state formation and regime maintenance strategies. Saudi Arabia's material politics makes that clear. It also helps us better understand the nature of Saudi power and the tensions inherent in the process of state formation. The state's reliance on subcontracted labor and multinational conglomerates for its material politics, for instance, reveals the ways in which Saudi Arabia exhibits features of combining nation (public) and capital (private). The privatization and outsourcing of state functions, however, is not exceptional or particular to the kingdom. Modern governmentality is characterized by the increasing corporatization of the state, with the private and public spheres becoming visibly more entangled and less discrete than they once seemed, especially in this period of late capitalism.[125] Bringing together the discursive, spatial, and economic underpinnings of the archive wars also foregrounds the fragility of Saudi Arabia's authoritarianism—its existence as a regime of dominance without hegemony. As a matter of fact, my archival and ethnographic materials reveal the ongoing confluence of two facts about how Saudi power manifests itself. On the one hand, the Saudi state appears strong, legitimate, and dynamic. It has managed to suppress and/or co-opt domestic popular political mobilizations and to delimit the rules and boundaries of discursive and material practices.[126] On the other hand, the state appears weak, decentralized, and incoherent. It is unable to centralize its archives, let alone its political authority, and struggles to fashion subjects along its evolving national ideals. The Saudi state has also failed to maintain regime legitimacy—which remains fragile—and regularly undermines, if not altogether sabotages, itself.[127] Far from being contradictory, these tensions trouble the ways in which academics and laypersons have come to think about the state itself in coherent and singular fashion and how we often collapse "state" with "regime." They dispel the myth of a cohesive and unitary state—authoritarian or otherwise—and instead make visible the multiplicity and plurality of state and regime, and the competing forces that shape it. They speak to the ways in which multiplicity is the form that the Saudi state has heretofore taken. It is only by attending to both facts of power at once, the top down and the bottom up, and the material practices associated with them that we can understand the machinations of power.[128]

"Archival thinking" is thus not simply about the politics of historical knowledge and its technologies.[129] Materiality is central to the production of knowledge as a disciplinary force that undergirds the ordering of political, economic, social, and spatial life.[130] The archive question is also the state question. The state's material politics reveal how state power manifests, how the state itself is a sort of material practice, and how this materiality shapes and is shaped by the construction and destruction of history. Rethinking the history of Saudi Arabia not through the lens of energy, security, or geopolitics but rather through the internal process of state formation by way of archives is to de-exceptionalize the state and reveal its complexities and specificities. Foregrounding everyday material practices of state making suggests new sites and modes for reading the state as an unstable work in progress that is riddled with tensions, contradictions, and rivalries. The archive wars thus raise questions about the politics of history, religion, and space, and also competing claims over these spheres of power well beyond the case of the Saudi state. Saudi Arabia is a paradigmatic site for understanding twentieth-century state formation as well as the fortunes, the battles, and the consequences of state consolidation and history's material and discursive infrastructures.

The best place to begin this story is the place that many readers might consider Saudi Arabia's paradigmatic site, the holy city of Mecca. Mecca is the birthplace of the Prophet Muhammad and the spot where he received the first set of revelations of the Quran. It is the destination of fifteen million Muslim pilgrims per year, with the Kaaba in the Grand Mosque dictating the *qibla*, the direction of Muslim prayer.[131] The Al Saud family stakes its claim to rule on its role as custodian of Mecca's holy sites, along with those in nearby Medina. In choosing Mecca as a prime locus of heritage making in the twenty-first century, the Saudi regime was partly nodding to Mecca's immense religious significance. It was also acknowledging a worldly fact: real estate in central Mecca is some of the most expensive in the world. A square meter of commercial space there reached upward of US$130,000 by 2010, a four-thousand-fold increase since the beginning of the previous decade. To put the price of real estate in Mecca in perspective, it was at least $30,000 higher per square meter than in Monaco and Hong Kong, considered the two most expensive places in the world.[132]

Finally, however, in choosing Mecca, the regime was targeting for demolition a built environment full of architecture that predated the Saudi state, thereby silencing the pre-Saudi past. That history, as we see in Chapter 1, undermined the state's image of Mecca as a dusty backwater saved for global Islam by Saudi armed protection and Wahhabi juridical rigor. When Al Saud's army of conquest encountered the city in the early twentieth century, it was abuzz with political and intellectual currents generated partly by a man who was not a Saudi and not even an Arab.

Chapter 1

OCCLUDED PASTS

WHEN HE ARRIVED IN MECCA FROM INDIA IN 1859, MUHAMMAD Rahmatullah al-Kairanawi (1818–1891) was already a prominent religious scholar. He was renowned for his intervention in the debates with the German Protestant missionary and Orientalist D. Karl Gottlieb Pfander on the abrogation of Christian Scripture and Muhammad's claim to prophethood, among other subjects. But he was also known for his involvement in anticolonial revolt.[1] Al-Kairanawi had called for armed struggle against British rule in what became known as the 1857 Rebellion. He then led two hundred mujahideen from Najibabad in Uttar Pradesh to Delhi. The British army crushed the rebellion and put out a call for al-Kairanawi's arrest. The scholar escaped to Bombay. From there, he sailed to the port of Mocha in Yemen and then walked more than a thousand kilometers north to Islam's holiest city, Mecca.[2] To the anger of Britain and other imperial powers, Mecca had become a haven for Muslim rebels fleeing repression. For some, it was a transit point on the way to Cairo, Java, and other destinations. For others, like al-Kairanawi, it became a permanent home.

The South Asian scholar-activists who sought refuge in Mecca, such as Imdadullah Farooqui and Abdullah ibn Muhyi al-Din al-Malibari, brought with them a panoply of anticolonial and modernist ideas—secular and religious, reformist and revolutionary.[3] Many came from far afield to seek their intellectual mentorship, and they helped shape the intellectual worlds of residents and more casual travelers as well.⁴ The fugitive scholars arrived in Mecca when the town, like others across the Ottoman Empire, was undergoing great changes propelled by internal and external challenges. On the one hand, insurrections and secessionist movements were unsettling the imperial seat in Istanbul. Already by the early 1800s, the empire had suffered significant territorial losses—and it was poised to suffer more. On the other hand, European domination of the global capitalist economy was accelerating, producing a more and more pronounced imbalance of power, including unprecedented European meddling in Ottoman affairs. To address these threats, the Ottoman government introduced a set of regulations and institutional reforms, better known as the Tanzimat, between 1839 and 1876. These aimed to safeguard the empire's authority and territorial integrity by modernizing its bureaucratic, military, economic, and cultural modes of governance. The reforms put control of Ottoman provinces in the hands of centrally appointed governors who stepped up the management of imperial subjects' everyday lives.⁵ The difference was especially noteworthy in formerly autonomous and semiautonomous regions such as the Hijaz, on the Arabian Peninsula's western coast—the location of Mecca and Medina.⁶

The combination of Istanbul's reforms and Europe's heightened intervention meant that several Ottoman provinces were caught in the web of nineteenth-century imperial rivalries.⁷ The Hijaz saw the Ottomans enhance their presence, particularly after an 1858 incident in which residents killed twenty-one European Christian merchants and diplomats. The killings were a response to mounting European privileges in the Ottoman Empire coupled with European attempts to end slavery on the Red Sea coast.⁸ The British responded by bombarding the port city of Jeddah, ninety kilometers west of Mecca. The Ottomans, to placate the British and assert central authority, executed the killers and sent additional troops to maintain order. The relative security that followed furthered the exchange of people, knowledge, and technologies between the Ottoman center and the rest of the world—an exchange only enriched when the Suez Canal opened in 1869.

Such was the backdrop to the Mecca in which al-Kairanawi and his colleagues thrived. It was also the context that led to the establishment of private and state institutions in the Hijaz that produced—via schools, religious endowments, travel, and print publishing—the conditions of possibility for the circulation of political ideas and shaping of political sensibilities.⁹ These developments helped link Mecca and the Hijaz to the intellectual and political currents that had emerged across the Ottoman East, including the decades-long Arab cultural reformation or renaissance movement known as the Nahda.[10] Such global concepts as modern constitutionalism, nationalism, political rights, and revolution—shaped as they were by transoceanic exchange—reached the Arabian Peninsula's shores in the late nineteenth century, not long after they began to circulate elsewhere in the Ottoman Empire.[11]

For many intellectuals, nationalists, and anticolonialists like al-Kairanawi, education was a central medium through which to improve socioeconomic conditions, raise political awareness, and foster attachment to the "imagined community" of the nation.[12] The school that al-Kairanawi established in Mecca in 1873, al-Sawlatiyya, accomplished just these things. It encouraged intellectual debate, promulgated reformist ideas, and issued calls for Muslim unity, all in keeping with the themes of its founder's writings and speeches. Al-Kairanawi's school stands out among its peer institutions for the extent to which it politicized and shaped the aspirations of students from the Hijaz and other parts of the Arabian Peninsula.[13]

If the nineteenth-century Hijaz witnessed an influx of South Asian scholars who influenced global Muslim thought, the early twentieth century transformed Mecca yet again, by way of travelers who brought with them ideas like nation-state nationalism and Arab nationalism. More pilgrims, scholars, and traders from the Ottoman Empire's Arab provinces and later on from the newly formed post-Ottoman states came to the Hijaz on the eve of and following World War I. Some remained in Mecca, Medina, and Jeddah.[14] At the same time, many anticolonial activists who were wanted by European overlords in Syria, North Africa, Egypt, and the Gulf coast sought refuge in the holy cities.[15] Like their South Asian predecessors, the new refugees brought (and took) with them political, cultural, and religious news, ideas, and aspirations that further enriched intellectual exchange and political solidarities.[16] But, ironically enough, the advent of the nation-state has rendered these actors invisible and their transregional networks mute.

This chapter addresses forms of historical erasure that are central to modern state formation. It takes up one of multiple strands of sociopolitical and cultural life—al-Kairanawi's school and its relation to the emergence of an intellectually engaged Hijazi middle class—in late Ottoman Mecca. It then attends to the ways in which Saudi institutions have occluded and repackaged this history since the state was formed in 1932. Diverse and connected historical realities elsewhere in the Arabian Peninsula, including in Riyadh itself, were equally erased from the state's evidentiary terrain. As the political and financial center, however, Riyadh is at the heart of the state-sanctioned history. It has received the lion's share of critical historical inquiry, even if the state's singular portrayal of this geographic territory remains dominant. Mecca, however, has received little scholarly attention, despite its immense religious significance and its standing as the Saudi state's first administrative capital. We cannot fully understand the making of history and state in Saudi Arabia, let alone social, cultural, and political life in the peninsula, without attending to the many ways in which Mecca's history has been effaced.

BREAKING WITH THE PAST

Official Saudi narratives portray Mecca as a timeless sacred space, a city not only sheltered from worldly corruption but also devoid of politics or culture, waiting for the ruling family to carry it into modernity even as they protected its holy places. Historical scholarship to date also limits discussions of Mecca either to matters of the annual pilgrimage or to the city's importance under Al Saud. The material record says otherwise: the city has a dynamic and, as it were, secular history that long predates the advent of Saudi rule. Mecca's people and its visitors were actually integral to fashioning political modernity.[17] Beyond the symbolic power it bestowed upon its rulers, Mecca was a space where intellectual debate flourished, honing the minds of thinkers who became central figures in twentieth-century politics and religion. The networks established in Mecca also informed some of the dominant popular political movements of twentieth-century Saudi Arabia. Yet these networks, some of the most recent evidence of Mecca's cosmopolitan past, are absent from histories of the Hijaz and of Saudi Arabia. They are missing, too, from histories of intellectual thought, cultural production, and political activism in the late Ottoman period. Such scholarly myopia and peripheralization, combined with the production of a singular, state-sanctioned historical narrative in Saudi Arabia, have enabled these depictions and the erasure of the city's intellectual and political significance to Saudi Arabia and beyond.

Unearthing these histories in Mecca is urgent. The Saudi state has been destroying the city's built environment in lockstep with the logic of historical erasure and state formation. As late as 2010, walking in the narrow winding alleyways of Central Mecca, one saw traces of non–Saudi Arabian pasts that were pivotal not only for intellectual, social, and urban history but also for Saudi state formation. Old neighborhoods organized along lines of ethnic origin, non-Arabic street and building names, classical Islamic and Ottoman architecture, and Ottoman cultural institutions and coffeehouses once threw the discrepancy between lived realities and written historical texts into stark contrast.[18] Since the late 2000s, the state has accelerated the destruction of these spaces, displacing the residents and rendering the unsanctioned histories they expose difficult, if not impossible, to discern.

It is striking—yet ordinary—that the Saudi state would occlude pasts that, in the case of Mecca, are central to global Islamic modernity, twentieth-century religio-political thought, and even the making of Saudi Arabia itself. Modern state formation necessitates the erasure of some pasts at the expense of others. The modern state is actively amnesiac, its creation resting on "an act of chronophagy."[19] It requires the destruction of existing subjectivities, socialities, and historicities, and their replacement with modes of being and remembering that are compatible with the modern state form, ones that will mask the symbolic and material violence of state making. In Arabia's case, Al Saud's military advances meant the reformulation of the shared histories of the conquered regions on the eve of Saudi state formation. The new rulers' attendant monarchical centralization, politico-religious socialization, and petrocapitalist development would transform the emergent national space and its sociocultural and political worlds. That the Saudi regime subsequently relied on US imperial and corporate support to manage the day-to-day affairs of state and to crush political opposition required the further elision of historical events and the crafting of a sanitized national past.

Arabia's pre–Al Saud social, economic, political, and cultural lifeworlds were the "old possibilities" that had to be destroyed to allow for "the creation of conditions in which only new (i.e., modern) choices can be made."[20] In "breaking with the past" and the "introduction of a new game of politics," Al Saud had to detach modern modes of belonging from the era before its conquests.[21] For not only were various parts of the Arabian Peninsula already connected to transnational political, economic, and cultural formations in the nineteenth century, to the chagrin of the Saudi state and the metahistorical narrative it propagates;[22] those connections, as manifested in the cultural and sociopolitical life of the Ottoman Hijaz in particular, also laid the groundwork for the Saudi state project. Al Saud, for instance, capitalized on the religious reform ideologies of South Asian scholars such as al-Kairanawi to produce a stricter form of Wahhabism in the twentieth century, one on which state ideology was later premised.[23] The new Saudi rulers also employed seasoned merchants, educators, and former bureaucrats from the Hijaz and elsewhere in the business of state building.[24] But by and large, they relied on elite foreigners who hailed from places ranging from the Levant to the United States to support their state project. Saudi rulers did so not because of the absence of Arabian expertise, as is commonly depicted, but because they faced stiff internal opposition. Those who came under Al Saud's rule opposed hiring foreigners to conduct Saudi state affairs when they themselves could perform the same jobs. They saw the foreign capitalists and workers as motivated purely by personal gain and accused them of doing the regime's bidding with little regard for the locals' desires or well-being. If anything, the foreign workers partook in the process of subject reformation, spatial reorganization, and historical revisionism that undergird modern statehood. Together and separately, these Arabian and foreign actors were crucial to the very success of Abdulaziz ibn Saud's state project. They had to be written out of official history, and wiped from the popular memory, lest the fact of their contributions compromise the state's historiographical self-representation.

The pasts foreclosed in the Hijaz and elsewhere in Arabia in the nineteenth and early twentieth centuries point to alternative modernities as well as futures. As we will see, Arabians had competing visions of the political future. These were inspired by the intellectual worlds they inhabited at the crossroads of imperial rivalries and anticolonial activism. Some traces of these worlds—Portuguese, Ottoman, Indian, Hasawi, Bahrani, Hijazi—perdured despite state efforts to erase them. Others were not as stubborn and have been relegated to the footnotes of history. Rendering some of these historical narratives visible, as this chapter does, reveals Arabia's multiple identities, histories, and potentialities, those presents and futures that could have been but never were. Doing so brings into conceptual view the intersection of state and archive making, history writing, and imperial formation. For it was against these futures past, what Gary Wilder refers to as foreclosed openings, that the organizing fiction of the Saudi state's origin was produced.[25] Decades later, that fiction was configured and structured in archives and commemorative spaces, enshrined as source materials—"facts"—for future historians. Bringing back the banished past also offers an alternative periodization and a more heterogeneous history of Saudi Arabia: one composed of ruptures and roads not taken rather than the smooth, linear progression that the modern state needs.

FORECLOSED OPENINGS: HISTORICAL POSSIBILITIES IN PRE–AL SAUD ARABIA

When al-Kairanawi arrived in Mecca in 1859, Ottoman administrators were living in the Hijaz for the first time. Their arrival signaled political and cultural changes that enriched an already-cosmopolitan Mecca and the intellectual debates that took place in its schools. Al-Kairanawi wanted to engage these scholarly networks. He sought to do so by opening a modern school that would allow him to spread his religious reformist message and his call for Muslim unity in order to confront European imperialism. To build the school, he needed to raise funds.

Fortunately for al-Kairanawi, his reputation preceded him. The Indian scholar quickly befriended one of Mecca's highest-ranking religious authorities and most influential jurists, the Shafi'i mufti (and historian) Shaykh Ahmad ibn Zayni Dahlan (1817–1886).[26] Through Dahlan, al-Kairanawi was able to teach at Mecca's Grand Mosque.[27] He also started to give private and public lectures about British colonialism and anticolonial nationalist politics, advocating a role for religious scholars in the struggle for national independence. By 1863, al-Kairanawi even counted among his friends the Ottoman sultan Abdulaziz I and the empire's supreme Muslim authority, the grand mufti (or *shaykh al-Islam*), in Istanbul.[28] He visited them both as an imperial guest, giving similar lectures. Impressed with his intellectual skills and anti-British commitments, Sultan Abdulaziz commissioned al-Kairanawi to write a book about the debates with Pfander, *Idhhar al-Haqq* (The Truth Revealed). The book was circulated after its publication in 1864 and translated into many languages. The sultan even financially supported al-Kairanawi in his remaining years in Mecca and appointed him to its governor's council.

In 1873, al-Kairanawi secured the funds he needed to open a school; the benefactor was an Indian woman, Sawlat al-Nisa', who was from Calcutta and was in Mecca on pilgrimage. He inaugurated the school he named after her—al-Sawlatiyya—in a crowded educational market. Meccans already had their own schools, most of them religious. Several notable families had provided funds and properties for traditional private schools in which established local ulama as well as those from Hadramawt, the Ottoman Empire, and the Indian Ocean taught. Although the majority of these schools restricted admission to boys, several provided a religious education to Mecca's young female population, such as the famous Ashiyya School and al-Qadriyya. Many boys who studied in these schools became influential religious scholars in the Arabian Peninsula.[29] The Ottomans, too, opened a school in 1860 to accommodate the arriving Ottoman administrators' families. The Rushdiye (al-Rashidiyya or al-Madrasa al-Rashidiyya) was a modern preparatory school in which Turkish was the language of instruction. Anxious about what they viewed as the Ottoman government's attempt at "Turkification," the people of Mecca altogether avoided it. The Rushdiye remained dedicated to the children of Ottoman administrators and their Meccan intermediaries, and thus had little influence on the city's cultural life.[30] Al-Sawlatiyya, however, made a big mark on the educational landscape by bringing together Indian and Ottoman reformist thought and practice.

At first, al-Sawlatiyya taught only Arabic and sharia studies, but soon it added social studies and mathematics.[31] It was one of the only schools in Mecca to incorporate secular subjects into its curriculum. Al-Kairanawi's school greatly reduced illiteracy and quickly earned the moniker "the mother of all schools in Mecca."[32] Its students hailed from all over the Muslim world. Within a few years, al-Sawlatiyya had opened branches throughout the Arabian Peninsula. Some of its graduates went on to open their own schools. Most notably, Shaykh Abdulhaqq Qari, who had studied with al-Kairanawi and later taught alongside him at al-Sawlatiyya, opened his own school, al-Madrasa al-Fakhriyya, in Mecca in 1878, also funded by wealthy Indian pilgrims.[33] Around the same time and also inspired by al-Kairanawi, Shaykh Abdulkarim al-Trabulsi opened what is considered the first regular Arab school in the Hijaz, al-Trabulsiyya, staffed by Syrian teachers.[34] These schools instilled in students the anticolonial, reformist, and modernist spirit of the time.

Al-Kairanawi's influence was so palpable that the Ottoman governor of the Hijaz, Osman Nuri Pasha, sought to extradite him to British India in 1882, fearing that his teachings were aggravating anti-Ottoman sentiments and might incite rebellion. Indeed, al-Kairanawi counted among his direct disciples future nationalist leaders, most prominently Sharif Husayn ibn Ali (r. 1908–1924) and Mecca's Hanafi mufti Shaykh Abdullah ibn Abdulrahman Siraj. Both would play a fundamental role in the so-called Great Arab Revolt of 1916 against the Ottomans.[35] But the governor's discomfort was no match for the sultan's unflinching support, as well as that of the people and ulama of Mecca, which allowed al-Kairanawi to continue his educational work undisturbed.

Al-Kairanawi's school exerted its influence amid two broader processes. The first was the spread of constitutionalism, appearing most prominently in the first and second Ottoman constitutional periods, which ran, respectively, from 1876 to 1878 and 1908 to 1915. These periods featured the promulgation of constitutions that delineated, and thus limited, the sultan's powers while establishing a parliament. The second constitutive process was the Nahda. A period and process of high intellectual reform, the Nahda entailed the articulation of new ideas about constitutionalism, socialism, feminism, and trade unionism, as well as the Islamic modernism that al-Kairanawi engaged, across the empire's Arabic-speaking provinces. Both processes were underpinned by new communication and transportation technologies that enabled the creation of scholarly networks that undergirded intellectual traditions and the circulation of the literature that teachers like al-Kairanawi, and later their students, produced. In 1882, despite his concerns that Mecca's inhabitants were becoming too politicized, Osman Nuri Pasha introduced the Amiriyya Press (al-Matba'a al-Amiriyya) to the city.[36] It replaced Cairo's publishing houses in serving the Hijaz's long-standing printing needs, and it strengthened existing networks of intellectual exchange to which al-Kairanawi and his peers were central. It connected Mecca's ulama, intellectuals, and political militants more tightly to debates in the Ottoman Empire and beyond. Through written texts—be they fatwas or opinions on Islamic jurisprudence—these actors were able to shape religious and political sociabilities among Muslim communities as far away as Indonesia, Mali, Zanzibar, and West Africa.[37]

These two broader processes of constitutionalism and intellectual exchange, along with a global wave of revolution, directed Hijazi attention to the relationship between ruler and ruled at a time when political rivalries among Mecca's traditional custodians, the Ashraf, were at an all-time high.[38] By the early 1880s, talk of constitutionalism and political change in Mecca had been so prevalent that the ruler Amir Abdulmuttalib ibn Ghalib (r. 1880–1882) arrested several Meccan notables on charges of sedition. He subjected the notables to a public whipping and sent them to prison in Istanbul.[39] But over time the arrests did little to deter Meccans from participating in intellectual and political life. More schools emerged in the early twentieth century as a result of al-Sawlatiyya and al-Kairanawi's influence. Pearl merchant Hajj Muhammad Ali Zaynal Alireza's Madrasat al-Falah (al-Falah School), for instance, opened in Jeddah in 1905 and Mecca in 1912, with other branches opening up in Mumbai, Dubai, and Bahrain.[40] Al-Sawlatiyya strengthened cultural and intellectual links across the peninsula and between the peninsula and the Indian subcontinent. It created a cohort of worldly teachers and students who were well versed in these different cultural and political worlds and years later wrote for *Barid al-Hijaz* newspaper (renamed *Sawt al-Hijaz* in 1932), a pro-Hashemite paper that became a sphere for literary and political debate.[41] Alireza gave outstanding students at his schools scholarships to pursue higher education in Egypt, India, and Lebanon. At times, he sent them to India to pursue various trades.[42] Al-Falah's teachers and graduates in the Hijaz became renowned scholars, poets, intellectuals, and bureaucrats, the likes of Muhammad Hassan 'Awwad, Hamzah Shehata, Abdulsalam ibn Tahir al-Sasi, Abdulwahhab Ashshi, and Ahmad Salih Qandil. They wrote about political, cultural, and economic issues that spoke to major debates of the time: Islam and modernity, the role of religion in politics, national belonging, cultural awakening, and economic development. Most went on to support Sharif Husayn in the 1916 Arab Revolt, through which he aimed to form, and rule, an independent post-Ottoman "Arab kingdom."[43]

AN "ARABIAN" NAHDA?

Al-Sawlatiyya and the schools that its graduates established politicized a generation of students who were coming of age at a time of escalating imperial confrontations, the entrenchment of the modern state system, and tribal jockeying for power in the Arabian Peninsula. All this turmoil produced competing visions of the ideal polity in Ottoman Mecca. The press was the preferred medium for these debates. If the press was already politicized in the years following al-Kairanawi's death in 1891, it became more so in the aftermath of the 1908 Ottoman constitutional revolution, which was jubilantly proclaimed on the streets of Mecca.[44] After the revolution, the new constitutional government in Istanbul, the Committee of Union and Progress (CUP), ordered city council elections in the Hijaz. The councils had both Turks and Arabs on them. Via these councils, the CUP aimed to centralize Ottoman imperial power while diffusing that of the Ashraf.[45] Mecca's Hanafi mufti Shaykh Abdullah Siraj, al-Kairanawi's former student, was elected as the city's representative in the Ottoman Parliament (*Meclis-i Umumi*). Mecca's municipality oversaw construction and market activity in the city.[46] The CUP also appointed Sharif Husayn ibn Ali as amir of Mecca on November 1, 1908.[47] Although he was a conservative and an opponent of constitutionalism, the CUP nonetheless addressed him in a welcome speech as the "Constitutional Emir" who promised to end Sultan Abdulhamid's despotic rule in Mecca.[48] Thereafter Sharif Husayn's family members, Bedouins, and Ottoman administrators mounted regular challenges to his power but to little avail. Also in 1908, the Hijaz railway reached

Medina. Although it never extended to Mecca, as was intended, the railway still allowed Ottoman armies to reach the region quickly when threats to imperial power arose. Along with Sharif Husayn's installation, the railway meant that by and large, peace reigned in Mecca until World War I.

In this atmosphere of relative security, the city's sociocultural and political life thrived.[49] The CUP used al-Amiriyya to publish the party's first local newspaper there, *al-Hijaz*, in 1908.[50] A government mouthpiece, *al-Hijaz* was published in both Ottoman Turkish and Arabic. It brought attention to administrative decisions meant to consolidate government control over the provinces and called for unity among Turks and Arabs in the empire.[51] *Shams al-Haqiqa*, the second Hijazi newspaper, was also published in Turkish and Arabic a year later, but targeted different segments of its elite readership.[52] The paper, however, regularly criticized the excesses of Mecca's Hashemite rulers, so Sharif Husayn shut it down.[53] Other local and regional newspapers and journals were established, and some were influential, but none lasted long. They were too critical of either the Ashraf or the Ottomans, and lacked the financial support necessary to survive the backlash.[54] The official gazette, *al-Qibla*, which was the mouthpiece of the Arab Revolt, was another critical newspaper that had a large readership and a longer life because it targeted the main challenger to the Ashraf's hold on power: Al Saud.[55] It started publishing in 1916, during the Arab Revolt, and was the first newspaper of the independent Kingdom of Hijaz under Sharif Husayn. Edited for its first four years by a Syrian, Muhibb al-Din al-Khatib, and later on by the Hijazi Nahda intellectual Al-Tayyib Tahir al-Sasi, *al-Qibla* was a pro-Hashemite organ in which Sharif Husayn himself wrote about political developments of his time.

The cultural and political renaissance, coupled with the relative safety of the Hijaz in the aftermath of World War I, allowed for another influx of pilgrims, scholars, and traders from the newly formed post-Ottoman states. Some remained in the Hijaz.[56] Khayr al-Din al-Zirikli (1893–1976) was one new arrival. He fled to Mecca in 1921, escaping the French after participating in the Battle of Maysalun in Syria. There, Sharif Husayn granted him the short-lived and long-forgotten Arab citizenship. Al-Zirikli owned the Arab Press publishing house. He was editor of influential daily Arab nationalist newspapers, such as *Lisan al-Arab*—which the CUP shut down shortly after its opening in 1918—and the Syrian *al-Mufid*.[57] He engaged Mecca's intellectuals, ulama, students, and rulers, and he played a significant role in spreading Arab nationalist thought in Arabia.

Through schools, texts, visitors, pilgrims, and their own mobility, Hijazis entered debates about nationalism and Islamic modernism, among the other types of solidarity developing in response to the transformation of everyday life.[58] The sources of transformation included encroaching European colonialism, Turkish nationalism, urbanization, new forms of taxation and land tenure, and the looming threat of the rising Al Saud clan.[59] The transformation was certainly uneven; it did not affect all parts of the Hijaz at the same time or in the same way. It nonetheless made possible new national imaginaries and the emergence of new forms of horizontal relations and identities. Put simply, Hijazis engaged in the same type of claim making seen elsewhere in the Middle East following the violent collapse of the Ottoman Empire and the end of the caliphate in 1924. According to Saudi Arabian literary critic Husayn Bafaqih, a new middle class emerged in the Hijaz between 1908 and 1924. Its members attended private schools such as al-Falah in Jeddah and Mecca. They read *al-Qibla* newspaper and prominent magazines like *al-Manar*, edited by the Islamic modernist Rashid Rida in Cairo.[60] Some of these young intellectuals, most of whom were men, immersed themselves in the modernist cultural production of Egypt, Greater Syria, and Iraq, as well as the "exilic literature" of Gibran Khalil Gibran, Mikhail Nu'aimi, and Iliya Abu Madi.[61] Their intellectual thought and political activism nonetheless grew out of their everyday social life in the Hijaz and the aspirations and struggles they shared with their compatriots there.

One of the political identities that these Hijazis espoused was Arab nationalism, particularly after the 1916 Arab Revolt that Sharif Husayn led from Mecca's Grand Mosque and through which he aimed to found an independent post-Ottoman "Arab kingdom."[62] The Arab Revolt was the first movement in the region to challenge Ottoman rule and call for Arab independence, albeit with the aid of British imperial power.[63] The new class of politically and culturally aware youths, inspired by the political teachings of al-Kairanawi and other Muslim scholars, called for greater independence and reform within the "imagined political community" of the Hijaz.[64] Early twentieth-century Hijazi intellectuals such as Muhammad Hassan 'Awwad published books—in conversation with the Nahda literature—on "cultural awakening," modernity, and the Hijaz as a unified region that needed protection.[65] They cited contemporary Egyptian volumes and included prefaces and introductions by fellow writers.[66] Following World War I, Meccans engaged with other political ideologies, including communist ideas and causes.[67] They also increasingly traveled to the newly formed post-Ottoman states, where they forged links to other Arab intellectuals.

Such intellectual exchange and youth politicization was occurring in eastern Arabia as well, along the Persian Gulf coast, and was equally important to these transoceanic intellectual networks. As the pearl trade became more lucrative in the early twentieth century, Gulf merchants and notables began to prosper and to form long-lasting personal, economic, and intellectual ties with peers throughout the Indian Ocean basin.[68] Ideas, as well as commodities, began to move more quickly between the Gulf, on the one hand, and the Red Sea and the Indian subcontinent, on the other. Many from the Gulf region had long traveled to al-Ahsa (in the Eastern Province of modern-day Saudi Arabia) to study in its Quranic schools or with Iranian- or Iraqi-educated ulama.[69] Through these scholars, students learned of regional political events, imperial rivalries, and anticolonial struggles. Some ulama, like Imam Hasan Ali al-Badr, of Qatif, were themselves involved in insurrection: he called for armed struggle against Al Saud in 1913 and later fought the British in the 1920 Iraqi Revolt.[70]

The Gulf merchants who traded in other Arab countries or in South Asia were exposed to nationalist movements and intellectual and literary debates. They regularly brought books back home with them.[71] Their exposure to modern education during their travels drew their attention to its absence at home.[72] Many merchants went on to sponsor modern schools and invited other Arabs and Indians to teach there. In Kuwait, for instance, such exchange led to the opening of al-Mubarakiyya, the first regular school (*madrasa nizamiyya*), in 1911.[73] Along with the al-Ahmadiyya School (opened in 1921)—which focused more on modern sciences and foreign languages—they hosted debates on tradition, culture, modernity, Islamic reformism, and nationalism.[74] The two schools attracted many Arab and Muslim intellectuals, most notably Rashid Rida, who came to Kuwait in May 1912.[75] During his stay, Rida's influence reached beyond the circles of rulers, intellectuals, and notables. He gave daily lectures and sermons attended by ordinary people—at least a thousand people a day according to conservative estimates.[76] Some were even able to ask him questions at smaller meetings. Kuwait's schools and the increased intellectual exchange they facilitated helped circulate the literature and ideas of the Nahda, Indian modernism, Islamism, Arabism, and later Arab nationalism, first within the Gulf region and then throughout the peninsula.

As in the Gulf, the Hijaz's intellectual production increased significantly following World War I. The war led to devastation and instability across the Ottoman Empire, which lost a quarter of its population. As the survivors strove to recover, they found their political horizons wide open. The defeat of the Ottoman Empire, the only form of political organization that its subjects had known, caused great anxiety, which European colonial schemes compounded. Nonetheless, the empire's eventual collapse and the end of the caliphate in 1924 led to popular mobilizations and created multiple visions for the future—not least in the Hijaz on the eve of its invasion by the forces of Abdulaziz ibn Saud.

In 1924, with Al Saud's forces massed nearby after a violent, two-decade-long war in which he conquered various parts of Arabia, the Hijazi educated class formed the Hijaz National Party (al-Hizb al-Watani al-Hijazi).[77] The elected party rejected Saudi-Wahhabi ideology and Al Saud's schemes to add the region to their expanding empire. Instead, it called for an independent constitutional monarchy, comprised of Jeddah, Mecca, Medina, and Taif, under Sharif Husayn's son, Ali, and an elected national parliamentary council. On October 4, 1924, Hijazi elites pledged allegiance to Amir Ali after his father, under pressure, relinquished the throne.[78] The same day, the party issued a statement to the "Muslim world" in Egyptian newspapers. The statement announced that the "will of the [Hijazi] nation" had prevailed: the Hijaz had become a constitutional monarchy that would seek guidance from the "Muslim nation" on how to run the affairs of the holy mosques. Given the looming Saudi conquest, the party also addressed Abdulaziz ibn Saud directly, assuring him that, with Sharif Husayn ousted, he no longer had reason to invade the Hijaz. He should let the "Hijazi nation live in peace and independence," the statement went on. The party also said the Muslims of the world would be to blame if they failed to save the country from Al Saud's imminent attack.[79] Abdulaziz also appealed to the world's Muslims. He called on the people of the Hijaz to elect "one of their own," though not a Hashemite, to rule under the guidance of "Muslim nations and peoples . . . like the people of India."[80] The Hashemite government and Al Saud began a war of information through *Barid al-Hijaz*,[81] and also through *Umm al-Qura* (which replaced *al-Qibla* newspaper),[82] respectively. In the end, Abdulaziz ibn Saud did not settle for Sharif Husayn's removal. He was intent on altogether terminating the Ashraf's rule and taking over the peninsula's western coast, which his forces did in December 1925.[83] Once he defeated his rivals in the Hijaz, Abdulaziz issued a general announcement. He justified taking over the region by claiming that the Muslim world had slighted his calls for them to share in governing the Hijaz. He therefore had no choice but to work with Hijazis, who sought him in droves asking for his help with attaining their freedom. He obliged.[84]

With the Saudi occupation in place, the Hijaz continued to experience literary and cultural renewal. Hijazis kept debating political rights (including those of women) as well as nationalism and the Arab renaissance. At one meeting of Hijazi intellectuals, the economist Muhammad Surur Sabban, who spent around two years in prison for demanding political, economic, and social reform, asked: "Is it good for the Arab nations to cling to the classical Arabic methods [*al-balagha al-'Arabiyya*] or should they succeed in reaching the standards of new development, follow the modernists' examples in breaking linguistic barriers, and use a general absolute method?"[85] In a response to Sabban's query as well as to his *Adab al-hijaz* (Literature of Hijaz, 1925), Muhammad Hassan 'Awwad published one of the first Nahdawi books in the Arabian Peninsula, *Khawatir Musarraha* (Authorized reflections) in 1926.[86] In this book, 'Awwad pointed out that the Hijaz was emerging from a "state of darkness" and beginning to experience "an intellectual revolution of the new against the old, freedom against tradition." 'Awwad called for the advancement of women, "proper national formation," and renewal in all aspects of life—namely religion, education, language, and literature.[87] Throughout the book, he refers to the Hijaz as the homeland and the country. As was common at the time, Sabban actually contributed the preface of 'Awwad's book, in which he enthusiastically writes, "We are merely the children of the homeland and want to reform it."[88] The book, in which 'Awwad chided the traditionalist ulama for standing in the way of progress, reached all corners of the peninsula (and by 1947 was translated into English and French). It stirred so much controversy that Abdulaziz ibn Saud appointed a council, headed by his son Prince Faisal, to investigate the author and "his intentions."[89]

Intellectuals from the Arabian Peninsula engaged with and contributed to the Nahda even if their names, ideas, and publications have been erased from historical memory and historiographical biases.[90] Yet the dominant literature on the Nahda continues to ignore the circulation of ideas and people in and through the Arabian Peninsula in the late nineteenth and early twentieth centuries.[91] There are two deleterious consequences. First, the literature omits the influence that Arabia's thinkers had on Nahda intellectuals, both secular and religious. This is to say nothing of the ways in which the Nahda actually shaped Arabia's Wahhabi movement, its doctrinal interpretations, and relationship to the past. Second, the literature's Arab-centric focus occludes non-Arabs like al-Kairanawi and his peers and their contributions to Arab intellectual, political, and cultural life. The cosmopolitan history presented here, selective as it may be, shows the very making of the Arab intellectual, far from but just as crucial to the Nahda's conventional centers in Beirut, Cairo, and Damascus.[92]

The social imaginaries, political awareness, and intellectual lifeworlds that flourished in the Hijaz persisted long after the advent of Al Saud. Members of the Hijaz National Party formed the Hijaz National Liberation Movement, which continued to call for Hijazi self-determination even after the Saudi state was founded in 1932. That some Hijazi elites supported Al Saud's state did not change that.[93] As Saudi Arabia became an established fact, some of these activists continued their political struggle but adjusted their tactics to account for heightened surveillance and the extent to which imperial powers were willing to go to safeguard the reign of Al Saud.[94] Many, however, gave up their activism and writing for government positions. The new Saudi state needed the bureaucratic skills the Hijazi intellectuals had acquired under the Ottomans. These foot soldiers of state formation later became implicated, through their employment, in the very erasure of their own histories.

FROM EMPIRE TO STATE: BURYING THE PAST

In 1902, Abdulaziz ibn Saud embarked on a war to conquer parts of Najd, the central plateau of the Arabian Peninsula where modern-day Riyadh is located. He saw these lands as his family's domain. In 1744, his ancestor Muhammad ibn Saud had established a Najdi emirate after joining forces with one of the area's many theologians, Shaykh Muhammad ibn Abd al-Wahhab.[95] Having studied in Baghdad, Basra, Damascus, Mecca, and Medina, Ibn Abd al-Wahhab was a product of the transoceanic and transregional intellectual networks of the eighteenth century.[96] He offered a different religious worldview based on Islamic orthodoxy, the primacy of Unitarianism—or the oneness of God (*tawhid*)—and purifying the *umma* of what he deemed to be improper innovation, such as shrine visitation and resorting to intermediation (*tawassul*). Muhammad ibn Saud realized the potential of this ideology to bolster his political ambitions, especially as it legitimated violent opposition to rival Muslim rulers and subjects.[97] He granted Ibn Abd al-Wahhab protection from the swords of neighboring rulers who accused the theologian of heresy.

In 1803, Al Saud expanded far beyond their traditional Najdi domains and occupied Mecca and, a year later, Medina. The Ottoman imperial government in Istanbul looked on with alarm. It had, until then, regarded Al Saud as an insignificant and provincial tribe whose arid plateau emirate was under nominal Ottoman control. But Al Saud's expansion exposed the imperial government's weakness by preventing Ottoman subjects from performing the pilgrimage, destroying Ottoman shrines and tombs, and calling on religious scholars to renounce their allegiance to the sultan.[98] Ottoman bureaucrats mobilized Egyptian forces in 1807 to crush Al Saud and reassert imperial sovereignty. It was only in 1811 that the Ottomans expelled Al Saud from the two holy cities. It took imperial soldiers another seven years to subdue Al Saud in their Najdi base of Dirʿiyya, which the Ottomans burned to the ground and rendered uninhabitable. Thereafter, the Ottomans kept a watchful eye on the ambitions of Al Saud, who regularly denounced the Ottomans as polytheists. The Ottomans began to intervene more directly in Arabian affairs.[99] Al Saud nonetheless emerged from the ashes to found another emirate, relocating their seat to the small oasis town of Riyadh in 1824. This time, they limited their rule to parts of Najd and eastern Arabia, at least until 1890, when the rival Al Rasheed clan defeated Al Saud there. Backed by Ottoman troops, Al Rasheed sent high-ranking members of Al Saud, including Abdulaziz, then fifteen years old, into exile.

Abdulaziz, who spent ten years in Kuwait during its cultural and political renaissance, would capitalize on his ancestors' religio-political narrative to ascertain his family's right to rule the peninsula, or large swaths of it. He was determined to restore his family to its former glory. When he conquered Riyadh in 1902, however, he had no intention of forming a state in the modern sense of the word.[100] He sought to assert power in the parts of Najd that his ancestors had ruled, through what he regularly referred to as his "revivalist movement." But by the 1920s, he had piled up victories over rivals across the Arabian Peninsula. Along with the major regional and global transformations of the time, these victories made state formation almost inevitable. Increasing Ottoman-British rivalry in the late nineteenth century and into the twentieth saw both empires vie for power by engendering Arabian rulers or propping up existing ones in the Persian Gulf and across the Arabian Peninsula.[101] Abdulaziz was one of many who sided with the British against the Ottomans in return for the promise of attaining hereditary political power and material support. The Great War and the subsequent emergence of the modern state system as the dominant expression of political power in the Middle East were the necessary conditions for Saudi state formation. Modernity had heralded new modes and technologies of governance, and Abdulaziz had to conform to the modern state system as the gold standard of international relations if he was to maintain his dominion.

If Saudi state formation was contingent on changing global structures, it was Britain's interest in the postwar Middle East that shaped Saudi state form and its expanding boundaries.[102] British interest was reflected in the political units that Abdulaziz established piecemeal: the Emirate of Najd (1902–1921), to which the Saudis added Hasa in 1913; the Sultanate of Najd (1921–1926); and later the Kingdom of Hijaz and the Sultanate of Najd and Its Dependencies (1926–1932), which adopted its current name, the Kingdom of Saudi Arabia, in 1932.[103] A pro-British hereditary monarchy ruling over large swaths of the peninsula bordering on British protectorates would safeguard British interests while eliminating the Ashraf's claims on the Hijaz, where their powerful base was located. In three decades, and with British prodding, Abdulaziz conquered all the regions that today make up the Saudi state.

Abdulaziz subsequently ruled the fledgling Saudi state with brute force. Violence, and the threat thereof, overshadowed the relationship between rulers and ruled. Abdulaziz had utter disregard for the modern political sociabilities of the peninsula's inhabitants, informed as they were by the same postwar Islamism, Arabism, and Arab and other forms of nationalism that he had experienced while in Kuwait. Even the Ikhwan—the troops who fought alongside Abdulaziz in his conquests—were not immune to his threats, especially after many of their cadres challenged his orders and staged a rebellion in 1928. The Ikhwan had been the first organized military force to accept Al Saud's project and Wahhabism's Islamic orthodoxy. They were socialized into it, like many Saudi Arabians years later, through the settlement and educational indoctrination and monitoring programs of Al Saud's "religious ritual specialists," better known as *mutawwaʻa*. But they rejected the boundaries of the new Saudi state because of the disruptive impact

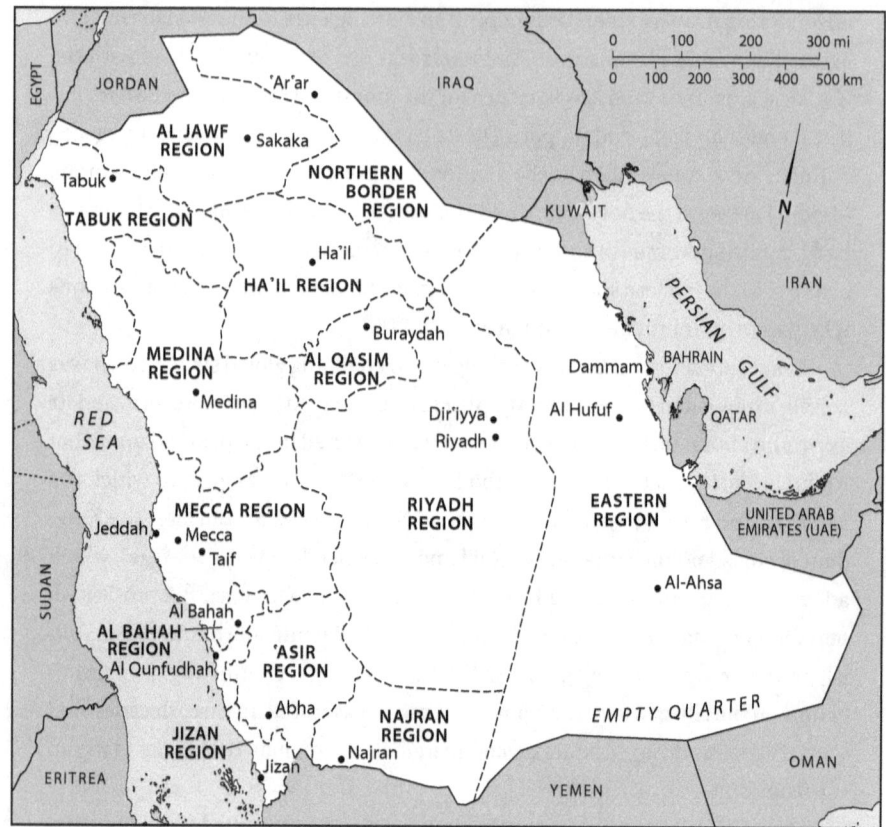

MAP 2. Regions, regional capitals, and main cities that Al Saud conquered between 1902 and 1934 and that today make up the Kingdom of Saudi Arabia.

they had on trade and migration routes. They refused as well to halt their raids on what they had long considered the infidel territories of Iraq and Transjordan, whose religious rituals they did not approve of.

The Ikhwan were motivated by religious and political beliefs as well as economic gain and territorial conquest.[104] Countering the spiritual and material practices of what Wahhabis considered non-Salafi, Sunni Muslims had consolidated the religious movement's identity and power. Labeling Shi'i and Sufi doctrines and practices as heretical, the Ikhwan propagated a rigid orthodoxy that informed Wahhabi identity and ultimately crowded out other religious and political sociabilities—even among Najdi Wahhabis. Establishment ulama and their Wahhabi enforcers considered places of religious and spiritual importance to be sites of contestation with those who did not conform to a strictly Sunni Wahhabi interpretation of Islam. Their ancestors, followers of Ibn Abd al-Wahhab, had attacked Shi'i shrines in Najaf and Karbala, which they saw as idolatrous, in the early eighteenth century. By destroying and curtailing access to such sites in Mecca and southern Iraq, they asserted their political power while preventing those of other faiths from performing their rituals.[105] Less than two centuries later, in the 1920s, when Abdulaziz denounced the Ikhwan's raids on the southern Iraqi cities, Wahhabis accused him of contradicting the religious message he had espoused. They declared that he had thus lost his legitimate claim to rule.[106] With British support, Abdulaziz crushed the subsequent rebellion of the Ikhwan, once his most loyal supporters.[107] His regime executed or imprisoned the revolt's leaders and many of their supporters. The British Royal Air Force went so far as to bombard the Ikhwan, who in early 1929 had raided the British protectorate of Kuwait.

Abdulaziz regularly relied on imperial support to defeat his rivals.[108] Nonetheless, he prided himself on his military prowess and unflinching ability to subjugate those who opposed his rule. In the early twentieth century, violent conquest was still a matter of great honor, and on the eve of state formation in 1932, Abdulaziz made it clear to the people of Najd that he would stop at nothing to consolidate his rule: "Do not forget that there is not one among you whose father or brother or cousin we have not slain. Aye, billah! it was by the sword that we have conquered you. And that same sword is above your heads. . . . We took you by the sword, and we shall keep you within your bounds by the sword."[109] The new ruler thus subdued the religious establishment, comprised of scholars, the Ikhwan, and the *mutawwa'a*.[110] The religious establishment also included Wahhabi inspectors (*muhtasibun*) charged with maintaining public order, morality, health, cleanliness, and honesty in business dealings.[111] Thereafter, the official religious establishment remained largely, though not consistently, deferential to the ruler's will.[112] State-allied religious leaders became the bedrock of political legitimacy, enshrining the notion of obeying the ruler as a religious obligation.

The new political sphere had no space for popular political will or the various aspirations, religious or otherwise, which had existed. The production of institutions and political practices that constituted the emerging state remained a dynastic affair. It relied on the bureaucratic expertise of those whom Al Saud's forces had conquered and who were subsequently excluded from Saudi national history: Hijazis and notables from other parts of the peninsula. The regime also depended on a constellation of "advisers" from the world over. Countering Ottoman rule and eliding the dynamic social, cultural, and political life in Ottoman Arabia, albeit describing such dynamism as nonexistent, shaped the discursive and material foundation of the Saudi state. The state-sanctioned narrative in Saudi Arabia's history textbooks portrays the Ottoman government as having promoted heresies that kept the Arabian Peninsula in an age of ignorance (*jahiliyya*) after it assumed power there in 1517.[113] Only a religious awakening, heralded by the new Wahhabi Saudi state, would cleanse the peninsula and bring it into the modern age. Modernity in Arabia thus hinged on the rule of Al Saud and rested on a particular religio-political, Najd-centered worldview.

In the earlier political entities that Abdulaziz's ancestors established in the eighteenth and nineteenth centuries, Wahhabi zealotry, nomadism, and the lack of resources, arms, and organizing power had allowed Ottoman forces and regional rivals to defeat them. Abdulaziz learned from his ancestors' experiences. He embarked on a project to settle the nomadic tribes in agricultural zones and socialize them into political Wahhabism. The ruling family quickly learned to contain tribal threats through financial tributes, marriage, coercion, imprisonment, and employment in the state's security branches.[114]

Abdulaziz espoused a singular yet more flexible Wahhabi ideology to legitimate and consolidate the modern state he claimed as his hereditary possession. Although religion remained subordinate to politics, the religious establishment played an instrumental role in political life well into the twentieth century. Loyal religious leaders and Wahhabi inspectors aided the practice of Saudi governance. The religious establishment first sought to influence religious learning in Mecca.[115] They did so through training ulama and religious leaders at the Grand Mosque and, with the help of officers, inspecting markets, religious practice, medical and educational facilities, and construction sites in the city. Ulama and judges based in Riyadh began to issue fatwas for the rest of the country. These were then enforced by religious officials (*nuwwab*, sing. *na'ib*), who represent or govern on behalf of a ruler. Religious socialization had a foundational role in Al Saud's imperial conquest, as it did in attempts to bind the conquered territories together politically and culturally. An officially sanctioned Wahhabism came to dominate the country even though the regime relocated its Sunni scholars from Najd to predominantly Sunni parts of the country, leaving the inhabitants of "non-Sunni regions, such as Qatif, Najran, and parts of Hasa . . . to continue relying on their own regional religious elite."[116] In this way, the production and dissemination of an officially sanctioned Wahhabism, bolstered by repression and the use of force, accompanied and shaped the early territorial empire and the post-1932 processes of state formation.

At the same time that the religious establishment socialized Saudi subjects, Abdulaziz set about securing the longevity of his lineage. He assigned his eldest sons to positions of power across the country and in 1933 designated Saud as crown prince. He hired many non-Saudi consultants to advise him on managing state affairs. Court historians and other intellectuals—Saudi and non-Saudi—wrote hagiographies of the new king. In them, they posit a continuous Saudi "state" from the mid-eighteenth century onward, whose territory at times includes most of the Arabian Peninsula. The narrative pivots on a religiously orthodox Al Saud clan "uniting" the allegedly premodern peoples of Ottoman Arabia—who had strayed from the practices of the prophet and his companions—into a "civilized" state whose nomenclature and that of its rulers are synonymous.[117] All Saudi subjects had to pay homage to this version of the country's history. Many, however, regularly challenged the official narrative, risking prosecution, exile, and imprisonment.[118]

Abdulaziz was a product of late nineteenth-century circuits of ideas and mobilities. But like most state builders elsewhere, once in power, he began to elide Arabia's pre–Al Saud diverse lifeworlds. The Saudi regime's attempts to centralize the ruling family's power increasingly silenced many subjects' varied senses of belonging, loyalty, and identity. But the emerging state's socialization mechanisms and disciplinary forces failed to control many of the peninsula's inhabitants. Where Al Saud had managed by 1932 to territorially consolidate their empire-cum-state, they were far from doing so politically, culturally, or economically.[119] The new state was one among multiple possible political formations that Al Saud had foreclosed.[120] The establishment of the state thus triggered political resistance and competing visions of the nation and state-society relations.[121] It also heightened regionalism and particularistic identities in the Hijaz in the west, 'Asir in the south, the Eastern Province, and various pockets in the central region of Najd itself. Inhabitants of the peninsula continued to have much in common with citizens of other states across the Red Sea, Persian Gulf, and Indian Ocean, and into the newly formed post-Ottoman Arab states.[122] Like them, many held on to political, social, and economic aspirations derived from the experience of modernity, transoceanic mobility, the emergence of the modern state system, early twentieth-century sociopolitical developments, and increased access to education at home and abroad. Consolidating Al Saud's early twentieth-century territorial empire into a state with an "authoritative identity" required obscuring these religious, cultural, and political realities.[123]

THE CORPORATE STATE

Al Saud largely failed to produce political legitimacy and a national ideology that united the people of Arabia, even as the idea of the Saudi state itself was becoming entrenched and legitimate.[124] Fearing secular nation-state nationalism and its populist manifestations in the region, the ruling family espoused a narrowly defined religious nationalism that initially did not resonate with most Arabians. Like all nationalisms, Saudi religious nationalism excluded many.[125] In addition to negotiating with locals, Al Saud had to rely on coercion—as well as British and US imperial backing—to rule the country and manage its resources. Events in the 1930s further hampered Al Saud's attempts at political, cultural, and economic hegemony. The Great Depression, followed by the outbreak of World War II in 1939, greatly constrained the ability of Muslims to perform the pilgrimage to Mecca and eroded the Saudi state's tax revenues.[126] The development of cultivated pearls in Japan in 1938 exacerbated the already-suffering Persian Gulf economies, dependent as they were on the pearl trade. The first decade following Saudi state formation was thus marked by poverty and disease. Even the discovery of oil in Saudi Arabia's Eastern Province in 1938 did nothing to improve the country's economy, occurring as it had on the eve of the war.[127] Not only did the war bring oil production to a complete halt, but it also interrupted the country's commerce with India and prevented the trade in dates, the state's second-largest source of income after the pilgrimage. Until the end of the war, the regime focused on its own survival and securing basic goods and medicines.

The Saudi regime was capital starved. It faced stiff internal opposition and lacked the infrastructure to construct the state and socialize citizens. To stay in power, Saudi rulers turned to subcontracting state functions to international, and later on to local, corporations. A prominent feature of late twentieth-century state formation, dependence on corporations has marked Saudi Arabia since its establishment. Of all the corporations, none was as imbricated in Saudi state and history making as the Arabian American Oil Company, or Aramco. In the first three decades of the state's existence, Al Saud heavily relied on the company in economic, diplomatic, security, planning, infrastructural, cultural, and social matters.[128] Aramco officials had realized the significance of Saudi Arabian oil before the US government did. For years, they urged policy makers in Washington to finance their operations there, but to no avail. It took a global war for the official relationship between Washington and Riyadh to transpire.

The war economy and postwar US foreign policy brought Abdulaziz ibn Saud closer to the United States. Saudi Arabia's strategic location in the war against Japan and Germany was not lost on the US government, which in 1941 even expressed the view that the "most crucial phase of the war will take place in the Near East."[129] The US government began to view Abdulaziz as the most important Arab and Muslim leader who could sway other rulers to side with the Allies in the war.[130] Given the importance of adding Saudi Arabia as an ally, the State Department recommended financing the Saudi king, partly with navy purchases of oil, despite its low quality and incompatibility with US naval equipment, and partly through a Lend-Lease Act in 1942.[131] So it was that in 1944 the US War Department made a formal request to build an air base in Dhahran, in Saudi Arabia's Eastern Province.[132] The need to build an air base for war purposes—rather than access to oil—preoccupied the Roosevelt administration from 1943 onward. In addition to discussing the Jewish settler colonial project in Palestine, building an air base animated the president's meeting with the king in February 1945.[133] Later that year, Abdulaziz granted the United States permission to build the base, positioning Saudi Arabia on the US side of the looming Cold War. Although the base remained nonoperational until after the war's end because of British resistance to US encroachment in the Gulf, it continued to play a central, if contentious, role in US-Saudi relations. The beginning of the Cold War only highlighted the importance of maintaining a US military presence in Arabia. The Saudi king also saw the merits of relying on US instead of British capital, the former not (yet) having the same colonial history in the region.[134] It was thus that Saudi Arabia abandoned its British protectors and came into the US orbit.[135]

By the time the US government lent its support to Abdulaziz in the early 1940s, Aramco was already deeply entrenched in many aspects of Saudi life.[136] The US alliance with the ruling family only reified Aramco's role in the country. From conducting land surveys, delineating borders, appropriating land, and building infrastructure to helping forge educational and foreign policy, Aramco executives acted as agents of Saudi state building, making decisions that affected the everyday lives of Saudi Arabian citizens. US officials in Saudi Arabia regularly complained to the State Department—with little effect—about Aramco's continued assumption of diplomatic functions despite the institutionalization of US consular affairs there.[137] Aramco became central to US foreign policy in Saudi Arabia.[138] Retired and active CIA agents joined Aramco's payroll, and vice versa, mostly in the Government Relations Department, while some simply used the oil company as a cover.[139]

As Aramco sealed its status as a state within a state, at least in the oil-rich Eastern Province, it sought to downplay its involvement in state affairs, all the while portraying itself as a force for good. Aramco's projects in the Eastern Province—in the fields of urban planning, education, and public health, among others—were necessary for the oil economy's proper functioning.[140] To better navigate the desert terrain, for instance, Aramco built an infrastructural network that linked the new geography of the petroleum industry. Asphalt roads made transportation possible between oil towns, camps, and ports in the Eastern Province. Aramco then oversaw the $50 million railroad project, which the Saudi regime fully funded and the Bechtel Corporation built in 1947 as a natural extension to the port at Dammam.[141] The railway connected several eastern cities with one another, and for the first time, with Riyadh, long before Aramco built the Riyadh–Dammam highway years later.

Having a docile but relatively educated labor force was crucial for Aramco. To deal with the shortage of skilled labor and to assuage heightening labor demands and government pressure, Aramco built training centers and educational opportunities for local Saudi Arabian employees and a few schools for their children. Ultimately, it was cheaper to train Saudi Arabians for nonexecutive jobs than to hire thousands of US and other expatriate workers. Aramco also opened hospitals for workers and residents alike in order to manage its employees' health and well-being. Eradicating communicable diseases such as cholera, which had taken a toll on workers, was of the utmost priority. Through these projects, Aramco sought to lay down the infrastructure of the modern oil economy while increasing its profits and privileges. By April 1952, a US finance commission had set up the Saudi Arabian Monetary Agency, effectively a central bank, in Jeddah.[142] Since then, the institutionalization of the finance industry has enabled the diversion of large amounts of oil money into banks in the United States and several Western European countries.

In addition to building a modern economy, the projects that Aramco and other corporations carried out undergirded the making of the state.[143] They furthered the regime's disciplinary control over a restive population while centralizing the ruling family's power.[144] Central to state consolidation was the ability to master the Saudi terrain and to project power over distinct and expansive geographies. This power projection allowed the regime to manage the population of the fledgling nation.[145] But as the regime's authoritarian rule and Aramco's extractive capabilities deepened, popular opposition to oil imperialism and to authoritarianism increased. Labor activism at Aramco and other corporations took off in the 1940s in opposition to oil imperialism, corporate overreach, and state authoritarianism. So did countrywide political mobilizations that espoused varied and predominantly leftist and Arab nationalist political ideologies.[146] The political solidarities that formed across geographical regions, socioeconomic classes, and sects, and struggles over the nature of power and the state, all seriously threatened Abdulaziz's rule. These only accelerated in the ensuing two decades, echoing popular politics across the Arab Middle East.[147] Multiple futures were still possible at the time, contrary to what the historiography would have us believe. The competing visions of the political future championed by Saudi Arabians—both at the popular and at the institutional level—also often divided them, creating fissures within the ruling classes and society at large. Many citizens who strove to change the nature of political authority within their country were caught up in the power struggle between King Saud (r. 1953–1964) and his brother and crown prince, Faisal ibn Abdulaziz (r. 1964–1975). The struggle was embodied by the comparatively progressive or conservative policies that each respectively pursued. Encouraged by popular demand and his political advisers, and in reaction to Faisal and his supporters in the ruling family, Saud adopted more radical measures. In 1960, he appointed the technocratic Council of Ministers that included leftists like Abdulaziz ibn Muammar and Arab nationalists like Prince Talal ibn Abdulaziz.[148] The short-lived Arab nationalist political system his regime formed was based on a constitutional monarchy, popular political participation, social justice, accountability, and comprehensive statewide modernization.[149]

Aramco, successive US administrations, and powerful members of the Al Saud family were united in their opposition to the direction being taken by Saudi Arabia under King Saud. They saw it as threatening to the ruling family's hereditary, authoritarian form of rule and the political economic order they all favored. When Faisal toppled Saud and ascended the throne in 1964, domestic and regional political groups increasingly opposed his authoritarian rule and ever-closer ties to the US government. Following the 1962 revolution in Yemen and the ensuing military confrontation between Egypt and Saudi Arabia and their proxies in Yemen (1962–1970), Egyptian president Gamal Abdel Nasser directed the harshest critiques against Arab monarchies, and Al Saud in particular. The Saudi rulers were, in his words, "'traitors' to the Arab nation, 'agents of colonialism,' and 'enemies of unity.'"[150] Faisal was anxious to pacify the domestic opposition and end public criticism of his regime and the unflattering image of himself as a US puppet.[151] With US backing, Faisal's regime crushed these popular movements and constrained the dialectic of radicalism that was gaining momentum in one of the major front lines of the Cold War.[152] The attendant Saudi state form shows how popular political life and the nature of political rule are mutually constitutive. They have shaped state policy since the emergence of Saudi Arabia in 1932. Indeed, Faisal's regime shut down secular political life and consolidated the religiously conservative, authoritarian state. Faisal and his corporate and imperial allies ensured that this history of contestation was subsequently elided in Saudi and US historiographies, which instead projected them as leading agents of modernization.[153]

The actions of the Saudi regime, the US government, and Aramco served their own narrow needs and not, as some scholars claim, those of the Saudi people.[154] Corporate and imperial interests required a materially and symbolically controlled Saudi Arabia. Aramco in particular was often an impediment to popular prosperity and well-being. The company, along with US officials, enabled nondemocratic politics, economics, and knowledge production, "distort[ing] development" and causing immense and irreversible damage to the environment.[155] When Aramco did make concessions, it was a result of labor demands, popular pressure, and at times, regime coercion. Former Saudi oil minister Abdullah al-Tariqi, a staunch critic of oil imperialism, put it this way: "The monopolizing oil companies in the Arab homeland are most invested in not improving the status quo and raising awareness among the Arab youths.... [They] resort to all measures, without exception, in order to maintain the status quo. They, like governments in modern states, utilize psychological, economic and political warfare, and like these governments, have specialized departments for the implementation of their policies, and . . . these companies cooperate closely with their home governments."[156] Like colonial states and companies elsewhere, Aramco hindered comprehensive development and tried to slow the country's modernization in order to maintain and expand its privilege there as long as possible. Also like other colonial states and companies, Aramco invested heavily in producing a sanitized history of the company, the regime, and the state, one that successive Saudi regimes used as a blueprint, revising its contours to accommodate political and social transformations.

CONCLUSION

During his lifetime, Rahmatullah al-Kairanawi wrote and lectured extensively about the perils of imperialism and the need to fight it, sometimes through violent means. His writings reached all corners of the Muslim world. Yet to the extent that Saudi Arabians have even heard about the shaykh, whom they recognize as al-Hindi, they were familiar only with his infamous book *The Truth Revealed* and his debates with Christian proselytizers. Selections of the book were assigned to the boys' curriculum, but the scholar and his work were detached from their historical and intellectual context. Saudi Arabia's official history, despite its slightly varying iterations since the 1970s, erased pre-1932 lifeworlds, imperial and corporate support, and the violence on which the modern state was founded. It also severed Saudi Arabia's subjects and spaces from the cosmopolitan pasts, identities, and intellectual trajectories that the Arabian Peninsula's geography had long allowed for, oriented as it was to the Ottoman world but also East Africa, Persia, and the Indian subcontinent. Regime members refer to these pasts as the "red lines" (*khutut hamra'*) of history, and they made sure to curate them out of state archives. The regime silenced these histories by controlling their evidentiary terrains through soft and hard violence. For a long time, Saudi Arabians who dared to publicly engage these occluded histories paid a heavy price for it. The regime's national cultural-intellectual field suppressed the peninsula's diverse transnational connections, identities, religiosities, and histories, and its people's political subjectivities and aspirations. Instead, it portrayed pre- and early modern state forms as insular, apolitical, and outside of history's inexorable march.[157]

It bears repeating that the Saudi ruling family's chronophagy has been of great utility for its contemporary self-representation. In both the popular and the conventional academic imagination, Saudi Arabia is an exceptional state that owes its existence more to divine power and the genius of Abdulaziz ibn Saud rather than to contingent factors such as imperial rivalries, global wars, and capitalist interests. Because of Abdulaziz, the monarchy wants its subjects to think Saudi state formation was a blessing that restored righteous rule to the birthplace of Islam. Because of Abdulaziz, conventional academic narratives say, Saudi state formation was a "stable," linear, and path-dependent process that escaped colonial occupation. In such narratives, the idea of the Saudi state was uncontested, in contrast to the tumult that characterizes the history of the nominally secular postcolonial states in the Middle East. It is a few short steps to the notion of a state outside time—and therefore immune to challenges present and future.

Taking seriously the intellectual landscape in nineteenth-century Ottoman Arabia and political movements that have challenged Al Saud since then reveals a multidimensional social history that has been flattened, obscured, and repurposed in the service of monarchical statecraft. The diversity of pre-Al Saud forms of belonging was all the more reason for the regime and its backers to diligently curate the country's official history. They dismissed indigenous modes of thought, activism, and economic and cultural life as insignificant, and occluded them from the state-sanctioned historical narrative. Doing so allowed the Saudi regime and its allied US oil company to project themselves as leading agents of modernization in a landscape empty of opposing ideas or figures.[158]

The Saudi regime is committed to globally propagating this image of itself. The stubborn insistence on Saudi Arabia being both anomalous and on the margins of global events has served to shield these portrayals, and the official Saudi Arabian history on which they are founded, from serious scrutiny. The consolidation of the Saudi state, and the very ability to maintain a sanitized global narrative, depended on religious legitimation and authoritarianism as well as on the imperial and corporate support that Al Saud have long enjoyed. Despite the critical scholarship that has emerged since the early 2000s, many academics and nonacademics alike continue to accept the regime's narrative. Wittingly or not, they refuse to see the centrality of Arabia since the nineteenth century to the regional and global circulation of ideas, movements, capital, and politics. Scholarship that includes Saudi Arabia as a case study, or as one site in a comparative framework, often reifies the state's conventional tropes. The regime's ongoing efforts to rub Saudi Arabia's multiple histories out of the material record, and to maintain a vacuous, one-dimensional narrative of Arabian history, have been remarkably efficient.

The ability to maintain such a dominant historical narrative has required authoritarianism and religious legitimation, to be sure, but also the collaboration of multiple internal and external forces.[159] Geopolitics and oil economics united US corporate and state interests with those of the political and religious elites in Saudi Arabia. These various constituents depended on Al Saud for their own interests and were thus committed to the regime's survival. From the Saudi state's inception, US corporations, and later on, the US government, protected the ruling family from pervasive, if erased, domestic anticolonial and anti-authoritarian mobilizations as well as from regional rivals like Nasser. This protection was discursive and material and had political, strategic, and economic motives. US corporate and political support consolidated Al Saud's authoritarian rule and empowered the regime to maintain an enduring historiographical self-representation. Yet those traces of the pasts that Saudi state formation and global capitalism have worked so hard to occlude have nevertheless persisted in private and public archives and libraries, in the built environment, and in people's individual, familial, and collective memories. They shed light on how older generations of intellectuals, activists, revolutionaries, and ordinary people operated against all odds. Far from romanticizing or resurrecting the heroic and activist subjectivities of those who have lived in Arabia, they also allow us to, as David Scott urges, "make the present yield more attractive possibilities for alternative futures," especially as the project for making and memorializing history intensifies in the twenty-first century.[160]

Chapter 2

A STATE WITH NO ARCHIVE

IN 1987, YAHYA IBN JUNAYD, IN HIS CAPACITY AS HEAD OF OPERAtions at the King Fahd National Library (KFNL), went on a scouting trip. On the lookout for rare books and manuscripts, he journeyed to Qasr Ibrahim, a fort located in Hofuf in the al-Ahsa region of Saudi Arabia's Eastern Province. An Ottoman governor had built the fort in 1555. Abdulaziz ibn Saud captured the stronghold from Ottoman forces in 1913, annexing the whole of al-Ahsa into his Kingdom of Najd in 1920 and the Kingdom of Saudi Arabia in 1932. The fort fell into disuse in subsequent decades.[1] Ibn Junayd had little idea of what might be at Qasr Ibrahim. To his utter shock, he found the fort's basement filled with bags of administrative documents that dated from the Ottoman era up to the 1930s. He took several of the sacks, along with some boxes he had found outside the fort, all of which were packed with records of legal transactions. Upon his return to the KFNL in Riyadh, Ibn Junayd described what he had unearthed to Prince Salman ibn Abdulaziz, then governor of the capital city (and who became king in 2015). The governor did not instruct Ibn Junayd to hand over his find to the King Abdulaziz Foundation for Research and Archives—the Darah—although the regime had at the time already commissioned the Darah with collecting historical documents. Instead, under the guise of heritage preservation, Prince Salman secured legal approval from the Ministry of Education for the librarian to house the documents he had located in the fort at the KFNL.[2] The task of archival preservation was missing from the KFNL's own mission statement.[3]

Ibn Junayd soon took a second scouting trip, this time northwest of Riyadh to the Red Sea coastal town of al-Wajh. From there, he journeyed a few kilometers inland to visit al-Wajh fortress (Qalʿat al-Wajh). The Ottomans built the fortress in 1617 to ensure the safety of the pilgrimage caravans as well as to surveil the movement of the pilgrims. The fortress had strengthened the status of al-Wajh—with its market and water wells—as an important and secure station on the pilgrimage route linking Egypt to Mecca and Medina. Its importance waned, however, in the decade following the opening of the Suez Canal in 1869, as travel by sea overtook that by land as the preferred mode of transportation from Egypt to the holy cities in the Hijaz.[4]

When Ibn Junayd entered the fortress, he found still more abandoned administrative records. Over the objections of outspoken locals, he took several samples to show Riyadh's governor. He then headed with his team to al-Wajh's old town, which was almost completely empty as well. There, buried under the sand within the town's abandoned houses, he uncovered numerous additional documents, well preserved from the elements inside the shelter of the abandoned houses. Some were Ottoman and Egyptian in origin, while others belonged to the Ashraf, the Hashemites who governed parts of the Hijaz under the suzerainty of the Ottomans starting in 1517 and against whom they revolted in 1916. Still other documents dated back to the more recent Saudi era. All were related to the pilgrimage, trade, and economic history of the region. Ibn Junayd again notified Prince Salman of his discovery. Salman wrote to the Ministry of Interior for permission for the librarian to take the documents he had found in Wajh, as well as others he had located nearby in the possession of the Coast Guard. They were all taken to the KFNL—where they still sit at the time of this writing. It was another successful collaboration between Ibn Junayd and Prince Salman. Both would be at the forefront of the twenty-first-century drive to secure as many historical documents on Arabia as possible.

The tale of Ibn Junayd's document hunts illustrates several truths about the history of archival production in Saudi Arabia and its relationship to the state. In the 1960s, as it entered its fourth decade on the throne, the Al Saud clan had a monopoly over economic resources and political authority, showed many of the trappings of absolute rule, and was a key "strategic partner" of the US government. But, as Saudi kings were acutely aware, they lacked domestic legitimacy. Religious, tribal, and popular oppositional mobilizations threatened their territorial integrity, especially as neighboring governments to varying degrees either disputed Arabia's borders (modern-day Qatar, Oman, the United Arab Emirates, and Yemen) or altogether challenged the nature of the Saudi state (Egypt and Syria).[5] Their status as "custodians of the two holy mosques" was contested at best. At its heart, Saudi power has been dispersed within a large and growing ruling family, fragmented by region, and threatened by recurrent, severe political crisis. Outside of their limited base in Najd and their elite allies across the kingdom, the rulers often had to resort to violence or the threat thereof to maintain their hold; everywhere, they relied heavily for political support upon the ideological common ground they found with important social strata in the Wahhabi reading of Sunni Islam. Saudi power was, and remains, control without hegemony.

In the late 1960s, however, the Saudi rulers understood that, in order to bolster their power against growing domestic and regional challenges, they needed to have a unifying history that built the cohesion of the imagined nation.[6] They promoted one around the religious awakening and the role of Al Saud as well as Muhammad ibn Abd al-Wahhab and his followers in bringing about what they regarded as an ideal Muslim community. They then hired historians from Egypt, Iraq, and Palestine who, in addition to working as schoolteachers, were employed at the Ministry of Education, where they refined the official historical narrative.[7] The emerging narrative additionally portrayed Al Saud as the anti-imperial modernizing saviors of the peninsula as well as its sole legitimate inheritors. In this framing, the Ottomans, and not the British, were the imperialists from whom the Arabs needed saving.

In the 1970s, the rulers institutionalized and centralized this narrative in school curricula and textbooks.[8] It was only a few years earlier, though, that they saw the need to centralize the administrative records of state institutions and establish a national archive. The goal was not to produce or evince the official historical narrative or to monumentalize the state and its power, as archives are so often deployed to do.[9] Rather, this initial top-down archiving drive was to hide, protect, and organize state secrets, not simply from the purview of citizens, but especially from that of top bureaucrats and ruling members of Al Saud. This, too, was common practice elsewhere. In places like Guatemala, Israel, France, the

United Kingdom, and the United States, the archive was at once a threat and a necessity. Decision makers invested heavily in curating national archives while regularly concealing documents from each other, challenging declassification laws, decentralizing records by way of dispersing them, and preventing access to documents.[10] As we will see, many of those in power in Saudi Arabia resisted all attempts at archival centralization and the sharing of government records. At least nominally, this national archiving project was treated with the same gravity as the roughly contemporaneous plans for the nationalization of the oil sector.

ARCHIVAL SOVEREIGNTY

The state is an effect of "ideological power." It is an effect whose dominance and legitimacy require ongoing reproduction and reification through the repetition of cultural practices. These include representations and performances as well as bureaucratic routines such as mapping, surveying, and urban planning.[11] Archiving is another such legitimating routine. Yet scholars have shown that the archival experience points as much to conflict and incoherence as it does to authority and centralization.[12] The archival operation, in fact, mirrors the making of the state in its constant flux and its continual negotiation and compromise between and among the political strata, economic elites, and grassroots as well as elite religious and secular groups. Like state formation, archives are not built on a tabula rasa: they are dependent on economic, institutional, political, and social dynamics that can either support or hinder these piecemeal processes. Archiving has been doubly arbitrary in Saudi Arabia, where the lines blur between the state and the ruling family, the private and the public, the corporate and the personal, distinctions that are not exclusive to Saudi Arabia's governance structures but are common elsewhere. This doubling of the arbitrary is one strategy of many in the regime's imperative of history making and erasing. Strategies such as these provide fertile ground to rethink many seemingly self-evident divides that we continue to rely on: secular-religious, public-private, corporation-state. A critical engagement with the mutually constitutive nature of history and state in Arabia also moves us beyond the seamless partitioning of the discursive from the material. Arabia is not some anomalous case distant from everything we know. It is a place where history and state are deeply and violently imbricated. Exposing the roots and consequences of these imbrications dismantles the binaries and divisions that are one source of epistemological blurriness.

In the case of Ibn Junayd's discoveries, and on many other occasions, archiving in pre–Gulf War Saudi Arabia was a matter of chance. As I show in this chapter, it was also an attempt to circumvent the official state-led history-making project. Indeed, the state archives that exist in Saudi Arabia have been assembled at the interstices of state formation and the violence that always attends that endeavor. This chapter connects the beginning of official archival praxis in Cold War Arabia to the necessity of managing elite rivalries over power as well as fending off threats to the regime from regional rivals such as Egypt's President Gamal Abdel Nasser and domestic popular political movements. Tracing the battles to produce a national archive from the mid-1960s until the late 1980s, it considers the institutional sites and infrastructural practices that support history making as integral to state formation and political legitimation.

The irony is that, fifty years and counting after the state-led archiving project was first proclaimed, Saudi Arabia still does not have a national archive, at least not one commensurate with the state's wealth and political weight. Can there be a state without an archive? Perhaps the better question is, what does it mean for a state not to have an archive? This is all the more salient given that the most functional and comprehensive archive housing state records in Saudi Arabia today is that of the formerly US-owned oil company, the Arabian American Oil Company (Aramco). Its archive remains outside the purview of the Saudi state even as the government fully owns the corporation, which was nationalized in 1980 and was, in 1988, renamed Saudi Arabian Oil Company (still referred to as Aramco). As a matter of fact, since the early 2000s, Aramco has turned down every proposal from Saudi state archives to share copies of its archival records as well as its employees' archiving expertise.[13]

Such a reality renders moot the Saudi regime's claims of having escaped colonialism in all its forms. In fact, it pushes us to think of the Aramco archive not simply as a corporate archive, or a postcolonial archive, but rather as a colonial one that indexes the complexity of statecraft and political sovereignty. The failure of state archives to secure Aramco's cooperation especially troubles the assumed coherence and stability of authoritarian regimes as well as the disaggregated nature of the state. The coherence of historical narration often masks the messy, arbitrary, and haphazard nature of archival production, and the ongoing struggles that undergird it. That these are often beyond the purview of scholars makes Saudi Arabia's belated archival production especially instructive. It has allowed me to foreground the social, economic, and political struggles that are endemic to both historical production and state formation, and the ways in which these overlap with, or diverge from, similar processes elsewhere. The case of Saudi Arabia complicates conventional thinking about archives—and about the authoritarian state itself.

CRISIS AND THE MAKING OF HISTORY

On November 2, 1964, Faisal ibn Abdulaziz Al Saud made history when he overthrew his brother, Saud, in a palace coup. Faisal had already built a reputation for himself as a ruthless man, and upon assuming the throne he did what anyone who had come to power in a coup would do: he purged the government of his brother's inner circle. The new king then moved to consolidate his rule against the many internal and external threats the monarchy was facing at the time. At home, the secular leftist mobilizations that had flourished in Saudi Arabia since the late 1940s imperiled the monarchy's monopoly on political and economic power. They took to the streets, issued petitions and pamphlets, and wrote in the burgeoning local press in their fight for social justice, economic equality, and political participation.[14] Abroad, the struggle between reactionary and progressive forces that was a hallmark of the Middle East during the Cold War pitted Al Saud (and other monarchies) against the most popular of Arab leaders, Gamal Abdel Nasser. In 1962 this conflict had become a hot war in Yemen, where Nasser sent troops to fight alongside republican rebels trying to overthrow the Saudi-backed hereditary imamate. Together and separately, these twin threats infuriated Faisal as he sought to end the dangers to Arab monarchical rule once and for all.

In the years after Faisal assumed the throne, thousands of dissidents were thrown in prison, where many of them experienced brutal interrogation and physical intimidation.[15] Others were exiled, placed under house arrest, and even killed, their personal papers confiscated or burned. As the newly minted king maneuvered politically and militarily to crush the domestic opposition movements, he was alarmed as well by the symbolic and material threat presented by Nasser. On the one hand, many local opposition forces were either allied with, or drew inspiration from, Nasser and popular movements associated with his persona. On the other hand, the war in Yemen was too geographically close for comfort. To make matters worse, Nasser regularly took aim at Arab monarchies in general, and Al Saud in particular, in various Arab media. Nasser's relentless war of information against the monarchy, which continued until his death in 1970, proved especially incriminating. As king, Faisal presented himself as the protector of the Muslim faith and regularly spoke of the importance of safeguarding Muslim unity in general and Arab solidarity, sovereignty, and independence in particular. Faisal even espoused political religion as a state policy in order to counter the dominant secular trends of the time. Yet Faisal had relied on US support to overthrow his brother and crush the popular, anti-imperial mobilizations that espoused the very same ideals that Faisal purported to defend. Saudi Arabian activists and various clandestine political parties criticized Faisal for these contradictions and for aligning the country with US imperial power at the height of decolonization. Although Nasser's propaganda machine, Sawt al-Arab radio, lacked accuracy and impartiality, it nevertheless found King Faisal, who blatantly enjoyed Washington's favor, to be an easy target.[16]

The indigenous socio-intellectual challenges that Faisal's regime faced were closely connected to the praxis of official historiography in Saudi Arabia. The mid-twentieth-century mobilizations had put forth a diverse set of political imaginaries that predate the consolidation of the Saudi state in the 1960s or the formation and institutionalization of a centralized, official historical discourse in the 1970s. For some, a sovereign republic rooted in economic justice and the political participation of all citizens—regardless of sect, class, gender, or regional and tribal belonging—was the ideal form of political organization. It was one that Nasser promoted in his daily Sawt al-Arab radio broadcasts. Others fought for a constitutional monarchy for which Al Saud were symbolic leaders at best, ones who nominated a sovereign "who reigns but does not rule."[17] The Al Saud monarchy, and the Saudi state form with which we are familiar today, was not yet portrayed in the popular imaginary as the only legitimate and permissible form of political organization. The monarchy had not yet mobilized educational institutions, cultural production, and the press as tools for these purposes.

Faisal needed to address lingering threats and to foreclose the conditions of possibility for such alternative futures. His regime developed a centralized system of mass education, which it mobilized as a tool with which to reconcile differences with opponents and strengthen ties with allies. Centralizing the historiographical self-representation of the Saudi state was key. To do so, the regime employed a network of non-Saudi historians, poets, and writers to advance an official historical narrative under the supervision of state-allied and state-employed religious bureaucrats. The goal was to solidify a homogeneous and religiously framed "Saudi identity" against competing secular populist ideologies.[18] It was an identity and a history that brought together Al Saud's genealogy with Wahhabi sectarianism, in a manner contrary to the liberal notion of historical progress dominant elsewhere in the world. Reshaping Saudi religious subjectivity was central to the institutionalization of political religion in Saudi Arabia. It was the frame through which the regime fended off the various threats it faced, and through which it entrenched a politically reactionary, religiously conservative state in the late 1960s.

It was no surprise that one of Faisal's first acts as king was to join the information war in which Nasser so clearly had the upper hand. The fledgling Saudi state bureaucracy had neither the technical nor the human infrastructure needed to compete with Egypt's multimedia juggernaut and seasoned government mouthpieces. Saudi Arabia lacked an archive from which it could deploy material evidence to bolster its claims or refute Nasser's accusations.[19] Intent on remedying the imbalance, Faisal pleaded with successive US administrations to intervene and prevent Egyptian propaganda against the kingdom. He also asked the US government for the technical equipment and training needed to bolster the regime's symbolic capital.[20] Distinct from his predecessor, Saud, whose reign featured a semblance of press freedom, Faisal invested in firm control of the production and circulation of knowledge about Arabia and the monarchy.[21] He started with an unofficial ban on any mention, oral or written, of King Saud and a cleansing of the historical record. The aim was to wash away any remnant of Saud's reign, the popular movements that had thrived therein, and any trace of the US-sanctioned coup against his brother. For Faisal, this had foregrounded the need to establish a central archive and control knowledge on the kingdom more broadly. In what is today one of Faisal's most lasting legacies, his regime issued a new media law that centralized the publishing industry in Saudi Arabia and strangled the nascent free press.[22] Thereafter, the new law required not only that the state be part owner of any Saudi newspaper but also that newspaper editors work closely with the Ministry of Information and its censors.[23] Newspaper owners and journalists contested and protested the new media law, describing it as a form of nationalization common to socialist countries and akin to the press law in Nasser's Egypt.[24] But the regime ignored their calls and, in the subsequent years, continued to invest in controlling knowledge production and improving Saudi Arabia's image abroad.[25]

It was in the context of these violent years that the regime undertook its first endeavor to construct a state archive. It was not coincidental that the country's first archiving law in 1966 should pass at the same time that the counterrevolutionary state tightened its grip. Postcolonial independence movements and nation-state formation in the region had led King Faisal's regime to the idea that, absent material evidence of the past, the nation and its makers had no history, and therefore no present.[26] Like its counterparts, the Saudi regime began to equate the absence of an archive that centralized state documents with the absence of history itself.[27] The absence of an archive was a source of weakness, a vulnerability that opponents could, and indeed did, exploit, especially at times of crisis. The regime thus needed to produce and control the archival record while managing the potential threats that are always embedded within it in order to maintain power.[28] Doing so would allow the regime to choreograph its own, sanitized version of the past and to reify its political, territorial, economic, and cultural claims, thereby bolstering its legitimacy. As important, an archival record would allow the state to conceal the rich leftist history of Arabia and the attendant violent counterrevolutionary measures. This is to say nothing of the dynamic pre–Al Saud intellectual and political networks that counter state claims about Arabia being stuck in an "age of ignorance" (*jahiliyya*) before the advent of Al Saud. At the same time, however, the regime needed to keep state policies, bureaucratic machinations, and family power struggles confidential, not only from the public but also from the various fiefdoms that constituted Saudi power. In other words, the king and his top advisers were afraid of the monarchy's many rivals, and especially of competing elements within Al Saud. These anxieties have shaped archival praxis in Saudi Arabia ever since, with the push and pull of the archival operation mirroring the rivalries endemic to the Saudi state. Authoritarianism, after all, has its limits.

SCATTERED ARCHIVES, FRAGMENTED STATE

In 1966, the High Committee for Administrative Reform decreed that the archive of the Ministry of Finance and National Economy (Amanat al-Mahfuzat) would become the national archive of Saudi Arabia.[29] Known as the Ministry of Finance until 1954 and initially located in Mecca, the ministry was formed in 1936 on the heels of the emergence of the Saudi state. Its archive, however, was not established until 1947.[30] As one of the young state's oldest and most powerful institutions, the ministry was the logical destination for the country's national archive. Under the leadership of Finance Minister Abdullah al-Suleiman (r. 1932–1954), the ministry had worked closely with the first king, Abdulaziz ibn Saud, and with Aramco, to put in place the political and financial structures that would ensure the viability of the state. Overseeing the state's emergent offices, it influenced all levels of policy making, leaving a significant paper trail in the process.

The Finance Ministry retained its authority over all matters of state until King Saud ascended the throne in 1953 and began the initial phase of state modernization and the creation of state institutions. His regime established a dozen ministries including the Ministries of Interior, Education, Health, Agriculture, and Transportation. It also merged the Ministry of Economy and the Ministry of Finance into the single Ministry of Finance and National Economy. One of the farthest-reaching reforms Saud ordered, however, was to move the seat of government in 1956 from Mecca eastward to Riyadh, the stronghold of both Al Saud and Al Al-Shaykh (descendants of Muhammad ibn Abd al-Wahhab). The Saudi regime had located government structures in the Hijaz—in Mecca and its surroundings, Jeddah and Taif—because of the region's relative institutional development during the late Ottoman period. The relocation of secular power away from Mecca was the first of many steps in distancing religion from politics so as to reconceptualize the nature of modern Saudi power. This was so even if the move was King Saud's way of distancing Faisal from his social base in the Hijaz—where he had served as minister of foreign affairs since 1930. Given Mecca's religious and historical significance for Islam and for the early Saudi state, the move to Riyadh had these symbolic connotations. Riyadh, long considered the birthplace of the conservative Wahhabi movement, became not only the political and financial heart of the kingdom but also the place where secular governmentality was articulated, exercised, and reproduced. After the administrative move to Riyadh, the regime maintained the practice of indirect rule, whereby it appointed lesser princes to key posts in geographically remote regions. As political power moved from the Hijaz to Riyadh, so did global capital and expertise, which the regime used to develop the neglected central Najd region of the kingdom. Administrative records, however, did not follow suit. For the most part, state employees left them behind to languish in deserted government buildings and state-owned depots.

In the wake of the 1966 archival law, the written records of the fledgling bureaucracy were supposed to be relocated, akin to the earlier transfer of the seat of power and its institutions, to Riyadh. In 1968, what had survived of the archive of the Ministry of Finance and National Economy—stored in depots in Mecca—was indeed moved to Riyadh and renamed the General Administration for Central Archives. But by and large, state institutions utterly disregarded other records they had left behind and did not move them to Riyadh, as the regime had instructed them to. Not all state records, however, met such a fate. In the absence of an institutional culture of preserving the bureaucratic paper trail, and before the 1966 archiving law, many documents remained in the personal possession of state functionaries, who kept the records at home. These men held on to the papers after leaving government, and the documents effectively became private property, and in some instances the object of inheritance disputes. Other factors compounded the challenge of document preservation. The political environment of the 1960s was volatile, and the country was in the midst of a massive state centralization process. Until then, those working in the emerging modern bureaucracy did not see the need to preserve the administrative records that had hitherto guided policy making and statecraft. To them, the past had no bearing on the future: institutional continuity and interinstitutional dynamics only partially rested on the production of knowledge. Other contingent and arbitrary factors such as the identities and interpersonal relationships of decision makers in a given institution were more important for them than the material records themselves.

Against this background of archival neglect emerged Faisal's newfound consciousness of the importance of evidentiary terrains for the longevity and legitimacy of the Saudi monarchy. So it was that his regime first commissioned the Ministry of Finance and National Economy in 1966 with collecting, classifying, and storing state records that were no longer in use (*al-watha'iq al-muntahiyya*). What, exactly, was meant by "no longer in use" was up for interpretation. Indeed, each state institution had its own definition of what constituted documents that were out of use, usually referred to as "archives" (*mahfuzat*). Records that were still needed for the daily business of government were simply called "documents" (*watha'iq*). Many bureaucrats took advantage of this definitional ambiguity to avoid depositing their "archives."

Other obstacles contributed to the failure of the first attempt at archival consolidation. In the aftermath of the 1966 royal order, for instance, only one mass transfer of administrative documents occurred (besides the Finance Ministry migration mentioned earlier). In 1970, the Mecca municipality, along with several state depots in Jeddah, gave their records to the General Administration for Central Archives in Riyadh.[31] Until then, the Central Archives had limited its work to cataloging the records from the Ministry of Finance and National Economy. But even these presented challenges that the archivists did not overcome for another two decades. On the one hand, the sheer number of documents strained the ministry's financial, spatial, and human resources. On the other hand, the archive personnel were not properly trained to handle the documents, many of which were already in a decrepit state. They had to wait until the 1980s, if not later, for the requisite human and technical expertise in document conservation to become available in the country. These collections thus continued to sit in improper storage conditions, this time in Riyadh as opposed to the Hijaz. To make matters worse, the few ministries and official institutions that actually adopted internal regulations for record keeping and began to maintain their own administrative documents did not employ technologies for conserving, sorting, classifying, or archiving their paper capital. This failure at once led to disarray and overaccumulation. The latter problem would surface time and again in the various iterations of the archiving project: state archives acquired reams of documentation through purchases from document traders, donations from former statesmen, the personal relationships of those who ran them, or the coercion and intimidation of officials in power. These were all matched either by disinterest in properly archiving the records or inability to do so.

Beyond these structural hindrances, most institutions did not even adhere to the royal order because of power struggles among the political elites. The 1960s were crucial years for state building in Saudi Arabia. Faisal's regime was embroiled in Cold War struggles in the Arabian Peninsula and the king made many promises to allies old and new to shore up his base of support.[32] He needed these allies particularly badly during the war in Yemen (1962–1970). Faisal could neither oblige the state institutions run by his backers to comply with the archiving law nor enforce accountability upon other powerful members of the ruling family. Doing so would jeopardize the fragile domestic balance of power the regime had established. Indeed, it was in the 1960s that Al Saud's power-sharing scheme came to rest on monopolies over particular ministries by certain branches of the ruling family, each headed by a son of Abdulaziz.[33] Faisal and later some of his sons have traditionally dominated the Ministry of Foreign Affairs. Al Sultan (House of Sultan ibn Abdulaziz) held the Ministry of Defense portfolio from the eve of Faisal's coup in 1963 until Salman inherited it upon his brother Sultan's death in 2011. (Salman, as already mentioned, was previously governor of Riyadh. In 2015, he became king, and his son, Muhammad, became the defense minister and later the crown prince.) Al Nayif (House of Nayif ibn Abdulaziz) has held the Ministry of Interior portfolio since the mid-1970s. These fiefdoms became entrenched while Faisal was king. In this way, each of these familial branches came to exercise complete control over the ministry it oversaw, which in the 1960s came to include the knowledge that each produced.

The 1966 law recognized the importance of archiving as a technology of state building and a central component of Saudi power. State institutions stopped discarding records, as had been common practice before the law, even if they refused to adopt the necessary requirements for the preservation of records or to deposit these in a central state archive. In the law's aftermath, many ministers—most of whom hailed from the ruling family—equated the sharing of administrative documents to a compromise of personal power. What began as a measure to strengthen the Saudis against internal and external threats actually opened more fissures among the ruling family, thereby weakening the state. Control over archives became a means by which state ministers jockeyed for power inside the state. The ministers refused to submit records to the central repository as a way to both protect secrets from each other and resist state centralization efforts, which meant the dominance of one branch of the family over the others. Despite regime attempts to confine intrafamily tensions to royal palaces, it was increasingly difficult to hide the skirmishes between ministries and other state institutions over the kingdom's documentary record. Faisal's archiving project also faced opposition from state-allied religious scholars, who saw this process as a form of undue reverence for secular power, or at least claimed as much.[34] Upon the death of Nasser on September 28, 1970, and the end of the Yemeni civil war soon after, the urgency with which Faisal's regime had embarked on archival production subsided, even as it continued to regard record keeping as a technical and political necessity. In this vein, the Saudi regime signed bilateral cultural cooperation protocols with Nasser's successor, Anwar al-Sadat, as well as with other countries like the United States.[35] These pacts aimed to keep any records on mid-twentieth-century social life in Saudi Arabia housed in foreign archives invisible to the gaze of scholars or others interested in the past. To use Mbembe's term again, it was an act of long-distance "chronophagy."

These foundational practices had detrimental effects on archival consolidation in the kingdom. From the 1960s on, such practices institutionalized a culture of secrecy and rivalry in all offices of the state, one that trickled down to various levels of the bureaucracy. Soon, civil servants and functionaries approached state records as forms of capital through which they, too, could attain and exercise power. In this way, access to records, or the lack thereof, took on an arbitrary nature that rested on informal interpersonal relationships, not simply top-down regulations against free sharing of documents. Civil servants often denied colleagues from other institutions access to records as a way to demonstrate their own clout, and then shared access if doing so meant personal gain. These petty rivalries turned archives into sites of contestation that furthered the dispersal of documentary records in Saudi Arabia. Archival practice thus revealed the multiple fissures in, and the incoherence of, the Saudi state.

CATEGORICAL DISTINCTIONS: THE DARAH AS A PEOPLE'S ARCHIVE

The architects of archival production in Saudi Arabia—those close to King Faisal—came to understand that the initial categorization of records as "in use" and "out of use" was simply not efficient. To assuage the regime's fears, they created a categorical distinction between "administrative records" and "historical records" in the opening years of the 1970s. This new system stressed the nature of documents and not the need to share them. The new category of administrative records encompassed all those that ministries and other state institutions produced as part of their everyday operations and thus were subject to institution-specific archiving rules. These papers were also referred to as "government records," and it was left to the discretion of each given institution whether to share them with the central archive or not. Historical records, in contrast, included documents that state functionaries had personally produced during their official tenure and which they had kept in their personal possession. They also included newspapers, journals, diaries, photographs, films, interviews, and nondiplomatic correspondence with men in the regime. All of these papers are still known as "people's records." Arbitrary as these distinctions may be, they inadvertently led to an epistemological division within the archival operation, one that has continued to govern the practice of knowledge production and its spatialization while reifying the fictional boundary between state and society.[36]

The first test of the new categorical distinction came in 1972, when the Council of Ministers—Saudi Arabia's cabinet—ordered the establishment of the Darah. King Faisal initially supported the Darah, but he died a mere three years after its formation. Even so, its first chairman was an ally, the intellectual, bureaucrat, and educator Shaykh Hassan ibn Abdullah Al Al-Shaykh (1934–1987), grandson of Muhammad ibn Abd al-Wahhab.[37] Under his leadership, the Darah would become an archive of "historical records" not generated by state institutions.[38] Housed in a small, isolated building in a residential neighborhood of the capital, it was assigned the task of collecting what cabinet members deemed less sensitive, nonadministrative documents, thereby circumventing the power struggles that were paralyzing archival practice. The Darah's founders claimed to be interested not in what "the state" produced but rather in what "the people" produced. They intended this distinction to reassure the jostling ministers that the Darah was not after official, and possibly incriminating or embarrassing, records. But the marketing of the state-owned Darah as a space for public or "people's" history was deceptive. It reinforced the separation between the rulers and the ruled while masking the fact that the "people's archive" was interested only in historical documents that spoke to the role of Al Saud in establishing the state. Under the directives of its chairman, the Darah aimed to memorialize the ruling family by producing material records of the Saudi Arabian past. It was the first attempt to set in stone a single teleological narrative of state formation that idolized Abdulaziz ibn Saud as the Muslim community's leader and the country's founding father, and to foreclose material evidence that countered such aims.

In any case, the Darah's reassurances failed to quell the power struggles that had plagued the previous archiving endeavor, for those in power were still not committed to the success of the archiving process. In 1974, two years after the Darah's establishment, a first-ever Saudi Arabian writers' conference that met in Mecca called for the establishment of another archive, a "documentary center," that would enable academic research, something that had not yet existed in the country.[39] Although the identities of those who issued the call is not clear from the sources, they must have included some prominent members, for the cabinet approved the recommendation that same year and commissioned several institutions with archiving experience, including the Darah, with planning a national center.[40] The Darah's representatives urged that the new center be part of the Darah, given the similarity of the missions to preserve the country's modern history. The government agreed.[41] The Darah was thus charged with setting the objectives of the new research center at a time when it was still unable to meet its own. Under the bylaws drafted by the Darah, the proposed National Center for Documents and Archives would collect and preserve both administrative documents—including those housed in foreign archives—and newspapers, manuscripts, workshop findings, and indexes. It was the Darah's attempt to circumvent its own mission, which had initially limited its responsibilities to collecting nonadministrative records only.

The Darah failed to achieve the ultimate goal of becoming Saudi Arabia's national archive and the country's first research center.[42] The government agreed that the Darah should house the new national center, but it rejected the proposed bylaws, namely, on housing administrative records. Instead, the government limited the new center's role to supporting the Darah, again leaving administrative documents without a central home. Had the Council of Ministers approved its proposal, the Darah would have been the only institution officially tasked with archiving both (administrative) state and (historical) nonstate records. The regime's caution, if not intransigence, about the centralization of administrative records points not only to the distrust among the ruling princes but also to the incoherence of the state, even in a highly authoritarian setting like Saudi Arabia. The king could issue decrees on a whim, perhaps, but his edicts would not have the force of law without the cooperation of several other power centers within the state. These would not openly defy the king. Instead, they would pretend to execute the orders while in reality altogether ignoring or stalling them. Sabotage via inertia is a time-tested strategy, and the office of the king usually tolerates such inaction because the stakes might be too low and a standoff with top members of the ruling family would tarnish the unified image the regime presents to its citizens and to the world. In some cases, the king has no real investment in seeing through the execution of his orders, announced in the first place just for show. As the archiving experience shows, the image of a cohesive, unitary Saudi state dissolves when the state's inner workings are explored. In the end, the overaccumulation of government records within the state's institutions and ministries as well as in its emerging central archives became a less known legacy of Faisal's reign, an example of his renowned attempts to consolidate power. In March 1975 Faisal was murdered before he was able to fulfill his archiving dreams.

Around the time of the establishment of the Darah's National Center for Documents and Archives in 1976, some cabinet members became concerned that the General Administration for Central Archives—originally slated to be the national archive—had failed to accomplish its mission. Indeed, ten years after the first archiving law, the regime, now under Faisal's brother, King Khalid

(r. 1975–1982), still lacked a system for regulating government records. It had no way of organizing, let alone gaining access to, administrative documents related to the daily management of the state and population. Meanwhile, the growing Saudi bureaucracy was churning out more and more paper that was accumulating in the hallways and basements of office buildings. The archiving challenge at the Ministry for Defense and Aviation was so insurmountable that the minister, Prince Sultan, asked the Council of Ministers for permission to destroy records dating from 1946 to 1975.[43] It is unclear whether this request was approved or the destruction carried out. But that one of the kingdom's most important ministries could not institute a proper archiving system speaks to the technical obstacles that Saudi state institutions faced. At the same time, the desire to erase what amounted to the ministry's entire history (it was founded in 1943) speaks to the level of anxiety about what the evidentiary terrain might reveal. Overall, the first decade of archival practice in the kingdom was marked by confusion, which led to the endemic loss of important government records, financial, diplomatic, and otherwise.[44] In the thriving oil economy of the 1970s, the retrieval of such records would become a serious matter requiring urgent intervention.

In 1976, the Council of Ministers put together a committee from the General Auditing Bureau and the Ministry of Finance and National Economy and tasked it with producing a "special system of regulations" for archiving government records. The goal was to solve the problems of overaccumulation and disorder that the archiving regimes had both suffered from and perpetuated.[45] The new regulations stipulated how, and where, all government records were to be collected or dispensed with, restored, categorized, or archived. It was a technical solution for a techno-political problem. It did nothing to convince, let alone compel, the lords of various fiefdoms to submit the records of their respective institutions. And once again, political events took precedence over archival centralization. King Khalid lacked the political will and wherewithal of his predecessor, Faisal. Yet his regime was confronted with some of the biggest challenges ever to face the monarchy—the free fall of oil prices in 1978, the takeover of Mecca's Grand Mosque in 1979, and the same year's uprising in the Eastern Province, to say nothing of the Iranian Revolution and war in Afghanistan, both of which had major consequences for political life in Saudi Arabia. The regime had more pressing matters to attend to than the centralization of government records. In 1980, the committee tasked with devising the special archiving system informed the minister of finance and national economy that it had suspended its work, having failed to bring order to the process of archival disarray.[46]

TAMING THE ARCHIVE: SECURITY AND THE POLITICS OF SPACE
In light of the recurrent failure of the archiving project, the Council of Ministers sought other solutions and different bureaucrats to take on the seemingly insurmountable task. In 1983, it ordered the establishment of another committee, this time under the leadership of the president of the Institute of Public Administration (IPA). This committee was charged with overseeing a second attempt at the formation of a national archive, also by the name of the National Center for Documents and Archives, one not connected to the Darah. In many ways, the IPA was well placed to take on this tall order. Established in 1961 during the reign of King Saud, the IPA is an autonomous government agency tasked with training government employees and improving human resources in Saudi Arabia more broadly.[47] The IPA had built a good reputation for streamlining government functions and maintaining an internal archive of its own. Other members of the new committee hailed from the kingdom's most important institutions, including the Ministry of Finance and National Economy, the General Auditing Bureau, the Ministry of Defense and Aviation, and the Ministry of Foreign Affairs. The committee was given the prerogative to develop a comprehensive regulation system for archives (*mashruʿ nizam al-mahfuzat*) with support from other Saudi institutions with relevant expertise.[48] The high-profile members met in the beginning of 1984 to devise regulation systems for archiving documents at all state institutions, as well as the proposed National Center for Documents and Archives.[49] Neither the cabinet nor the king approved these systems for another five years, despite the prominent status of the members of the committee, made up as it was of high-ranking politicians who were otherwise influential. Approval of the systems finally came in 1989.

In 1988, to further calm the political elites' fears, the regime administratively incorporated the National Center for Documents and Archives into the office of the Council of Ministers, Saudi Arabia's cabinet, itself a major producer of government documents.[50] The new archive was housed inside the council's gated and heavily secured compound, like those that had popped up all over Riyadh.[51] The council, headed by the king, appointed its own office's president and secretary general, and the president of its own Bureau of Experts, to work directly with the general manager of the National Center of Documents and Archives to ensure the archive's proper functioning. Three other members of the Council of Ministers, appointed to three-year terms by royal decree, would also oversee the operation.[52] Incorporation into one of the kingdom's most powerful political bodies was meant to reassure elites that the confidentiality of their important documents would be protected inside the council's compound, where they would remain classified and beyond the reach of other institutions or the public. Indeed, the new relationship was intended to give the national archive the security and prestige it required to induce government institutions to cooperate.[53]

Yet instead of playing a constructive role, the committee members put in place to "save" the Saudi archiving project hindered its proper functioning. These men were politicians appointed for their status and influence, and not for their expertise or investment in the production of a central archive. They were, in fact, guilty parties in the power struggles that had plagued the archival operation since the 1960s. The incorporation of the National Center into the Council of Ministers impeded the centralization process as well. Despite paying lip service to the importance of producing a national archive, the Council of Ministers did not extend to the archive's employees the prerogatives and privileges they needed to do the job. Nor did the national archive receive the financial, institutional, and political support it needed to collect, preserve, and archive the kingdom's dispersed historical source material. At the same time, the Council of Ministers failed to force most ministries to adhere to the national archive's regulations and bylaws, again reflecting bureaucratic competition and the constitutive instability of archives.[54]

If the choice of committee members gave the archiving project a semblance of seriousness, it simultaneously confirmed the fears that many in the archiving industry had about the government's commitment to centralizing documents. For the selection of such a high-profile committee projected the will to construct a national archive that itself lacked executive dispatch. Such political maneuvering was most evident in the meager physical space the archive was allocated for the colossal task at hand. The repository was no monument to state power, as national archives so often are. Rather, its sixty employees occupied a few cramped floors of one building in the council's compound.[55] Its operational budget was insignificant. The so-called national archive was thus out of sight, its existence and lifeworld sequestered from the physical and political context in which it was formed.[56] So insignificant was this archival institution that researchers often confuse other repositories for *the* national archive. Among US publications, as Robert Vitalis pointed out to me, Kiren Aziz Chaudhry's *The Price of Wealth: Economics and Institutions in the Middle East* is a case in point. In her book, Chaudhry goes as far as to mistake the IPA archives for the Saudi national archive.[57] Among the small community of foreign scholars I met in Riyadh between 2009 and 2011, none had even heard of the IPA, let alone the National Center of Documents and Archives. It was no surprise, then, that practitioners in Riyadh's broader archiving industry, as well as the archive's own nonexpert managers, dismissed the National Center as a nonfunctioning office that was more about political jockeying and maintaining state secrets than anything else. In the absence of physical space and political will, boxes of randomly collected administrative and historical documents piled up at the council and various ministries well into the second decade of the twenty-first century—and the contents began to disintegrate.

Before the establishment of the National Center in the compound of the Council of Ministers, those in the archiving industry had regarded the lack of unified regulations for archiving and categorizing documents as the single largest obstacle to centralization. Indeed, different state institutions adopted outdated systems of categorization that were incompatible with Arabic-language materials, making it almost impossible to locate a document. Following the establishment of the center and the sanctioning of national archival regulations in 1989, archivists came to see the failures of state archives as political. Many ministries refused to organize their records according to the new regulations, let alone surrender them to the national archive. Unlike in the United Kingdom or the United States, where government documents are consolidated in a national repository, "the same will never happen in Saudi Arabia," according to a managing archivist at one of Riyadh's state archives. "The academic, historical, and political culture is very different here. We simply do not trust each other. And of course, the nature of the regime has everything to do with it."[58] Indeed, state ministries continued to view successive regimes' interest in their documents with deep suspicion, preferring to squirrel the records away in spare rooms or rented warehouses on the outskirts of Riyadh, where many still sit today. Archival praxis in Saudi Arabia has been replete with such terms as "neglect," "ignorance," "disregard," "lack of responsibility or expertise," and "backwardness" to describe what archivists perceive as the failures of the industry. Saudi Arabian archivists are apt to use such terms to describe the failures of the regime to preserve documents and achieve archival consolidation.

By the end of the 1980s, those who were genuinely committed to the archiving project were well aware that theirs was not a purely technical challenge.

The regime's ostensible drive for archival consolidation was paralleled by utter negligence in developing the necessary infrastructure, in effect ensuring that archival centralization would remain a permanently unfinished project. If overaccumulation and neglect symbolized the reality of archival praxis writ large, then anxiety, instability, and resistance undergirded the logic of its infrastructure.[59] The Saudi archive is both the sine qua non of the modern state and a "constant threat" to it.[60] State officials, ministers, and members of the ruling family feared that open access to documents would expose bureaucratic ineptitude, in a state with one of the world's largest budgets, or, worse, implicate them in nepotism, corruption, and the crushing of all forms of opposition, religious and secular. The revolutionary decades of the 1950s and 1960s posed one particular problem for the archiving regime.[61] Its evidentiary terrain could expose Faisal as a power-hungry ruler who betrayed his half brother Saud, responded most violently to peaceful activists seeking a more just and egalitarian life, and did his utmost to crush Arab nationalist solidarities—and for mostly personal gain with the support of the United States. The authorities were also especially loath to make public the records that demonstrated the centrality of the British, and later the Americans, to the making of the Saudi state and its oil economy.[62] The Gulf War started within a year of the national archive regulations, spelling the end of this phase of archival consolidation. Under these circumstances, it was not surprising that other, less "official" archiving projects emerged to document the kingdom's past.

HIDING IN PLAIN SIGHT: ACCIDENTAL ARCHIVES AND EARLY PIONEERS

In the shadow of the top-down archival centralization efforts that took off in the 1960s, the Institute of Public Administration and the King Fahd National Library started performing the task of gathering the kingdom's scattered written records.[63] In so doing, these two state-owned institutions managed, inadvertently, and without being part of the regime's archiving production and centralization plans, to accomplish what the regime ostensibly could not. It might be ironic that some of the most relevant developments in the history of archival production in Saudi Arabia occurred outside of, but alongside, the regime's concerted and decades-long official archiving plans. But such a reality is far from exceptional. It helps us understand not simply who has power but also how power works. The

Saudi regime and its state project was far from an inevitability. As in other historical instances, the singularity of a unified state is a fragile façade. The multiplicity of state institutions renders any state project multiple, fragmented, and made up of competing parts. There was never one path to one state. And the Saudi regime, like any other, could not control or even have knowledge of the maneuvers, visions, or interests in its various institutions. These early "accidental archives" signal these multiplicities and competitions. They also squarely locate archival production as a site of immense power: its accumulations for some, its loss for others.

The IPA, which oversaw the 1983 official attempt at saving the archiving project, had established an archive twenty years earlier in 1963, the Center for Documents (Markaz al-Watha'iq), which is separate from the IPA's internal archive for the records it generates. As per regime directives during Saud's reign in 1961, the IPA started "collecting, classifying, and cataloguing the administrative records of the Kingdom of Saudi Arabia."[64] It required ministries to send it copies of official administrative documents for educational purposes. And unlike the national archive, the IPA was able to secure the cooperation of many state ministries in this endeavor since its very inception. The compliant institutions included the Ministries of Justice, Hajj, Finance and National Economy, and Municipalities and Rural Affairs, as well as the Riyadh, Mecca, and Ha'il Principalities; the Consultative Council; the Council of Ministers; the Arriyadh Development Authority; the Royal Court; and the King Saud University.[65] The IPA has an institutionalized archiving system whereby state ministries can deposit non-"secret" records, which has made its categorizing logic and search engines more efficient than other archives. Unlike all other archiving institutions, it does not purchase any of its archivable documents.

The IPA was the first Saudi Arabian public institution to collect and categorize official administrative state records (*al-watha'iq al-idariyya*) from various government agencies.[66] These records include, but are not limited to, agreements, treaties, correspondence, memoranda, laws, supreme decrees, royal orders, contracts, speeches, religious proceedings, telegrams, and planning regulations. Many documents date back to 1925, seven years before the creation of the Saudi state. The IPA's own existence as an institute responsible for training, research, consultation, and administrative development in the kingdom rested on access to these documents. In order to organize the massive influx of paper, the institute established its own Public Administration of Libraries and Documentation.[67]

The IPA archive completed this extensive processing of material despite the fact that, until 1980, it had just five employees, who were not specialists in the field. And unlike other repositories of primary-source documents in Saudi Arabia to date, the IPA began digitizing the material records it possessed in 1979 and within nine years had digitized approximately forty thousand documents.[68] As of my last meeting at the IPA, in 2011, its archive had approximately 104,000 documents available in its digital system (it has since digitized tens of thousands more). The institute sought to make these documents available as references and training tools for government employees and for its own students of business and government administration. Even though the IPA's repository was never meant to be a public archive for research purposes, it has made its archived material readily available to researchers since the late 1970s.[69]

The IPA was never intended to be a central state archive, either, but its managers succeeded in centralizing state documents even before the country's first archiving law in 1966 went into effect. Its archive has actually categorized, archived, digitized, and made available more documents than any of Riyadh's official state archives. The success of the IPA archive is largely due to the fact that it emerged as an important administrative institution before regime intervention in the archival operation in 1966. The IPA's investment in administrative training, administrative continuity, and education has distinguished it from other platforms whose primary function was archival. For many of those in power, the official, royally decreed archives housed "historical" documents that could be deployed for legal claims and political purposes. By contrast, regime insiders saw the IPA as a safe destination for the records that their institutions produced—for the records were simply used to train the institutions' employees. That the IPA was not intended to receive any state records classified as "secret" built trust as well, despite the fact that its archive contains many documents so designated that are at times declassified and accessible. The IPA archive continued to grow, and in 1991, it was renamed the Administration for Saudi Government Documents (Idarat al-Watha'iq al-Hukumiyya al-Sa'udiyya).[70] Six years later, it was renamed a second time, as the Center for Documents and Archives, and administratively incorporated into the IPA's Public Administration for Libraries and Documents (al-Idara al-'Amma li al-Maktabat wa-l-Watha'iq). By 1998, the center housed the documents of fifty government institutions.

While the IPA archive housed a relatively small portion of the records that the government produced, its robustness may seem odd, given the repeated failures of the official archiving projects to get off the ground. Did the rulers not worry that the IPA's success in collecting documents from recalcitrant ministries would make the official efforts look weak or incompetent by comparison? Did they not fret about the fairly open access to administrative documents at the IPA? Were the rulers not bothered simply by the IPA's duplication of what was supposed to be the national archive's work, precisely the sort of bureaucratic inefficiency they were so keen to conceal in the ministries? In reality, no one in the regime's upper echelons realized the full extent of what the IPA was doing or understood its implications. And ultimately, for them, the official archiving projects were a performance intended to contain the state's many secrets and a means to discipline and outdo each other. In any case, the IPA archive's success is still more evidence of the messiness and lack of cohesion inside the formation of one of the world's most autocratic governments, prone to depicting a hermetically sealed state wrapped in an easily understood past with little possibility for alternative futures.

The second of the two successful archiving experiments in the 1980s also took place outside the regime's official archival centralization plans. In the fall of 1982, King Fahd was hospitalized abroad, having allegedly suffered a heart attack upon hearing of the massacre of Palestinian refugees at the Sabra and Shatila camps in Beirut (Fahd had succeeded his brother Khalid months earlier). To celebrate his return, wealthy merchants and political elites donated the money to erect the King Fahd National Library as a way to honor and commemorate the ailing king, on whom they depended for their wealth and status. The ruling family then offered the land on which the library stands today. KFNL was subsequently declared Saudi Arabia's National Library.[71] The library was built on what were then the northern edges of the capital city. Today, given the rate of urban sprawl in Riyadh, the renovated library sits on prime real estate, in the business district close to the city's first two skyscrapers and at the intersection of two major roads. Prince Salman was made chairman of the library. Modeled on the US Library of Congress, the KFNL is the country's reference library and aspires to be caretaker of the totality of Saudi Arabian intellectual production. Under the leadership of Ibn Junayd, the first Saudi Arabian national to earn a doctorate in library sciences, the KFNL soon became the central repository for everything published in the country. These publications included books (common and rare), dissertations, newspapers, magazines, manuscripts, photographs, and maps published since the creation of the Saudi state in 1932. Archiving primary source documents, however, was not part of the library's mission.

Ibn Junayd was appointed head of operations at the KFNL in 1986 and when the library opened its doors three years later was promoted to secretary general, a post he held for six years. During his tenure, the library developed a modern infrastructure that has enabled it to become the academic and cultural landmark it is today. Over the years, it also unintentionally, and at times accidentally, amassed more than two million primary source documents, mostly administrative ones, largely because of the personal interests of its secretary general. The document hunts that opened this chapter are but the two most colorful examples of Ibn Junayd's efforts and finds. His first experience with historical documents dates back to the early 1970s, when he headed the manuscripts department at the central library at the King Saud University. The library had just acquired the private collection of the notable Meccan merchant Sulayman ibn Abdulrahman al-Saniʿ, and Ibn Junayd was responsible for overseeing its transportation to Riyadh. While going through the boxes of books in Mecca, Ibn Junayd found a roomful of administrative documents that the owner had unknowingly included in the price of the collection. Ibn Junayd did not alert the sellers to the "treasure" he had discovered. As he went through the collection once it reached its new home in Riyadh, he categorized and archived the documents, legal manuscripts, and correspondence that he found and in the process became an aficionado of historical documents. Two years later, he pursued a master's degree in library sciences and information at Missouri State University, and in 1984 he earned a doctorate in library sciences and documents from Cairo University. He returned to Riyadh and started working on local document collection at a time when there was no interest in, or ability to, procure Saudi Arabia's dispersed written records.[72]

At the KFNL, Ibn Junayd started collecting locally produced books through Saudi Arabian historians and the many contacts he had made at the King Saud University and, later, the Imam Muhammad ibn Saud Islamic University. It was through such contacts, as well as random encounters and private-public endeavors, that the KFNL acquired its archival collection. After his first few trips, including those to Qasr Ibrahim and al-Wajh, Ibn Junayd put together a two-man team to visit other abandoned Portuguese and Ottoman forts around the kingdom. Yanbuʿ and Najran were among the many destinations. There, they often found rare political, economic, and legal administrative documents. As he did in the Qasr Ibrahim and al-Wajh instances, Prince Salman provided the official backing needed for the KFNL team to take the documents to Riyadh. In its first few years, the KFNL collected one million local historical documents, the majority of which were administrative. It also housed a substantial collection of nonadministrative documents that various families had donated to the library. Many of the original documents in the library's collection were badly damaged and required rehabilitation, a field that would remain nascent in the kingdom for at least another decade. The library staff made copies of all the documents, regardless of their quality, and began work on its internal archiving system. The KFNL's historical documents project was an individual effort that took years of labor and personal struggle, earning Ibn Junayd great respect in the field of libraries and archives. By the 1990s, the KFNL was selectively making its documents available to researchers, at a time when other state institutions were still at loggerheads over the drive to centralize the country's written record.

The archives of the IPA and the KFNL developed their own standards for collecting, classifying, and archiving the historical documents they had obtained. With minimal expert support and financial backing, it took them years to go through their documents. In the case of the IPA, the archiving process had become standardized. State institutions automatically sent duplicates of what they deemed administrative documents to the IPA for the sake of institutional continuity, efficiency, and training. Nonetheless, the archiving regime, along with its foot soldiers, continued to deny the IPA the status of "archive" in the full sense of the word. What distinguished the KFNL from other archives in Saudi Arabia is that it had no protocol dictating the genre of documents it would house. The library accepted all genres of documents, which were either haphazardly acquired or donated as part of diffuse individual efforts. According to the archivists at both institutions, all the documents, without exception, were archived and cataloged, with many made accessible to researchers.

CONCLUSION

The archival artifacts at the IPA and KFNL narrate episodes in Arabian history that the royally decreed archiving projects would rather efface—periods of time that the Saudi state would rather "consume."[73] Some records dated back to the pre-Saudi era, to the late Ottoman past and the vibrant transregional connections it had made possible. Others revealed the Saudi regime's "state thinking" and administrative logic. These "collections" were but pieces of a large puzzle, many of which did not fit together. The remaining pieces were still strewn across the country, not only in discrete archiving and state institutions but also in homes and private libraries. Few of the IPA and KFNL documents furthered the official state-sanctioned historical narrative, which had been in circulation for a long time, initially spun out by Aramco in the 1940s and codified in state textbooks in the 1970s. Although they may not have intended it initially, the very presence of the IPA, KFNL, and other private archives frustrated the regime's project to centralize government records, to silence the ideas and people outside the vacuous and hagiographic narrative that the regime hoped its citizens and its competing bureaucrats would well remember and revere.

If the national archive and the power of the modern state are co-constitutive, and Saudi Arabia does not have a national archive, what does that say about the Saudi state? It teaches us that states are not unitary, that they are always messy: they are not simply made up of buildings but rather of the people who inhabit them, make them, and move within them. We should take care, first of all, not to cast the Saudi case as exceptional. All archives are built brick by brick, with many detours, false starts, delays, turf battles, and political struggles along the way. While specific regimes of law govern different archives, at the end of the day, the declassification of records is at the discretion of governments, who have at their disposal an arsenal of mechanisms to "legally" prevent certain documental collections from seeing the light of day long after their declassification dates. Such a reality is as true of archival practice in Washington and London as it is in Tel Aviv and Riyadh. This is to say nothing of the ways in which the digitization of archival records—touted as the democratization of archives—have enabled governments to vet and take stock of the records in their possession and to then manage them in more strategic ways. After all, it is archivists who curate the thousands of records they receive regularly, and much is missed in the process. Common are stories of archivists who learn of records in their possession only after researchers happen upon them. Chaos and overaccumulation are features of every archive. And policies change, as do the agendas and prerogatives of the people involved: Why, in the Saudi case, did Prince Salman route valuable records to the KFNL, and not to the Darah? Was it simply because he was the library's chairman? Did he heed Ibn Junayd's call without paying it much thought and in the process was introduced to the potentialities of historical production? We are inclined to read coherence into the past, when the interventions of historical actors, whether as individuals or in groups, are often the opposite of coherent.

It is ordinary as well for there to be gaps in the archival record. Such breaks are constitutive of the archive. The elision of state documents is a form of bureaucratic violence that, in ordering the writing of history, structures everyday life and the very making of the state. Archivable documents, whether in Saudi Arabia or elsewhere, undergo vigorous processes of selection and reselection at every turn, from their production and storage to their categorization and archiving.[74] Archivists are makers of social memory, their mediation part and parcel of the historical operation. The multilayered spaces in which they perform the labor of vetting documents and structuring knowledge reveal the political, social, and economic choreography of documents. The lifeworld of documents casts doubt on historical praxis as an objective affair while adding nuance to our understanding of the power structures that undergird the writing of history.[75] For official history is not simply written by the victors. Stripping away its multiple layers and exposing the artifice of its production reveals the proactive planning as well as the incompetence and arbitrariness that often constitute the making of history.

If the Saudi archiving experience is not exceptional, it does have special features that, in turn, bespeak the particularity of the Saudi state-building project and Saudi Arabian political economy. In the words of Yahya ibn Junayd: "In Saudi Arabia, the national archive only exists in name. Without the proper physical place, the archive is nothing. Space is the most important thing."[76] The humble quarters of the so-called national archive, inside the forbidding walls of the Council of Ministers' compound, demonstrated the utilitarian and anemic character of the regime's archival commitment as well as how history can constitute a nagging insecurity of one of the world's most authoritarian regimes. Not only did this location restrict access for researchers in general, whether citizens or foreigners; it also made a special effort to exclude women, who are not allowed into the compound except on very rare occasions and only when accompanied by a male legal guardian (*mahram*). The enforcement of this exclusion replicated and bolstered common gender apartheid practices in the kingdom. It also designated the archive as a space that is not accessible to women because of the "exceptional" social and legal norms and traditions in Saudi Arabia.[77] In reality, archive representatives resorted to myriad criteria—academic affiliation, research topic, nationality, "seriousness," and political values—to deny access to male researchers as well. The exclusion of men is not as easily justified, but it is regularly practiced nonetheless. This performance of strict archival guardianship produced the Saudi archive as a fully functional institution without having to address the fact that, as late as 1990, there was still no national archive in existence. The performance of archival inaccessibility largely succeeded, it must be said, in reifying the existence of an archive that does not exist. The pretense of a national archive was, for the Saudi regime, a necessary show of strength in the face of persistent weakness.

Chapter 3

ASSEMBLING HISTORY

> In Saudi Arabia, the nation suffers from severe
> memory loss [*al-watan mafqud al-dhakira*].
> Yahya ibn Junayd, *interview on March 21, 2011*

IN 1996, THE KING ABDULAZIZ FOUNDATION FOR RESEARCH AND Archives, or the Darah, launched a yearlong national program to survey and collect historical documents on Saudi Arabia and its rulers.[1] The national survey proved just how dispersed historical documents were—and how hard to obtain. Less than five years later, the Darah sponsored another similar initiative.[2] Yet these programs did not prove as fruitful as the Darah's stakeholders had hoped. They needed to devise more drastic measures. So in the following decade, the Darah expanded its surveying efforts. Among other things, it deployed its two mobile laboratories for document sterilization and restoration to targeted locations across the country in search of historical records. The mobile units were meant to assist the Darah in its theretofore-failed mission to centralize the country's historical source materials (Figures 1 and 2). The Riyadh-based cultural organization had by then convinced few former bureaucrats or scions of prominent families and tribes to donate or sell the records in their possession.[3] Most remained skeptical of the project's aims and intentions. The Darah's managers were hard pressed for an alternative solution. By approaching people at their doorsteps and offering them free, on-site preservation services—without asking them to give up any records—Darah managers hoped their employees could persuade recalcitrant citizens to temporarily share their documents. The Darah employees explained that they did not intend to make copies of the documents. They simply sought

FIGURE 1. The Darah's mobile document-sterilization and restoration laboratories on one of its scouting trips. The writing on the truck reads: "Together we preserve the nation's memory." *Source:* Photograph taken by author at the Darah's Center for Restoration and Preservation of Historical Materials in Riyadh, 2010.

FIGURE 2. Darah employees gathering abandoned old records in a historical site in Saudi Arabia.
Source: Photograph taken by author at the Darah's Center for Restoration and Preservation of Historical Materials in Riyadh, 2010.

to sterilize them for posterity. The mobile labs were the proof of their benign intentions.

Many Saudi Arabians gave the Darah employees their papers, albeit with some suspicion. Sitting inside the comfort of their homes, they watched the technicians work through their windows to make sure that none of their possessions went missing.[4] The technicians, for their part, patiently endured the stench of chemicals in the small quarters of the high-tech mobile vans. Day after day, hour after hour, they pored over the documents as they preserved—and secretly made copies of— historical records before bringing the originals back inside to their owners. But not every document was returned. The mobile laboratory technicians described regularly and furtively confiscating documents that they deemed incriminating of the political elites. Just following orders, they said. Through these legitimate and not-so-legitimate means, they managed to secure a variety of records: Ottoman and early Saudi Arabian legal and religious manuscripts, land deeds, cadastral surveys, records from the sale of dates, diplomatic correspondences, and documents from pilgrimage caravans. Of those, they were instructed to flag anything related to Abdulaziz Al Saud for immediate processing.[5] While some document owners learned of such theft through contacts years after the fact, most remain oblivious. The entire process was a spectacle of archiving as a regime of silencing.

In the past, Saudi Arabia's top rulers had impeded archival centralization as a way to undermine rivals and bolster their own power. In the early 1990s, at least a few of them began to endorse the archival project. For them, the Gulf War was a game changer. It featured heightened popular opposition to the regime, a belligerent neighboring Iraqi government that nevertheless garnered support from various Arab pockets, and a global recession that saw a fall in returns on Saudi investments worldwide. These were a few of the ramifications that the regime had to contend with. The war exposed Saudi Arabia's political, military, and economic weakness. It shook Saudi leaders to the core and convinced some of them that an overhaul of the political-economic system was necessary if Al Saud were to maintain their hold on power.

For Salman ibn Abdulaziz, Riyadh's governor at the time, this entailed a shift in the grounds for political legitimation, subject formation, and economic diversification. Salman's agenda rested on restructuring the kingdom's postwar legitimation mechanism away from its conventional religious trappings. Instead, he suggested rooting it in secular material heritage centered on "his" city, Riyadh. The regime would have to develop the archive and historical space as the locations in which to wage the post–Gulf War battles over national (re)production, political legitimacy, and social formation.[6] On the one hand, the archive, as a social category, both produced and memorialized much of the lived realities it purportedly described.[7] On the other hand, the process of making the archive is the process of restructuring political logics and producing institutional space for these logics. As such, the regime not only had to revise its history. It also had to materialize and monumentalize that revised history through manuscripts, historical records, archives, and the built environment.

Salman was a postwar architect in every sense of the word: he had a vision for a new Saudi Arabia, the bureaucratic apparatus to sketch it on paper, and the will and resources to achieve it. As one of the most trusted confidants of his brother, King Fahd (r. 1982–2005), he secured backing for his vision.[8] Salman had also built a strong and diverse support base since becoming Riyadh's governor in 1963. He threw his full weight behind the cultural redevelopment of the capital city. But when a stroke incapacitated King Fahd in 1995, Crown Prince Abdullah, who became the de facto regent and then king in 2005, was less enthusiastic about Salman's plan and historical worldview. Yet he did not outright oppose him. Abdullah at least agreed that the influence of the religious establishment needed to be minimized, if not eliminated. Exactly how to do that would be worked out in the coming years.

Shortly after the war, the rulers, with Salman at the helm, breathed new life into the national archiving project. Saudi Arabia had entered the last decade of the twentieth century without a national archive to call its own, and Salman was intent on changing that. For him, it was of the utmost importance to territorialize a usable national past that would bolster Al Saud's legitimacy and undergird its postwar political power.[9] Assembling the past became central for the new conception of state power.[10] Together with his allies in the regime and among the economic elites, Salman also sought to capitalize on both space and history by creating new capitalist ventures through cultural heritage and development. Culture became a key arena for struggles over the postwar political economy, with heritage making in particular being politicized in unprecedented ways. Salman would rely on the Darah, along with his other prized institution, the Arriyadh Development Authority (ADA), to assemble the past and its spaces.

The Darah, established in 1972 as part of that decade's low-grade archive fever, got a second lease on life in the 1990s. With Salman as its new chairman, the Darah received the financial and political backing it needed to augment its document collection capabilities. Riyadh's other archives in the making—including the National Center for Documents and Archives—were not so fortunate. They did not have any significant political backing in the postwar period. It was around this time that Salman began to portray himself as a history aficionado, "a leader of historians." Unlike the prince's half-hearted efforts in decades past, his renewed commitment to archival production overhauled the archival landscape. Indeed, one archivist recounted how "we cannot label the Darah's work prior to the mid-1990s as 'archival' by any stretch of the imagination. The archive was neglected; it was dead."[11] This time, it had the political and financial backing of one of Saudi Arabia's most powerful decision makers. But as we will see, power has its limits. By 2014, when I concluded my research in Saudi Arabia, the country still lacked a functioning national archive.[12] Like Faisal before him, Salman faced many challenges to centralizing the archive: from other members of the ruling family, politicians and bureaucrats, activists and archivists. The decentralization of power is what held Saudi Arabia's top rulers in check. Salman understood that. It was only as king, years later, and by resorting to great violence and repression, that he would upend the political-economic system and implement his vision.

The vast operation of document collection in Saudi Arabia casts doubt on archives everywhere: the politics of their making, the truths they engender, and the futures they call for. The complex processes of archive formation that this chapter attends to are not exceptional. Although they are common to archives across borders, their machinations are sociopolitically and historically specific. But rarely is the process of archive making—which, like state making, is always ongoing—visible to those outside the archival operation. The fraught conditions of archive formation remain opaque and lend themselves easily to notions of objective truths. If we are to challenge the amnesiac impulse that marks all national projects, the Saudi case is an instructive one. It can help us rethink the archive, the state, and how power constitutes itself.

THE POLITICS OF COMMEMORATION

Constructing a national archive was the first step in the labyrinthine post–Gulf War effort. Saudi Arabia suffered only light physical damage during the war. Saddam Hussein's regime launched several Scud missiles into the kingdom, in retaliation for the monarchy's decision to side with Kuwait and provide US and coalition forces with bases from which to attack the Iraqi army. There was some loss of Saudi life and property, but it paled in comparison to the carnage and destruction in Kuwait and Iraq.[13] Yet the sociopolitical and economic ramifications of the war for the kingdom were immense. Never had the Al Saud monarchy been so excoriated by Saudi Arabians—and the Islamist Sahwa movement in particular—as the contested and militarily dependent state that it was. Never had its imagined historical, political, and religious legitimacy been cast into such doubt, with opposition movements putting forth reform agendas as well as outright alternatives to Al Saud's rule.[14]

It was thus that King Fahd's regime turned, belatedly by the standards of the modern state, to the projects of history making and commemoration as instruments to reform Saudi subjectivity and political identity. These categories would no longer center primarily on religion, given Islam's looming potential to undermine Al Saud's hold on power.[15] As local Islamist movements grew bolder in their demands for political and religious reform, the regime continued to respond, perhaps even more visibly, with a religiously framed political rhetoric. All the while, its on-the-ground policies signaled a different reality, one in which secular nationalism would replace religion as the basis for political legitimacy and social engineering. Saudi Arabia's revised official history and its emerging sites of commemoration would be rooted solely in Al Saud's secular past. Not only would historical revisionism slight the Wahhabi movement that had enabled the monarchy's ascent to power; it would altogether sideline religion from social, political, and cultural life—past and present. Through the practice of history, a form of secularization would eventually take shape. History had become a more intense form of politics than ever before, its instruments and institutions weapons and sites for reconfiguring the postwar polity. The archive became a preferred postwar site for the production and reproduction of state power and sovereignty. Among many things, it was a technology through which the regime reworked the relationship between secular and religious powers in Saudi Arabia.

With this in mind, the Saudi state invested hundreds of billions of dollars over the following two decades in the production of Saudi Arabia's material heritage.[16] Producing source materials for this soon-to-be archivable vision of the past, and constructing the national archive that would house them, were necessary steps for the postwar memorialization impulse to have a permanent legacy. Eventually, in years to come, this narrative in the making would become the only one that researchers in Saudi Arabia's archives and heritage sites could extract. To start, the regime needed to centralize primary source documents on the history of Saudi Arabia and, crucially, to foreclose those parts of the past deemed outside of History. These included official records on late Ottoman Arabia, the centrality of the Wahhabi movement to Saudi state formation, anti–Al Saud revolts since the 1920s, and Saudi intervention in Yemen and Egypt, among others. These were scattered around the country, gathering dust in abandoned warehouses and government buildings, sitting in private archives or with tribes and families, and circulating in the black market. Many were located around the world, held in foreign archives but also by foreign regimes and individuals as well as by private auction houses like Sotheby's and Christie's.

In the past, secrecy was the organizing logic of Saudi Arabia's archives. They served as hiding places for the secrets of those in power, to be shielded from one another and from the population at large. The new phase of archival production was not limited to collecting the records in state institutions alone, but it included those in all corners of the country. Archival production was instead marked by monumentality and the public "performativity" of history.[17] The archiving regime publicly stressed history's civilizational promise and disciplinary effect as a way to convince people to submit or share the records in their possession. This new message adorned dozens of billboards that dotted Saudi Arabia's highways when the Darah embarked on its first national survey of historical documents. The billboards proclaimed "the importance of historical documents to safeguarding the Saudi nation." The history-making project and the collection of records were promoted as a collective endeavor in which all Saudi Arabians could—indeed, must—partake. The regime framed archival operations in civilizational terms that equated history with modernity.[18] At stake, it seemed, was nothing less than the kingdom's standing as an equal among "civilized nations."

As with Faisal's archive, however, the post–Gulf War archival operation was born in response to popular opposition and political insecurity. King Fahd's regime was not simply attempting to capture history retrospectively, as those in power regularly do. It also sought to shift the multisited terrain of postwar political opposition to a centralized struggle over the making of symbolic and material history. In doing so, it would co-opt or silence the sort of mass religio-political opposition that emerged during the war. In other words, the regime would channel political opposition into struggles for inclusion in the historical past rather than economic redistribution or political equity. Archival institutions in Riyadh, where the regime's ideological and material power remained strong, became the grounds upon which it preferred to fight these battles and pacify its political opponents. Little did those in power anticipate that in trying to contain old rivals, new ones would emerge, this time even from within the archival establishment itself.

HISTORY BEFORE THE "FACT"

As Darah employees traversed the country in 1996, they were in a rush to collect historical evidence of the rise of the Saudi state. The regime had just announced January 16, 1999, as the beginning of the yearlong centennial celebration (Figure 3). With less than three years to go, time was of the essence.[19] For the regime, the centennial presented the perfect opportunity to enshrine the revised historical narrative and entrench the new set of power relations between the religious establishment and other government sectors. It was the pinnacle of postwar social, economic, and political reengineering, and it would have great consequences for everyday life in Saudi Arabia. The country's first official nonreligious celebration did not mark the creation of the state in 1932, as one would expect. It commemorated Abdulaziz's capture of the oasis town of Riyadh from its previous rulers, the Al Rasheed clan, as the historical anchor and originary moment on which the ruling family based its legitimacy.[20]

Although the capture of Riyadh occupied a prominent role in the national imagination prior to this moment, the state had been unable to celebrate or memorialize the event. Abdulaziz had attempted to celebrate the Hijri semicentennial of the takeover of Riyadh on July 20, 1950.[21] In preparation, Abdulaziz assigned a committee of the most prominent writers and historians of the time to work on a book on the kingdom's history, geography, population, and cities. The regime also requested that the Arabian American Oil Company (Aramco) produce books, exhibitions, and short films for the event. However, the semicentennial celebration was canceled because many of the state-employed religious leaders had not yet wholly succumbed to the political will of Al Saud. They opposed attempts to revere the secular leadership and denigrated such acts as heretical and sacrilegious. When the king relented under pressure from the powerful religious institution, it set an even stronger precedent against historical preservation, commemoration, and the glorification of rulers. At the end of the twentieth century, however, the religious establishment no longer posed an obstacle. Historical records and other artifacts would finally monumentalize this moment.

FIGURE 3. Poster celebrating the Hijri centennial of Al Saud's conquest of Riyadh. Caption reads: "Unification and Construction 1319h–1419h." *Source:* Photograph taken by author at the National Museum in Riyadh, 2010.

In May 1996, as Darah employees expanded their attempts to collect historical documents, the High Committee for the Centenary Celebrations had commissioned the Arriyadh Development Authority—both of which were chaired by Salman—with building a state-of-the-art cultural center that would host the activities of the yearlong centennial.[22] With less than three years to pick the site that would host the historical event, the ADA worked around the clock with experts from the world over: Germany-based landscape consultant Boedeker, Wagenfeld & Partners; the architects Moriyama & Teshima, Ali Shuaibi, Rasem Badran, and Martyn Best; engineering consultant Buro Happold; cultural and museum consultants LORD; exhibit designers Reich & Petch; urban design consultant Albert Speer & Partners; historian William Facey; and editor and writer Arthur P. Clark, among many others who joined the effort. Together, they chose Abdulaziz ibn Saud's Murabbaʿ Palace (Qasr al-Murabbaʿ) in downtown Riyadh as the focal point of the celebrations.[23] Abdulaziz's seat of power was located there from 1938 until his death in 1953. The ADA redeveloped the whole area at a cost of $182 million. The redevelopment encompassed the palace and was steps away from the landmark al-Masmak Fortress, site of the 1902 conquest of Riyadh. The new institution was named the King Abdulaziz Historical Center. On this occasion the center would stand as a national icon. It would include a public park, the Directorate General of Antiquities and Museums, Murabbaʿ Palace, traditional adobe buildings, the King Abdulaziz Foundation for Research and Archives (the Darah), the King Abdulaziz Public Library, the King Abdulaziz Mosque, the King Abdulaziz Auditorium, Riyadh's landmark water tower, and the national museum.[24] Two and a half years was a short time to complete the whole complex, so the planners decided to put all their effort into building the national museum, where the centennial's indoor events would take place.

The three-million-square-foot center became part of what has since been known as Historic Riyadh. In the capital's postwar urban master plan, this area is slated to become the country's primary destination for a fledgling secular tourist industry whose blueprint was also conceived in the aftermath of the Gulf War. According to the ADA, which oversaw and planned all centennial projects, "The goal is for it to become a cultural center and a respectable civilizational front that reflects the history of the Arabian Peninsula, the eternal message of Islam, and the historical role of the Kingdom of Saudi Arabia, the foundations on which it was built and the effort spent on its construction to motivate the sons of this nation to persevere anew in the path of construction started by King Abdulaziz."[25] Yet when preparations for the centennial got under way, it became evident to experts, officials, and members of the ruling family that there were no functioning local archives or cultural institutions able to produce material evidence for the official historical narrative and the scholarly publications that they envisioned. Even the Darah was not equipped for the task. The kingdom had to depend on other sources for its own history, namely the Saudi Aramco archive and personal libraries of the company's former employees and of former Saudi bureaucrats. It also relied on the Egyptian, Russian, Ottoman, British, French, Dutch, and US archives.[26] The centennial's engineers therefore needed to start from the very beginning: with the archive itself, in order to construct and centralize what they understood to be the facts of history.

In the absence of a national archive or organized local historical sources, the Darah offered to take on what seemed like a gargantuan task. Since its establishment in 1972, the Darah had been confined to a small space in Maʿzar, a mainly residential upper-middle-class neighborhood in Riyadh. Although easily accessible, its location had lost the importance it once had as urban sprawl pushed the city center further north. Before planning for the centennial began, the Darah was more excluded than ever before, both spatially and intellectually. Until then, it was "yet another dysfunctional government institution."[27] The Darah had achieved little of its mandate to document the past of the Arabian Peninsula. Its biggest achievement until then had been the acquisition of copies of foreign documents: seventy thousand from the British Foreign Office and the India Office combined and five thousand from the Ottoman Foreign Ministry and Council of Ministers archives in Turkey.[28] Local documents amounted to only 3,300. As late as 1989, the Darah's managers had complained that their annual budget had been flat for fifteen years and that they were denied the appropriate space, autonomy, and personnel:

> One of the most important problems that the National Center for Documents and Archives at the Darah faces is the lack of an appropriate building befitting of its [the Darah's] stature and importance among scientific institutions, one that provides modern, state-of-the-art equipment as well as maintenance and safety, seeing that it houses documents and manuscripts, ones that may not be replaceable. And one of the constraints is the lack of manpower specialized in

indexing, classification, and translation; another is the difficulty of acquiring the documents available at different government institutions, and insufficient financial capacity to buy documents and manuscripts or provide the necessary tools or equipment such as computers. One of the administrative problems is that many citizens offer documents and manuscripts in their possessions for sale to the center, but the process has to go through several officials, which then impedes the acquisitions of these documents and manuscripts, which are considered an irreplaceable treasure.[29]

Despite failing to achieve its stated goals in the first two decades of its existence, the Darah was commissioned by the centennial planners to produce the evidentiary terrain of the state-sanctioned history of the Arabian Peninsula, with an eye to the state-building process that led to the creation of modern Saudi Arabia.[30]

The Darah had improved its chances of being chosen as the site of the post–Gulf War project of archival centralization once it came under Salman's wing. The life history of the so-called founding father was to be at center stage on this momentous occasion. According to al-Semmari, the Darah's secretary-general—and since 2015 the adviser to King Salman's Royal Court as well as general supervisor of the National Center for Documents and Archives—the Darah would collect "documents [both original and duplicate forms], manuscripts, books, magazines, photographs, sketches, paintings, films, and oral traditions . . . with the aim of preserving the history of the Kingdom of Saudi Arabia, along with its geography, literature, thought, and architecture."[31] The Darah's goal, however, was still to "particularly focus on the history of King Abdulaziz [ibn Saud]."[32] Collected historical documents on older regional and national political formations—not to mention the layered and multisited regime and corporate violence undergirding the state-building project—would be excised from the postwar material record, destined for rotting boxes in decrepit basements.

Al-Semmari regularly spoke of the alarming state of historical and administrative documents in the kingdom and the urgency of rescuing them. In an opening speech at a symposium on historical documents, al-Semmari noted: "The ambitious program that the Darah embarked on to survey national historical sources across the kingdom revealed to us the massive number of historical documents, but the state of these documents actually terrified us, given their neglect and bad storage conditions. Many of the national historical documents remain stacked up in boxes or bags inside warehouses not suitable for resisting rough weather conditions . . . but the Darah's designated teams . . . were able to save, transport, and preserve many of them."[33] The postwar political economy had placed the Darah at the center of the archiving industry, and Al-Semmari was justifying the Darah's newfound clout.

By the turn of the twenty-first century, the Darah's future seemed infinitely more promising as it moved from Ma'zar to the new King Abdulaziz Historical Center, site of the centennial celebration and now a landmark of the fledgling tourism and culture industries. In so doing, the Darah gained access to state-of-the-art buildings conducive to the storage and maintenance of valuable historical artifacts. In the first year of its renewed life, the Darah's annual budget averaged $3 million.[34] It counted ninety-four full-time employees on its payroll, a feat compared to the staff of other archives in the country.[35] Almost overnight, the Darah raised hopes that it would revolutionize historical and cultural production in the kingdom and become a first-rate international institution. Acknowledging past failures, al-Semmari explained the importance of documenting the past:

> I am proud to inform Your Highness [Prince Salman] that the Darah has many programs and plans that will accomplish a large part of its ambitions and goals to compensate for what we have failed to accomplish in the past. . . . Our judicious state [*dawlatna*] whose history goes back to the fifteenth century and its formation to the eighteenth on the basis of Unitarianism, spread security and stability in the Arabian Peninsula due to the nobility of its principles and goals. What our judicious state has accomplished . . . is closer to a miracle than an accomplishment, and we should be interested in documenting and preserving its history and accomplishments so future generations can turn history pages that are glowing with that which is impressive. This cannot be achieved without caring for historical source materials, most important among them are documents, the backbone of history.[36]

Al-Semmari was reassuring those in the archiving industry, whose cooperation and support he needed, that the Darah was ready for this big assignment.

The Darah quickly became the most powerful actor in the industry of Saudi historical production. The political motivations for this transformation were clear to its employees as well as to others involved in archival practice.[37] From its relaunch, the Darah earned the unqualified support of Salman, the designated gatekeeper of history for the ruling family. In his keynote address at the Symposium on Historical Documents in 1996, Prince Salman explained:

> Due to the lack of cultural awareness in this country, there were periods in our history in which, we can say, the researcher would get exhausted in order to obtain the facts, to truly grasp the history of this great country.... Unfortunately, we now have two, three, or maybe four books that we rely on to write our own modern history, in addition to a couple of Orientalist books.... With the presence of intellectuals and researchers, the conditions are now ripe for us to search for historical facts and historical records, and we should fully support them in this endeavor, especially with the presence of universities across the kingdom as well as cultural centers, above all the Darah, to which the government, headed by the king and his crown prince, give full confidence and support.... We should, as citizens throughout the kingdom, avail and give our documents to the Darah.[38]

It was the governor's way of publicly supporting the Darah and signaling its importance and institutional hegemony in the emerging cultural landscape. Other state institutions would play a supporting role at best. Salman's speech was intended to transcend the personal rivalries and power struggles that had marred past archival centralization. It also laid the groundwork for government claims that equated history with secular modernity in order to posit document collection as a national duty for all, citizens and state institutions alike. Almost overnight, "the search for historical facts" became of paramount importance. Ironically, the National Center for Documents and Archives at the Council of Ministers complex was ignored; as were the King Fahd National Library (KFNL), which once earned Salman's patronage, and the only operating, semicentralized state archive at the IPA.

A CROWDED ARCHIVING LANDSCAPE

The Darah complemented its worldwide search for historical records by sponsoring conferences on the history of Saudi Arabia and its past rulers. Together, these efforts unintentionally heightened competition among members of the ruling family, many of whom contested Salman's version of the past. For reasons that are not altogether clear, Salman was amenable to incorporating the history of his late brother, King Saud (r. 1953–1964), into the official narrative of the past. Salman began to make his stance public in the mid-1990s. Faisal had ordered the elision of Saud from the material record when he assumed the throne through a coup in 1964.[39] Salman overturned this decision three decades later. In the late 1990s, and to the chagrin of many in the ruling family, Salman ordered the Darah to host conferences, workshops, and research projects to document Saud's long-censored history. One of King Saud's daughters, Fahda, even presented a research paper on her father's eleven-year reign; this occurred at the Darah in January 1999, during the centennial celebration.[40] Fahda argued—using Saudi, Lebanese, Egyptian, British, and US archival sources—that Saud was the force behind many of the decisions, agendas, and events that official history has ascribed to his brother, Faisal. For instance, Fahda maintained that Saud, and not Faisal, actually masterminded the so-called Ten-Point Program. Among several things, the program abolished slavery, set the agenda for the development of modern educational and health programs, built state institutions, and called for a constitution.[41] Essentially, Fahda publicly accused her late uncle Faisal of silencing her father's past and rewriting the history of the kingdom. Faisal's descendants stormed out of the room in protestation.

Seeing this opening, Fahda embarked on a project to document her father's history using his personal papers and belongings but also primary sources from state and personal archives around the world.[42] She then turned the material artifacts she had collected into an exhibit on the life of King Saud, which opened at the Darah on November 26, 2006. A pictorial book on Saud was launched alongside the exhibit.[43] The Darah had also organized a simultaneous symposium on the late king's history, which resulted in the publication of a multivolume history of King Saud.[44] Although the exhibit contested many accepted truths, it made no mention of the constitution that Saud had announced in 1960: Fahda had the evidence for it, but she knew it would be too provocative a claim (too much too soon, she seemed to think).[45] With Salman's blessing, the exhibit was well attended and widely covered in the media, prompting unprecedented discussions of Saud's rule. Many visitors even donated documents on Saud that were in their possession. The event was so successful that Fahda turned it into a mobile exhibition that subsequently toured Saudi Arabia and neighboring Bahrain.

The positive reception that the exhibition on Saud elicited alarmed some in the ruling family, especially the pro-Faisal factions and his descendants. They accused King Saud's family of "hijacking history" and filed official complaints within the ruling family, to no avail.[46] They also claimed that the Darah, under the tutelage of Salman, was involved in a project of rewriting official Saudi history. Prince Turki al-Faisal, chairman of the King Faisal Center for Research and Islamic Studies, was especially known to express this view to researchers visiting the center. To counter this narrative and protect Faisal's legacy, his children and grandchildren demanded the Darah host a conference on Faisal. They began to collect documents, photographs, and other artifacts on his life and legacies. They contacted state and private archives worldwide in search of historical documents that evinced their version of the past, which was becoming less authoritative than it had once been, at least inside Saudi Arabia. In 2009, they launched their own mobile exhibition titled *Al-Faisal: Shahid wa shahid* (Al-Faisal: Witness and martyr). By then, however, Faisal's descendants had abandoned some of their historical claims, such as those about the Ten-Point Program. They conceded that the latter was King Saud's doing when Faisal himself had pointed to the Ten-Point Program starting in the late 1960s to portray himself as a "reformer" and a "modernizer." Patrons in several of the exhibitions on Faisal that I attended feigned admiration, but their whispers said otherwise. The same was true of debates in various intellectual salons that took place in Riyadh and Dammam. Many of the intellectuals in attendance there, however, ridiculed the very premise of these exhibitions and the futility of clamoring over "accomplishments," even if they appreciated the resurrection of Saud.

With state archives endorsing one or the other of these historical narratives, the mobile exhibit became an alternative and preferred mode of knowledge production among the ruling family. Members of Al Saud used it to circulate their own version of the past, which in reality only slightly deviated from state-sanctioned historiography. Under the direct control of Salman, the Darah managed the historiographical rivalries among different factions of the ruling family and the attendant histories they proffered. While the Darah unprecedentedly advanced historical research on King Saud and pushed for the revision of official historiography to include his accomplishments, it did so within the discursive bounds of its own historiographical agenda. Incorporating King Saud's history in the official narrative was a step in the right direction, according to some descendants of King Saud. But the Darah still had a long way to go to do so in a truly meaningful way. As Fahda was keen to emphasize, Salman and the Darah allowed the discussion only of some of King Saud's state-building and infrastructural accomplishments. His role in mid-twentieth-century political and social life in

Arabia and the way he was overthrown were off-limits.[47] Fahda has, as a result, endeavored to establish a "documentation center" that would help researchers access materials on her father. The historical records Fahda has collected have been published on Saud's official website.[48]

The historiographical struggle between the descendants of both kings were triggered by, and overlapped with, heightening competition among Saudi Arabia's state archives. But Al Saud's generational archive battles also furthered the institutional rivalries and the race for the collection of historical records. When, in 1996, the Darah proposed assuming the mantle of Saudi Arabia's national archive, industry officials made their opposition known. The proposal for a national strategy that the Darah put forth was especially alarming to them. Therein, Darah managers made several demands that they deemed necessary for the success of archival centralization and the safeguarding of the country's national history. They requested that the Saudi Council of Ministers issue edicts to compel rightful owners of historical documents to hand over either the originals or duplicates to the Darah. The decrees would target individuals as well as state and cultural institutions, whether they had organized archives or not.[49] For al-Semmari, these bureaucratic interventions would prevent the duplication that runs rampant in the archiving field as well as the financialization of material heritage. Such centralization of archival efforts would also serve as a "serious step to constructing a national archive in the Kingdom" and "achieve continuity in the archival collections, which should naturally be all housed together in one place."[50] Although al-Semmari stressed the importance of cooperation within the archiving industry, he also requested that the Darah establish and supervise special committees that would decide the accessibility of the collected documents. In other words, according to the proposal, the Darah would have the mandate to collect all documents. It would also have the power to foreclose the future of certain documents and the ability to banish the histories they tell from official memory.[51] As I elaborate later in the chapter, while the regime upheld the Darah as the country's main repository for historical documents, the Darah's proposed national strategy did not secure royal sanction. Doing so ultimately put every other institution in the industry on the warpath. The Darah was at the forefront of an intraregime and regime-society war over the ownership of history, and thus of the future.[52] Where state archives historically struggled to obtain documents because of elite rivalries, they now also had to contend with an official project, with the Darah as enforcer, to curate the documentary landscape in accordance with a singular, teleological, and secular view of the past. Riyadh's main archives were concerned with the Darah's ambition to carry out the centralization of the kingdom's documents and to enshrine some "facts" while obscuring others. They started to work in circumstances of hyperprotectiveness in order to circumvent any laws that would have them surrender their documentary capital. Although most of their employees worked for the state, they labored to prevent the Darah from succeeding.

These rivalries inadvertently triggered the commodification of historical documents in the mid-2000s. An illicit market for (real and forged) historical documents only furthered their dispersal and complicated archival production. Together and separately, the heightened rivalries, historical contestations, and financialization of documents caused a protracted archive war between and among members of the ruling family and the managers and employees of Riyadh's state archives. Archive managers lamented the failure of the National Center for Documents and Archives—the country's intended national archive—yet they rejected the Darah's centralizing mission, and Salman's political project more broadly.

Even Aramco emerged as one among many institutionalized interests within the Saudi state. When Darah managers embarked on a project to document the history of oil (*mashruʿ tawthiq al-naft*) in 2008, Aramco consistently refused their requests to duplicate the records in the oil company's possession. Both the Saudi Ministry of Petroleum and Mineral Resources and the Ministry of Finance held duplicates of some Aramco documents. Those records that have actually been archived at both ministries are, however, classified, and the Darah has not able to access them.[53] Salman's favored institution also failed to secure Aramco's archival training cooperation. Aramco signed contracts with the Darah in 2008 and again in 2011, promising to share many of its records as well as its archiving expertise. Yet the company reneged on its obligations in both contracts.

In fact, Aramco had decided to join the impulse for archival praxis, announcing in 2007 that it would establish the King Abdulaziz Center for Knowledge and Culture in Dhahran. Construction began a year later. The center would house, among its various departments, an archive of carefully choreographed rare documents, images, footage, and books, with the aim of "manag[ing] and maintain[ing] records of the social heritage of Saudi Arabia."[54] Aramco was not willing to share its corporate records with other state institutions. Instead, it would produce an archive of its own for public consumption, one that told a sanctioned history of the company. "Sensitive records" would remain out of sight, secured at Aramco's corporate archive. As Aramco's public relations director, Tariq al-Sh'aifan, explained in 2010, "The archive is the golden treasure that Aramco will always sit on. Even after the end of oil, these records will never see the light of day. They will remain behind the sun. It is life and death for the company but also for the state."[55] Indeed, despite Salman's backing, the Darah failed to access, let alone control, Aramco's archive or benefit from the company archivists' long experience.[56]

Salman, and the regime more broadly, did not expect such a struggle over archive making to emerge or to escalate as it did. They nonetheless took advantage of it in order to achieve their primary goal: taming both the archival landscape and popular political opposition. This was not lost on many of the regime's wartime critics. Some of them had nonetheless joined the postwar archiving project, despite significant opposition from their allies and constituencies.[57] Their faith in the regime had slightly increased as Crown Prince Abdullah became the de facto regent. One journalist who had protested the regime during the Gulf War reasoned: "We know that the government is using us in the name of inclusivity and nation-building to curtail our opposition. But maybe if we work within the system, we can gain more rights, maybe we can force our own histories into the national narrative and into history textbooks."[58] Another activist who also joined the postwar heritage-making effort in the mid-1990s explained that too many friends and relatives had been imprisoned because of their wartime activism. He did not want a similar fate. At the same time, he insisted: "The rulers finally heard the people and understood that we should have a voice, that the status quo was not sustainable. This time, they were serious about change. And history is as good a place as any to start."[59] Others I spoke with who also fell within this category were weary of the rulers' increasing disregard for religion. They believed they could reform the system and recenter the place of religion if they worked from within. When all else failed, some of them did all they could to encourage document owners not to hand over their troves to the Darah.

The institutional war over archive formation eventually drew in the owners of private archives and others in the historical industry. These equated the Darah with Salman and saw its work as a regime attempt to further silence those outside of official historiography. They began to fear for the documents in their possession, which they now saw as not just personal property but proof of their place in Arabia's past and present. Maintaining records of these pasts, which did not fit into the state-sanctioned history, became all the more important for them. Without much power, there was little they could do if confronted with Salman's orders to submit their possessions. But Darah employees met with the utmost resistance in collecting documents from notables, traders, tribes, and former functionaries, none of whom were under the state's thumb. They were, after all, powerful members of the society on which the Saudi regime's stability and balance of power depended. To coerce them into surrendering what the archiving regime had deemed part of Saudi "heritage" would risk this balancing act, especially because the regime had not issued any heritage preservation laws that would so compel them.

The Darah's practices thus alienated allies and foes alike. Those who could began to evade its requests for the historical documents in their possession. The Darah strategically attributed this marked resistance to a lack of appreciation of national heritage, or "a lack of cultural awareness," to use Salman's words. Remarkably, even representatives of Riyadh's other state archives who were wary of the Darah's political project ascribed Saudi Arabians' reluctance to a state of "backwardness" and "uncivilization" in the kingdom.[60] This "unenviable cultural state," they said along with the Darah's managers, came from a century of religious "intolerance" in which the official religious establishment considered the preservation of archeological and historical artifacts to be un-Islamic innovation (*bidʻa*). For those in the official archiving industry, national education and awareness programs were necessary to combat decades of official discourse that not only denied the legitimacy of preserving historical artifacts but also damned it as heretical.

Whether this justification was true or not—given the diversity of views on the matter among religious scholars—those in archiving and in urban planning said as much in interviews as well as in industry publications. They used this rhetoric to explain the acts of vandalism against historical sites and monuments that became all too common in the 1960s and also had become a matter of municipal concern.[61] If the "lack of awareness" did indeed explain some Saudi Arabians' reluctant approach to documents and historical sites, it certainly did not capture all the reasons, specifically since the 1990s. That the Darah was doing the regime's bidding in reifying a singular official history that many in the kingdom contested was not lost on most Saudi Arabians, within and outside of the archiving industry.

The Darah ignored these ulterior motives and increased its efforts to centralize archives. Using people's alleged ignorance as justification, it embarked on a multimedia national campaign to raise awareness of the importance of historical artifacts, and of commemorating the past, to "modernizing and civilizing of the nation." Without the documentary evidence of the past, the logic went, the nation could not achieve the modernity befitting a petrostate with the wealth and geopolitical weight of Saudi Arabia. The modern Saudi Arabian citizen suddenly needed a documentary and material history, an archive, to become part of History itself. It was in this spirit, and with these goals in mind, that the Darah put up its billboards and deployed its mobile labs.[62] With all these tactics, it quickly became clear to those in Riyadh's archiving industry that the Darah's mandate was no longer limited to collecting the history of the country, with a focus on its first king. The Darah instead aimed to centralize all archival documents in order to remove from sight those papers that countered the official historical discourse. And when it could not achieve that, it would consolidate its archival power precisely by further dispersing the country's material history. Like history and archival production more broadly, state institutions became key battlegrounds for both wrestling with the present and envisioning the future.

INSTITUTIONAL HEGEMONY: THE DARAH'S CENTRALIZING MISSION

With this many vested interests in the archival process, the Darah's employees struggled to collect historical documents. This was despite Fahd al-Semmari's reassurances and Salman's unbridled support. At first, several collectors donated their papers to Salman's designated institution. Others took the Darah up on its promise of "the restoration and conservation of documents, manuscripts and newspapers... as long as the Darah received a copy of these items," often asking for monetary compensation for originals or copies of their documents.[63] As with any archive, the records were strictly vetted. Many, however, remained inaccessible to most of the Darah's employees and the few researchers who were allowed into the archive. By 2003, the Darah had cataloged only fifteen thousand of the supposedly "massive [cache of] historical documents" it acquired. In subsequent years, it managed to finish with only several more thousand. This lack of access exacerbated suspicion among the owners and managers of other state and private archives, who subsequently questioned the real motives behind the Darah's project of documenting Saudi Arabian history. Given these suspicions, the Darah had to go to even greater lengths to secure primary source artifacts and to prove its competence.[64] The official seal bestowed on the Darah gave it unrestrained powers, which its representatives did not hesitate to abuse in pursuit of their mission, as the practices of the mobile laboratory preservationists indicate. The Darah quickly earned a reputation for aggressive and unethical tactics in acquiring all of the records of the country's diverse past.

The Darah eventually managed to collect an impressive cache of documents because it did not rely solely on donations and solicitations.[65] It could not, given the resistance it faced. The Darah, in fact, had to purchase the bulk of its records—upward of five million documents—in the years between 2006 and 2011. It was able to do so because of Salman's backing. As of 2014, Darah employees had yet to vet the papers. However, they expect all of them to contain historically valuable information, even if they knew that at least some were forged. Of the five million documents, approximately 1.5 million (in both original and duplicate form) are local administrative and historical records, duplicates of which are housed in the capital's other archives, including the National Center of Documents and Archives, the archives of the KFNL, and the IPA. Many were purchased from local and regional document traders as well as auction houses. Like its counterparts in other Gulf Arab capitals, the Darah purchased foreign documents related to Saudi Arabia, mainly from British, Ottoman, and Arab national archives as well as those of the United States, France, Germany, the Netherlands, Italy, Russia, and India. These were diplomatic, economic, and political documents, but they also concerned religious issues, mainly to do with the Muslim pilgrimage to Mecca and Muslim-Christian relations. The copy-and-paste archive has been organized to cover the history of the Arabian Peninsula, particularly that of Saudi Arabia. Documentary records showcasing Abdulaziz ibn Saud in heroic terms took precedence; they were placed in a special folder and slated for immediate classification and cataloging, with the stated intent of making them available to researchers.[66]

Where records that pertain to Abdulaziz and some of his sons were expedited, the vast majority of the Darah's documentary inventory continued to sit in boxes in its basement. This disarray stood in stark contrast to the state of alarm with which the Darah described the condition of historical documents in the kingdom, which it equated with a lack of civilization, a scar on the nation. If the Darah had indeed saved historical documents from destruction, as its director claimed throughout the opening decade of the twenty-first century, it continued to endanger them by keeping them locked up in improper storage conditions, away from scrutiny. As late as 2011, an employee at the Darah's Center for Restoration and Preservation of Historical Materials described the "wretched state of the Darah's historical documents." He confirmed that the Darah had neglected its records and lacked the will to "save" them.[67] He further explained that archiving documents and making them available to researchers is not as difficult as archive managers made it appear. Without any additional funds or manpower, according to another colleague who worked there, the center would be able to restore and/or preserve between 120,000 and 150,000 documents per year. Yet, since the center's founding and at least until 2015, the staff there had worked only on historical documents that Salman and his brothers, and the Darah's director, sent directly to the preservation department, bypassing the Darah's official procurement and processing protocol. The preservationists spent their remaining working hours restoring and preserving newspapers and manuscripts, both of which are highly time-consuming tasks (Figures 4 and 5).

FIGURE 4. Employee at the Darah's Center for Restoration and Preservation of Historical Materials laminating a historical manuscript. *Source:* Photograph taken by author at the Darah's Center for Restoration and Preservation of Historical Materials in Riyadh, 2010.

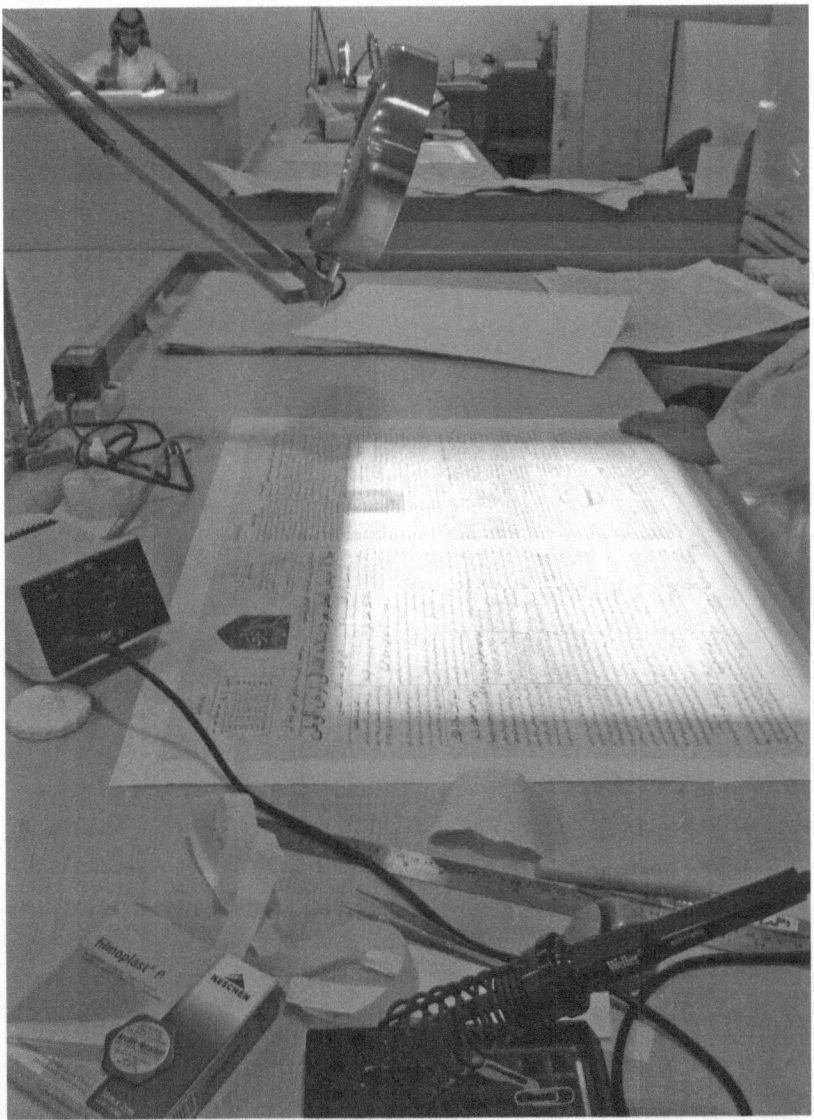

FIGURE 5. Employee at the Darah's Center for Restoration and Preservation of Historical Materials conserving and subsequently digitizing a copy of Saudi Arabian newspaper *Umm al-Qura*. *Source:* Photograph taken by author at the Darah's Center for Restoration and Preservation of Historical Materials in Riyadh, 2010.

Despite what the archiving industry viewed as documentary neglect, the Darah continued to invest in collection above all other archival functions. It became clear to those in the industry that the necessity of finding the "facts of history" lay not in the facilitation of critical scholarship—as Salman had once proclaimed—but in a desire to memorialize the postwar state-sanctioned historical narrative. Documents that evinced alternative histories would be collected, but then set aside, not out of incompetence but as part of the official archival project. Instead of serving as a research archive, the Darah began to put out its own historical publications, purportedly based on its archival collections, to which few outsiders had access. That the Darah showed no will to sort, classify, catalog, or make its massive "documentary conquests" available confirmed fears about its intent to privilege one historical narrative, distressing both the community of historians as well as those in the ruling family who are being written out of the country's past.

AN INDUSTRY AT WAR

The 1999 centennial celebration inadvertently set off a race to collect Saudi Arabia's historical source material. By the turn of the century, the Darah's attempts at hegemonizing the archiving operation at other archivists' expense, and without benefit to the community (of producers and researchers alike), turned archival praxis into an archive war proper. The KFNL, the King Abdulaziz Public Library, the King Faisal Center for Research and Islamic Studies, and the National Center for Documents and Archives all entered into fierce competition with the Darah. In the attendant atmosphere of hostility and secrecy, the other archives hid their most prized possessions and canceled many of the annual exhibitions in which they displayed their treasures. Archive managers feared that the Darah—and not, ironically, the national archive—would secure legal sanction from Salman to requisition what they saw as rightfully theirs.[68] This tactic was one among many that the archive managers adopted in order to safeguard their possessions and what they saw as the country's "real" history. With the exception of the Darah, Riyadh's archives invested most of their resources in digitizing their documental collections in the event that the Darah succeeded in confiscating them. At the same time, they all adopted stringent rules for access, further constricting the ability to conduct archival research in the kingdom. These archival anxieties were heightened when Salman became crown prince in 2012 and then king in 2015.

The archive wars of the first decade of the twenty-first century generated a local and international market for historical documents, turning cultural artifacts into highly prized commodities. Indeed, few document experts and enthusiasts were unaware of the archive wars raging in Riyadh. Those working in document markets (*souk al-watha'iq*) in Jeddah, Riyadh, Cairo, and Sanaa, in auction houses such as Sotheby's in London and Christie's in New York City, and in the world's largest colonial and postcolonial archives followed the archive battles in the Saudi capital. An illicit market for real and forged historical documents flourished in Arab capitals and continental Europe, which only complicated archival consolidation. As purchasers at Riyadh's archives scoured markets for Saudi Arabia's dispersed source materials, they found that document merchants (*tujjar al-watha'iq*) had beat them to it: using their commercial networks, the merchants had acquired the documents first and sold them at exorbitant prices to buyers in Riyadh. The merchants took advantage of the high demand for historical documents to play Riyadh's archivists against one another in bidding wars. In many instances, archive representatives would battle it out in auction houses, paying hundreds of thousands of dollars for a document on King Abdulaziz ibn Saud, and even more than that for papers that evince Saudi Arabia's official history. The Darah, with Salman's financial backing, managed to acquire the largest number of documents, including those classified as "rare" and with the most value to the historical operation, aggravating tensions in the industry.

As these markets for authentic records expanded, a market for forged historical documents also quickly took shape in Saudi Arabia.[69] Forgeries of existing documents that would then be sold to multiple buyers became so prevalent by the end of the decade, and weighed so heavily on the budgets and reputations of archives, that the regime had to intervene. In January 2010, the Shura Council unanimously approved a draft penal code to replace the kingdom's Anti-Forgery Law of 1960. It comprises thirty-two articles dealing with fraud and its negative repercussions for the national economy. Forging historical documents to "distort the Kingdom's history" became a punishable offense, although it is not clear if the regime has prosecuted anyone on these new fraud charges. According to the council's chairman, Abdullah Al al-Shaykh: "Manuscripts are an integral part of the Kingdom's annals.... Heritage is considered an important reference for the Kingdom's history and serves as an invaluable asset that should be preserved and protected for the good of the nation."[70] This legal intervention was one of the first occasions on which Saudi Arabia's religious establishment partook in the economy of historical preservation, which it had long disregarded. At the same time, the regime was cautioning, with the threat of legal and religious sanction, those who would attempt to challenge the official historical narrative.

Within a few years, Riyadh's archives had drained their reserves and could no longer afford the inflated prices they had paid for documentary evidence. The endeavor to reclaim the dispersed Saudi artifacts had come at great expense, upward of $100 million in the first decade following the centennial celebration.[71] The Saudi regime had to reevaluate its priorities, delineate a more rigorous artifact selection process, and limit its budget. The directors of three of Riyadh's archives (the KFNL, the Darah, and the King Faisal Center for Research and Islamic Studies) agreed to change the rules of their bidding wars at the upscale auction houses. Whichever institution first announced that it would bid on a particular document would face no interference from other Saudi state organs, with the proviso that it give the other archives duplicates of the document. As the archive wars ground on, these rules succeeded in maintaining the market price of documents while sparing the archives' budgets and guaranteeing access to the documents.[72] On other fronts, however, the archive wars continued. On the one hand, the emergence of a competitive market for documents was accompanied by a scattering of all types of historical source material among different institutions. On the other hand, the institutions disregarded a century's worth of state records for the sake of collecting as many documents as they could before their competitors did so and before any new law forced them all to surrender their troves to the Darah.

Although directors and employees of Riyadh's archives are candid about the archive war, it has largely remained within the confines of the industry. The incident that opened the introduction to this book, detailing the lifeworld of the historical documents that South Asian laborers discovered buried under a construction site at the Grand Mosque in Mecca in 2010, remains an exception. The Mecca discovery nonetheless expanded the discursive field in which these struggles operated and so led to archival battles playing out at the Darah's *Rare Manuscript Exhibition on Saudi Arabia*.[73] It was not simply Islamists who criticized the Darah for cutting the Wahhabi movement out of the country's official history. Managers of the

KFNL, already critics of the Darah's practices, were equally upset. While at the exhibit, they discovered some of the rare manuscripts that the laborers had found in Mecca. According to Saudi Arabia's Manuscripts Law, issued by the Council of Ministers in 2002, the KFNL was tasked with receiving and preserving local historical manuscripts. Yet the Darah had neither informed the KFNL about these manuscripts nor shared duplicates as the law required.

Reporters were quick to cover the brawl at the exhibition, along with the struggle over the manuscripts and the writing of the country's history. For two weeks, the country's major newspapers investigated the rivalries between the various archiving institutions and ran editorials about the politicization of history writing. For the first time, the Saudi Arabian public became aware of the struggles pitting cultural institutions against one another. It was perhaps the first and only instance in which all the actors involved in the production of official history contributed to this debate. Public discourse became so disturbing to the archiving regime that Salman had to intervene to silence the warring factions and remind everyone that all national documents should be sent to the Darah. He also directed the media and state censors to abort the story. The publicity had already compelled the Darah's secretary general to give a statement to the media:

> There is no conflict between the King Abdulaziz Foundation [the Darah] and the King Fahd National Library over the collection and preservation of historical manuscripts. The Foundation and the Library have a long history of cooperation, so that if the Foundation receives any documents, it falls under this cooperative agreement. There is no encroachment taking place. The two institutions play complementary roles.... Apart from this, Sulaiman Al-Senai', head of the King Fahd National Library, is also a member of the foundation, and there has been constant cooperation between the two bodies.... The preservation of the historical manuscripts by the Foundation or the Library serves one national goal, which is to enable the public to have access to these rare and invaluable manuscripts that document the country's culture and history.[74]

Although directors of the various archives may have cordial personal relations, sitting on the same boards and committees, their institutions were locked in a state of war. This conflict is all the more paradoxical given that the archives, except King Faisal's, are owned and operated by the state and promote the same state-sanctioned historiography. Again, history making and archiving reveal the contentions, complexities, and impulses otherwise hidden in flattened narrations of a singular and easily discernible Saudi state. In al-Semmari's words, "They play complementary roles . . . and serve one national goal." Yet those in the archiving industry view the Darah as the authoritarian state's "destructive cultural arm." Without exception, they spoke of the politicization of history writing and accused both al-Semmari and Darah archivists of pandering. Yet this view was also held by many of the Darah's own employees, some of whom were critical of the Darah's own secular history-making project. They internally slowed down or sabotaged the collection and cataloguing processes. At times, they even provided me with documents I had not requested because they exposed one state secret or another. Indeed, the separation between state institutions and opposition forces were often blurry. At the heart of the charge is that the Darah was invested in rewriting history in order to privilege certain historical events and Al Saud personalities at the expense of others, and also to arrange the material evidence according to how the Darah's patrons would like future generations to understand the past.[75] In this scheme, the Darah's main objective was to hoard as much of the documentary record as possible and then to produce "scholarship" for the public, whose access to the actual documents it has restricted. Indeed, through the Research and Publications Department, the Darah focuses its resources on histories of Al Saud and life in Najd,[76] written by the same state-approved historians who have marketed the Saudi national fiction for decades.[77]

In less than a decade, the Darah was transformed from a marginal cultural institution invested in documenting modern history—religious and secular, popular and state—to one in charge of curating and materializing the state-sanctioned and largely secular history of the ruling family. Not only did the Darah receive the support of the regime; it also earned the sanction of the religious establishment. Reiterating the regime's position, and Salman's in particular, Grand Mufti Shaykh Abdulaziz ibn Abdullah Al al-Shaykh (b. 1943), who was appointed in 1999, asked citizens to present their rare documents to the Darah because "it has all the resources for efficient conservation."[78] Even the Council of Senior Scholars called on all private libraries to transfer their rare manuscripts to the Manuscript Center at the Darah—not only for the preservation of the kingdom's historical past but also in the greater interest of students and researchers. These calls put archivists elsewhere in the country on alert. They also mobilized those in various opposition movements, and importantly, regular citizens, who fought the regime by hiding historical records, stalling, and blatantly lying to the Darah about artifacts in their possession. All the while, they built their own private and secret archives and, in some cases, digitized them.

ARCHIVAL DECENTRALIZATION AS RESISTANCE

The Darah's policy has led to the containment of source materials: "removing them from sight" in the words of some, "imprisoning" in the words of others, instead of letting the documentary evidence "speak for itself." The main grievance against the Darah is that its myopic view of the past destroyed the material evidence of other political, economic, social, and cultural formations that thrived before and under Al Saud. These conflicting visions of the past also took up the way in which imperial rivalries have shaped the form of the modern Saudi state. To reveal either the alternative histories or the imperial influence, especially in material form, was to counter Al Saud's political, historical, and legal claims and to implicate members of the ruling family in the erasure of inconvenient historical truths. Archivists unaffiliated with the Darah asserted that they were well aware of the "red lines" that constrain their archival and historical endeavors. At the same time, they claimed that the documents in their possession evinced a diverse past that could be an asset, and not a threat, to the monarchy. To affirm this position, most of these archivists stated that they did not have "secret" or confidential records.

Yahya ibn Junayd, the former head of operations at the KFNL and former secretary-general at the King Faisal Center for Research and Islamic Studies, agreed that battles over the representation of the past are detrimental to the creation of a proper "national archive." However, he saw merit in the dispersal of documents. He marshaled as evidence the fact that both the "nonfunctional" National Center and the Darah held millions of untouched historical documents in their basements, and yet neither had properly treated, cataloged, or archived them. The archiving regime was not even able to safeguard the valuable Mecca archives, according to Ibn Junayd, so it lacked the will or the ability to handle the millions of other historical documents around the country.[79] Ibn Junayd thought that dictating the centralization of the country's historical documents by law, whether at the Darah or at the National Center, would be a disservice to both the archival industry and the country. He argued that the dispersal of historical documents guaranteed that the various archival institutions cared for their documents and made them available to researchers. He explained: "The point is not to 'park' the historical documents, but to classify and properly archive them. This requires a level of expertise that we do not have here. Historical documents are not just crucial for history alone, but for economics, law, and social studies. They all need the archive. But we do not have the right concept about what archives should be. The archive is the nation's memory, a sign of civilization, a landmark of modernity. In Saudi Arabia, the nation suffers from severe memory loss [*al-watan mafqud al-dhakira*]."[80]

Saudi archivists critical of the official archiving regime agreed with Ibn Junayd. Commenting on the state of archival affairs in 2011, many archivists lamented the inability to produce a "proper" national archive. Others deemed the failure to centralize historical documents as purely political. For them, millions of historical documents languished in boxes because of the political agenda of those in power. They therefore saw dispersal as a way to counter the failure of political will to develop a centralized archive on the one hand and resistance to the regime's attempt to centralize and hide documents on the other hand. Even the national archive's vice president Khudran al-Damuk, who was part of the archiving regime, agreed that those in power were not invested in making the archival operation successful. In response to a 2008 critique of the national archive's failures that appeared on *al-Yasir*, an online libraries and information blog, he commented: "The national archive had a late beginning, yes, but it has become a landmark since His Royal Highness Abdulaziz ibn Fahd became in charge of it, and despite bureaucratic obstacles that stand in its way and that of other state institutions. These obstacles are on their way to being resolved, and involve other parties and outside forces."[81] In an interview with me in 2011, however, the vice president was more candid: "The strategies that the National Center has adopted to collect documents are specified in the protocols and regulations on documents and archives, which are more than capable of accomplishing the center's objectives but *only* when there is an efficient government administration [*al-idara al-fa'alla*] overseeing the country's institutions, which are the basis for generating documents, and the National Center, with much of the burden falling on the center itself to support the huge operation."[82]

Archival practitioners—regime supporters and critics alike, with the exception of the Darah's secretary-general—agreed that those in power simply do not want a functioning central archive, albeit for different reasons. Like the Darah's architects, they also saw this failure as a civilizational one, a sign of backwardness, in comparison to states that are "civilized," "developed," or "modern." The practitioners felt this way despite being cognizant of and open about the politicized nature of the state-sanctioned history and its memorialization. For them, the archive, in its physical and symbolic monumentality, is a marker of modernity. It promised to "elevate" Saudi Arabians to the level of other nations, something wealth and religious morality have failed to do.

ARCHIVAL PERFORMATIVITY: OF ARCHIVAL STATUS QUOS

If the archive is indeed about the future, as Derrida would have us insist, then what is the decades-long performance of archiving in Saudi Arabia really *doing*?[83] In the years leading up to the 1999 centennial celebration, the Saudi regime was at the height of its drive to memorialize its past through the King Abdulaziz Historical Center, and the Darah in particular. It directed much of its time, expertise, and financial resources to the yearlong spectacle of monumentalizing the so-called founding father and his descendants. Yet in the same year as the centennial, in 1999, the Ministry of Finance froze funding for two key Darah projects: document conservation and computerization. Both operations were crucial to the survival and future accessibility of documents—and the Darah considered them of existential importance. The ministry had previously approved the two projects, but in the years following the centennial, it would ensure that they were shelved. Before the dust had settled on the centennial celebration grounds, the ministry also rejected the Darah's proposed $9.5 million annual budget for the year 1999–2000. Instead, it approved less than one-third of that amount.[84]

Unbeknownst to most of those in the archiving industry, including Darah employees themselves, the Darah had received budgetary authorization to do little more than collect historical documents. The Council of Ministers had turned down the Darah's proposal for a national strategy, mentioned earlier, despite having commissioned it with centralizing Saudi Arabia's historical documents. The Ministry of Finance—whose archives were the target of the country's first archiving law in 1966 and thereafter made up the first collection at the National Center—continued to generously fund official archival collection and centralization in Riyadh. The ministry, however, held back the necessary support for other functions such as conservation, archiving, cataloging, and digitization, unless the documents in question evinced the official history as sanctioned by

Salman's Darah. The official postwar campaign to document the young country's state-sanctioned history and to centralize its dispersed material record never aimed to produce a functional state archive, as some in the regime regularly claimed. Rather, the goal, at least in the period under study, was to take possession of the scattered state- and privately owned historical documents in order to warehouse them, displaying only those very few that evinced the official history. The regime thus paid lip service to collecting the country's historical documents as a national duty, all the while empowering the Darah to hoard millions of records in order to create and consecrate facts on the ground.

How can we understand this archival performativity? Abdullah, whether as crown prince or as king, never expressed much interest in the archiving function even as he halfheartedly supported his half brother, Salman, and his vision of the postwar political economy. That his longtime ally and nephew Abdulaziz ibn Fahd oversaw the National Center for Documents and Archives throughout much of the twenty-first-century archive wars only confirms Abdullah's disinterest in developing a national archive throughout his reign. Abdullah had also sponsored an annual, two-week heritage festival organized by the National Guard that he, too, oversaw, starting in 1985. But the Janadriyya Festival under Abdullah was a cultural event that celebrated the diverse heritage of Saudi Arabians throughout the kingdom, and not a singular, Najd-centric Saudi identity, the sort that Salman has long called for (and accomplished at the Janadriyya Festival since assuming the throne). The festival also stressed Islamic unity and often featured speakers from neighboring Arab states. It was not an archival project: it did not aim to produce knowledge, create facts on the ground, or memorialize Saudi Arabia's official history. Far from it.

In the aftermath of the Gulf War, Abdullah fully backed the 1999 centennial and the production of an official secular history that privileged Al Saud only. The latter was reaffirmed in the aftermath of the September 11, 2001, terrorist attacks in the United States and those inside Saudi Arabia in 2003. On the face of it, Abdullah supported Salman and his choice of empowering the Darah over other archival institutions. Salman was a force to contend with, especially for all matters related to Riyadh, and Abdullah, known to be an appeaser, could not afford to antagonize him. Instead, he indirectly undermined him when it came to archival policies and actions. Abdullah and his allies supported archival centralization only as long as it served their interests and insofar as it helped relegate religion from everyday life and solidify Al Saud's history. During Abdullah's reign, the archival operation was primarily a spectacle for centralizing documents—which, ironically, overlapped with Salman's archival intentions—while paying lip service to the importance of maintaining Arabia's material history.

The lack of necessary support from the king, coupled with political maneuvering, explains why the Council of Ministers never passed into law any of the Darah's centralization proposals. Such laws would have seen the Darah become the country's only functioning national archive, benefiting Salman and compelling the regime to pursue the archival process to its logical end. Abdullah and his allies thus obstructed the work of the Darah and other state archives through bureaucratic means, making sure that they would not make available most of the documents in their possession. The regime's noninterference in the archive wars likewise sabotaged archival praxis, which stayed at the level of collection, where the regime wanted it. In this way the regime maintained the balance of power that undergirded the status quo while keeping archive managers focused on the dispersed material record. In other words, Abdullah's regime consolidated its archival power precisely by further dividing, dispersing, and hoarding the country's material history. As Huda al-Abd al-Ali, one of the few archivists to have seen most documents in the storage facilities of all the archives examined in this book, explains: "This attention to historical documents has led to their further dispersal in different locations, which has especially reflected negatively on the state of documents, as well as on academic research and development projects. The lack of coordination and planning among those collecting documents has caused repetition, redundancy and not knowing what has already been collected and what has not. And all the efforts and activities have revolved around the issue of collecting documents, which has delayed all other operations, such as classifying, organizing, availing or enabling the writing of the country's actual history."[85]

Despite the archive wars within the regime, the monarchy, and society writ large—and between them—the wars nonetheless ultimately bolstered the material heritage of Al Saud without exposing the "state secrets" that had made the rulers so anxious. Much remained hidden from view: the material evidence of British and US imperial support of Al Saud's authoritarian rule and state-sanctioned violence; collaboration among the political, economic, and religious elites to maintain power; rivalries within Al Saud; corruption and nepotism; and the place of Ibn Abd al-Wahhab and his Al Al-Shaykh descendants in state formation. The archiving industry's management and organization methods further entrenched the obstacles to finding this material record, let alone accessing or reviewing it. The industry could not have done so without Salman's endorsement and scheming, even if he ultimately failed to secure Abdullah's real backing.

CONCLUSION

Abdullah and his allies achieved their objectives in several ways. First, the organizations they ran institutionalized the epistemological if blurry divide between "administrative" and "nonadministrative" documents, with each category managed by the national archive and the Darah, respectively. Through the latter institution, they have been able to categorize and prioritize the genres of institutional documents, ensuring that those considered "important" remained in their home institutions and out of the national archive. All other documents, regardless of their nature, would end up in unsuitable storage units at the national archive. Second, they set up the Archives and Documents Protocols, which prioritized administrative records and structured the ways in which this knowledge was organized and consumed. Third, by singling out the Darah as the central repository of national historical documents, they ensured it had ultimate physical, spatial, and technical control over the country's material record. Finally, through the Ministry of Finance, they controlled how archiving institutions allocated their funds and ensured that archival praxis was limited to collection and centralization.

It was thus that the ruling members of the monarchy deployed their legal, institutional, and financial power to compete with one another while attempting to delineate what could and could not be recorded, remembered, or iterated.[86] Despite this archival standoff, Abdullah and Salman ultimately had the same aims: to conceal historical records. Archives are dynamic and generative of particular realities, politics, and ideals. Archival praxis has allowed the Saudi regime—in its multiplicity—to assemble the past, to consolidate much of the country's dispersed material history in state warehouses with no intention to archive the records or make them available. Through the archive, they have attempted to foreclose the multiple histories, geographies, and futures of Arabia while fighting one another and political opponents and containing threats to their monopoly on power. Indeed, even as Saudi rulers faced off through the archives, they at once battled other common enemies who opposed the Al Saud regime. Having sparked the archive wars, Abdullah and his allies, as well as Salman, then appeared to intervene in the archival operation only when the warring institutions required a benevolent mediator,[87] as during the spats over the documents discovered underneath Mecca's Grand Mosque, or when the rivalries were becoming too expensive.

The writing and rewriting of history reveal the depth of the state's vulnerability and its mercurial relationship to the past. The stakes of the contemporary struggle to produce a national archive differed from those triggered by the country's first archiving law, which King Faisal issued in 1966. Both struggles, however, reveal the precariousness and incoherence of the state at the same time that they signal its dynamic and multiple nature. Such archival performativity also reveals the political geography of Saudi Arabian society and the regime's technology of assembling the Saudi social through the physical control of the archive. This became even clearer after Abdullah's death and as Salman ascended the throne in January 2015.

For most of his tenure in office, whether as Riyadh governor (1963–2011) or defense minister (2011–2015), Salman did not have unbridled power to surpass the Council of Ministers and impose his postwar plan, whether in the capital or in the rest of the country. As king, however, he finally did, to the chagrin of so many Saudi Arabians. In his first three years on the throne, Salman brutally put an end to the power-sharing system that had at once kept prominent branches of Al Saud in check and allowed them to rule over institutional fiefdoms that regularly hindered state centralization. Once these institutions were under his absolute control, the new king dealt with other obstacles to the implementation of national policies and his vision of Saudi Arabia in particular, marketed since 2016 as Vision 2030.[88] He unleashed security forces against all pockets of dissent, opposition, and criticism regardless of political orientation—especially the Sahwa movement—creating a reign of terror not seen since Faisal's years.

Salman did not spare the archiving industry his heavy-handed rule. Not only did he strengthen the Darah and support its mandate, but he also sidelined the already ignored National Center for Documents and Archives at the Council of Ministers, initially meant to become the country's national archive. The newly conceived National Center for Archives and Records at the Royal Court would henceforth assume this responsibility. None other than Fahd al-Semmari became its general supervisor and the adviser to King Salman's Royal Court. With these changes, Salman heightened the centralization of historical and administrative records, and, for now, seems to have put an end to the archive wars. While Salman appears to have defeated all his rivals, upending the conventional power-sharing scheme and creating fear among the masses has cost him dearly: opposition to his rule has skyrocketed. He has created new enemies among Saudi Arabians who in prior years were at least superficially willing to work with the regime, in the archiving industry, too. How this heightened opposition will affect the archival function is yet to be seen. So far, Salman has continued his investment in archival centralization, but it is not yet clear to what end.

Institutional acts of history making and placing speak to how historical time and space are being captured, retrospectively, by the Saudi "victors" while elucidating the multiple silences that constitute Saudi Arabian history and politics. They also put into question the coherence of historical narration and memorialization, and expose archival anxieties, uncertainties, and rivalries among the architects of state building and their agents. The weaponization of history has also been deployed in an attempt to pacify or co-opt those who otherwise opposed the Saudi regime even if it engendered new rivals. To study the multipronged war over the consolidation of archival power in Saudi Arabia—in its marked belatedness, commodification of records, and competition over production of social memory—is, then, to underscore ruling ideologies, spatial politics, and layered temporalities. Far from exceptionalizing Saudi Arabia, such an approach speaks to mundane practices and struggles that go into the making of archives writ large. For in their own ways, all archives are sites of war that embody and reflect inter- and intrastate and state-society relations and struggles over power: the power to subjugate the past to the politics of the present and to dictate the future.

Chapter 4

HERITAGE AS WAR

> Stone gives a false sense of continuity, and a
> deceptive assurance of life.
> Lewis Mumford, *The Culture of Cities* (1938)

IN THE AFTERMATH OF THE 1991 GULF WAR, AN ARMY OF URBAN planners, economists, historians, archeologists, and tourism consultants descended upon Riyadh. Under the aegis of Prince Salman ibn Abdulaziz's High Commission for the Development of Arriyadh (HCDA), they brainstormed ideas for the redevelopment of the capital city. All eyes were on the political, economic, and social challenges that the country was facing in the late twentieth century. The executive arm of the HCDA, the Arriyadh Development Authority (ADA), which oversaw the centennial celebration, was charged with producing a regulatory planning document that would govern Riyadh's development.[1] The ADA then worked closely with the Ministry of Municipal and Rural Affairs (MOMRA), along with Dar Al Riyadh and the renowned US planning consultancy Harland Bartholomew and Associates.[2] Together, they came up with a long-term urban development strategy and mechanisms for its implementation. Work on the comprehensive strategic plan for the city began in March 1996, around the same time that the Darah began its first national survey of historical documents.

Covering an area of five hundred square kilometers, the comprehensive plan, known as the Metropolitan Development Strategy for the Arriyadh Region (MEDSTAR), aimed to enhance the centralization of the Saudi state. It would transform Riyadh into the true administrative, cultural, economic, and historical center of Saudi Arabia.[3] The plan delineated an urban vision for Riyadh in the coming fifty years based on a twenty-five-year strategic plan and a ten-year executive one.[4] As the city's planning authority, the HCDA approved MEDSTAR in 2001. The Council of Ministers followed suit in 2003 and put the Ministry of Finance at the HCDA's disposal. Saudi Arabia's national urban strategy, five-year development plans, and regional development schemes were put in the service of remaking Riyadh.[5] Achieving the city's new corporate identity became a national priority. The "historic district" (Al-Mantiqa al-Tarikhiyya), now known as Historic or Old Riyadh, was at the forefront of a newly conceived city center. The new center would encompass the Governance Palace District (Mantiqat Qasr al-Hukm), the royal court, the Diplomatic Quarter, and the public park at Riyadh's old airport.[6] The urban sprawl that Riyadh experienced since the 1960s had shifted the city center farther north, leaving some of these designated areas distressed and disconnected from the city's urban fabric. Salman was intent on reversing this development.

Cities are always in the making; they are never fully made or remade. They capture the desires, anxieties, struggles, and histories of their inhabitants, and especially of those in power. Riyadh's reimagined postwar urban identity revealed Salman's fears and some of the goals he hoped to achieve through the built environment. First, MEDSTAR would bolster Al Saud's historical legitimacy, and undermine that of the Wahhabi movement, through investment in particular historical sites. The cultural production of the past and the creation of a national heritage became key to Saudi Arabia's postwar material politics. Second, MEDSTAR would exploit Riyadh's historical sites—most of which were made of adobe and had deteriorated—for recreational purposes. Historical tourism would become a new means of real estate development and capital accumulation.[7] Private-sector participation would especially encourage local economic growth based on historical tourism.[8] Finally, through urban planning, and the production, territorialization, and commercialization of Al Saud's history in the built environment, the rulers would use their bureaucratic power to dominate postwar political opposition.[9] It was a main strategy to focalize the political opposition around institutions of historical preservation—to institutionalize dissent—in the name of social inclusion.[10] Together, these practices of "cultural governmentality" aimed to reshape Saudi sociabilities while financializing the heritage industry.[11]

The last decade of the twentieth century featured the acceleration of the remaking of historical areas in Riyadh and the creation of a heritage industry therein.[12] The Ministry of Finance—first under Fahd and then Abdullah—unprecedentedly approved a multibillion-dollar budget for the cultural redevelopment of Riyadh. Where Abdullah used his leverage to discreetly control the process of archive formation, doing so with the redevelopment of Riyadh, Salman's stronghold, proved riskier. This was a gamble that Abdullah was not willing to take, certainly not as crown prince, but not even as king, with Fahd and then the late defense minister Sultan ibn Abdulaziz as his main rivals.[13] Supporting Salman in the effort to remake Riyadh was in Abdullah's interest for other reasons. Producing heritage would increase Al Saud's legitimacy—or so he thought.[14] Investing in historical sites would create new revenue streams for the state and ultimately strengthen the economy. Abdullah was also a proponent of stripping the religious establishment of all influence and decision-making power, and so in this, too, his goals overlapped with those of Salman. In this vein, the regime launched a concomitant domestic tourism plan. It was rooted in Al Saud's secular history and reviving an imagined Saudi culture while revitalizing largely neglected neighborhoods of the city that were derelict. Just as the changing postwar political economy injected archival praxis in Saudi Arabia with new life, it also entailed a radical shift in ideas about the political, economic, and historical utility of space.[15] Spatial politics are what Michel-Rolph Trouillot would call doubly historical. They are sites of social history and history making. In Arabia, this duality intensified following the 1991 Gulf War.

HERITAGE IN CONTEXT

The construction of heritage can be a violent process. Authorizing state-sanctioned narratives and the spaces that materialize them are belligerent acts. Crafting and territorializing a singular history out of many entangled ones necessarily relies on the destruction, containment, and/or silencing of the countering evidentiary terrain—of people, places, and things. In this sense, the construction of the past—to play on Carl von Clausewitz's well-known maxim—is the continuation of war by other means.[16] As networks of knowledge production and transmission, *lieux de mémoire* are everyday sites of violence that embody ongoing social relations and the attendant struggles over power.[17] In times of peace as in war, they are terrains of symbolic and material contestation whose creative destruction can be deployed as political spectacles and projections of power. In its varied forms, then, heritage is as much a cause for celebration for some as it is one of mourning for others. Heritage reflects the power to subjugate the past to the politics of the present and to dictate the future, both of which are intrinsic to state and subject formation. It is in this context that memorialization came to constitute a key node in the postwar architectural reformulation of the Saudi state.

The announcement of the centennial in 1996 inaugurated the cultural redevelopment of the capital city just as it had heralded historical and archival production. In the aftermath of the Gulf War, it seemed that only stone could save Al Saud, give it permanence, and consecrate its rule in the built environment. Almost overnight, long-neglected sites in Riyadh were considered worthy of commemoration and became targets of state intervention: Murabba' Palace (Qasr al-Murabba'), Governance Palace (Qasr al-Hukm), Justice Square (Sahat al-'Adl), Red Palace (Al-Qasr al-Ahmar), and the city's various state archives.[18] Equally important to MEDSTAR and the historicization of the capital was the redevelopment of Dir'iyya, the historical hometown of Al Saud located on the outskirts of Riyadh. These spaces monumentalized official historical knowledge in the quest to normalize the social order and pacify opposition. As sites of heritage and tourism, they were also new sources for economic production and capital accumulation.[19] On the one hand, they were the bedrock of a national tourism plan that was, and continues to be, in the making.[20] The plan had the domestic population as its primary target. In ensuing decades, the country would open up the tourism industry to a regional and subsequently to an international audience, first through a combination of hajj-tourist visas and then through tourist visas alone, in order to better exploit the kingdom's resources.[21] On the other hand, heritage sites were used as infrastructural and technological spatiotemporal answers to the postwar predicament, thereby enabling capital investment within and surrounding emerging sites of memorialization.[22] Manipulating and managing the built environment with petrocapital surplus, the political and economic elites wanted to transform surplus capital into a regular source of income while territorializing and spatially circulating the official version of the past.[23] Such reordering of urban space reveals practices of history making and political legitimation as inextricably linked to the production of economic value in the built environment.[24]

Constructing the necessary infrastructure for a national tourism strategy would take years, if not decades. Its success also relied on the cooperation of the official religious establishment, which had in the past objected to memorialization practices and to opening up the country to both domestic and international visitors for recreational purposes. Until the 1990s, the state had regarded—or at least claimed—preservation as a heretical form of memorialization that countered the religious and cultural beliefs of the ruling class. This is not to say that all establishment ulama were in agreement on the topic. They regularly debated the issue and often distinguished between the preservation of historical versus religious sites. Many considered the latter only as a mediated form of worship and an association with, and thereby a diminution of, the oneness of God.[25] Their position, however, did not mean that they supported the preservation of nonreligious sites: some were either ambivalent about it or thought it was unnecessary. Others outright opposed it as heretical.[26] According to ADA planners, some religious scholars as well as religious ritual specialists (*mutawa'a*) regularly showed up at different cultural and historical sites, such as the National Museum and Dir'iyya, while the sites were under construction and after completion. They harassed workers and accused them of being unbelievers and practicing religious innovation (*bid'a*).[27] Despite the variance in opinion among religious scholars and enforcers, many Saudi Arabians used these as justifications to sabotage historical sites in the kingdom. At times, such manifestations were simply everyday acts of vandalism.[28]

For archeologists, museologists, and historians I spoke with who were working on the postwar cultural redevelopment project, this was an uncontroversial reality they had to contend with and try to assuage. It was also one that Salman, his son Sultan (president of the Saudi Commission for Tourism and Antiquities), and the Darah's Fahd al-Semmari regularly, if subtly, addressed in their speeches.[29] For much of its history, then, the state actively resisted the very idea of memorializing people, objects, and buildings. Unlike in other countries, historical memorialization strategies were not yet central to political aesthetics and regime maintenance. They were therefore not worth the time and energy the state would have to expend on them. Until the turn of the twenty-first century, those in power thus largely pandered to the religious establishment and prevented the commemoration and monumentalization of space, including the building of museums and memorials as well as the showcasing of statues and other artifacts.

With the exception of sites such as al-Hijr (Mada'in Salih) that were geographically distant and predominantly isolated, the integrity of most historical and archeological sites in the country was compromised by regime negligence. Saudi Arabia's newfound petrowealth in the 1970s increased vehicular-driven development, which led to the partial or complete demolition of many places now considered historically significant.[30] This reality was concomitantly exacerbated as land values in Riyadh rose in that same decade and land speculation came to shape the built environment as well as social and economic life.³¹ These rapid urban transformations led some Saudis, in the 1970s, to embark on projects of historical preservation, such as regional museums and archival undertakings. The regime tolerated these fringe projects because it saw them as local manifestations of cultural nostalgia that did not threaten the regime and its fledgling official historiography. Yet state institutions stood idle when such sites were attacked either by the religious establishment or private individuals. They remained silent even when state institutions that had been vocally antipreservation were responsible for the demolition of historical sites. Historical preservation remained marginal to state affairs for the first five decades of Saudi Arabia's existence.

The regime's approach to material history began to change as it entered its sixth decade of rule. The popular religious opposition that mobilized against the official religious and political establishments across Saudi Arabia during the 1991 Gulf War as well as the subsequent global economic recession unsettled Al Saud's rule. As discussed in the introduction, the war undermined the official religious establishment, which thereafter publicly lost the mass support it claimed to have. It became a direct target of postwar government reform, institutionalization, and pacification. Religion, asceticism, and the protection of the "Wahhabi awakening" were no longer necessary pillars of Saudi sovereignty. Under Salman's tutelage, the ruling elites in Riyadh began to make technical decisions that ensured the built environment matched the regime's new historical imagination. ADA executives obliged. Al Saud no longer sought to legitimate their rule through association with the region's religious past, thus subsuming themselves to religious authority. Instead, the official religious establishment was conscripted in support of a new phase in state aesthetics, one that relied on the relegation of the role of religion in state formation, legitimation, and monumentality. In a seemingly paradoxical move, establishment religious leaders endorsed the memorialization of secular history—which sidelined Muhammad ibn Abd al-Wahhab's past. Starting in the early 2010s, they began to hail sites of commemoration in Saudi mass media as exemplary modernization projects.³² This sort of utilitarian move to abandon the history that had no small part in empowering Saudi rule seems self-contradictory. Here Arabia once again reveals how the intersections between power and history can dismantle what we believe we know. Many religious leaders who were not in the service of the state—and their supporters—opposed the state's memorialization plans. As happened at the Darah's *Rare Manuscript Exhibition on Saudi Arabia* in 2011, they publicly contested them, along with other Islamists, in Riyadh's emerging heritage sites.

In many ways, claims to state land and state aesthetics were easier for the regime to realize than the centralization of the kingdom's dispersed administrative and historical records. Space was an equally, if not more contentious, domain. But those who resisted the regime's spatial plans could not contest or subvert space as they had done with the historical records in their possession. They simply could not match the regime's financial, legal, political, and technological power. These were represented by the powerful MOMRA, and in the case of Riyadh more specifically, the ADA. Just as the ADA oversaw the planning for the centennial celebrations, it also spearheaded the postwar project to remake Riyadh in the image of its ruler Salman.

W(H)ITHER THE PAST: MODERN RIYADH

The modern history of Riyadh begins elsewhere, in Dir'iyya, the historic home of Al Saud. Located twenty kilometers northwest of Riyadh, the walled adobe town overlooking Hanifa Valley was the capital of the political entity that local chieftain Muhammad ibn Saud and religious scholar Shaykh Muhammad ibn Abd al-Wahhab established in 1744. The politically motivated alliance sought to counter increasing Ottoman power, both symbolic and material. It was nonetheless justified based on the rejection of the folk rituals that the central government in Istanbul had allegedly encouraged in Ottoman Arabia, including the worship of saints and pilgrimages to shrines. The Ottoman government did not immediately react to the politico-religious reform movement, although it cautiously watched its adherents even as they broke out of Central Arabia and conquered parts of the Arabian Peninsula to the east, north, and south of Dir'iyya.

It was only when the Saudi-Wahhabi forces began their assault on the holy cities of Mecca and Medina in 1803 and disrupted the Muslim pilgrimage, which was under the realm and protection of the Ottomans, that Sultan Mustafa IV saw the need to intervene. He could not mobilize his own troops, however, preoccupied as they were with crushing various rebellions and opposition movements across the empire. The sultan therefore requested the military help of Mehmet Ali Pasha, viceroy of the autonomous Ottoman province of Egypt. Mehmet Ali had imperial ambitions of his own and had his eye not only on the holy cities but also on the Red Sea trade in coffee. He agreed to send troops, under the leadership of his son Ibrahim, to the Hijaz and did so in 1807. It was only in 1811 that they were able to reclaim Mecca and Medina and push out the Saudi-Wahhabi forces. But Mehmet Ali did not stop there. His troops continued to fight these forces in other territories they had conquered. In 1817, the Egyptian troops reached the town of Dir'iyya.[33] Emerging as victors after a yearlong siege of the fortress, they subdued the rebellious Al Saud clan and exiled their leaders from Dir'iyya to Egypt and Istanbul. After destroying much of the town, the troops set what was left on fire.[34] The damage to the site was so extensive that Al Saud and their allies could not make Dir'iyya their seat of power again.

In their next attempt to secure political dominance in the region, the children of Muhammad ibn Saud and Ibn Abd al-Wahhab managed to establish another, albeit much smaller political formation in 1824. With Dir'iyya all but in ruins, they had to relocate their seat of power to the tiny oasis town of Riyadh. The latter became the capital of their emirate until 1891, when a rival tribe known as Al Rasheed conquered it and displaced Al Saud as the region's rulers. In 1902, another member of Al Saud, Abdulaziz ibn Saud, conquered Riyadh and from there began a bloody war of conquest across the peninsula that lasted almost thirty years. In 1915, he allied with the British, who then provided him with annual subsidies of money and weapons at least until 1924.[35] Abdulaziz's takeover of Mecca and Medina coincided with the fall of the Ottoman Empire and, specifically, the end of the caliphate in 1924. It was also a time when the nation-state was becoming the gold standard in the Middle East. What started off as a religio-political movement at the turn of the twentieth century had by 1932 morphed into a modern state, the Kingdom of Saudi Arabia, with Mecca as the initial seat of power. Nonetheless, the following decades heralded waves of development that saw the once-isolated one-square-kilometer oasis town of Riyadh transform into a metropolis, which by the late 1990s covered an area upward of 632 square kilometers.[36]

The sacking of Dir'iyya in 1818, coupled with rapid and largely unregulated urban development in Riyadh since the 1950s, meant that there was little by way of material heritage that Al Saud could claim as their own in the 1990s and onward. Any previous memorialization efforts were highly divisive and had escaped institutionalization and professionalization. Historical preservation was simply not a bureaucratic concern at least until the 1990s, which is when Dir'iyya came to hold historical significance. Prior to that, the Museum of Archeology and Ethnography, for instance, showcased material life from the diverse regions that made up the modern Saudi state.[37] When it opened in 1978, the museum included a minor exhibit on the adobe fortress town. The exhibited artifacts were portrayed as remnants of a town destroyed by the Ottomans when they vanquished the Saudi emirate in 1818. In this early cultural and historical imaginary, Dirʿiyya represented just one among many of Arabia's demolished material lifeworlds. By the mid-1990s, the top ruling elites' view of the past had changed. The town's political and economic potential became central to postwar political governance. Dirʿiyya would receive a complete makeover: it would no longer be one among many demolished towns but a distinct site of heroism and victory that would stand at the forefront of Riyadh's urban redevelopment plans.[38] Until then, what little had survived of Dirʿiyya's adobe palaces, markets, towers, stables, and alleyways continued to deteriorate as a result of the regime's neglect and the vagaries of Central Arabia's weather.

The distressed state of material history was not limited to the fort town. The regime also neglected, and in some instances even destroyed, spaces in central Riyadh that bore traces of Al Saud's rule in the early twentieth century. This included Governance Palace District (Mantiqat Qasr al-Hukm), the one-square-kilometer walled-in adobe town that Abdulaziz lived in with fourteen thousand other inhabitants following his conquest of Riyadh in 1902.[39] State neglect also affected Murabbaʿ Palace, located two kilometers north of the old city walls. Abdulaziz and many of his sons moved there in 1938, six years after safeguarding Al Saud's monarchical grip on power and establishing the Kingdom of Saudi Arabia.[40] Comprising one-third of the old city, the new adobe complex housed several palaces, dwellings for the king's servants and aides, and some administrative buildings. This move heralded the beginning of an era in which living outside the city wall became possible. The area between the old city and the complex, al-Futah, was the first that urban planners developed in the 1940s.[41] As residents moved to the new dwellings, the older parts of Riyadh were neglected. Within a decade, the city wall was all but destroyed.[42]

Urban planning continued without much attention to architectural preservation, and the city witnessed a major wave of spatial development under Saudi Arabia's second monarch, Saud. In 1953, Riyadh altogether abandoned traditional construction techniques after King Saud commissioned a modern, concrete palace complex northwest of the old city, in al-Nasriyya. Only three years later, the king ordered the transfer of Saudi Arabia's administrative capital and its bureaucratic infrastructure from Mecca to Riyadh.[43] It was a turning point in the history of Riyadh, one that started with the planning and construction of al-Malaz district north of the old city. With its modern quarters and government ministries, al-Malaz housed newly arrived government employees, whose lifestyles became the envy of other town dwellers. As scholar and architect Faisal al-Mubarak points out, "Al-Malaz was comprised of a large-scale housing development encompassing 754 single-family homes, 340 apartment units, and a plethora of supporting facilities including a municipal hall, a library, a fire station, schools, a market, and recreation and health facilities."[44] The al-Malaz development quickly set the ideal for Saudi Arabian urban development and architectural design. Al-Mubarak, who has written extensively on urban development in Riyadh, describes the project:

> Following the transfer of government ministries to Riyadh in the late 1950s, the government sought to attract the Hijazi employees to Riyadh, the traditional base of Al Saud. At the behest of King Saud, a 500 acre satellite suburb, Al Malaz, was inaugurated 5 km to the north of the walled town. The Saudi government assumed responsibility for direct financing of housing construction of the Malaz suburb to house civil servants, who were newly moved from the Western region.... The Al Malaz suburb stood as an antithesis to the traditional mud communities surrounding the walled town. By the end of the 1950s, Riyadh had a population of 300,000, and covered an area of about 100 km^2 as opposed to the original 100-acre [0.4 km^2] "heart of Arabia."[45]

Riyadh's inhabitants quickly grew disdainful of adobe homes, associating them with backwardness and a bygone era of insecurity and poverty. They so longed for the comforts of modern housing and easier transportation that by the 1960s most had abandoned the old city's dwellings, leaving its built life to deteriorate. Its historical markets and economic life nonetheless persisted and enabled the old city to retain its commercial importance despite its outdated and rundown infrastructure and buildings, many of which became warehouses. Shortly after, property owners—those elites who had supported Abdulaziz in his wars of conquest and in return secured massive land grants in Historic Riyadh—began to demolish built structures in the old city to make way for taller buildings and wider roads that could accommodate automobiles and the new commodity market.

As the state's security apparatus strengthened and Riyadh became a relatively safer and more comfortable place to live in, more people moved there for economic, educational, and other purposes. Unequipped for such an increase in residents, and with the absence of an urban regulatory power, the city witnessed a bout of urban chaos and unregulated construction. By the late 1960s, the latter had become a main concern for King Faisal's regime, which was occupied with crushing leftist political mobilizations and intent on modernizing the city as a way to better govern Riyadh and its population.[46] It was with this in mind that Faisal issued the first archiving law in 1966, which coincided with the establishment of the country's first archeology department at King Saud University by archeologist Abdulrahman al-Ansari. Barely two years later, Salman also formed the High Commission for the Evaluation of the Riyadh Master Plan to oversee the city's first strategic plan (1968–1972). Known as the Doxiadis Plan after the Greek firm that concocted it, the master plan was first approved by the Council of Ministers in 1973.[47] It was meant to regulate the city's urban plan until the year 2000. Rarely do master plans reflect the lived realities and needs of urban dwellers, and urban planning in Riyadh was no different. If anything, the Doxiadis Plan actually reflected the ideological Cold War politics of its architects more than it did environmental, social, and other realities on the ground.[48] The successive stages of its implementation turned Riyadh into an alienating city for most of its inhabitants, one that would grow along these initial guiding principles.

Doxiadis planners were at the forefront of modernist city planning, having worked with governments in Lebanon, Iraq, and other parts of the world, with planning Islamabad one of their foremost achievements.[49] In planning Riyadh, Doxiadis feigned interest in conserving cultural and architectural heritage in the planning of Riyadh.[50] According to Saudi state planners, including the deputy minister of town planning, Saleh al-Hathloul, the plans and regulations that Doxiadis called for did the exact opposite. Not only did they fail to emphasize historical preservation, but they also advanced the state's active disregard of material heritage. State officials actually considered historical sites, long deserted by their residents and rendered ghost towns, to be a security challenge. Municipalities and urban development agencies regularly tried to demolish these sites on the grounds that they attracted crime, drug use, and prostitution.[51] In rare cases where heads of municipalities valued historical preservation, they devised creative solutions short of demolitions, such as enclosing or covering up historical sites to keep them out of the sight and reach of people who might otherwise try to cause them harm.[52]

The unprecedented influx of petrocapital in the 1970s intensified processes of built urban disorder. As investment in Riyadh's property market became more lucrative, historical spaces fell to the wrecking ball. Infrastructure in the old city was transformed, its narrow streets and adobe homes replaced with roads wide enough to accommodate cars and small buildings. Such transformations struck at the heart of everyday social life in Riyadh. At the time, Al Saud had more pressing development concerns to attend to: the bureaucracy was frail; the economy required organization and regulation; and infrastructure, social welfare, and education, among other sectors, were lacking. Historical preservation simply fell by the wayside. The capital, along with Saudi Arabia's other cities, endured waves of state-sanctioned demolitions as part of the modernizing regime's mundane practices. Such unbridled construction, which nonetheless stalled by 1978 as a result of dwindling profit margins in the real estate industry, molded Riyadh's cityscape and future physical development. It also led to the destruction of spaces that, especially since the 1990s, have been considered historically significant. It was no surprise that these colossal shifts in urban and social life coincided with public discussions of historical commemoration and the first indigenous archeological excavation missions.[53] Indeed, many Saudi Arabians were traumatized by the loss of their familiar way of life. A few even wanted to preserve what they saw as their tradition and culture. In the absence of state support, those few, however, had to operate away from public reach and scrutiny. They found in archeology, with its often-remote excavation sites, a safe attempt to dig up the past and try to preserve it.[54]

INSTITUTIONALIZING RIVALRIES

Successive Saudi regimes dismissed historical preservation in their first five decades of rule. They nonetheless needed to tame elite rivalries over Riyadh's physical development, contain the city's built environment, and centralize the profitable construction industry. It was for these purposes that in June 1974 Salman ordered the establishment of the High Commission for the Development of Arriyadh under the auspices of the Riyadh municipality.[55] The ADA, its executive branch, was established years later, in 1983. The role of the HCDA was to manage the architectural, cultural, economic, environmental, and social development of the capital city, and competition over land acquisition and construction. In 1975, the regime restructured the High Commission's supervision. It placed it under the Ministry of Municipal and Rural Affairs created earlier that same year.[56] It was an attempt to centralize urban planning in Saudi Arabia. MOMRA's power has increased steadily since then. Upon assuming his position as minister of interior on October 11, 1975, the late Prince Nayif ibn Abdulaziz (1934–2012) centralized the kingdom's sixteen principal municipalities (*amanat*) as well as 269 local and regional municipalities under MOMRA. The MOMRA minister was given a rank equivalent to that of the deputy minister of interior and, like him, reported directly to Nayif. It was an attempt by the highest echelons of the new regime to rein in the escalating elite rivalries over construction.

As a highly sought-after position, the MOMRA ministerial portfolio has changed hands every three to five years.[57] Its minister had final say over the spatial strategies across the country, including the distribution of land grants and the expropriation of land. He also approved every public and/or development project throughout the kingdom, including the development of historical and archeological spaces, which continued to suffer under this arrangement.[58] Where MOMRA was successful in containing some rivalries, it simultaneously created new opportunities for corruption and nepotism concentrated in MOMRA itself. Its officials are notorious in Saudi Arabia for abusing their powers for the sake of land grabbing, commonly known as *tashbik* (enclosing with a fence). They regularly forced developers to pay them commissions in return for construction and other permits. The extraordinary surplus oil revenues of the 1970s and the sprawling desert land surrounding many of Arabia's cities had allowed for expansive development. This was especially true in Riyadh, which was experiencing a heavy influx of internal migration. Control of property rights and of development permission was thus the vastest sphere for elites to engage in their own massive enrichment and to maximize profits "in order to accumulate ... as much capital as possible."[59] With MOMRA responsible for national urban planning, many of its infrastructural and development projects failed and had already started to outgrow the city limits as delineated by the Doxiadis master plan.[60]

In practice, MOMRA failed to centralize urban planning or to take over Riyadh's physical development. In 1983, likely with pressure from Salman, the Council of Ministers extended the powers of the HCDA and declared it an independent authority in charge of planning the capital. MOMRA's powers in Riyadh were relegated. At the same time, the Council of Ministers mandated the establishment of the Projects and Planning Center (Markaz al-Mashari' wa-l-Takhtit). This would ensure that the HCDA's newly formed executive arm, the ADA, would plan and execute all basic infrastructural projects and development in the city.[61] It was yet another endeavor to better profit from the built life of Riyadh and prevent the haphazard path that the development of the city had taken.[62] If the planning commissions of the capital and other cities came to enjoy greater authority, they still needed the approval of the minister of municipal and rural affairs. MOMRA, therefore, continued to manage and oversee all development projects across the kingdom. As al-Mubarak explains:

> Giving the government the preponderant role in underwriting urban growth of Saudi cities, urban management is heavily controlled from the central government in the form of simple and unified physical urban planning practices adopted by the central urban planning authority in the capital. As such, the central municipality [amana], which derives its financing and authority from the Ministry of Municipal and Rural Affairs, retains substantial control of urban development over the entire city despite the explosive growth over the last seventy years. Consequently, Riyadh's urban development has been run by an unwieldy and bloated bureaucratic municipal organization.[63]

In this order of things, the minister of municipalities and rural affairs personally controlled the everyday life of Arabia's cities and their built landscapes. He also approved any deviation from the national spatial strategy and the country's urban master plans.[64] More often than not, these deviations were dependent on personal relations. This was the case, for instance, with the massive demolition of central Medina that occurred in the 1970s under its governor, the late Abdulmuhsin ibn Abdulaziz, who held the position from 1965 to 1985.[65] The bloated bureaucracy and rivalry among its leaders have shaped urban development in Arabia since the mid-twentieth century.[66] They strengthened arguments for, and practices of, the privatization of state functions, with great consequences to social and political life in Saudi Arabia. In the east, Aramco remained another layer of the state in the palimpsest of power that is Saudi Arabia long after the 1960s consolidation of the state and the nationalization of oil (1972–1980). Similarly, the Saudi Binladin Group, discussed in detail in the next chapter, prevailed in the western part of the country. In the central region, namely in Riyadh, the top ruling members of Al Saud, and Salman in particular, along with their institutions and regimes of local and foreign consultants, reigned supreme.[67] The centralization of state functions, especially the management of the built environment, like that of the archival record, proved as challenging as ever. Salman cut his professional teeth and developed his institutional power and capacity in this cutthroat political economic environment.

In the meantime, as political and economic elites, elites-to-be, and regular Saudis engaged in the real estate market throughout the 1960s and 1970s, Riyadh continued to grow in size as in population.[68] By 1976, at the height of the post-1973 oil-price hike, MOMRA had to update the Doxiadis master plan. It hired the French urban planning firm SCET International to do so.[69] Building on the Doxiadis plan, the one that SCET finalized in 1982 caused the remarkable urban sprawl that has turned Riyadh into the world's fastest-growing metropolis, extending over 1,500 square kilometers by 2004.[70] Both versions of the master plan only paid lip service to the importance of conserving historical and architectural heritage. According to Saudi state planners, these master plans have ensured, in theory and in practice, that the city's historical and architectural heritage was disregarded. Indeed, the master plans seriously underestimated population growth in the city, despite the warning of ADA planners. They also primarily accommodated the interests of the political and economic elites, who sought "economic prosperity and social stability through manipulating the spatial system."[71]

These interests shaped the built life of Riyadh as it entered "a new era of government intervention in the land and housing market as a major supplier, financier and subsidizer."[72] By 1984, land in Central Riyadh reached an average price of $3,000 per square foot.[73] With some of the highest land value in the Middle East, Riyadh attracted the attention, and rivalry, of investors, developers, and political and economic elites who operated with little oversight or accountability. As a result, few significant architectural remnants of the original walled oasis town of Riyadh and its outskirts survived the urban growth of the first few decades of Saudi Arabia's existence. Many were destroyed beyond repair in the drive to modernize the capital, which, until the last decade of the twentieth century, was all about getting rid of the old and replacing it with the new.

TERRITORIALIZING THE PAST: THE HISTORICAL BRANDING OF RIYADH

As with the national archive, or the lack thereof, the Al Saud monarchy entered the twenty-first century with little material heritage to call its own. Much of it had not survived the vagaries of time, environmental factors, and capitalist development. Such an absence would not have been a concern had the regime not decided to reconfigure the political, economic, and cultural pillars of its rule following the 1991 Gulf War. Its new, postwar conception of state power, which Salman advocated, relied on a particular ordering of urban space that highlighted Al Saud's secular past, promoted historical tourism, and capitalized on land as an economic resource.

In the rulers' imagination, the success of Al Saud's ancestors in forming two distinct emirates in the Arabian Peninsula at different times since the eighteenth century was enough justification for the family's sole and permanent control over the state's territory and its resources. Salman regularly alluded to such a reality in the historical talks he gave across the country before becoming king in 2015. While he tempered his tone in such public addresses, he was more candid in private ones. In the words of Salman himself, "We inherited the land and everything on it from King Abdulaziz" (*Al-malik Abdulaziz warrathana al-ardh wa ma 'alayha*).[74] Salman sought to territorialize this reading of the past in the built environment through construction and memorialization in Riyadh and negligence and creative destruction elsewhere. This was not merely a matter of renovating particular sites of national importance for the purposes of hosting foreign dignitaries or receiving school children as part of national identity building, which very much animated the renovation of Masmak Fortress in previous years.[75] Rather, the postwar policy was a new and comprehensive national policy with cultural, economic, and spatial dimensions.[76]

Following the announcement of the centennial in 1996, ADA planners, project managers, and an "army of consultants" embarked on a multibillion-dollar constellation of projects to update Riyadh's previous master plans and to rebrand the capital city.[77] The first phase of the King Abdulaziz Historical Center—the National Museum—was one of several deliverables the ADA had to achieve in time for the yearlong celebration in 1999.[78] That the three intervening years saw the price of crude oil plunge to an all-time low did not hinder these projects. Remarkably, even when the price of oil dropped to $12 per barrel in 1998,[79] the rulers still approved the multibillion-dollar Dir'iyya Redevelopment Program.[80] By then, heritage was already instrumental for those in power. They were therefore willing to invest in all the heritage sites that evinced the ruling family's secular history. For the first time, urban planning in Riyadh took on a heritage-oriented direction that showcased the regime's serious attempts to mold history anew through construction and memorialization in Old Riyadh. As a high-ranking official at the ADA proudly told me: "When the ADA began thinking about heritage sites in 1980s Riyadh, the government was not willing to financially support any of our proposed projects. Even in Dirʿiyya, little was actually done then. There was simply no political will. Any claims to heritage development in the capital before the 1990s is a joke. But since then, the rulers have spared no expense. Especially Prince Salman. Whenever the Ministry of Finance rejects a proposal, the prince makes sure that the necessary funding is at our disposal."[81] Interestingly, when Salman encountered any resistance from those more powerful than him, he personally funded the construction of heritage sites. He did no such thing with regard to archival production. He did not need to, for his goal of simply centralizing archives without availing them converged with those of Abdullah. For many of the experts I spoke with over the years and who worked on Riyadh's cultural and urban redevelopment, the 1990s was a turning point: it was a clear break with what came before, and Salman single-handedly transformed the city's urban landscape.

As Riyadh's governor, Salman also became the executive director of the newly formed High Commission for the Development of Dirʿiyya. He had unlimited powers to see the redevelopment of the town through to its completion, with the ADA responsible for planning and execution.[82] Ruling members of Al Saud, and the respective bureaucratic institutions they administered, saw the utility of perhaps temporarily setting aside some of their decades-long rivalries. This was necessary to prepare for the centennial celebration and, importantly, to materialize their family history in the built environment. Many cooperated with Salman, who emerged as the architect and executor of the plan to bolster his family's history and secure its future. The historian and archeologist Ali al-Mughannam, who oversaw the making of the National Museum and the redevelopment of other cultural and historical sites in Riyadh, remarked:

> Prince Salman is the architect of Riyadh [*muhandis al-Riyadh*] in every sense of the word. He is the architect of culture in the kingdom. Salman was the real force behind the museum. On the occasion of the centennial, he found the opportunity to build the National Museum. He understood early on the importance of history to power and legitimacy. He wanted the King Abdulaziz Historical Center to become a reality, and as one of the most powerful princes in the kingdom, he pushed others in power to make this happen, providing it with an unlimited budget that the ADA managed. The Riyadh Municipality

does not have the financial capacity or freedom to fund such projects, especially given the costs of the land expropriations that took place. National projects like these must not be constrained by the usual bureaucratic procedures. At last, the centennial highlighted the importance of history and culture.[83]

Salman managed most of the heritage redevelopment projects in Riyadh and ensured that they received the financial, technical, and legal support they required.

One of the key stumbling blocks for developing heritage in Central Riyadh, and at the King Abdulaziz Historical Center in particular, was that of land tenure. Some of the country's elites owned the hundreds of small homes in Old Riyadh that the regime aimed to enclose and incorporate into the center. Many Saudis from lower socioeconomic classes lived in these rundown buildings. Inhabiting these would-be national spaces accelerated their deterioration. As Riyadh governor and one of the kingdom's most powerful ruling members, Salman settled the contentious issue of land tenure. The regime wanted to legally reclaim these properties in the 1980s for commercial development purposes, before the heritage-making project was conceived. At the time, it sent lawyers and planners to Washington, DC, where they carefully studied eminent domain cases heard by the US Supreme Court.[84] They found that the 1954 *Berman v. Parker* Supreme Court decision had set the precedent for future public use cases in the United States by ruling that private property rights were sufficiently respected as long as owners were justly compensated for their properties. They returned to Saudi Arabia and sought a similar precedent under sharia, or Islamic law, for the confiscation of both private property and endowments (*waqf*). They found one in the concept of *hikr*, better known as *subrah* in Arabia, whereby the owner retains the title but leases land to the government on a long-term basis.[85] The regime then used a combination of these legal concepts to transfer the ownership of contested properties to the regime throughout the 1980s and 1990s.[86] When they failed to do so, they executed long-term leases with the original owners. These legal strategies were subsequently used elsewhere in the kingdom.[87] By 1996, the regime had acquired and vacated most of the lots surrounding the Historical Center, but the reasons for having done so in the first place had changed. With the sudden politicization of vernacular architecture, the ADA enclosed these sites with a metal fence to prevent intruders from damaging what little had remained of the built structures.

Capital and technical experts labored to turn the historical neighborhood into the center of modern-day Riyadh.

As with Salman's Darah, the ADA also surfaced as the institutional hegemon in charge of Riyadh's cultural and historical redevelopment, sidestepping MOMRA in these endeavors. The Supreme Commission for Tourism (SCT)—renamed the Saudi Commission for Tourism and National Heritage (SCTH) in 2015—was established in 2000 to support the regime's project for revising, centralizing, and materializing official Saudi Arabian history.[88] The SCT, under the leadership of Salman's son, Sultan, supported the commemoration of the state-sanctioned secular past in historical spaces and heritage sites in Riyadh. Despite calling for the preservation of historical sites elsewhere in the country, the SCT's mandate was largely limited to Riyadh's historical landscape. In a few instances, the SCT received funding it had applied for to preserve ancient archeological sites outside of Riyadh, such as the northwestern site of Al-Hijr (Mada'in Salih), which was granted the status of World Heritage Site in 2008. Mada'in Salih did not threaten the regime's historical self-image. On the contrary, the regime relied on these sites to refute claims against its Riyadh-centric cultural policy and its wholesale destruction of historical sites in places like Central Mecca, which the SCT has done little to prevent. The regime also used such sites to evince its modernizing capabilities and to argue that, in appreciating history and caring for its remnants, Saudi Arabia was part of a community of modern states.

Following the Gulf War, the regime sought to produce a new narrative about itself and enshrine it in built life. This reinforced the historical branding of the capital city, which engendered new forms of power and citizen-subject formation.[89] This came at the expense of the diverse pasts of the country's other regions—such as those in Mecca, discussed earlier—and the alternative histories they portend. These material practices enabled the Saudi state to reproduce itself and proved central to the maintenance and architectural reformulation of the postwar state.[90] It was in this spirit that political, economic, religious, environmental, cultural, and disciplinary forces converged in Riyadh, forging one of the most expensive cultural and urban redevelopment state projects in modern history.

HISTORY'S NEW HOME

As the centennial approached, the project for historical commemoration in Riyadh assumed a great sense of urgency. Most historical sites there were completely dilapidated. Construction work had started on a few others in the 1980s but not in view of the objectives of postwar preservation. These sites had to be brought in line with the new vision for Riyadh. In the updated master plan, Riyadh was to become an ideal "First World city" that sets the standard for future economic trends but without losing sight of its national past and heritage.[91] To this end, the regime allocated an open budget for the redevelopment of the capital.[92] Governance Palace, the King Abdulaziz Historical Center, the Red Palace, Riyadh's adobe homes (in al-Dahu), and Dir'iyya were at the center of the state's monumentality, political aesthetics, and financialization practices.[93] So pervasive has the remaking of Riyadh been that much of the script of this urban landscape has been revised and rewritten several times. But master plans and development records from the 1970s, coupled with interviews with experts, shed much-needed light on the politics of urban planning and its goals, and how these have changed over the decades, as Salman grew stronger in the 1990s and especially since he ascended the throne in 2015.

Governance Palace District

Located within the old city walls, the Governance Palace District (Mantiqat Qasr al-Hukm) occupies a central role in the postwar national imagination. The idea to develop the area, originally known as the Imam's Palace and more recently as Justice Palace, first came up in the early 1970s, during studies and discussions for the Doxiadis master plan. It was then that Riyadh's mayor, Abdulaziz ibn Salman ibn Thunayyan (1966–1976), was made aware of the dilapidation of Masmak Fortress. Concerned, he commissioned preservation expert Franco Albini, who worked in tandem with Doxiadis planners, to come up with solutions. In 1974, Albini recommended the preservation of the whole district, and not just the fortress. The mayor instructed him to develop a comprehensive plan, which Albini completed in the next two years.

As SCET International began revising the Doxiadis master plan for Riyadh in 1976, Thanayyan accepted another position, and the redevelopment of the district fell by the wayside. This was compounded by the fact that the mayor's office was not able to expropriate land within the district and faced other obstacles that prevented the area's redevelopment until two decades later.[94] By 1979, the regime disregarded Albini's recommendations and approved the preservation of Masmak and nothing else. In the same year, Salman's High Commission for the

Development of Riyadh established the Qasr Alhukm Area Development Office, which subsequently commissioned Ali Shuaibi's Beeah Group Consultants to revise the design of the whole district. The High Commission approved the design in 1983 but brought in its newly formed ADA to oversee the project. After a thorough review, the ADA overhauled the project goals and set up a competition for its design and execution. Over the subsequent years, the ADA commissioned different architectural and engineering firms to revise the design and execute the plan. Although these steps delayed the project, the main obstacle was the lack of political commitment and financial support for the preservation of the site.

The ADA eventually chose Beeah Group Consultants, architects Rasem Badran and Saleh al-Hathloul, and British engineering consultants Buro Happold to draw the redevelopment plans for the site. Unlike most of those involved in the belated redevelopment project, Badran and al-Hathloul, and urban planner Ali Shuaibi, were concerned with the loss of what they understood to be "Saudi tradition." They had already sought its costly rehabilitation through vernacular Najdi architecture throughout Riyadh. They attempted to do the same at the Governance Palace District. But the project goals, steeped in financial considerations and the economic rejuvenation of that part of the city, diverged from their own. At the time, the regime had allocated the project a limited budget that constrained the work that the architects could do. The regime was simply uninterested in preserving the district's material heritage and did not heed the recommendations of Badran, Shuaibi, and al-Hathloul.[95] Indeed, they were hired with the explicit mandate to revitalize the Governance Palace District and to restore it as "the political, administrative and commercial center of the City."[96] In the site's redevelopment plans, focus was on restoring the city center's role as an administrative hub and seat of power as well as a crucial node in the city's economic matrix.

The Governance Palace District received renewed attention in the mid-1990s, in line with the country's postwar plan. The ADA was commissioned with redeveloping the district, this time with an eye toward restoring its historical and architectural significance. ADA planning records are imbued with the cultural significance of the site as the capital of an earlier emirate that an Al Saud ancestor—Imam Turki ibn Abdullah ibn Muhammad—had established in Riyadh (1824–1891) after the Ottoman destruction of Dir'iyya. The palace was also the seat of Abdulaziz ibn Saud's fledgling government until 1937. In the postwar imagination, the district became "the most important area in the Kingdom after the two holy mosques [in Mecca and Medina]."[97] Its buildings and structures, however, were already crumbling or had fallen apart by then. In fact, in 1953, King Saud ordered the complete demolition of the palace and some of its surrounding buildings. He had them replaced with other spaces that housed the new government in Riyadh, including its courts. Restoring as much of the buildings as possible was suddenly of utmost importance. The ADA planners regularly reiterated that before their intervention in the 1990s, very little restoration or development work had been done on the site. They even had before-and-after photographs to show for it. So extensive was the damage that the ADA had to completely reconstruct many of the buildings on what planners speculated was the location from which Imam Turki had ruled. With this premise, ADA planners hoped to turn the revitalized Governance Palace District into a reimagined city center, one that would be the commercial, cultural, and political anchor of modern-day Riyadh.[98]

The rejuvenated district included minor remnants of Riyadh's original city wall; palaces; a re-creation of the mosque that Imam Turki prayed in; and date palm–lined squares such as al-Safa (Sahat al-Safa), Justice (Sahat al-'adl), and Imam Muhammad ibn Saud. Masmak Fortress and several markets, al-Suwaiqah and Deerah prime among them, were also among the district's landmarks. Much of the construction work had been completed by 2017, which is when the redevelopment entered its third and reportedly final phase. Already, however, ADA planners complained that they had failed to achieve the goals of the project. Although they had come to terms with having had to architecturally reconstruct much of the structures—even parts of the city wall itself—the district had yet to become a city center in all senses of the word. Cars remained the primary mode of transportation—an issue that the planners had hoped to overcome—and traffic was rampant. Few residents went there for the district's historical resonance. The planners lamented that most visitors were low-income and working-class Saudi Arabians and non–Saudi Arabians alike, there to enjoy the public spaces on offer. They were not the target group of the planners or the regime more broadly. With the residential and financial center of the city having moved northward decades earlier, this part of Riyadh was simply still out of the way for most.

The King Abdulaziz Historical Center

If the Governance Palace District was slated to be the anchor of a revitalized city center in Riyadh, the nearby King Abdulaziz Historical Center was its crown jewel.

FIGURE 6. Aerial view from northwest, before intervention, King Abdulaziz Historical Center, Riyadh, 2004. *Source:* Aga Khan Award for Architecture. Courtesy of architect Rasem Badran.

The center, located at the old Murabbaʿ Palace, was largely built in the years following the 1996 announcement of the centennial. The ADA commissioned the center's designers to "look forward and develop a concept that will place the complex at the forefront of cultural development both within Saudi Arabia and internationally."[99] The terms of reference (TOR) were imbued with mentions of the importance of Al Saud's "historic past" and how it would "help frame its future."[100] The center includes the King Abdulaziz Foundation for Research and Archives (the Darah), the National Museum, the King Abdulaziz Memorial Hall, the King Abdulaziz Mosque, the King Abdulaziz Public Library, the King Abdulaziz Auditorium, and traditional adobe buildings (Figures 6 and 7).[101] Several squares, gardens, public parks, and the landmark Riyadh water tower surrounded the center and turned it into a green haven in the middle of the city.

ADA planners were enthused to show off the highlight of the Historical Center and yearlong site of the centennial celebration: the National Museum, the first of its kind in Saudi Arabia. The idea of creating a national museum, like the archive before it, was not new. King Saud had been a patron of the arts and took a special liking to museums, which he first encountered in Egypt and then other

FIGURE 7. Presentation panel with general views of new and rehabilitated structures, public spaces, and landscaping, King Abdulaziz Historical Center, Riyadh, 2004. *Source:* Aga Khan Award for Architecture. Courtesy of architect Rasem Badran.

countries he visited. During his reign, Saud received a proposal for building a national museum, but as with other cultural projects, it fell by the wayside given the country's more pressing development needs.[102] In 1973, King Faisal also dismissed a similar attempt, seeing it as "marginal, wasteful, and unnecessary," especially given the local and regional challenges his regime was facing.[103] Alternatively, several regional museums emerged over the years, largely the fruit of independent local efforts that aimed to safeguard and exhibit their region's past. The actual National Museum, which did not materialize until the turn of the twenty-first century, was in fact an afterthought. It was concocted by Salman and his ADA planners after brainstorming for the centennial celebrations that the government had just approved.

Where international firms were eager to take on the project, not all designers and planners in Saudi Arabia were as enthused. Al-Hathloul explained that he simply could not understand why the "crash project," as he called it, was conceived only three years before the centennial. But the rulers had given it their full political and financial support, and it was a fait accompli. Foreign consultants quickly flooded the capital city in 1996. The ADA and its international regime of experts began work right away.[104] Despite the faltering economy, the regime authorized the Ministry of Finance to fully fund the endeavor, which was led by Japanese-Canadian architectural firm Moriyama and Teshima, along with British engineering firm Buro Happold. For Salman and his team, urban design—and the integration of the site with the urban fabric—was a priority. This was one of a dozen teams to actually satisfy these conditions. That they did so in a timely manner was an added bonus that got them the contract. Together with the ADA, they would construct what then was the regime's most important development site. It took hundreds of archeologists, historians, curators, preservationists, collectors, urban planners, architects, engineers, and construction workers to see through the completion of this project in less than three years. They labored, night and day, in two twelve-hour shifts. Crown Prince Abdullah even visited the site on several occasions, conversing with laborers and managers alike and conveying the importance of the museum and its timely completion. Work on the project was completed mere days before the centennial celebrations began, a feat the regime continues to boast about.

The National Museum has since circulated the revised official historical narrative of Saudi Arabia through its state-of-the-art technologies and nine acres of exhibition space featuring artifacts—both originals and replicas. A teleology leading up to Al Saud as emancipators of the peninsula undergirds the organization of most of these spaces.[105] As with the Governance Palace, however, the ADA has yet to accomplish the site's goals, short of having hosted the centennial celebrations. Rarely do Saudi Arabians—its primary target—visit the museum, unless they are on mandated school visits. The museum's consumers remain foreign dignitaries on diplomatic visits, embassy personnel and their families, and architects, artists, and academics. For the most part, low-income residents are the ones to go to the King Abdulaziz Historical Center to enjoy its outdoor public spaces. They rarely went there to access its indoor facilities or exhibitions, for which they had to pay. According to an ADA museologist, this is a struggle that all museums in the Gulf states face, but one that he thinks will be overcome with time and education. Nevertheless, the National Museum of Saudi Arabia has become an architectural landmark in central Riyadh, a product of world-renowned global expertise, petrocapital, and Al Saud's political power.

The Red Palace

A replica of a residence in Italy, the Red Palace in Old Riyadh was the three-year home to the second king, Saud. He later used it to conduct government business and to host state dignitaries, Gamal Abdel Nasser being one of many. The building itself was a 1950s architectural landmark, built by Muhammad Binladin's contracting company.[106] In the early 2000s, it was subsumed within the greater flow of deification of Abdulaziz and his sons and came to be included in Historic Riyadh. In its new life, the Red Palace was slated to become a science museum heralding the ruling family's modernizing accomplishments. After decades of utter neglect, the Red Palace became part of the project to memorialize the state-sanctioned version of Al Saud's history, which until the centennial had completely silenced any mention of the second Saudi king. As Princess Fahda, King Saud's daughter, elaborated: "There is a slight official push to document my father's history, but it is not enough and has met with great resistance. The palace he built, lived and worked in for years is being turned into a museum that is not about him. Can you imagine that happening in any other royal palace? They bring King Saud in only to silence him further."[107] The ADA project managers responsible for the development of the Red Palace corroborated internal Al Saud struggles over the Red Palace's future, which delayed its planning and execution. Planners had initially understood the project as intended to highlight the architectural capabilities of the early Saudi state while developing the site in line with the area's economic rejuvenation policy. Doing so would signal that the palace was an architectural ode to King Saud's accomplishments, something those in power were not ready to do. Although Salman was able to bring Saud back into the official narrative, attempts to manage Saud's history as they had done in other sites and with other kings created tensions among those in power. Speaking of the Red Palace Development, its project manager Khalid al-Hazzani explained:

> We did not want to get into the politics of it. As a compromise, we decided that instead, we would have a future "Kings' Museum" in a different location in which each king receives equal attention. For the Red Palace, we put aside two rooms only as a replica of what they had looked like under King Saud. But those in the rest of the palace, we changed them so they do not reflect his life and accomplishments. We needed something politically neutral and yet exciting, something that people would come to regularly. We decided not to turn it into a "museum" after all. We wanted it to be more interesting, and "museum" often elicited the exact opposite of interesting for people here. In the final plans, the place is going to be very interactive, informative, very high-tech so it attracts children, our primary target group. We want Saudi children to learn about their country and rulers' scientific accomplishments. It will have a historical archive and a library also, so students can come study here. It will also have an internationally recognized fine-dining restaurant with one of the largest indoor fish aquariums in the world.[108]

The rebirth of the Red Palace as a science museum—if this is indeed still the plan—sheds light on the process of elision central to the making of national history. The redevelopment of the Red Palace, like the archival record and the material heritage, will silence the contentious life history of this second Saudi king. When the museum temporarily opened its doors to visitors in March 2019, there was little evidence of any serious renovation efforts. For the few weeks it was open, the museum hosted three exhibitions, one of which was on the 1991 Gulf War and Iraq's invasion of Kuwait.

Al-Dahu's Adobe Homes

In the late 2000s, the redevelopment of historical Riyadh started to also encompass the area west of Murabbaʿ Palace. The only surviving homes from the era of King Abdulaziz were located there. These, too, became part of the broader King Abdulaziz Historical Center (Figures 8 and 9). Once a joint endeavor between the

FIGURE 8. Aerial view of adobe houses, before intervention, King Abdulaziz Historical Center, Riyadh, 2004. *Source:* Aga Khan Award for Architecture. Courtesy of architect Rasem Badran.

FIGURE 9. Adobe house, before intervention, King Abdulaziz Historical Center, Riyadh, 2004. *Source:* Aga Khan Award for Architecture. Courtesy of architect Rasem Badran.

ADA and the Saudi Commission for Tourism and Antiquities, the project quickly fell under the former's sole custody owing to bureaucratic inefficiencies, land disputes, and other obstacles. The complex work of adobe preservation on these homes began in the late 2000s.[109] Some of the properties are slated to become boutique hotels that will give tourists an opportunity to experience "traditional" life in Najd, what some scholars and critics sarcastically refer to as "going native in the city." This dose of reality will include living in small adobe houses without modern luxuries, wearing traditional garb, and experiencing traditional Saudi cuisine. Social life there will revolve around the renovated market and mosque, a tribute to what many consider the traditional "Muslim city."

Urban planners and architects, including al-Hathloul, had put forth their understanding of what tradition meant. They relied on images and archival records from Aramco and oral history interviews with those who had lived long enough to have witnessed that pre-automobile era (which planners considered material heritage's biggest technological enemy). Shops in al-Dahu, however, were all modern, with heritage commodities produced in China, India, and Indonesia, destinations from which the service labor market in the historic area also hailed. The built surroundings, from the mosque to the pedestrian walkways, were replicas and variations of what had once existed—or rather, what planners assumed had once existed.

Dir'iyya: From Tragedy to Tradition

The new reinvigoration of Riyadh's historical landscape saw the pouring of more than US$28 billion, as of 2011, into the renovation of al-Turaif District in the adobe fortress town of Dir'iyya.[110] Located twenty kilometers northwest of Riyadh, this walled town overlooking Hanifa Valley was the capital of the so-called first Saudi state (1744–1818). King Saud was the first monarch to express interest in the abandoned town. He was particularly concerned with unregulated construction taking place in the town's al-Turaif District, where his ancestors are thought to have resided. He wanted the government to purchase all properties there.[111] With limited financial resources to purchase the titles to the land and develop it, he requested that people from lower socioeconomic classes who needed housing be allowed to temporarily move to al-Turaif neighborhood. This would prevent others from seizing property within the site, suggesting the existence of political rivals who would have been able to establish property claims that, in turn, would have been construed as ownership rights, either because of their status or their political connections. The hundreds of people who relocated there built shoddily planned homes on the site's many ruins.

Despite its best efforts, the Department of Antiquities failed to change the social and physical realities of al-Turaif District. People continued to live there even though the site earned protected status in 1972.[112] In 1973, King Faisal, who had dismissed a proposal for a national museum, also rejected an Egyptian consultant's proposal to develop Dirʿiyya using the most advanced technologies and museological techniques at the time. Construction continued unabated until King Fahd purchased the adobe town in 1982 and expropriated its inhabitants.[113] According to ADA engineer and Dirʿiyya project manager Abdullah al-Rukban, it was only in 1986 that the ADA even started to think about how to redevelop historical Dirʿiyya. That year, an ADA team held brainstorming workshops and solicited serious studies on the matter. Even then, there was no budget or political will—it was just "ink on paper." The ruling family generally regarded Dirʿiyya as a doomed place (*makan mash'um*) that only resurrected memories of defeat and weakness.[114] Dirʿiyya therefore remained marginal to the rulers' political or historical consciousness, at least for another decade.

In the mid-1990s, the rulers discovered Dirʿiyya's political, economic, and social potential, and so King Fahd's regime approved its redevelopment as a heritage site under the ADA's management.[115] Prince Salman was to chair the High Commission for the Development of Dirʿiyya, the project's supervisory body.[116] Salman's son, Sultan, chairman of the SCT, was a committee member. It was the ADA's biggest heritage project yet. The development agency worked closely with the SCT and the Municipality of Addirʿiyah—the main consulting institutions—to rehabilitate the fort town and develop it as an international cultural tourism site.[117] This was the first serious effort to redevelop Dirʿiyya and its cultural and historical dimensions. Historical preservationists and experts in "commercializing heritage sites" from Canada, Egypt, Morocco, Spain, the United States, and the United Kingdom visited Dirʿiyya and submitted proposals for its redevelopment.[118] Companies from the world over collaborated over conception, brainstorming, planning, preservation, and execution.[119]

Actual work on the site began in 2004, after the Ministry of Finance approved the project's historic budget. The larger structural redevelopment work took off a few years later, toward the end of that decade. The planning regime did not want to simply display the space. They wanted to somehow inject life into this otherwise deserted place and to invigorate cultural and economic vibrancy in its vicinity. Lead consulting historian and Dir'iyya project manager Ali al-Mughannam explained the goal and importance of the project:

> We do not want to turn Dir'iyya into a site of historic tragedies, because history is full of tragedy. We want it to be a location of learning, of belonging to the country and increasing the sense of loyalty to it. We want it to teach our children the meaning of tradition [*turath*] and its importance. How did people live in adobe houses? How did they survive, live, and defend themselves, not too long ago, purely from local production? The Dir'iyya Redevelopment Project is thus cultural, educational, and developmental, it takes into account the residents of Dir'iyya and includes them. It connects people to their past.... It reminds us of our identity, our tradition as Saudis.[120]

The main point of contention among the different parties involved in developing the site was whether to reconstruct or attempt to preserve the severely deteriorated adobe structures. The challenge for reconstruction, according to the planners, was the lack of accurate depictions of the site and what the whole of it had actually looked like before the 1817 Ottoman invasion. Existing images were rudimentary, partial, and did not hold up to expert scrutiny. Those who had inhabited the site in the previous century had also built extensions on the different buildings, further complicating the conservation process. The ADA refused to demolish the town and then reconstruct it based on "imagination" and "conjecture."[121] The pressure to do so, however, was so great that the ADA considered resorting to an experimental software that a renowned British structural engineering company was developing at the King Abdullah University of Science and Technology.[122] The program would deduce what an original building had once looked like based on three-dimensional images of the remnants of existing building structures. But the engineers, and their speculative software, failed to convince the Dir'iyya planners of the viability of the program. After months of expensive consultations, the planners rejected the proposals and instead decided to conserve as much as possible of the existing buildings.

In 2006, the SCT decided to submit the al-Turaif District of Dir'iyya for inscription as a UNESCO World Heritage Site. Since then, redevelopment necessarily assumed a different trajectory that prioritized the organization's stringent regulations, goals, and definitions. The planning regime commissioned consultants who worked daily to meet the conditions of UNESCO and the International Council on Monuments and Sites (ICOMOS), one of the three advisory bodies of UNESCO's World Heritage Convention. Yet planners simply could not adhere to all the regulations. Although most adobe structures are short-lived, engineers preserved Dirʿiyya with the help of the world's best human expertise and most advanced technologies. In some instances, structural engineers reconstructed buildings or parts thereof as they had existed over two centuries ago based on the closest visual approximations. To commercialize the space, they also needed to develop a completely new, modern infrastructure for water, power, and sewage—aggressive practices that unavoidably affected the integrity of the site. They sought to make Dirʿiyya accessible to pedestrians and those with disabilities, which also necessitated building new roads, walkways, and ramps.

The regime's actual goals for the site, then, conflicted with those of the heritage convention. The former's aim was primarily to turn the site into the country's foremost tourism destination in order to circulate the state's official legitimating order. ICOMOS was primarily concerned with the impact of the planned Living Heritage Museum, whose blueprint seemed to especially threaten the integrity of the site. In its review of the nomination of al-Turaif District of Dirʿiyya, the ICOMOS report stated that "the museum and tourism development programme must in its turn be no more than a part of this [management] plan, and must be completely subordinated to the conservation of the property's attributes of integrity and authenticity, under the surveillance of a scientific conservation committee."[123] It further stated:

> ICOMOS considers that the architectural integrity of many buildings has been affected by the history of the property and by its abandonment for more than one and a half centuries. The buildings that have not been rebuilt or restored are in ruins. The integrity of these ruins and remains from the old town is, moreover, subject to erosion and to substantial natural degradation in a manner that is specific to adobe. ICOMOS considers that the structures on which work has been carried out have been profoundly transformed and that they can no longer be considered to demonstrate integrity. The overall architectural integrity of the nominated property is therefore inadequate. . . . The severely degraded state of the property partially reused at the end of the 20th century

did not allow the carrying out of simple repairs in order to make its reuse possible; this led in most cases to reconstructions and interpretations of the past state, or even to mere architectural similarity. For example, the enclosure wall was rebuilt in stone, although it was originally earthen, and Unit 5 of the Salwa Palace was entirely rebuilt using modern techniques.[124]

ICOMOS concluded that, because of the planners' intervention, the conditions of authenticity, architecturally speaking, had not been met. It recommended deferral until the state adhered to the requirements. ICOMOS stressed that conservation goals should be prioritized, and everything else, such as museology, should be subordinated to that goal.

Given these conditions, the reality of the built environment of Dirʻiyya was alarming, as the architectural integrity of its sites was regularly abused. Those working on the project faced many political obstacles and interventions. Most shocking to them were the historical ambiguities and inaccuracies, silenced and presented as historical truth by the rulers based on political motives. For instance, the team of planners, archeologists, and historians working on the site simply could not find evidence locating the actual house of Muhammad ibn Saud, Al Saud's first amir of the Dirʻiyya settlement and the one who initially harbored the religious preacher Muhammad ibn Abd al-Wahhab in 1744.[125] Visitors to the site, however, were to be directed to Salwa Palace as the historical home of the first amir. There were major discrepancies in these and other historical details, which the technocrats resolved on the basis of political interest. Further, as the project consultants surveyed the site in the initial stages, they found artifacts and rare material evidence that dated back to earlier settlements.[126] Again, the technocrats ordered the archeologists to disregard any material heritage that did not refer to Al Saud's era.

This historical reimagination extended to the country's religious founders as well. In its new life, Bujairi, the area where Ibn Abd al-Wahhab lived, was compromised. ADA planners did not renovate or conserve buildings in Bujairi, located a few hundred meters across from Salwa Palace (Figures 10 and 11). This was true of the mosque where Ibn Abd al-Wahhab prayed. With direction from the political decision makers, they demolished these spaces and instead built a stone amphitheater-like seating area from which visitors can look out at Al Saud's original seat of government. Such an irony was hard to miss, especially when

FIGURE 10. Renovation of part of the structure thought to be Salwa Palace, where Muhammad ibn Saud lived in the Turaif District of Dir'iyya. On the near left-hand side of the photograph is the Bujairi District, where the mosque in which Muhammad ibn Abd al-Wahhab prayed once stood. *Source:* Photograph taken by author, 2010.

FIGURE 11. Bujairi District of Dir'iyya, across from Turaif District, under construction. *Source:* Photograph taken by author, 2010.

compared to the global expertise that the ADA relied on to preserve what little it could of the original homes that Al Saud lived in, the mosques where they prayed. The irony is all the more glaring when contrasted with the iconic status and grandeur of Qatar's national mosque, the Muhammad ibn Abd al-Wahhab Mosque.

When I first visited the al-Turaif District with ADA representatives in 2010, I was quickly led to the seating area where the mosque once stood. It was still under construction, and yet I was directed to "sit and look out at al-Turaif Quarter and the beautiful Salwa Palace." It was still surrounded by cranes. At the time, the ADA had no plans to rebuild Ibn Abd al-Wahhab's mosque in the vicinity. It also did not intend to commemorate the shaykh in any other way. This, however, has been revised since my last visit in 2014. The ADA added the Sheikh Mohammad bin Abdulwahhab Cultural Foundation. The "westward sloping roof providing a charming view of Al-Turaif Quarter" now includes a mosque, also in the shaykh's name.[127] It is not clear to me who ordered the addition or its timing.[128]

Despite these political maneuvers, Dirʿiyya's al-Turaif District earned the long-sought status of a UNESCO World Heritage Site. It did so on the basis that it "illustrates a significant phase in the human settlement of the central Arabian plateau, when in the mid-18th century Dirʿiyya became the capital of an independent Arab State" and showcases "Najdi architecture and its ingenious use of adobe."[129] One of the conditions for inscribing a historical place as a World Heritage Site is its potential contribution to the world through tourism. Yet Saudi Arabia then lacked an international tourism strategy and forbade travel to the country for touristic purposes. The regime had spent a vast amount of resources on developing a local tourism industry, with its cultural and historical heritage in Riyadh wholly aimed at Saudi Arabian citizens. Indeed, the careful manipulation of Riyadh's built environment in the name of heritage, modernity, and progress starkly contrasted with the utter disregard—"voluntary dilapidation"—that many other historical sites in the kingdom have experienced. This is not to mention the destruction and remaking of Mecca and Medina.[130] Such spatial reordering was the first phase of implementing the regime's political imaginary, one that reinscribed a hierarchy of national belonging and identity in the built environment with the aim of shaping national subjectivity, and perhaps in the future, collective memory as well.

The second phase of the postwar plan began when Salman ascended the throne in January 2015, and especially since his son Muhammad was promoted to crown prince in June 2017. Salman unprecedentedly consolidated his rule in the few years since becoming king. As I detail in the conclusion of this book, he upended the conventional power-sharing scheme within the ruling family and violently centralized all power in the office of the king and crown prince. The regime subsequently subsumed many of the existing postwar political, economic, and cultural plans into what the crown prince has marketed as Saudi Arabia's "new" Vision 2030.[131] The ambitious national blueprint that had as its goal nothing short of overhauling everyday life in Saudi Arabia also appropriated existing plans for international tourism, claiming them as its own.

The new structure of centralized sovereignty has entailed the suppression of all domestic sociopolitical movements, the incarceration of thousands of ordinary Saudi Arabians as political prisoners, and the curbing of the religious establishment from all aspects of everyday life. The relegation of the religious establishment was complete and put on display for all to see. The new reality was publicly instantiated in everyday life in December 2018, when Formula E held a racing championship in Dir'iyya. The event also included concerts by world-acclaimed performers such as Enrique Iglesias and Black Eyed Peas, which took place in Muhammad ibn Abd al-Wahhab's Bujairi Quarter.[132] That the festive championship was organized by none other than then-chairman of Saudi Arabia's General Sports Authority, Turki Al-Shaykh, a descendent of Ibn Abd al-Wahhab, sends a clear signal of Salman's victory over the religious establishment. Indeed, despite the many revisions to the Dir'iyya plans, including the addition of the Ibn Abd al-Wahhab foundation, the evidentiary terrain still displays the primacy of Al Saud and their secular past.

CONCLUSION

Much has been written about the antagonistic politics, constructed nature, and destructive tendencies of heritage making; the destruction of the Bamiyan statues in Afghanistan and of artifacts in Palmyra comes to mind. Yet rarely do everyday forms of violence such as transforming Riyadh into "history's new home," for instance, evoke sustained and broad-based international outcries, even as they directly affect how people live in the present and commemorate their pasts. In fact, state projects of heritage making often receive global recognition from international media outlets and multilateral institutions. This is as true of the *New York Times* and *National Geographic* as it is of the United Nations Educational, Scientific, and Cultural Organization (UNESCO) and ICOMOS. Not only are these institutions largely silent on the contentious construction of heritage in places such as Saudi Arabia (and Israel, the United States, and elsewhere); they also ultimately serve to legitimize and endorse the national history-making projects. Such recognition conceals the political and technocratic nature of memorialization. It decenters the precarity of political authority and allows the regime to depict historical preservation as apolitical. But in Saudi Arabia, the regime's turn to commemoration in the aftermath of the Gulf War is a political strategy. It aims to renegotiate the state, counter ongoing claims against and within the ruling family, and bolster ties with the economic elites by creating new opportunities for capital accumulation. It is a strategic move that speaks directly to intraregime rivalries as well as the sociopolitical and economic challenges that various Saudi rulers had to contend with in the changing political economy of the 1990s.

The territorialization of Al Saud's history in the built environment manifested through widespread destruction in some places and reconstruction and memorialization in others. As with the production of archives, studying the making of Riyadh reveals the contentious, oft changing, and at times contradictory process that went into building the capital since the 1990s. Doing so allows us to see how this process addressed several crises at once. Political aesthetics and its monumentality set in stone the changing relationship between religious and secular power in Saudi Arabia. It heralded a form of secularization through new ideas of historical time, progress, and capital accumulation. The production of heritage facilitated the regime's transformation of the Saudi landscape into a revenue-generating asset and encouraged local economic growth. Capital accumulation through heritage and urban development in turn reaffirmed the regime's faltering ties to local elites. Finally, the regime channeled political opposition into struggles for inclusion in the historical past, rather than doing so through economic redistribution or political equity. Space, and sites of heritage in particular, like archives, became the regime's preferred battlegrounds. These battlegrounds constituted one register of violence upon which the regime operated. The regular erasure of historical voices, enclosure of primary source records, and destruction and reconstruction of spaces became the field for forging a collective identity, one that shapes and is constantly shaped by dynamics and various forms of profit and speculation in Saudi Arabia.

Saudi Arabia's conventionally national project of producing heritage and organizing history spatially discloses an ongoing cultural production of the Saudi past, but one that remains unstable and contested and dependent on vast capital resources.¹³³ The politics and economics of petrocapitalism have enabled the Saudi state to mask the pervasive and multilayered violence it has inflicted on space, place, people, and history. Analyzing the practices and politics that undergird urban redevelopment lays bare such violence, even if the sense of vulnerability and defeat has overwhelmed a population that continues to pay a heavy price for fighting for a more egalitarian and politically inclusive future. Planning documents, what Henri Lefebvre calls representations of space, are like archives, political devices for the construction of the past through forms of present engineering.¹³⁴ They are central modes of making history, ones that tell us about the contested politics and materiality of place and reveal the "false sense of continuity" that stones inspire. Only by performing such an analysis can we discern between "what happened and what was said to have happened."¹³⁵

Chapter 5

BULLDOZING THE PAST

AS ABDULAZIZ IBN SAUD COMPLETED HIS CONQUEST OF MUCH OF the Arabian Peninsula in the early 1930s, his regime embarked on the slow and arduous business of state building. Securing the political, economic, social, and territorial viability of newly formed Saudi Arabia occupied the king and the heirs to his throne. Breaking with the past, which accompanied the development of state institutions, was equally important. The modern state, as we have seen, necessitated the erasure of prestate histories and the incompatible truths and socialities they mobilized. In the case of Mecca, this meant, among other things, masking the cosmopolitan Ottoman lifeworld to which Shaykh Muhammad Rahmatullah al-Kairanawi belonged and the thriving socio-intellectual networks that had connected him to his peers and students. Producing the past initially centered on writing and rewriting Saudi Arabia's official historical narrative. Historical documents and repositories of primary source records subsequently became the regime's preferred sites for materializing the organizing fiction of the Saudi state's origins. Toward the end of the twentieth century, the archive also came to include the built environment. If the memorialization of secular history in Riyadh was critical for the consolidation of post–Gulf War Saudi authority, it was complemented by the destruction of another form of historical memory in Mecca.

The early 2000s featured the accelerated demolition of sacred and historical sites in Central Mecca and the replacement of its thousand-year-old topography

FIGURE 12. People praying under construction cranes at Mecca's Grand Mosque during the third phase of the mosque's expansion, which began under King Abdullah ibn Abdulaziz in 2011. *Source:* Saad Alghamdi / EyeEm via Getty Images.

with imposing steel-and-glass skyscrapers. Cranes dotted the skies of Islam's birthplace, as smog choked its Grand Mosque (Masjid al-Haram) and the millions of pilgrims who visit it each year (Figure 12). Construction sites and earthmoving heavy equipment became part of the city's landscape. They marked the movement of pilgrims through dense roads crammed with pedestrians, automobiles, and buses. Over one hundred mixed-use developments were under construction around the mosque. Internationally acclaimed luxury hotels; designer, serviced apartment buildings; and malls lodged inside concrete skyscrapers have replaced the archeological, historical, economic, and cultural landscape of this rapidly developing city.[1]

As a holy sanctuary, Central Mecca is meant to be sacrosanct. Alterations to its physical environment are religiously sanctioned in rare circumstances, and then only to better serve pilgrims. Even then, the alterations must be judicious, sparing, and carefully executed. Before Al Saud conquered the Hijaz in 1925, they had accused its Ottoman rulers of propagating a so-called age of ignorance (*jahiliyya*) and of failing to tend to the holy cities of Mecca and Medina.[2] Once in power, Al Saud promised to "cleanse" Arabia of what they considered heretical practices. In the past, Muslim caliphs and imperial rulers had rarely designated Mecca their political capital. But their imperial ambition had rested on exercising sovereignty over the holy city and capitalizing on pilgrimage revenues and trade networks by tending to the infrastructure of the pilgrimage. Such practices persisted through the modern period.

As did those before them, the Saudi rulers utilized the logic of serving the two holy mosques as a main pillar of rule, this time to confer legitimacy on their Najd-centered state-building project. Maintaining the religious infrastructure entailed the mosques' upkeep and the building of secure roads, tunnels, bridges, sewage systems, transportation networks, and lodging facilities. These were meant to improve the pilgrimage experience and ensure pilgrims' safety. The expansion of the Grand Mosque—and thus the destruction of its surrounding areas—began in earnest in the 1950s and increased in the years after the 1973 oil-price hike. Yet the transformations that the city experienced after the turn of the twenty-first century were not only unprecedented but also unfathomable a mere decade earlier. Redevelopment became centered on the overhaul of the neighborhoods surrounding the mosque. The regime, in concert with the Saudi Binladin Group (SBG), summarily brought down whole mountains around the mosque with the force of dynamite. They destroyed much of Islam's material history, as well as places of religious and historical significance such as the Prophet's alleged birthplace. Abbasid and Ottoman architecture were also targeted and replaced with commercial megaprojects.

Despite bulldozing the past in Islam's holiest site, the Saudi state continued to employ religion, and the religious significance of Mecca in particular, for purposes of its own legitimation. To justify such destruction, the regime relied on those religious scholars who argued that memorialization was an innovation: it turned places into sites of visitation, a practice that countered Wahhabi religious and cultural beliefs.[3] The use of religious legitimation and the destruction of religion's material infrastructure were nonetheless peculiar. Such deliberate destruction was a stark contrast to the painstaking preservation of more recent, dilapidated sites associated with Al Saud's heritage in Riyadh. Some of the same decision makers and planners who oversaw the remaking of Mecca simultaneously decried the loss of what they saw as traditional Saudi identity and culture. They related such tradition with Al Saud's stronghold in Najd and sought to resurrect it in Riyadh's built environment.[4] Thus in one city, Riyadh, planners spared no expense to replicate an imagined secular past. In the other city, Mecca, they managed the erasure of a much older topography, whose history, on the face of it, informed Saudi sovereignty and subjectivity.

With the regime's post–Gulf War crisis of hegemony, Mecca came to serve different political and financial purposes, ones rooted in grandiose infrastructural projects and aesthetics whereby secular time overwhelmed religious temporality and subjectivity. Megadestruction was at the heart of reinventing postwar Mecca, but there was also more at stake for the Saudi state. Parallel to the regime's postwar heritage-making effort in Riyadh, Mecca offered a two-pronged solution to looming political and economic challenges. First, the territorialization of Saudi Arabia's history necessitated the destruction of spaces that contested the official rendering of the past. That many of those spaces were located in Central Mecca, one of the most visited cities in the world, and evinced a vibrant pre–Al Saud history made the city's built form a target for state intervention.[5] Second, Mecca offered much-needed lucrative investment opportunities for a regime that had suffered financially from decades of military spending and its adverse effects on the economy. Turning Mecca into a neoliberal city was at the heart of the postwar twinned process of real estate and heritage development.[6] The symbolic importance of megaprojects and their material logic are indeed interdependent, with processes of memorialization being imbricated with questions of property development, speculation, and diversification.[7]

Despite the distance that separated them, Riyadh and Mecca played complementary roles in the postwar vision that Prince Salman ibn Abdulaziz advocated. In the capital, newly constituted heritage would generate political and financial rewards while pacifying popular political opposition. In contradistinction, it was the multibillion-dollar material dehistoricizing of Central Mecca that would produce similar political economic outcomes: the projection of new forms of infrastructural power, strengthened ties with local capitalists, and restructured property markets. Actors in Mecca's redevelopment industry were intimately tied to the same networks of capital, power, culture, and knowledge production that had structured Riyadh's redevelopment. These included Kings Fahd (r. 1982–2005) and (later) Abdullah and Salman; the religious scholars who either opposed or supported Mecca's redevelopment; and capitalists such as the Binladin family who reaped billions of dollars from construction bids. Just like in Riyadh, alliances shifted. The interests of different power centers sometimes overlapped, and other times diverged. In the process, development plans, goals, and trends changed. But for the better part of the twentieth century in Mecca, two of the most powerful families in the world, Al Saud and the Binladins, reaped unimaginable wealth in the name of modernization while ensuring that the religious capital of Islam would become unrecognizable to its inhabitants.

SAUDI ARABIA'S "ROYAL BUILDER"

Despite Mecca's political, economic, and religious importance, Saudi Arabia's top rulers largely outsourced its physical administration to the Binladin contracting company starting in the mid-twentieth century. The Al Saud family did not have the administrative training to govern a modern state. The regions that came to make up the Saudi state were historically, geographically, culturally, and politically diverse and largely disconnected from one another. The bureaucratic finesse required to thread the regions together, symbolically and materially, was lacking. As the center of the Sharifate and the Ottoman Province of Hijaz, Mecca had more developed bureaucratic and human resources. When the new rulers first conquered Mecca in 1925, they made it their administrative capital for the following three decades. Jeddah became the headquarters of diplomatic representation and Taif the summer capital. This guaranteed the gradual transfer of bureaucratic expertise and economic resources to the rulers and their allies.

The sons and closest confidants of Abdulaziz, who became Arabia's new notables, headed the fledgling bureaucratic institutions across the country. Throughout the 1930s, Al Saud increased their influence and secured, initially with the help of British imperial support, a modicum of sovereignty across the newly conquered vast geography. Describing the state of law and order in Saudi Arabia in 1945, Nils E.

Lind, the attaché at the American legation in Jeddah, wrote in a memorandum: "Every town of 1000 or more population with its outlying district is governed by a Nejdi Amir, appointed by the King. The Amirs are responsible directly to the King for the maintenance of law and order, for the collection of taxes and to serve as the last word in any dispute, throughout the districts they govern.... The Amirs can appropriate unoccupied land for their own use in their districts and any investments made can be sold on leaving the post."[8]

The rulers needed to tighten their reign over these loosely governed regions, but they lacked the necessary financial and technical support. Until the exploitation and sale of oil in commercial quantities in the aftermath of World War II, state income consisted of pilgrimage revenues, the sale of dates, taxation, and financial tributes from regional governors. Even when oil revenues began to trickle down to state institutions in the 1950s, they simply were not enough to accommodate the nascent state's capital-intensive needs.

Aramco supported Al Saud and took up those state functions that were crucial for the development of the oil economy. Urban planning was prime among these. The new oil cities that Aramco built—Dhahran, Dammam, and Khobar—were meticulously engineered, planned, and connected to the region and the world. These material manifestations of Saudi Arabia's new oil economy replaced the much older and once prosperous cities of Qatif and Hofuf, turning them into underdeveloped hinterlands. While Aramco took up some development projects in Riyadh and elsewhere in the country, it operated mostly in the Eastern Province. Al Saud relied on other sources of capital and expertise to develop the infrastructure of the rest of the country and to balance Aramco's growing influence. The Binladin family, with its patronage tie to Al Saud and access to capital and know-how, gave the regime leverage over Aramco and other international engineering firms. Muhammad Binladin, who in 1931 was a rising builder of Yemeni origin and had borrowed money to build a construction company, was the most crucial figure in the network of economic elites that would come to serve as the state's private financiers and contractors, especially at times of low oil prices.[9]

Binladin highly impressed Abdulaziz ibn Saud with his vision, acumen, and willingness to take on the ruling family's public and private projects for significantly lower rates than Aramco, Bechtel, and other international companies. He built Al Saud's palaces and government buildings, sometimes at no cost. To earn the trust of the rulers and break Aramco's monopoly on development projects,

Binladin relied on Hadrami merchant diasporas operating across the Indian Ocean and Southeast Asia, and their circuits of capital, to undertake public projects for free or on the promise of future payment.[10] The regime did not always live up to its promise and regularly failed to pay the contractor. Yet the gains for Binladin in terms of closer ties with Al Saud and the subsequent prioritization in receiving development projects was worthwhile. The relationship paid off. By 1953, Binladin was overseeing the expansion of the Prophet's Mosque in Medina. The project's success earned the Muhammad Binladin Organization, as the Saudi Binladin Group was known until 1989, its second, even larger contract: the expansion of Mecca's Grand Mosque. The company broke ground there in 1955, demolishing some major religious and historical landmarks in the process. By then, Muhammad Binladin had been crowned the country's "director-general of construction works of King Abdulaziz," or the "royal builder." On July 22, 1955, King Saud named him a minister of state.[11] Binladin even lent money to the regime in subsequent decades during times of economic crisis and low cash flow. The Binladin family and Al Saud grew symbiotically richer, stronger, and more politically and economically entrenched.[12]

Abdulaziz, and Saud after him, made sure Binladin received some of the country's largest construction contracts, mostly in the Hijaz but elsewhere too. It was under Faisal, however, that the Binladin family's prosperous fate was sealed, despite the oft-contentious relationship between the two. After assuming the throne in 1964, Faisal faced major political and social challenges. The national financial crisis only made things worse for him. Binladin bankrolled Faisal's regime then, essentially saving both the economy and the monarchy. Faisal reciprocated by guaranteeing Binladin the majority of infrastructural bids in the kingdom and the wholesale "development" of the western region, or the Hijaz. At the height of the Cold War and its turbulent manifestations in Arabia in the 1960s and 1970s, Faisal actually diverted major infrastructural resources to the Muhammad Binladin Organization. Together, state and company also worked to secure the southern border with Yemen, especially toward the end of the Yemen War (1962–1970).[13]

In many ways, the Muhammad Binladin Organization facilitated the regime's control and authority over the western region of the country. One of its chief accomplishments was developing a complex network of roads that defied the Hijaz's desolate and rugged topography.[14] This was crucial for connecting the region's cities and hinterlands with one another and with the center, Riyadh. In addition to expanding infrastructure, Binladin built airports, hospitals, mosques, and universities. The introduction of new technologies and opportunities for capital investments in the 1970s only consolidated the Binladin–Al Saud relationship.[15] Before long, the company became the de facto decision maker over the built environment in Mecca and Medina. It shaped both cities' social, political, and economic life, not just the physical space of the two holy mosques. Where Muhammad Binladin initially had made a career for himself in the 1930s by preserving homes in the historical al-Balad area of Jeddah, by the end of the century, his family amassed a great fortune through the redevelopment of Mecca and Medina and the destruction of Islam's historic and religious sites there.

PLANNING MECCA (1968–1991)

By the 1970s, the exponential increase in Saudi Arabia's oil revenues heralded a wave of demolitions across the kingdom. Mecca was no exception among Saudi cities, despite the added concern of administering the mass movement of Muslim pilgrims. Just as the management of vehicular traffic was the main target of engineering plans in the 1960s and 1970s across much of the globe, so did it preoccupy engineers in Mecca. Only five years before the 1973 oil boycott, the Saudi Ministry of Interior commissioned the architectural firm RMJM (Robert Matthew Johnson Marshall) to draw up plans for the whole of the Hijaz, including a master plan for the city of Mecca. Already by 1968, RMJM saw the urgency of improving the city's road infrastructure and increasing the accessibility of the Grand Mosque and its surroundings. The firm's plan, completed in 1973, rested on expanding Mecca's road network while maintaining its historically rugged terrain.[16] The plan was riddled with designs for tunnels that cut through the city's mountains to funnel cars from highways into the city. Parking lots would be spread out across Central Mecca to house the cars once they arrived.

The scale of the proposed urban development in the 1970s was dwarfed by that of early twenty-first-century Mecca. But already, experts and concerned citizens alike expressed concern about the plans. They were especially worried about the changes that took place in the wake of the 1973 oil price hike. The Hajj Research Center was the most vocal in expressing concern. Hijazi architect Sami Angawi and others initially formed the center to document the number of hajj-related deaths.[17] The center quickly outgrew its initial mandate and became invested in all aspects of the pilgrimage to Mecca. The city's built environment and its Islamic architecture came to lead the center's priorities. As early as 1976, the center warned of the destruction of the social and physical fabric of the city:

> Modern Mecca has all the worst characteristics of modern cities throughout the world without their redeeming qualities. Present day Mecca is noisy, ugly, dirty and smelly and has been sold to a new god: Money. The modern architecture is appalling (with one or two notable exceptions) and is out of human scale; land and property speculation is rife resulting in central urban decay and severe social problems; trees and landscaping are almost non-existent and where they exist they lack imagination. The situation is so bad that either nobody notices or cares about Mecca or is too embarrassed to talk of it. Mecca is the scene of inter-ministry conflict and personal ambitions of land and property speculators.[18]

Personal and institutional rivalries, and the corruption that marred state institutions, ensured that various ministries, institutes, elites, and experts converged over the management of Mecca's built life. This resulted in great confusion and redundancy. The kingdom's fledgling centralized state planning seemed to altogether forgo the management of Mecca's built environment. Where the Ministry of Municipal and Rural Affairs (MOMRA), established in 1975, managed the minutest details of Riyadh and other cities, when it came to Mecca, supposedly the kingdom's most important city, MOMRA was nowhere to be found. It lacked any influence, authority, or ability to contest urban developments.

In a damning report, the Hajj Research Center blasted the multiple institutions that had overlapping and conflicting powers over the city's physical space and called for stronger planning controls. At the height of the 1970s construction boom, those who wrote the report suggested that all development work in Central Mecca be halted. They recommended the establishment of a department at MOMRA that would safeguard Mecca's historical, environmental, and social integrity. The department would be independent, immune from political and economic pressures, and strive to end wasteful spending and make better use of the country's resources. The report recommended the following:

> Development which does not require proximity to the Great Mosque should be positively banned from the center and offered attractive sites in other parts of the city where access would be much easier. The method whereby development pressures would be reduced is to pursue a strong policy of decentralization. . . . All civil engineering works must be designed to be in harmony with the natural environment; conservation and rehabilitation of traditional buildings; reparation of damaged traditional buildings and landscape; no destruction or demolitions of the natural landscape; limits to growth of all areas and sectors; four stories to be the maximum building height of all buildings in the main valleys; two stories to be the maximum height of buildings on mountains and hillsides; and no further development to be allowed in the mountains and hillsides.[19]

Like other Saudi Arabian cities, 1970s Mecca experienced urban transformations that alienated many of its residents.[20] Undaunted, the regime dismissed such cautionary statements as nostalgic expressions for the past. With unregulated urban development still the norm, rivalries continued and perhaps even deepened. Where the young monarchy's first urban intervention in midcentury Mecca was dictated by legitimation concerns, the situation looked different by the 1970s.[21] Political expediency, competition over lucrative contracts, and the interest of property speculators superseded that of pilgrims, residents, the environment, and planned urbanization.[22] Intraregime rivalries became increasingly visible in Mecca's built life and pointed to the lack of planning coordination and organizing. Where religion played a more significant role in late-1960s Saudi Arabia as a counter to secular leftist mobilizations, within a few years, its material life was already being effaced in places like Mecca.[23]

Several bureaucrats tried to rein in the rivalries shaping Mecca's built form and to regulate construction in the city. They had to grapple with some of the same challenges and obstacles that had hindered archival centralization in Riyadh: popular and religious opposition, institutional and intraregime competition, and corruption and crony capitalism. In Mecca, there was the added challenge of a private corporation with the almost unbridled power to decide the city's fate.[24] While the Binladins had free reign in Mecca, they would not have touched religious or historical sites there without direct permission from the king himself. Having worked together for decades, both the top rulers and the scions of the Binladin family were well aware of the "red lines" that neither could cross. The various monarchs, for their part, were well aware of the urban transformations taking place in Mecca. They sanctioned the demolition of historical and religious sites but did not otherwise intervene in the company's daily affairs. In return, the company fulfilled its mandate without any opposition and guaranteed the interests of its main allies in the ruling family. Despite outsourcing state functions to a company in Mecca, the rulers regularly paid lip service to the importance of the city and to investing in its comprehensive development.

Shortly after King Fahd assumed the throne in 1982, he decided to expand the holy mosques in Mecca and Medina and appointed the Muhammad Binladin Organization as the main contractor. The king wanted Egyptian architect Muhammad Kamal Ismail to oversee the projects. Ismail was renowned for his work on mosque architecture in Egypt and for having designed the 1940s government office complex—the Mugamma'—in what is today Cairo's Tahrir Square. Ismail had previously impressed Saudi Arabia's first king, Abdulaziz, and his son, then viceroy of Jeddah and foreign minister Prince Faisal, when they met to discuss a proposal for building the Saudi Foreign Ministry in 1952. The Binladins, who had a long-standing professional relationship with Ismail, immediately endorsed the king's choice. The "teacher of generations" (*ustadh al-ajyal*), as Ismail was known, earned King Fahd's trust. It seemed to matter little to the king that the SBG had already commissioned Ismail to draw up similar, albeit smaller plans for the expansion projects even before Fahd became king and without informing the previous regime.[25] Seeing Fahd's ambitions, the company convinced Ismail to expand the scope of the original plan. SBG executives rightfully argued that the mosques in both cities were not large enough to absorb the growing number of pilgrims. With the Prophet's Mosque in Medina requiring more immediate attention, construction began there. Still, the contractor and the regime knew that given the projected population growth, the number of pilgrims would soon surpass the targeted capacity even before both mosques were completed. Yet the revised plan remained the same.[26]

That Ismail was on the Binladin payroll and acted as an intermediary between the Al Saud family and the company is indicative. It spoke to the deeply entrenched ties between family and company.[27] As a blindly trusted confidant, Ismail had final say over the architectural and design plans of the mosque expansion projects. In theory, Saudi kings had to approve all architectural designs in Mecca and Medina. They regularly partook in pompous ceremony to convey their guardianship over the two holy mosques. In practice, however, the top rulers barely participated in the decision-making process, glancing over cursory presentations that the company delivered.[28] They were more concerned with the timely completion of the expansion projects as evidence of their modernization capabilities. Infrastructural expansion projected a sense of power that the monarchy relied on. The direction that urban planning took was at the discretion of the company. It was of little concern to the rulers as long as the construction was profitable, safe, and did not engender any serious opposition.

It just so happened that the Egyptian architect saw the two cities as sacred and hoped to minimize damage to religious and historical heritage. In the documentation of the expansion works, Ismail regularly summons the language of preservation and the importance of historical artifacts.[29] When the engineering firm Dar al-Handasah was commissioned to produce Mecca's comprehensive master plan, which it published in 1985, it also so happened that its planners prioritized maintaining Mecca's distinct mountainous topography.[30] Given the size of the Grand Mosque, the urban development of the city throughout the centuries, and the increasing numbers of pilgrims, it was impossible to sufficiently expand the mosque without infringing on Islam's material history. When expansion works began years later, Ismail's intervention in the built environment was nonetheless cautious. He avoided the destruction of historical artifacts when possible and safeguarded such artifacts when not.

Ismail's guiding principle was the maintenance of what he saw as Central Mecca's spirituality and humility. He planned a pedestrian-only area around the Grand Mosque. Using the tallest existing building surrounding the mosque at the time—fifteen stories—as the benchmark, Ismail set out "regulations to limit the height of high-rise buildings in Makkah." He also recommended "the removal of upper floors where necessary, and the adoption of an architectural style and form which would be compatible with the heritage of the site and its importance."[31] Ismail's caution was paralleled by the absence of centralized urban planning and any supervision over the development of the city. That the regime commissioned several master plans for the city made no difference; the Binladin company disregarded them anyway. Even the Mecca Development Authority (MDA), established in 1987 to oversee urban development, had no control over what went on in Central Mecca. According to a former deputy minister of MOMRA and member of the board of directors of the MDA:

The Ministry of Municipalities has no say when it comes to the holy cities. This is the problem in Mecca. It is not like Riyadh where there is a functioning, efficient, and empowered planning authority like the Arriyadh Development Authority. There was a body called the Mecca Development Authority [Hay'at Tatwir Makkah al-Mukarramah], but it was prevented from intervening in Central Mecca. I was a member of the authority by virtue of being deputy minister for twenty years; none of us had any say in urban planning there. Binladin made all the decisions. Contractors do not care about the design part of "design and build," they just build, and this is what you get when you hand over a city to a contractor.[32]

The company's selective execution of master plans was not anomalous. It persisted long after Ismail produced his own master plan for Mecca in 1991, two years before the mosque expansion project he was overseeing was completed.

If urban redevelopment in Mecca diverged from that in Riyadh, building the city nonetheless resembled the centralization of state archives. Both were marked by haphazardness, informality, and competition. Just like the archive, the planning document is a historical device over which different forces organized, competed, and struggled. The regime increasingly used planning documents—Mecca's urban master plans to be specific—as political tools to accomplish its aims. When necessary, it showcased the plans as material evidence for its alleged careful management of Central Mecca. In reality, it gave the Binladins free rein over building the city. With such minimal supervision, Mecca, whose development was increasingly following global construction trends, was bound to experience what seemed like chaotic urbanization and unregulated expansion. It is remarkable that despite all of the drastic transformations that beset the city before the 1990s, it nonetheless remained largely recognizable to its inhabitants.

PROFITEERS OF PILGRIMAGE

Under the supervision of Muhammad Kamal Ismail, those overseeing construction, renovation, and urban planning projects respected, to the extent possible, the sanctity of some of Central Mecca's religious and historical sites. Several project managers made impromptu design alterations on the ground in order to work around what they deemed historically significant.[33] Mecca's residents regularly intervened, also on-site, to prevent workers from demolishing what they considered valuable artifacts, with some success.[34] But by the mid-1990s, as commemoration came to condition Riyadh's urban redevelopment, the regime's approach to Mecca, and the scale of developments there, also changed. It was barely a few years after the completion of Ismail's expansion plan when the regime set out to redevelop the whole of Central Mecca. The area in question extended out almost a kilometer from the mosque in all directions. It encompassed people's homes and livelihoods, historic buildings and architecture, and significant religious sites.

The new comprehensive vision for the city rested on real estate speculation and profit-driven commercial megaprojects. There was a major lull in the construction industry starting in the late 1980s as a result of the oil glut. The attendant stagnant domestic real estate prices and the global recession of the 1990s necessitated the opening of high-return domestic markets that were, to the extent possible, exempt from market competition and the volatility of trade, manufacturing, and other forms of economic life.[35] Megaprojects in Mecca offered exactly that. They served as an important vehicle for the transfer of state revenue to indigenous capitalists as well as through tenders for infrastructure and site construction. They also functioned as a convenient mechanism for the restructuring of property markets by razing poor neighborhoods, connecting new urban spaces to transportation infrastructure, and building parks and other urban beautification sites. Through these mechanisms, the new comprehensive vision sought to capitalize on pilgrims' spending power and to attract visitors year-round in order to sustain Mecca's economy beyond the pilgrimage season, a challenge similar to what seasonal destinations often have to contend with. Before the regime announced the redevelopment plans, those closest to King Fahd, Crown Prince Abdullah, and other high-ranking bureaucrats began purchasing properties encircling the Grand Mosque at below-market prices. It was not uncommon for them to fully appropriate lands from their legal owners through coercive means.[36] With the help of their allies in the regime, they then sold those back to the government at inflated prices. Those close to the regime also entered into silent and public partnerships with some of the region's major real estate developers. Oftentimes, getting approval for such transactions came at a price: including these ruling members as major investors in the projects, although this was a common practice throughout the kingdom.

Mecca became part of Saudi Arabia's late twentieth-century efforts to diversify its petroleum economy. For the regime and its allies, Mecca served as one of several dynamic series of solutions for the post–Gulf War economic (and political) crises. The real estate market there was more insulated from the global property market than the petroeconomy could ever be.[37] Instead of attempting investments in new areas as capitalists often do, those in Saudi Arabia relied on the regular destruction of existing spaces and the rebuilding of new ones in their stead. Regime strategies of memorialization, and its dialectical opposite, destruction, at once became a new field for the production of a collective Saudi identity. In the postwar period, the regime accelerated the destruction of Mecca's major landmarks. The war exposed the limits of Al Saud's hegemony to be rooted in a particular ordering of urban space, both ideologically and materially. The built environment of the city posed a problem for both Al Saud's postwar revisionist history and their notion of what modernity should look like or "do" in Mecca.

Because Al Saud could not rely on the past to commemorate their rule outside of Najd, they manipulated the built environment to anchor their rule for future generations. At the same time, by signing off on upscale megaprojects steps away from Mecca's Grand Mosque, the regime was able to further capitalize on pilgrimage revenues through increased rents, unearned income, and fees. It would benefit from retail spending, capital flow, investment opportunities, job creation, and transportation revenues, all of which were central to strengthening the national economy. Doing so exponentially increased returns on profit compared to previous decades and signaled the regime's willingness to expand domestic property markets and share the profits with local elites. According to a high-ranking urban planner at SBG:

> This is a young monarchy, with little history beyond Najd, facing a crisis of legitimacy. But they are going to change that, and it is starting in Central Mecca [Makkah al-Markaziyya]. It is an easy target; the majority of its residents are elderly, foreigners, or transient, and Binladin already controls all of it. It is not like Historic Jeddah [al-Balad], for example, where owners of the historic homes, who hail from historically powerful families, either live or work there or within driving distance. It has been much harder to do what we are doing in Mecca there. In Mecca, we are able to work in complete secrecy; whatever the world discovers is always after the fact. And of course, in Mecca, you have the best return on your investment, so the more you build, the more you profit. This is the logic of what you are seeing in Mecca today.[38]

As the primary destination of the pilgrimage, Central Mecca historically had a profitable rental market. Meccan property owners often rented their houses year-round and relocated to Jeddah or other cities.[39] Those who continued to reside there were more often than not elderly and perhaps not as connected to the congested city's social fabric. The SBG and other contractors often worked in secret, under cover of night, when conducting controversial business. Unlike property owners in Jeddah and Medina, many of whom remained close to their cities, Meccans rarely learned of such schemes in time, and were not able to protest, let alone prevent them. Even Saudi Arabia's elites who hailed from Mecca and were vocal about the loss of its material heritage, among them the likes of former petroleum minister Ahmad Zaki Yamani, were powerless in the face of political and corporate decisions.

If the people of Mecca failed to affect SBG's urban designs, the provincial governor did not fare much better. Historically, Mecca's governors were close allies of the king, who appointed them there for their allegiance and obedience. Prominent sons of the first king governed the city for eighty-six years in the twentieth century. They were dismissed from their posts if they diverged from the king's directives. The governors simply could not challenge the king or the existing alliance between family and company. If Riyadh's governor Salman exerted his power in the capital city, Mecca's governors could not. Although they massively enriched themselves through construction contracts, they were beholden to the will of the king there. In the reconceived postwar economy, Mecca's built lifeworld succumbed to considerations that had little to do with the city or its inhabitants, and everything to do with the regime's plan to secularize and financialize space. When "Islamic geographies" became sites of extensive intervention, materially signified through political aesthetics, there was nothing that anyone could do.

Official religious discourse sanctioned the destruction of historical and religious spaces such as the Prophet Muhammad's home and mosques attended by his immediate family, even when not all official religious scholars were in agreement on the matter. As discussed in Chapter 4, those who support this position claim that the destruction of these places is necessary to prevent them from becoming shrines and sites of visitation, a practice that is permissible in most readings of Islam outside of Wahhabism.[40] These scholars rely on official Wahhabi doctrines that forbid monumentalization as a mediated form of worship and view the association of material structures with God as sinful.[41] Calls for these targeted acts of destruction are commonplace and have been especially successful since the 1990s. The religious scholars, then, found common cause with decision makers, developers, contractors, and other elites in the construction of megaprojects on landmarks a stone's throw away from the Grand Mosque.

Despite the variety in scholarly opinion on the preservation of religious sites, the state has adopted this stance as official rhetoric, using it, conveniently, to justify its urbanicide in Mecca. Many high-ranking state officials I interviewed over the years said as much even about the demolition of nonreligious historical sites that predate the rule of Al Saud, especially those that belong to the late Ottoman era. Within the belated archive wars, the late Ottoman era's social, intellectual, religious, and urban networks—to which al-Kairanawi and other cosmopolitan scholars and activists belonged—countered the state's historiographical and material self-representation. Many of the planners who oversaw the remaking of Mecca concurred. Both politicians and planners were unfazed by the threat that Mecca's built environment posed for the ruling family and the family's need to destroy modern history that was not its own, let alone in Mecca.

DEHISTORICIZING SPACE: SPATIAL LOGICS IN THE AGE OF MEGAPROJECTS

The multibillion-dollar Development of King Abdulaziz Endowment Project (DOKAAE) on Mount Bulbul, overlooking the Grand Mosque, was the engine that propelled the massive redevelopment of Mecca in the image of its political rulers and contracting allies (Figures 13 and 14). DOKAAE was conceived and approved in the mid-1990s. Design plans began in 1999 and were finalized within two and a half years. As the developer of this first of Mecca's megaprojects, SBG actually took on much of the $15 billion in construction costs.[42] The company reached an undisclosed deal on repayment with the ruling family, with the mutual goal of increasing returns from pilgrimage revenues and stimulating Mecca's economy and real estate market—in which both family and company were heavily invested.[43]

Building DOKAAE required demolishing the southern part of the mosque's immediate surroundings, the most profitable and desired real estate in Mecca (Figure 15). Many of these were endowment lands largely belonging to the Hashemite Ashraf, South Asians, and other Muslims, both individuals and governments. The Turkish government, for example, was a major owner of these lands.[44] Endowment owners have contested the regime's schemes but failed to regain what they claimed was legally theirs. The regime, in fact, devised multiple legal

FIGURE 13. A general view of the Grand Mosque on the second day of Eid al-Adha in Mecca, November 17, 2010. *Source:* Reuters/Mohammed Salem.

FIGURE 14. The other side of the Development of King Abdulaziz Endowment Project (DOKAAE) in Mecca. *Source:* Photograph taken by author, 2010.

FIGURE 15. A Saudi Binladin Group construction site across from the Grand Mosque in Mecca showing the depth of destruction. *Source:* Photograph taken by author, 2010.

as well as illicit maneuvers to transfer the ownership of endowment land to top Al Saud rulers.[45] One of these was turning DOKAAE into a new religious endowment belonging to the descendants of the first Saudi king, Abdulaziz, which the regime did only in 2001, shortly before construction began.[46] In so doing, the regime single-handedly disregarded the ownership rights of the properties strewn across the site, and it gave their owners little time to contest the regime's appropriation of these lands.

The DOKAAE's planners claimed that once the initial project investment and expenses were recovered, the endowment's revenues would provide for the maintenance of the Grand Mosque, as endowments were meant to do.[47] Many within Mecca's contracting industry and the Mecca Development Authority were skeptical of these claims. Instead, they believed that contrary to sharia, the endowment's revenues would go to the SBG, members of the ruling family, and other investors; only a fraction would be diverted to the maintenance of the Grand Mosque. The endowment model that DOKAAE followed has not been made public, so it is difficult to comment on its financial infrastructure. More evident in such a project is how the nature of twentieth-century Saudi power has blurred the line between private and public sectors in Saudi Arabia. This was apparent not only in funding for DOKAAE provided by both the ruling family and the privately owned Binladin corporation, but also in the nature of the endowment's ownership, future returns, and planning. Indeed, Mecca's megaprojects bring to the fore questions on the divide between political rulers and economic elites, as well as between those members and the state itself. Rulers have long exploited this fine line to justify their political and economic transgressions and abuse of power.

In early 2002, SBG began clearing ground on Mount Bulbul to commence construction work on DOKAAE. The Ajyad Fortress, an eighteenth-century Ottoman military site that once defended the Grand Mosque against invading forces, stood there (Figure 16). The fortress was one of the endowments that the Turkish government had inherited from its Ottoman predecessors.[48] Mecca Province's then governor Prince Abdulmajid ibn Abdulaziz Al Saud (r. 2000–2007) denied rumors widely circulating in 2001 that neighborhoods surrounding the Grand Mosque, such as Ajyad, al-Shamiyya, Harat al-Bab, and Misfila—which Muhammad Ismail actively sought to preserve less than a decade earlier—would be demolished or significantly altered.[49] Yet in a feat of major secrecy in 2002, SBG demolished the fortress. The whole of Mount Bulbul—two million cubic meters of

FIGURE 16. View of the Grand Mosque while congregational prayers are being held during hajj, 1889. The Ajyad fortress that was destroyed, and where the Development of King Abdulaziz Endowment Project (DOKAAE) now stands, appears in the upper-left corner. *Source:* Al-Sayyid Abd al-Ghaffar, physician of Mecca, photographer (public domain).

rock—fell to the force of dynamite to make way for the 1.5-million-square-meter development project.[50] According to a Meccan historian:

> Only a year after Abdulmajid denied these rumors, the Saudi Binladin Group started working on the Ajyad site. And then one day, the contractor announced that the Ajyad Fortress would be destroyed and barely hours later, began demolition work, not giving people any time to react. There was a lot of confusion at the time, because no one actually knew when the destruction would begin. I asked my father, who lives there, to visit the site right after Binladin's announcement. He did, and confirmed that very little of the fortress was left. I was called in as a participant on a television talk show that day, and they were debating the future destruction of Ajyad and other historical sites in Mecca. I said, "not will be demolished," but rather "already demolished." It is already demolished. Everyone was shocked. I said the regime should not use pilgrims or

the pilgrimage, or the endowment itself, as an excuse to destroy history. Without oil revenues, this would not be possible. That's why they say Yemen's historical heritage is lucky, because they simply do not have the needed resources to destroy it in the name of development and modernization.[51]

Mere years after these comments, Saudi Arabia and its allies launched a brutal military assault against Yemen. In addition to the death and suffering the war has wreaked, the Saudi regime deliberately targeted archeological and historical sites, with great impunity. Since March 2015, the kingdom has cleansed much of Yemen's cultural heritage.[52]

The DOKAAE project managers again explained that the development was intended to bolster the "young regime's" history while upgrading the quality of services available in Mecca and providing upscale investment opportunities to local and international investors.[53] But targeting material heritage is a weapon in the regime's arsenal, as its record in Mecca reveals. Ajyad Fortress is a case in point. The Hashemite sharif Surur ibn Msa'id and a group of Hijazi craftsmen and builders had constructed the fortress in 1781, when the Ottomans had sovereignty over the city. The fortress and the neighborhood where it stood were but two of many historical places sacrificed to Saudi historical territorialization and financial diversification. In addition to using the safety of pilgrims to justify these demolitions, the regime and SBG maintained that the mosque's 1980s expansion designs—which they had planned together with Muhammad Kamal Ismail—had led to the destruction of many hotels and residential buildings, limiting the temporary housing supply that pilgrims relied on. The destruction of such sites as Ajyad and others like it was therefore necessary to allow for the construction of new accommodations. At the same time, both company and regime suggested, wrongfully, that many of these spaces had become visitation sites, contrary to Wahhabi religious ethic, and had to be destroyed. Indeed, to counter Turkish as well as global criticism of the wholesale destruction in Mecca, the regime went as far as claiming that the Ajyad Fortress was an Islamic, and not a Turkish, artifact, ironically suggesting that its destruction was religiously legitimated.[54] After much criticism, the regime scaled back on such reasoning and instead argued that Ajyad was neither a sacred site nor a historical one. That it had lost its function as a fortress that protected the Grand Mosque in light of the "restoration of security in the Saudi era" justified its demolition.[55] The demolition, however, engendered so much public criticism that some regime representatives retracted the contradictory claims and announced that the Saudi Binladin Group did not demolish the fortress. Rather, the developer had relied on "world-renowned experts" to professionally dismantle the eighteenth-century site and move it to a government warehouse, where allegedly it is currently stored.[56] These representatives insisted that the regime would reconstruct the fortress on a different mountain once the redevelopment of Central Mecca was complete. This was so despite the availability of video footage of the SBG dynamiting Ajyad Mountain.[57]

Dwarfing the Grand Mosque and those praying in it, DOKAAE is one of the largest religious endowment investments in the world. At the time of writing, one of its many towers is the tallest building in Saudi Arabia and among the tallest in the world. It also lodges the largest clock in the world, dubbed "the capitalist clock" by those who oppose the new urban vision for Mecca.[58] This last-minute design addition was built on the ashes of Mecca's original Hamidian clock, once located at Dar al-Hukuma in Ajyad neighborhood. The clock used to sound a loud alarm to inform government employees and the area's residents of prayer time. The idea of the current clock "came to establish a recognized Islamic timing for prayers and also create an internationally visible landmark."[59] Other urban planners in Mecca, including a former deputy minister of MOMRA, concurred that such a "disaster," referring to the clock, was possible only because of the absence of regulated planning in Mecca.[60]

State monumentality was precisely the goal of redevelopment in Mecca. Mecca's infrastructure represented "the violence at the heart of sovereignty" and was intended to project power and to legitimate the normative economic and social orders.[61] It also embodied "the memory traces of the collective unconscious" of twenty-first-century capitalism, to resurrect Walter Benjamin's description of the Paris arcades.[62] Indeed, when told, in a private meeting, that the clock and the tower itself were "ugly" and were being publicly criticized, King Abdullah responded in a way that perfectly summed up the relationship of petrocapital, space, and political aesthetics: "Let the next king demolish it and build something that he likes better."[63] Decisions to demolish and rebuild what had cost immense time, money, and labor were thus made with a stroke of a brush. Such was the fate of the existing multimillion-dollar King's Palace on Mount Abu Qubays, overlooking the Grand Mosque. Covering an area of over one hundred thousand square meters, the palace had required the demolition of historical and religious artifacts for its construction in the early 1990s. In the mid-2000s, the SBG, with regime approval, decided to move the king's Mecca quarters to the top two floors of one of the DOKAAE towers and to turn the existing mansion into additional prayer space.

If the regime made arbitrary and at times hasty decisions to demolish and rebuild in Mecca, it also resorted to state ulama to legitimate the aestheticization of politics, which in turn reshaped religious practice. Such legitimation began with Mecca's first megaproject, the DOKAAE. One of its towers, Abraj al-Bayt, includes a massive prayer hall facing the Grand Mosque.[64] There, pilgrims with means can pray as if they were inside the Grand Mosque but without leaving the hotel. In 1998, then grand mufti of Saudi Arabia Abdulaziz ibn Baz (1993–1999) declared that pilgrims can perform congregational prayers (*salat jama'a*) anywhere around the holy mosque and it would amount to praying in the mosque.[65] This included, and indeed legitimated, the newly built international hotels adjacent to the mosque, such as those in the DOKAAE, on one condition: the buildings had to remain connected to the cement foundations of the holy mosque; they could not be separated by an actual road.[66] Effectively, people who can afford the $4 million apartments or pay upward of $3,000 per night for a hotel room during the pilgrimage do not have to hear, smell, touch, or be near other pilgrims. They can pray from the luxury of their homes or hotel rooms.

Originally, this measure was intended to keep Saudi kings from praying with the people and allowed them to do so in the king's palace. It was later expanded to allow the affluent to make their pilgrimage experience just that much more luxurious and exclusive while offering them high-return investment opportunities.[67] The lucrative construction projects have in reality changed the religious experience of modern hajj, along with other Islamic rituals. They have, for one, radically increased class inequalities and created "gated communities" in which rich worshippers can separate themselves from the crowds. This separation defeats the purpose of the pilgrimage and the sense of spiritual communion it is meant to generate. It also counters the importance of eliminating distractions and eroding national, class, and other identity markers through the humble, white robes that pilgrims wear (*ihram* clothing).

Despite these and other consequences, the "infrastructural link" became an underlying condition for the other construction projects in Central Mecca, for which the DOKAAE henceforth acted as a model. DOKAAE was also a platform for justifying the need to develop the areas immediately surrounding the Grand Mosque, where real estate value was the highest. By the time the SBG broke ground on the DOKAAE site in 2002, property prices had already increased at an exponentially inflationary rate. By then, too, the region's most prominent developers had started to invest—in partnership with some of the most powerful members of the ruling family—in the construction of other development projects in Central Mecca. The project increased market confidence, one of the state-owned project's primary aims.[68] The economy started to show signs of recovery and the real estate market in Mecca ballooned. This, in turn, led to a new construction boom that eventually accomplished the regime's goals: in 2011, the regime and development companies were already investing $20 billion, with another $120 billion expected in the following decade.[69]

Mecca's new economic and urban plans occurred at the expense of those who lost their homes, livelihoods, and heritage for the sake of the latest redevelopment of Mecca. Other centuries-old sites were demolished to make way for more multibillion-dollar mixed-use developments. The Jabal Omar Development Project and Al Shamiyya Development Project, named after the historical neighborhoods they were to replace, were among the largest. Like all spaces surrounding the Grand Mosque, the one on which the Al Shamiyya Development Project stands was historically remarkable. Al-Kairanawi's school, al-Sawlatiyya, was located there for more than one hundred years. The country's first regular school for girls opened there in 1943 (Madrasat al-Banat al-Ahliyya), followed in 1947 by the establishment of another girls' school, Madrasat al-Fatat al-Ahliyya.[70] The Jabal Hindi Fortress also rested on Mount Qu'ayqa'an that once stood there. Built in 1806, the fortress was renovated by Ottoman governor Osman Nuri Pasha in 1882 and again in 1916 under Sharif Husayn ibn Ali. After Al Saud's conquest, the fortress housed two national institutes: the Saudi Scientific Institute (al-Ma'had al-'Ilmi al-Sa'udi), established in 1928, and the preparatory school for studying abroad (Madrasat Tahdir al-Bi'that) between 1939 and 1949.[71] In 1951, the first Saudi radio station (Iza'at al-Sa'udiyya) took as its headquarters a space adjacent to the fortress. Even developments in Mecca that occurred in the first few decades after the Saudi takeover were targets for demolition; they were reminders of Al Saud's earlier weakness and their reliance on the Hijaz and its people. This and other areas surrounding the Grand Mosque have been completely severed from their past.

As plans for postwar development projects began to materialize, the barely exploited real estate market in Central Mecca brought theretofore-unforeseen profits as well as the rejuvenation of the Saudi economy. These investment opportunities paved the way for the regime to dominate a speculative land economy rooted in a return to primitive accumulation through expropriating private property and dispossessing people of their homes, businesses, and histories, ultimately transforming property relations.[72] Petrocapital circulated through Saudi Arabian banks—many of which are partly or largely owned by regime members or their allies—in the form of loans to contractors and Mecca's real estate market. In this way, the construction projects further enveloped the economic elites into Al Saud's fold and tied them to the regime's political and economic longevity at a time when Al Saud were politically and economically vulnerable. With the absence of an international tourist industry in Saudi Arabia, Mecca was doubly important. The city was the kingdom's gateway to the world's Muslim pilgrims. As of 2013, those who went on the lesser pilgrimage, or Umrah, could join organized travel packages to different parts of the kingdom outside Mecca and Medina if they obtained an Extended Umrah Tourist Visa, known as the Umrah Plus visa.[73] Mecca was also a regular destination for many Saudi Arabians who do not necessarily travel around the country for holiday, yet regularly visited the city. Mecca provided a lucrative landscape for the regime's postwar politics, both symbolic and material.

WHAT'S "PRIVATE" IN PRIVATE PROPERTY?

The Jabal Omar Development Project was the first megaproject to be signed after DOKAAE. SBG was initially the primary developer of the $5.5 billion mixed-use commercial megaproject but was later sidelined.[74] Slated for completion in 2020, the project is located west of the Grand Mosque on the site where the Prophet allegedly lived with his wife Khadija for twenty-eight years. Covering two square kilometers, the development contained other historical sites as well.[75] The longtime residents of Jabal Omar, who had moved there throughout the past century, hailed from all corners of the world. They resisted the surveying attempts of employees of the Mecca Development Authority and the Jabal Omar Development Company. The residents attacked, mugged, and scared off the employees.[76] In a way, the residents of Jabal Omar were somewhat better off than residents of other neighborhoods who lost their homes in return for meager compensation. For example, some of the area's property owners came from prominent families with political leverage and were able to delay the company's work in order to negotiate better deals than the ones property owners in nearby neighborhoods received. As a city planner explained:

> If you look at it from the point of view of justice, you cannot estimate what my home is worth. No matter how much money you want to give me, I live across from the holy Ka'ba, and that is priceless. You simply cannot compensate people for that. But on the other side, if you are responsible for developing the city, you cannot leave this area in ruins [*kharab*] with rundown, thirty- to forty-meter lots, it is a problem. What they did in Jabal Omar in terms of financially compensating owners is somewhat better than in other places and guaranteed them a permanent income. Very few refused.[77]

Although there were rundown lots across the city, the neighborhood itself was far from being "in ruins," as those who benefit from the megaprojects so often suggest. Also contrary to these claims, the Jabal Omar concession was not fairer than those of other development projects. Many continued to reject the final compensation packages that the company offered, which entailed paying owners five years' worth of rent and taking them in as partners with shares commensurate to the worth of their properties.[78] According to company officials, they would pay owners dividends once the project was completed and started to generate revenues. If "very few refused" as the company claimed, it was because owners were subjected to "acts of intimidation, injustice, and bullying," in the words of some owners' lawyers. Although many of their lawsuits against the development company were dismissed, some languished in the courts as late as 2017.

Other property owners have suffered similar fates.[79] The $10 billion Al Shamiyya Development Project, located north of the Grand Mosque and actually falling within the sanctuary, offered property owners one of two options: selling at significantly below-market prices or accepting shares in the development as a form of compensation.[80] In 2006, after a three-year study, the High Commission for the Development of Mecca—established in 2000 to plan the redevelopment of all areas close to the haram—gave the project its final stamp of approval.[81] The site looked like a magnificent one-kilometer-deep crater stretching across three million square meters when I visited in 2011. The mixed-use development would offer Mecca upscale international hotels and short-term and permanent residences, as well as state-of-the-art commercial facilities and markets. It was meant to absorb an additional four hundred thousand residents, a prayer space for four thousand pilgrims, and an underground bus station and parking lot with a capacity of 10,500 vehicles.[82] Considered one of Saudi Arabia's largest and most ambitious construction projects, its overseeing developer, Al Shamiyya Urban Development Company, was a partnership between SBG, Al Oula, Al Sagheer, and Dallah Albarakah.

The powerful private company resorted to eminent domain in order to purchase properties there for approximately 10 percent of their actual worth.[83] Many who refused both options were forcibly evicted. Their properties were either fully expropriated for little compensation or expropriated through *hikr*, in which the government became a "partner" in the development of the expropriated land.[84] Moreover, owners were not able to obtain financial compensation from the Monetary Agency's compensation fund because they refused either option. This is in spite of the fact that Al Shamiyya neighborhood was home to some of Mecca's historically prominent families and many intellectuals and ministers—including former petroleum minister Ahmad Zaki Yamani. The livelihoods of political and economic elites remain dependent on good relations with the regime, and they were thus more likely to agree to undisclosed forms of compensation than to show public opposition.

Mecca's redevelopment forced at least a hundred thousand residents from different socioeconomic classes out of their homes. Former residents received meager compensation in return and were left without legal recourse. Some were relocated to new settlements farther away, on the edges of the city, from which it was difficult to regularly visit Central Mecca. Many ended up in slums less than a mile away from the Grand Mosque, hidden from visitors' eyes by the Abraj al-Bayt Towers and other megadevelopments (Figure 17).[85] Regime officials and their allies in the city's construction industry regularly argued that many of Mecca's landowners have not lived in their properties for decades and could not, as such, seriously maintain their property rights. Such a legal claim has no precedent in the kingdom.[86] Speaking of the Hijazi landowners with contempt, the officials denigrated them for having "abandoned" their properties and rented them out all these years, stating that if they really cared about Mecca as they claim, they would have lived there. They should, according to detractors, be thankful for any compensation they receive from the regime.

FIGURE 17. Slum in the shadow of the Grand Mosque and the Development of King Abdulaziz Endowment Project (DOKAAE). *Source:* Photograph taken by author, 2010.

Although the desire for profit animated Mecca's redevelopment projects, such statements and accusations have great salience in Saudi Arabia. They build on a century-long sense of Najdi disdain toward the people of Hijaz, some of who are nonetheless close regime allies and owners of the very development companies that have been operating in Mecca for decades.[87] This has made it easier for the regime to dismiss complaints about private property reclamation. Practices of land reclamation are obviously dependent on political power and its legal or judicial, security, and public relations arsenals. Claims to property are clearly designated within Saudi law, and the regime frequently speaks to the importance of respecting private property. The implementation of such rights in everyday life, however, was vague at best, with property claims easily trumped by those with political and economic power, as in the case of endowment land in Mecca but also private land across the kingdom.

Owners of capital have been able to claim much of the privately owned land in congested Central Mecca, as elsewhere in the country, at little cost, through private-public initiatives. The lack of strong property rights and a judicial regime to enforce property laws allows rentier regimes and individuals to maximize their surplus capital with minimal expense and without legal repercussion. At first glance, this seems paradoxical given the petroregime's heightened dependence on land for capital accumulation. But as Wallerstein explains of capitalism more broadly: "Because capitalism has been built on the juridical foundation of property rights, we assume that it requires and capitalists desire that property be sacrosanct and that private property rights extend into ever more realms of social interaction, whereas in reality the whole history of capitalism has been one of a steady decline, not an extension, of property rights."[88] Political power is more likely to protect the interests, and capital, of the economic elites than to uphold the rule of law. The entrenched political and economic interests reveal the difficulty of separating the political from the economic. After all, many of these elites circulate in both spheres and rely on one another to further their own power.

Tracking processes of real estate development in one of the world's most high-value property markets provides a good lens for understanding postwar transformations in Saudi political authority. It sheds light on the increasing privatization of prayer space and the reorganization of property relations in the primary destination of the Muslim pilgrimage. The history of spatial development in Saudi Arabia is a complex one. It entails powerful members of the ruling family who can enclose a property they desire despite its legal owners. It also includes people close to those with political authority who purchase land slated for development well below market price, only to resell it to the government at exorbitant prices. Key members of the Saudi regime—kings Fahd and Abdullah—regularly shared privileged information with the Binladin family in particular, enabling SBG to preempt a number of planned development projects by purchasing those properties or securing the bids for their redevelopment before their incorporation was announced. The implicated Al Saud members and the Binladin family have benefited immensely from these processes. They siphoned tens of billions of dollars from state funds intended for the development of the Holy Mosque Expansion Project since the 1980s. One of the largest development projects in the world, the expansion project acted as a main front for their personal enrichment as well as that of their subcontractors and allies.[89] Billions of dollars in "public" funds were transferred to these beneficiaries through similar projects, in the form of either direct cash or mansions that the SBG built for them in Mecca and elsewhere.

These practices bring into view an otherwise occluded social history and the economic, political, and cultural phenomena that punctuate it. They reveal a relentless blurriness in the confident divides between religious and secular, public and private, and past and present. And finally, they show how state formation was just as much about destruction as it was construction. Relegating religion from the state's material politics, territorializing secular history, and financializing what was once sacred and historical space varyingly shaped Mecca's built environment and its social relations. Not only did these operations of rule have to conform to changing domestic threats, alliances, and political economic conditions; they also took shape in, and were connected to, the rapid ascendancy of neoliberal forms of governance. The past several decades were indeed marked by accelerated urbanization and privatization. While the relationship between the political and the corporate capitalist classes predated late capitalism, it nonetheless has become increasingly imbricated, co-dependent, and visible in recent decades. The Saudi case demonstrates this reality, showing how the erosion of private property rather than its protection is becoming the norm.

MODERNITY, RESISTANCE, AND THE POWER OF THE PAST

With the accelerated destruction of hundreds of sites in Islam's holiest city, Mecca has undergone a drastic and irreversible change. The archeological sites that recorded the temporality of Islam, Ottoman rule, and political, economic, and cultural life before and in the first few decades of Al Saud's rule are today nothing but demolished remains. These unrecognizable remnants are a powerful testament that the very evidence of the peninsula's alternative history threatens the new foundation of the Saudi state. They reveal the official historical discourse as thoroughly constructed, shallow, and permeated with power relations.

Concerned urban planners, historians, and architects had challenged top-down designs for Central Mecca. They even donated several master plans that would have preserved all surviving historical sites, safeguarded private properties, and turned Mecca into a sustainable city. Like the Hajj Research Center and Muhammad Ismail before them, these were based on limiting Central Mecca to religious purposes, and moving all residential, commercial, and entertainment facilities to nearby satellites. A confidential group that the regime itself commissioned to produce alternative plans for Central Mecca proposed a similar design: the Grand Mosque and its immediate surrounding should be restricted to low-rise buildings that are less congested; satellite towns should be built two kilometers away from the Grand Mosque, on vacant land, and then connected to rapid transit; and high-rise buildings should be restricted to those satellites, which the mountains surrounding the Grand Mosque would hide from sight. According to members of this group, doing so would preserve the sanctity and visual openness of the place while managing congestion and the safety of people in more efficient and feasible ways.[90]

The regime dismissed these plans as unfeasible and allowed Mecca's redevelopment to proceed unhindered. Given the scale of the megaprojects and the speed with which the regime wanted the redevelopment to take place, developers compromised on quality. More alarmingly, they failed to meet internationally recognized safety standards. They risked the lives of hotel guests and the millions of pilgrims who visited the city each year, whose safety and comfort the regime used to justify the mosque expansion to start with. SBG planners admitted as much. They did not know what the proper emergency protocols were in the event that a fire broke out in one of the towers, especially if it caused debris to fall directly onto those praying in the Grand Mosque and its piazzas. Mecca Development Authority employees were happily surprised when the few emergency incidents that occurred in the towers since 2008 passed without serious casualties. They had expected the worst, having failed to convince SBG and the regime to take the time to improve safety standards.

Time was not on the regime's side. In the 1990s, Saudi Arabia's rulers were rushed to monumentalize their power, foreclose Mecca's diverse historical landscape, and exploit the city's investment potential. Real estate in Mecca was scarce and among the most expensive in the world. A square meter of commercial land in Central Mecca cost upward of $130,000 in 2010. It reached $400,000 per square meter in 2013, compared to an average $21,000 per square meter in New York City.[91] Capitalizing on these opportunities, while they still could, served the rulers' broader aims. Sami Angawi, a Jeddah-based Meccan architect who has been at the forefront of local opposition to the construction affronting Mecca since the 1990s, explained: "The Hijaz as a whole, but Mecca in particular, threatens Al Saud because it is layered with histories that tell a different past than the one they want us to believe. Yes, Wahhabi ideology is conveniently at play, but let us be clear, this is about politics and profit; they get to finally recreate the holy city in their image, erase our much longer past, while reaping unimaginable profits, all in the name of necessity and development."[92] The redevelopment projects therefore complemented Al Saud's selective invocations of the past by demolishing material evidence that countered the official historical discourse. As in other cases, Saudi Arabia's state-sanctioned history was premised on and necessitated a relentless erasure. As in other cases, too, the relentless drive to erase, demolish, rebuild, and renarrate exposed a deep and abiding insecurity about claims to historical, cultural, and religious legitimacy.

Such urban reordering has met with little mass indignation inside Saudi Arabia. A Meccan historian of pre-Islamic Arabia lamented the destruction of heritage in Mecca—the Prophet Muhammad's birthplace—and its redevelopment into a fictitious place that is disconnected from its material past:

> Cultural heritage holds no significance for the majority of the Saudi Arabian population. Schools and the educational system in general do not instill a sense of appreciation for these matters. Indeed, there is a large gap between history and reality, between history and its material terrain ... as if our prophet became one in a fictional place, not right here, in Mecca. There is a flagrant flattening of Islamic history. . . . My family had an idea of what was going on

in Mecca, we were all too aware that Islamic heritage was missing and being destroyed.... I grew up learning that Wahhabism works on destroying Islamic heritage, but of course, this is primarily political. Religion is simply the suitable guise through which politics is expressed. They [Al Saud] are not going to say they would have preferred for the Ka'ba to be in Riyadh, they are simply not going to say that, so they acquire their legitimacy through other means.[93]

Despite the critical disposition, the scholar seemed to agree with the logic of the archiving regime's civilizing mission, which had fueled the awareness campaigns: that ignorance, and the lack of education, were heritage preservation's worst enemies. Saudi Arabians have indeed been socialized through educational curricula, sermons, media, and official rhetoric into a Wahhabi religious ethic. Encouraging outright opposition to acts of commemoration and the preservation of religious heritage, if not all forms of heritage, was sometimes part of that worldview. Yet not all have bought into this rhetoric. There is a plethora of evidence that challenges claims that Saudi Arabians summarily support Wahhabi iconoclastic zeal. The decades-long and multipronged domestic attempts to challenge, against great odds, the state's urban planning project, specifically, the destruction of religious and historical sites, are one example. Citizens have used official and unofficial channels to contest the destruction of religious and historical sites in Mecca. They also opposed the form that redevelopment in Mecca has taken. Some even publicly or privately regarded the violence done to Mecca's built environment as a crime against humanity, the environment, and history, one that is compounded by the resounding silence such transgressions have met.[94]

Attempts at contestation have, however, been discreet and circumspect given the cost of contestation is high. Saudi Arabian citizens have been arrested for much less than voicing opposition to regime designs. They feared a similar fate for speaking up. Dozens of urban planners, architects, and scholars at institutions involved in the redevelopment of Mecca, such as the Mecca Development Authority, SBG, the General Presidency for the Affairs of the Holy Mosques in Mecca and Medina, and MOMRA were themselves personally opposed to the nature of redevelopment they oversaw in Mecca. Without exception, they believed that alternative plans that respected the sanctity of the place were possible and equally profitable.[95] Their voices were silenced and ignored. Along with several hundred Saudi Arabians I interviewed across the country for these purposes, they felt a sense of defeat and futility; the regime, and in the case of Mecca, the SBG, were too powerful and overwhelmed critics.

Many Saudi Arabians opposed the demolition of Mecca's material history but did not speak out against it out of fear of regime repression, not "lack of awareness." Still, even they did not know the politics behind the effort to redevelop Mecca. Saudi Arabian scholars, archeologists, and laypersons not connected to the planning industry did not see the redevelopment of Mecca as a consequence of Wahhabi belief, as the regime often claimed and as international media often repeated. But they also were not aware of the political economic motives of the project. Instead, many deemed these destructions a necessary evil, collateral damage from the need to accommodate a ballooning Muslim population in a now-easily-accessible pilgrimage destination that should offer its sophisticated visitors more than just its material heritage. This is not surprising. None of the institutions responsible for Mecca's built life engaged with the community about the city's future. The heightened secrecy that surrounded Mecca's redevelopment, coupled with scant reporting on the topic until the late 2000s, made access to information difficult. When local newspapers covered the redevelopment of Mecca, they did so within a framework that praised the modernizing power of the Saudi state. International media and preservation agencies began to critique the topic in a serious and sustained manner only in 2010, and more so after 2013, blaming Wahhabi forces for such destruction.[96] By then, most of the areas around the Grand Mosque had already been demolished. The few scholarly attempts to account for or to theorize recent transformations to Mecca's built environment blamed Wahhabi iconoclasm as well as the need to accommodate the ballooning number of pilgrims.[97] In these ways, state institutions and their partners shrouded Mecca's development in secrecy, thereby shielding it from more pronounced scrutiny until it was too late.

In addition to altering social and economic life and exacerbating class inequities and distinctions among Meccans and pilgrims alike, these development projects have thus far created much anger among residents of Mecca.[98] Responses to such urban injustices and dispossession rarely circulate in the media. As another historian of Mecca explains:

> Those who live in Mecca are, on average, older, retired Saudi people. The ability to protest there was rather meager. There are also no channels of

protestation in the kingdom; when you do they quickly throw you in prison. We cannot march or protest. Since the creation of the state, they have neutralized all peaceful means of expression, so all we have is the press, which is controlled by Al Saud. How is it that our prophet's home is now under the Haram's public lavatories? How did this happen? The media empire of Al Saud have made this possible; they market it as "expansion" [*tawsiʿa*], they do not let people know what is really happening, they do not tell you at what expense they are expanding, in the name of modernization. There is a regulated elision of history, and the media cannot report it. When have international journalists been allowed into Mecca? So even if there were people in Mecca protesting the regime's demolitions, their voices were not relayed, they could not be heard.[99]

Several groups and individuals nonetheless continued to protest—through institutional channels and outside of them—the destruction of historical sites and architecture, the regime's plans for the city, and the forcible expulsion, displacement, and violent treatment of residents.[100] At times, the regime heeded popular calls when they did not entail serious revisions to their original plan, and at other times they paid lip service to the need to do so.[101] For the most part, protestation has been largely silenced, co-opted, or otherwise intimidated. This was a sensitive topic in Mecca in the late 2000s, and as a researcher there at the time, I had limited access to many of those who tried to block or alter the redevelopment plans, whose stories I therefore cannot include here.

The Saudi regime has carefully managed contestations of its latest urban plans in Mecca, especially those coming from within the official religious establishment itself. In 2008, when the Saudi Binladin Group began demolition work in the Grand Mosque in preparation for the King Abdullah Expansion Project, there was an outcry from Mecca's religious leadership, who knew nothing of the construction plans and subsequently leaked the news to the public in an attempt to generate support. Shaykh Salih ibn Abdulrahman al-Hussayin (d. 2013), president of the Affairs of the Holy Mosques in Mecca and Medina and former member of the Council of Ministers, demanded to see the Saudi Binladin Group's expansion plans.[102] When SBG refused, the shaykh, who had worked closely with King Abdullah in the past and still had access to him, wrote directly to him. Abdullah had already heard of the popular concern. He consequently asked Bakr Binladin, SBG's chairman, to share the plans with the shaykh. Upon finding out that the current plans were a repeat of the earlier King Fahd Expansion Project, which planners and religious leaders alike had deemed inefficient and problematic, the religious institutions met with Binladin and explained to him the multiple ways in which the plan was impractical. When Binladin ignored the religious leaders, Shaykh Hussayin again wrote the king, this time suggesting that the Ministry of Higher Education commission a working group of Saudi-educated engineers and planners to evaluate Binladin's work. The king agreed, and the working group has since appointed dozens of local and international consultants to produce a "more appropriate" plan, the first stages of which were completed in 2010. But in the process, and with regime knowledge, the SBG continued its work unabated. King Abdullah's relationship with the company was strong. It could not be shaken or threatened by such complaints, even if from a prominent religious leader. Throughout this whole process, the Mecca Development Authority was not even consulted.[103]

This was not the only time Shaykh al-Hussayin intervened in the regime's expansion plans. In 2008, the king issued a royal order (that was never heeded) to stop the destruction of Islamic and historical sites in Mecca and Medina. He assigned the Saudi Commission for Tourism and Antiquities (SCTA) responsibility for the protection and management of historical sites in the holy cities.[104] But those who knew anything about Mecca's built environment were well aware that it was already too late to "save" Mecca. Despite the royal order, SCTA officials, including its secretary-general Sultan ibn Salman, lamented their continued inability to carry out their mandate in Mecca and called for the urgent protection of the few remaining historical artifacts and sites, especially the Mecca library (Maktabat Makkah al-Mukarramah; Figure 18).[105] Confirming widespread fears, in 2009 an international company won the competition to redevelop the site on which Mecca's library stands, itself built in the early 1950s on the site where historians think the Prophet Muhammad was born.[106] The new plan was to turn that space into a bus stop, which was later revised to a metro stop. When news of the development became public, Saudi newspapers and the blogosphere attacked and criticized it.[107] Muslim voices from outside Saudi Arabia also made their concerns heard. Again, Shaykh Hussayin appealed to the king and requested that the library's integrity be respected. The project was temporarily halted. After all, the regime was not sure if it could mitigate the potential fallout, given that the plans were receiving increasing global public criticism.[108] In 2010, in an effort to garner some legitimacy, the regime responded to the criticism by restructuring and increasing the powers

FIGURE 18. The library at the Grand Mosque in Mecca. Built in the early 1950s, the library stands on the site where historians speculate the Prophet Muhammad was born. *Source:* Photograph taken by author, 2010.

of the Mecca Development Authority (MDA), allegedly to regulate development. But the MDA continued to have no say in the development of Central Mecca, powerful as the Saudi Binladin Group was. An MDA executive remarked:

> Development in Mecca does not follow a master plan. It is random, disconnected, and dependent on economic and political power. In Medina, all historical sites were destroyed a long time ago, but at least redevelopment occurred according to a well-thought-out master plan. They had a functioning Higher Committee for the Development of Central Medina, with a technical staff slightly less qualified than its counterpart in Riyadh, so development there was sustained and made sense. In Mecca, nothing makes sense. You have the added problem of Mecca's other religious sites, Masha'ir, Mina, Muzdalifa, and Arafat; they are part of the city, but they are treated, along with the masjid [Grand Mosque], as if they have no connection to the city. You cannot plan a city when you have parts of it that are out of your control or authority. It is only

this year that it seems that things are getting more regulated. Unfortunately it is too late.[109]

The MDA indeed proposed several carefully-thought-out master plans for the city it allegedly oversaw. It also attempted to intervene in the SBG development plans in the central area, which it deemed problematic. All its plans in Central Mecca were supplanted by SBG's proposals. The MDA's leadership not only failed to implement any real changes to the urban development of Mecca but also in the purported mission to safeguard the sanctity of Central Mecca and avoid unnecessary destructions there. MDA leaders, who regularly spoke in public about the institution's accomplishments and spectacular future plans, inadvertently acted as spokespeople for the regime. Meanwhile, the SBG continued to make all decisions concerning the city's planning and development.

Saudi popular scrutiny of Mecca's urban planning increased immediately after 2010, when the scale of destruction became impossible to cover up or justify. An ailing King Abdullah promptly responded to Saudi citizens by issuing a video of himself supposedly reprimanding SBG chairman Bakr Binladin and commenting on SBG's expansion plans for Mecca's Grand Mosque.[110] This performance was meant to counter allegations circulating online and in Saudi popular discourse that the ruling family had sold the holy city to material interests and greed. It showed that the "Custodian of the Two Holy Mosques" was indeed involved in the country's most prized geographic and historic possessions that had given him his prestigious title. In reality, the king simply put on a charade of royal supervision of construction in Mecca, pretending to threaten the SBG chairman with ending his contract if he did not deliver the expansion project in time. The speediness with which projects were completed was the marker of the monarch's accomplishments, and thus the central priority. The king singled out "Mecca's spirituality" (*ruhaniyyat Makkah*) as the most important goal. In saying that, the king expressed concern with the process of construction and the disturbances it would cause, as opposed to the physical shape the city would take and its effects on religiosity and spirituality.

Those who had warned that "to allow major economic activities to overshadow the essential religious function of the holy city would be to destroy its essential, spiritual nature" were completely ignored.[111] In 2011, almost a decade after postwar construction in Central Mecca had begun, the regime announced a yearlong international competition for the Mecca Master Plan.[112] In so doing, decision makers made it evident to all those challenging the already established plans for Central Mecca's development that they had no intention of altering them. The master plan would be finalized and approved only after the blueprints were set in stone. As a matter of fact, as late as 2015, the regime was still commissioning firms to draw up a master plan for the city. Foreign journalists were eventually allowed into Mecca, but only after most historical sites were already demolished and construction plans either finalized or in the process of completion.

After freezing the destruction of the library at Mecca's Grand Mosque in 2009 as a result of popular outcry and the ulama's criticism, the regime once again gave SBG permission to demolish it.[113] In the updated plan that the SBG proposed in 2013, the site was still slated for destruction, this time to become home to the mosque's imam, with a new "presidential palace" adjacent to it. King Abdullah died before the execution of this plan, and the library was not demolished under his watch. The future of the site, and whether the new regime under Salman would go through with the demolition, is still not clear. Currently, two spaces house Saudi kings, both only steps away from the Grand Mosque: the royal palace—connected to the Grand Mosque by tunnels—and the last two floors of one of the towers of the King Abdulaziz Endowment Project. If built, the new "presidential" palace will not only be closer, physically, to the Grand Mosque; it will also sit on top of the Prophet's alleged birthplace. Whether the plan is executed or not, this remains a symbolic gesture that parallels the recent religious marginalization. It will not be lost on the people of Arabia, religious or not, or on the millions who will visit Mecca each year.

Since the turn of the twenty-first century, Mecca's built environment has conformed to Saudi Arabia's postwar vision for secular national heritage while strengthening religious tourism, investment opportunities, and economic ties with elites. The demolition of parts of the Grand Mosque and its historical surroundings did not begin in the 1990s. But it was only in the years following the 1991 Gulf War, when several members of the regime decided to relegate the political influence of the religious establishment and the place of religion in political life, that Mecca's urban plan came to rest on the city's complete overhaul. During Fahd's and Abdullah's regimes, Islam lost most of its material heritage in Mecca. What Abdullah's regime preserved of Islam's heritage would be displayed in museums and exhibitions throughout Mecca, which the monarchy has used as evidence for its historically oriented modernization efforts.[114]

In roughly the same period, Salman was able to create a heritage industry in Riyadh, one that materialized Al Saud's past alone. Yet since the time that Salman became known as the gatekeeper of history in the late 1990s, he did not express much concern for the destruction of heritage in Mecca, let alone anywhere else outside of Riyadh. Despite the various power rivalries, Salman's Riyadh-based project conformed to Fahd's and Abdullah's visions for Mecca. In fact, when Salman became known as a history aficionado, regional power brokers reached out to him. Various ministries had rejected their proposals for preserving historical sites in their towns at their own expense. They hoped that Salman would intervene. He did not. Salman's son Sultan, who headed Saudi Arabia's tourism sector from 2000 until 2018, publicly decried the destruction of heritage in Mecca on several occasions during his tenure. His powerful father stood idle, paying lip service to the important steps the regime was taking to safeguard the religious capital's heritage.

Turning Mecca's infrastructural developments into discourses of government, the Saudi regime has marketed the city's overhaul as necessary to prevent what it sees as unorthodox rituals of site visitation and reverence, to accommodate the increasing numbers of Muslim pilgrims, and to enhance the infrastructure of the pilgrimage. In the words of Mecca's governor, Prince Khalid Al Faisal (r. 2007–2013, 2015–), modernization is meant to transform Mecca into the most beautiful "First World" city in the world.[115] The religious capital of Islam was to embody the urban model for development and become "a model twenty-first century" global city.[116] In line with the erasure of the city's material life and evidence of its past diversity and cosmopolitan history, its governor also submitted the city to a process of Arabization, whereby all street and building names would shed their non-Arab names.[117]

Upon assuming the throne in 2015, Salman criticized previous urban planning practices in Mecca and promised to do justice by its heritage. His son Crown Prince Muhammad blamed the SBG for all of Mecca's ills. In November 2017, he imprisoned SBG chairman Bakr Binladin and at least one other member of the Binladin family in a countrywide purge of rival political and economic elites. He then appropriated most of SBG's contracts and incorporated the lucrative redevelopment of Mecca into his portfolio, promising to turn Mecca into a tourism destination that would rival Dubai and Paris.[118] Turning Mecca into a veritable tourist destination, and not simply planning with the pilgrimage in mind, has since become a celebrated goal. Father and son also publicly pledged to salvage material history in Central Mecca. Instead of caring for what little is left of it, however, they have continued Abdullah's urban policy directions. They have commodified religion using the same existing patterns, calling on the building of yet more museums that showcase Mecca's Islamic history. In fact, one of the crown prince's stated goals in his Vision 2030 for Saudi Arabia is to build "the largest Islamic museum" in the world.[119]

Achmed Rasch, who manages exhibitions in Mecca—and whose father, Bodo Rasch, designed the clock tower in the DOKAAE development—best embodied such pretense when he "suggest[ed] that the best way to preserve the history of Mecca and to make it accessible to millions of visitors would be to set up a museum," and not, for instance, to leave Mecca's central district intact and build accommodations on its outskirts because, for him, that would increase traffic.[120] It was a way to justify the logic of capital, which "celebrates the defeat of the past at the same time as it appears to mourn it."[121]

CONCLUSION

The turn of the twenty-first century heralded waves of wholesale demolitions in Mecca. The attendant land speculation and construction of multibillion-dollar commercial megaprojects steps away from the Grand Mosque led to the unprecedented overhaul of Mecca's physical space as well as its once-mountainous landscape. The new spatial reconfiguration accomplished the central objectives of the post–Gulf War regime. It created high-return domestic investment opportunities that strengthened the postwar national mono-economy and promoted its diversification while further aligning the interests of economic elites with those of the rulers. Indeed, according to some estimates, pilgrimage revenues are expected to "exceed $150 billion by 2022."[122]

Mecca's spatial redevelopment also ensured the permanent erasure of particular episodes of Arabian and Islamic history and of the very possibility of living history, thereby territorializing the state-sanctioned historical narrative in an attempt to reproduce or bolster its legitimacy. Exceptional as they may seem, such practices of spatial redevelopment are part of mundane global urban phenomena, capitalist development, and political governance, deployed under the guise of religious asceticism and the need to better serve a ballooning population of Muslim pilgrims. That some of the strongest voices of protestation emanated from within Mecca's highest religious authorities signals the complexity of these processes. Ultimately, Abdullah's regime and the Saudi Binladin Group prevailed over the religious and secular forces that protested the city's transformation—as did Salman's regime, albeit within a different political economic power structure.

Without understanding the Saudi state's theological politics, we cannot appreciate how and why "Islamic geographies" are now the site of such extensive intervention, materially signified through state aesthetics. Not only were those in power able to defeat dissenting voices; they also silenced and erased their very attempts to do so. The political theorist Neera Chandoke observed that "spatially and socially the city condenses the contradictions of social formations. It responds both to the logic of accumulation and to social struggles."[123] State development practices in Mecca, at a multitude of scales, are embedded in and produced through the very tangible material of urban history—the bricks and mortar and streets and gutters rebuilt and ripped down in the remaking of the city. The Saudi state's material politics speaks to how the regime aims to reengineer the social order—to supplant its religious foundations for political legitimacy with a secular national mythology built around the selective history of Al Saud family. While this effort at the making of history reveals itself in the built environment, it simultaneously transforms the Saudi landscape into a revenue-generating asset, one that has consolidated the power of the ruling family and its economic allies.

These multiple valences—cultural, social, political, and economic—are at once evident in the regime's efforts to generate symbolic and material capital, legitimate its genealogy, and monumentalize its power. Together and separately, projects of political commemoration and capital accumulation in Riyadh and Mecca mediate and reproduce state sovereignty and legitimacy while reshaping Saudi society and the economy. They are sites where different social orders, time, and densities exist in the same social space and for different ideological and material goals. The erasure of alternative accounts of state formation through commemoration in Riyadh and violent destruction in Mecca is, at heart, a performance of state power and also of its limits. It is a continuation of Al Saud's state-building project and the deep-seated violence to the everyday, the spiritual, and the temporal.

Conclusion

THE VIOLENCE OF HISTORY

BORN TO A NOTABLE FAMILY OF CONSERVATIVE RELIGIOUS SCHOLARS, Abdulaziz, a graduate of the Sharia College in Riyadh and al-Azhar University in Cairo, was a cleric who held high-ranking positions in some of the most influential religious bodies in Saudi Arabia.[1] Articulate and mild mannered, Abdulaziz was nonetheless scathing in his critique of regime policies that he himself had fostered throughout his decades-long bureaucratic career. Like many of his colleagues who worked in the different institutions that made up the religious establishment, Abdulaziz was dependent on the regime for his salary. Still, he was disgruntled about the increasing marginalization of religion from politics, law, and history that marked the post–Gulf War era.

For Abdulaziz, the sidelining of Muhammad ibn Abd al-Wahhab from the country's official history was a grave matter. He himself had legitimized the practice by going to Dirʻiyya and the National Museum on official public relations tours in the mid-2000s. His voice was shaky as he regretfully admitted as much. But this, to him, was a symptom of a larger and more damning problem that had plagued the country since the early 1990s, especially after Crown Prince Abdullah became the de facto ruler in 1995. Those years, accordingly, saw the beginning of an unprecedented regime effort to relegate religion from public life, transform official socialization and nation-building programs, and further disempower the clerical class. These efforts only accelerated following the September 11, 2001, terrorist attacks in the United States and those in Saudi Arabia in 2003. The commercialization and rebranding of Mecca embodied the new direction the country was taking and that Abdulaziz vehemently opposed.

A "SECULARIZING" NATION?

Despite the "vulgar secularization" he was critical of and that he and his colleagues aided even though it countered their own beliefs, Abdulaziz saw providing advice (*nasiha*) to the rulers as a religious duty (*wajib*). It was through advice and not confrontation, he half-heartedly argued, that clerics could best ensure that rulers fulfilled their responsibilities in a manner that conformed to religion and safeguarded the well-being of the community (*umma*). That Al Saud regularly disobeyed the "word of God and his prophet" was not lost on him. Neither were the bitter rivalries among the ruling classes. But if Abdulaziz feared the repercussions of opposing those in power, he was terrified by the alternative to a regime led by Al Saud. Surely the clerical class that had for decades done the bidding of Al Saud would not fare well in a post–Al Saud state not run by one of their own. Like many clerics, Abdulaziz patiently yet begrudgingly advised the rulers in the hope that a more opportune moment would present itself, one more sympathetic to and in support of the rule of clerics.

For Abdulaziz and his colleagues, that moment came in the spring of 2011. The Arab uprisings that began in North Africa and subsequently led to the overthrow of several Arab leaders unsettled Arabia's rulers. The loss of staunchly pro-Saudi presidents in Tunisia, Egypt, and Yemen threatened Al Saud's geopolitical, economic, security, and cultural interests in the region. Only a week after the January 2011 revolution in Egypt, Saudi Arabia sent a delegation of bureaucrats and archive managers to Cairo to meet with the Supreme Council of Culture and its secretary general, the interim minister of culture.[2] The regime was anxious that Egypt's postrevolutionary government would abandon the protocol that King Faisal had signed with Anwar al-Sadat in the early 1970s. The protocol ensured a moratorium on mid-twentieth-century Saudi records housed in Egypt's state and national archives. The delegation sought to reaffirm Egyptian-Saudi cultural relations and ensure that the agreement on access to information between the two countries remained intact despite potential changes in the power structure. Getting access to historiographical sources of the events of the 1950s and 1960s was simply nonnegotiable for the Saudi regime, and the Darah worked closely with Egyptian archivists to ensure the records remained inaccessible.

The emergence of mass popular forms of Arab solidarity, reminiscent of the popular politics of the mid-twentieth century and those following the 1991 Gulf War, promised to alter the social landscape in Saudi Arabia. As neighboring Bahrainis took to the streets on February 14, 2011, a heightened state of anxiety prevailed among the highest echelons of power in Riyadh. Beyond the corridors of power, the reaction was different. Almost overnight, the Saudi blogosphere was replete with excitement, hope, and the promise of political possibility. By early March 2011, Saudi Arabians from all walks of life were calling for their own countrywide "day of rage" to demand political participation, social and economic justice, equal development, employment opportunities, and an end to corruption.[3] Those members of the religio-political opposition movements of the 1990s who had given up their activism and joined the regime's postwar cultural redevelopment project, and years later, Abdullah's post-2003 National Dialogue program of the liberal period (*infitah*), were now split.[4] Some maintained that reform within the system was still the best way to nonviolently effect change, especially given the regime's repressive history. Others became more critical of their own roles in supporting exclusivist and narrow regime goals by operating strictly within the bounds delineated by those in power. For them, the Arab uprisings were evidence that reform was futile. They would join oppositional efforts and try to pressure the regime in more confrontational ways.

Abdullah's regime responded to these efforts by (re)criminalizing protests and imposing heavy fines and prison terms for sharing protest-related information or photographs. The most powerful men in the kingdom—Abdullah, Sultan, Nayif, and Salman—set their differences aside and quietly mobilized their secular and religious forces to drum up support across the country. They visited the political and economic elites as well as powerful tribes to ensure their continued allegiance. Importantly, security forces and intelligence officers canvassed urban and suburban areas and monitored all social and online activities. They arrested hundreds of citizens in the first two weeks of March alone, and hundreds more in the ensuing months. They intimidated scores of others who had intended to participate in the protests. For Abdulaziz and other clerics, this was the moment they had been waiting for. They believed they could regain their privileges and foreground religion in everyday life in return for supporting Al Saud against mounting criticism and opposition. They acquiesced to the orders they received from the rulers.

The country's senior ulama issued a statement a week before the planned March 15, 2011, "day of rage" supporting the ruling family and denouncing all forms of political protest as Western imports.[5] Using verses from the Quran, they advised Saudi Arabians to communicate peacefully with the rulers and provide them with advice so the rulers could implement reforms accordingly. During Friday sermons, mosque prayer leaders across the country preached the same message of political loyalty they received from the Ministry of Islamic Affairs in Riyadh. Those who did not were intimidated, arrested, or replaced. Clerics cautioned that protesting against the political leaders was not only a punishable crime but also sacrilegious. By 2011, the religious opposition—the Sahwa and its splinter groups as well as other Islamist movements—still presented the most serious challenge to Al Saud's authority. The regime thus used the prayer leaders to spread the warning far and wide: they would not deviate from the official message the way many had during the Gulf War. Mosques were the only spaces where gathering was legal. The regime sought to prevent them from becoming breeding grounds for political opposition and organizing. On a weekly basis, security forces—often undercover—surrounded and infiltrated certain mosques in which they suspected political activity. They crushed many plans to protest following Friday prayers.

The state security apparatus succeeded in preventing mass protests and breaking up the budding forms of solidarity that were emerging across sectarian, regional, class, and gender divides. It resorted to unbridled violence in the Eastern Province, where the local Shi'a population was nonetheless able to sustain peaceful protests for at least four years. The religious establishment, which had long lost credibility among many believers and nonbelievers, did little by way of preventing people from expressing dissent. Effectively, the clerics and the discourse they promoted covered up for the systemic violence that the security forces unleashed against citizens in the latest wave of popular opposition. By downplaying the massive security measures and highlighting the religious foundation of the state, the rulers sought to show the world that they were legitimate and popular leaders because they ruled according to "religious law," unlike other, "secular" Arab regimes. They also wanted to use their purported credentials as protectors of Islam and the two holy places in order to dismiss political opponents either as "secularists" or "fifth columns" who took their order directly from foreign powers such as Iran. The discursive performance was meant to publicly counter the domestic Islamist opposition. In reality, it was the security arm of the regime that had, as always, safeguarded the monarchy.

In the process of supporting Al Saud, the religious establishment did not regain the privileges and powers it had lost in the 1990s. On the contrary, as Abdulaziz lamented, the religious establishment's intellectuals and foot soldiers simply played a disciplinary and surveillance role like other state functionaries and employees. They continued to do so, even as the rulers reminded them that it was the secular leadership that decided the country's fate and the place of religion in it, and no one else. A sick King Abdullah even publicized this stance through his son, Mit'ib, in 2013. According to Mit'ib, the king "stressed the importance of national dialogue as well as the need for religious dialogue, but that it is also equally important for religion not to interfere in politics."[6] In fact, while Mit'ib reiterated his father's message that religion had no role to play in politics, Saudi Arabia's security forces were cracking down on members of the religious establishment who had misunderstood the rulers' orders following the 2011 mobilizations as a sign of dependence and power.

The Custodian of the Two Holy Mosques' message that religion and politics could not mix was broadcast on every major local and regional media outlet, without any significant official or popular reaction. This would not have been possible, let alone during a time of widespread popular discontent, if the religious establishment had any power. It was a turning point for Abdulaziz and others like him, who only then realized the extent to which the regime was willing to publicly pursue the marginalization of religion from the state (*tahmish al-din min al-dawla*). Abdullah's regime continued to pay lip service to the importance of Islam. It then used religion as a guise to justify arresting those who disobeyed any of its orders. The state, after all, was always open to hearing advice (*nasiha*), or "morally corrective criticism."[7] Confrontation and criticism were therefore not justified or tolerated. That the Saudi rulers have a history of not heeding *nasiha* did not matter. Despite the selective invocation of religion, it was clear that the state no longer relied on Islamic authority. It continued to institutionalize its approach to religion and to rely instead on Al Saud's secular history to inform political processes and the territorialization of history. As Talal Asad observes: "It is precisely in a secular state—which is supposed to be totally separated from religion—that it is essential for state law to define, again and again, what genuine religion is, and where its boundaries should properly be. In other words, the state is not that separate. Paradoxically, modern politics cannot really be separated from religion as the vulgar version of secularism argues it should be—with religion having its own sphere and politics its own. The state (a political entity/realm) has the function of defining the acceptable public face of 'religion.'"[8] A form of secularization had already taken shape, and the self-ascribed Islamic state was beginning to publicly delineate the proper bounds of religion and religious forces without much concern for a backlash. The archive wars, and the shift to secularized forms of politics in Saudi Arabia, began in the 1990s in response to a particular set of political, economic, and social crises. The terrorist attacks in the United States and Saudi Arabia at the turn of the twenty-first century, and the Arab uprisings a decade later, only reinforced the postwar project that some political elites called for.

The belated institutionalization, territorialization, and financialization of secular history accelerated with Salman rising up the ranks of power, becoming minister of defense in November 2011 and crown prince in June 2012. Linking the stability of the state to the secular leadership of Al Saud only four months after Abdullah's comment on the separation of religion from politics, Salman reiterated the importance of Al Saud's history to the "Saudi nation." During a meeting with the Darah's secretary-general Fahd al-Semmari, Salman noted that "the unity of the nation is cemented by the Kingdom's founder King Abdulaziz through the participation of citizens. His mission was carried out by his sons, King Saud, King Faisal, King Khalid and King Fahd. These are the main pillars of the stability, security, and unity that we enjoy in the Kingdom."[9]

Salman's comment underscores the political importance that the regime came to attach to its historiographical self-representation, which only intensified as he ascended the throne in January 2015. Salman, after all, was one of the masterminds of the postwar project. In the past, he had used his personal power, capital, and connections in Riyadh to ensure that the Darah and the Arriyadh Development Authority (ADA) managed archiving and urban planning practices, respectively, in line with his vision of the past and of the ideal future. As king, he was no longer limited to the capital city and had the power to enforce his vision on a national scale. This was possible only once he upended the conventional power-sharing schemes in the kingdom and consolidated his power. Only then was he able to confront other challengers of his vision, including family members, political groups, and popular and establishment religionists. As we have seen, Salman experienced these challenges and "red lines" firsthand in his long tenure as Riyadh governor. He would not let them stand in his way as king. During his reign, the postwar development plan would come to full fruition, with great consequences to both the archive wars that shaped the postwar cultural and urban landscapes and the nature of power in Saudi Arabia. History would yet again elide the violence that undergirds ongoing practices of state formation and the shifting nature of power.

SALMAN'S SAUDI ARABIA

In his fifty-odd years as governor of the capital, Riyadh, Salman had built a reputation as a firm, pragmatic, and uncompromising ruler. He commanded fear from both friend and foe. Salman was instrumental in conceiving the postwar national development plan. As we have seen, the top-down plan promised to overhaul social, economic, and cultural life in the kingdom. It aimed to gradually diminish the power of the religious establishment, foreground the importance of secular dynastic history, and diversify the national economy. There was a lot at stake for those who had theretofore benefited from the status quo. But the beneficiaries were not the only ones who feared the severity of a Salman regime. With Salman holding absolute power, Saudis of all political stripes and socioeconomic classes worried about what Salman's Saudi Arabia would bring, especially as the new king doubled down on his vision for Saudi Arabia.

Salman amassed great power through his prestigious position as governor of Riyadh, long considered the heart of the ruling Al Saud monarchy. The Darah, ADA, and other institutions he oversaw there—largely manned by professionalized graduates of Saudi universities—ran like clockwork. This was a significant feat, considering the history of institutional decentralization as well as incompetence in Saudi Arabia. Together and separately, they worked to implement the regime's postwar vision, even if their scope was restricted to the capital. By the mid-2000s, and especially as the price of oil rose to an all-time high in the aftermath of the US invasion and occupation of Iraq in 2003, many of the economic and cultural plans conceived in the previous decade began to materialize under the framework of the Metropolitan Development Strategy for the Arriyadh Region (MEDSTAR). The strategic development plan was managed by the ADA, through which Salman has engendered new loyal elites, construction moguls, and employees. That sidelining religion was central to the plan provoked the ire of many, not least Islamists and conservatives. But Salman had close ties with the religious establishment, over which he nonetheless exerted great power that he used to manage both clerics and foot soldiers to serve his own agenda.

More than anything, Salman embodied the potential to undermine what many saw as the pillars of Saudi rule: traditional alliances within the ruling family and between the ruling family and the country's economic elites and religious clerics. Even within Al Saud, it is not surprising that many dreaded the prospect of Salman ascending the throne. After all, he was the final arbiter of disputes between members of his family and of transgressions and crimes that they themselves committed. That the "family prison" was located on his estate for decades speaks to the role he occupied within the monarchy. He was known to be ruthless toward those who did not heed his orders or toe his line, a lesson that has served his son and crown prince, Muhammad, rather well. Indeed, many of Muhammad's claims to reform religion, state, and economy in the kingdom are continuations of his father's three-decades-long efforts.

Upon acceding to the throne at the age of seventy-nine, King Salman did just as many had expected and feared. His regime reorganized government and regularly reshuffled top administrators in the bureaucracy. It also espoused an unprecedentedly belligerent foreign policy, the devastating effects of which have been all-too-tangible in Yemen, Syria, Libya, and Qatar. Gone were the days of the more cautious (even if destructive) Saudi foreign policy that characterized the previous few decades. If Salman's reign is marked by the kingdom's muscle flexing abroad, that is equally the case inside the country. Salman's regime went to great lengths to silence all forms of criticism.[10] Not only did it criminalize opposition to the Saudi-Emirati war in Yemen and both countries' belligerent posture toward Qatar.[11] In its first few months in power, the regime also indefinitely detained or disappeared dozens of Saudi intellectuals, activists, religious scholars, and writers. It placed others under house arrest or on no-fly lists. But even as he became king, Salman suffered from mild Alzheimer's disease. He thus increasingly entrusted many functions of the state to his son Muhammad, who has since centralized most powers of the state.[12]

Muhammad is a product of his father's upbringing and political ideologies, even if he has shown himself to be less cautious, discreet, and tactful than the ailing king. He came of age working by his father's side while the latter oversaw the making of the capital into a sprawling metropolis. Immediately after Salman appointed him deputy crown prince in April 2015, the regime began quietly arresting hundreds of citizens, including religious scholars, preachers, writers, journalists, activists, and bureaucrats. These ranged from people who opposed the regime outright to those who called for political, economic, and other reforms, even if within an Al Saud–led state. Those familiar with Saudi regime tactics understood these wide-ranging arrests as punitive and a prelude to unpopular policy changes. The regime wanted to preempt and silence all forms of criticism and dissent.

It was in this broader context of local opposition and foreign-policy failure that Muhammad began to consolidate his economic power in order to strengthen both his political and his financial positions. To start with, his personal wealth paled in comparison to that of his cousins, who had amassed great fortunes when their respective fathers ruled the country as kings (Fahd, 1982–2005, and Abdullah, 2005–2015) and ministers of interior (Nayif, 1975–2012) and defense (Sultan, 1963–2011). Making matters worse, Muhammad came to power at a time of low oil prices. These led to a ballooning budget deficit that saw the regime burn through its foreign-exchange reserves, which shrank by $208 billion between 2014 and 2016 alone.[13] Seeing the financial crisis as his main weakness, Muhammad proceeded to secure control of important economic institutions such as the Saudi Arabian Monetary Agency, the Council of Economic and Development Affairs, and the newly formed Supreme Council of the Saudi Arabian Oil Company (Aramco). Even Aramco, which had largely maintained its autonomy and was shielded from interference by members of the ruling family, came under the control of the rising prince.

Muhammad then began to snub many of the country's traditional economic elites and slowly strip them of their privileges. This was most evident in the contracting sector, where he made it very difficult for the historically dominant construction conglomerates to conduct their business. At times, he canceled existing contracts and transferred them to his own front companies and those of his allies. From early on, Muhammad targeted the Saudi Binladin Group (SBG), long noted for its sheer size, market share, and operations, especially in Mecca and Medina. But SBG was not an easy target. Its long-standing networks extended to the highest echelons of the ruling family as well as throughout various strata of economic elites.

The collapse of an SBG-owned crane in Mecca in September 2015 presented the perfect opportunity to weaken the company, primarily because it resulted in the death of over a hundred people.[14] King Salman quickly halted work on that and other SBG projects in Mecca. A speedy investigation revealed that SBG was only partially responsible for the crane collapse, with stormy weather conditions the main culprit behind the tragic accident. Yet the company paid an unusually heavy price: In the name of anticorruption and reform, the regime prevented SBG from taking on new business and confiscated many of its existing contracts, especially in Mecca and Medina. It then transferred those contracts to front companies linked to the king and his son Muhammad, thereby increasing their share of a lucrative market that had been largely closed off to Salman and his sons. That same month, authorities in Mecca shut down one of the main arteries from Central Mecca to neighboring Mina at the height of the annual pilgrimage (hajj), secretly reserving it for the sole use of a VIP-designated car transporting a member of the ruling family. The resultant stampede killed 769 people according to official Saudi sources, although most independent observers put the estimate closer to 2,400.[15] This was the highest casualty rate for any "accident" in the modern history of the hajj. The regime, however, was not as quick to investigate the incident and pursue the perpetrators. The investigation remained pending years after the incident.

The symbiotic relationship between business-economic and political interests is a common feature of all modern states.[16] It was not limited to Saudi Arabia, let alone SBG or the contracting industry. Since the consolidation of the Saudi state in 1932, and especially during times of economic and political crises, cash-strapped Al Saud regimes have relied on merchant financing for their own survival. This was a central way through which the authoritarian monarchy engendered loyal economic elites, who would reap the benefits of close ties to the regime and finance the state in times of need. In this way, the survival of economic elites was strategically tied to the longevity and enrichment of the regime, which relied on these rival sources of rent, revenue, and financing. The symbiotic relationship was further institutionalized during the regime's consolidation in the 1960s, under King Faisal. It has since characterized economic and political life writ large in the kingdom. Any and all successful business ventures require an alliance with one prince or another to secure permits and avoid intimidation. Those economic elites who attempted to bypass this ritual either have been excluded from new deals or have had existing projects suspended. The regime also used commonly accepted maneuvers such as inflating costs, signing phantom deals, encouraging massive kickbacks, and contravening the law against its economic allies when they fell out of favor, as has been the case with the SBG. This is the stark reality of regime-business relations, which is common knowledge to all in Saudi Arabia.

Muhammad ibn Salman was not so much upending this historical relationship between the regime and economic elites as much as he was shrinking the circle of those who benefited from it—and positioning himself at its center. Not surprisingly, this has created many enemies—both among the economic elites and among their beneficiaries in the ruling family. It is this factor that explains why several of the wealthiest families began to move some of their capital abroad as early as 2015. At the time, the heads of such families—including Bakr Binladin and Saleh Abdullah Kamel—publicly expressed their dissatisfaction with the economic direction that Salman's regime was taking under the tutelage of Muhammad.

As deputy crown prince, Muhammad continued to tighten his grip on the contracting industry. In April 2016, he announced the ambitious Vision 2030.[17] Much like the still-operational MEDSTAR, which inspired it, Vision 2030 centers on the reorganization of the economic, infrastructural, social, and cultural spheres. Focusing on diversifying and streamlining the Saudi economy, it lauded the role that a predominantly young Saudi population would allegedly play in achieving this vision. In a slight diversion from MEDSTAR, Vision 2030 touted the new, open lifestyle it would enable, which would better accommodate Saudi youth. In it, the regime expresses the expectation of "increase[d] household spending on cultural and entertainment activities inside the kingdom from the current level of 2.9% to 6%."[18] Yet the regime has cynically deployed this seeming accommodation to "Saudi youth" only to legitimize its authoritarian schemes. Muhammad has not consulted Saudi citizens or studied the needs of a population whose middle class is shrinking and whose poverty rates are increasing. Instead, the regime has predominantly relied on foreign consulting firms such as McKinsey, notorious for severely inflating its costs and producing plans so disconnected from reality on the ground as to render them useless.[19] The voices of the very youths whom Muhammad claims to be saving have been ignored. Many were even silenced when questioning how Vision 2030 could achieve its promise of increased employment opportunities and better living conditions given that thousands of Saudis actually lost their jobs in 2016–2017 alone. Citizens and potential investors were equally alarmed in the fall of 2017 when the regime announced that it would not balance the budget by 2020, as promised, instead postponing the deadline to do so until 2023.[20]

By mid-2017, as Muhammad's economic and political ventures came under heightened scrutiny, he opened new fronts in his war against Saudi Arabians, often using "development" as a form of warfare. For instance, he began a new war against the Shi'i inhabitants of 'Awamiyya in the Eastern Province. 'Awamiyya was home to the renowned Shi'i cleric and Al Saud critic Shaykh Nimr al-Nimr, whom the Saudis executed in January 2016.[21] It was also home to many of the opposition activists who took to the streets to protest the regime starting in 2011.[22] In early May 2017, the regime began demolishing al-Musawara, an old neighborhood in 'Awamiyya and home to three thousand Saudi Arabians, mere months after unilaterally announcing its intentions to "redevelop" the neighborhood. Without consulting the people of the town, and under an almost-complete media blackout, the regime ordered residents to evacuate, providing them with temporary yet inadequate housing in a nearby town. It then sent in contractors with their bulldozers to demolish the neighborhood. Security forces used live fire against peaceful protesters who had refused to evacuate their homes, killing several of them. Armed confrontations ensued, and the regime escalated its campaign by shelling the neighborhood and killing twelve to twenty-five people before the last inhabitant managed to escape.[23]

In demolishing and reconstructing the town, the regime would kill two birds with one stone: it would uproot some of the most radical anti–Al Saud activists while opening up a new investment frontier to Salman's companies and those of his allies. Such private-public endeavors are not new. As with previous Saudi rulers who regularly blurred the line between public and private for their own personal enrichment, Salman's regime relied on such ventures, especially during times of financial duress—in keeping with the corporate underpinnings that have sustained the Saudi state since its inception. And in this case, the Eastern Province provided a particularly lucrative opportunity. Throughout the twentieth century, most of the Shi'i towns in the east were actively ignored by the construction drive of the Saudi state. These underdeveloped towns now constitute new investment frontiers for a cash-hungry regime that at once sought to assert its control over Shi'i neighborhoods and make them more legible for security purposes. Indeed, this was not simply about sectarianism or flexing the regime's muscles in the face of growing regional challenges. Driven by financial motivations, the regime nonetheless justified its military assault on people and infrastructure in the name of counterterrorism.

In the past, the scale and mode of such violence has usually been limited to Saudi Arabia's Shi'a population. But the belligerence of Muhammad—who became crown prince on June 21, 2017—was not. As the bombs dropped on al-Musawara, with the aim of "redeveloping" the town, the regime also intensified its silencing campaign across the country. It arrested hundreds more Saudis who were still skeptical of regime policies or called for serious reforms. Those included writers, intellectuals, bureaucrats, activists, clerics, and preachers: not only were they arrested but their families also were regularly terrorized through armed house searches, if not direct threats. Several cultural producers who simply refused to voice their support for domestic and regional policies met a similar fate. For the latter, remaining silent came at great cost. The regime, however, especially bore down on the Sahwa, which by 2017 was still the most popular of the (Sunni) Islamist movements in Saudi Arabia. The crown prince blamed the Sahwa for all of Saudi Arabia's ills. Using social media to call for constitutionalism, civil rights, and political reform, the Sahwa targeted Muhammad's corruption, economic policies, and unwillingness to embark on political reform. Sahwa followers saw these as further disenfranchising the Saudi population, its youth in particular. It was also around this same time that the Saudi and Emirati regimes escalated tensions with Qatar, accusing the neighboring state of supporting the Muslim Brotherhood—which has historically challenged the legitimacy of establishment Wahhabism and the Al Saud monarchy—and what they viewed as fundamentalist Islamist groups in the region. This belligerence quickly turned into a full-blown embargo.

As security forces intensified the countrywide silencing campaign, the crown prince convened hundreds of foreign dignitaries, investors, business leaders, journalists, and public relations experts, among other speakers, at the first meeting of the Future Investment Initiative, held on October 24–26, 2017, at the Ritz-Carlton in Riyadh.[24] There, Muhammad announced his plans to build a $500 billion high-tech city on the northwestern coast of Saudi Arabia. The prince pitched this utopian, sustainable "gigacity," or Neom, as the solution to the country's ailments but also as a lucrative global investment opportunity and socio-technical experiment rooted in "religious tolerance" and sustainable development.[25] It was the beating heart of the prince's Vision 2030. Set on the pristine northern desert coast of the Red Sea, the proposed economic zone was marketed predominantly to investors as an unprecedented global hub and the "world's most ambitious project . . . for a new way of life." The earmarked location remains "unspoiled" today because large parts of it were designated a military zone in the early 1960s and closed off to civilians, given its proximity to Israel as well as Egypt, at the time Saudi Arabia's prime adversary. It mattered little to the cheering investors that the Saudi regime had expropriated this very land in the 1960s without compensating those who claimed ownership over it or that the regime planned to dispossess the few thousands who remained of their homes and properties.

The site allotted to Neom reflects the changing geopolitical realities and a desired shift in the center of economic power away from the oil-rich Persian Gulf in the east to the Red Sea in the west. It is meant to signify a shift away from oil production but also one in which neighboring Israel is no longer considered an adversary or a threat. This is not surprising. Informal relations between Saudi Arabia and Israel can be traced back to the 1960s, when Israel militarily assisted King Faisal's regime in his proxy war against Gamal Abdel Nasser in Yemen (1962–1970).[26] These relations further improved under King Abdullah. During this period, Saudi-Israeli relations were becoming more of an unspoken reality. In 2006, Abdullah's regime blatantly sided with Israel in its war on Lebanon, in which 1,109 were killed—the vast majority of them civilians—4,400 were injured, and more than one million were displaced.[27] It also supported Israel in its brutal wars on Gaza in 2008–2009, 2012, and 2014.[28] It was during Abdullah's reign that officials from both countries began expressing cordiality toward each other in public for the first time. Such overtures have only increased and become more official since Salman ascended the throne. As a matter of fact, since announcing Neom, the regime has embarked on an aggressive media campaign, using the country's most renowned cultural producers, to pave the way for the normalization of ties with Israel and to further silence any criticism of the regime's policies.[29]

Neom thus promised a geopolitical restructuring, and not just technological, cultural, and economic rewards. The optics are seductive, not least to a global audience of investors, politicians, planners, and cultural producers, who are more interested in pursuing profits and personal gain than in acknowledging the forms of violence that have conventionally undergirded similar reformist claims in Saudi Arabia. In so doing, such an audience reinforces Saudi rulers' own exclusion of citizens and, like them, mobilizes "the Saudi youth"—this elusive and allegedly homogeneous group—only when it benefits their own interests. Few, if any, have expressed a desire to understand, let alone acknowledge, the diverse lived realities, needs, and political affinities of people in Saudi Arabia before uncritically perpetuating the regime's ostentatious, top-down narratives, claims, and plans.

The regime's pervasive disregard for people in Saudi Arabia is not new. But given the difficulties of entering the kingdom, coupled with the heightened surveillance of, and punitive measures against, popular opinion and social media in general, the experiences, desires, and opinions of Saudi Arabians have been absent in all but the most critical of analyses. With the crown prince adopting so many policies in the name of Saudi Arabians, and youth in particular, it is all the more urgent to discern where citizens stand in all this, even if they do not factor into the calculations of those in power and their global allies. It is a stretch of the imagination, for example, to conclude—as many have—that normalization with Israel would have much traction among citizens just because of the heightened state of sectarian, anti-Iranian, and anti-Shi'a sentiments in the country. But this is what the regime wants the world to believe. It is one thing for people's interests to converge with those of the Israeli state on some policies. It is another to then assume that fear of Iranian power trumps both the political affinities that Saudi Arabians feel toward Palestinians and widespread Saudi opposition to Israeli settler colonialism.[30]

Similarly, Saudi Arabians covet the economic security, access to entertainment, and lifting of social restrictions that the crown prince has promised. That does not translate to support for the regime, or for the crown prince in particular. Economic indicators were never sufficient measures of people's political desires, as some theoretical models such as rentier-state theory would like us to believe. According to the latter, the regime has historically pacified Saudi Arabian citizens with oil wealth in what is better known as the "authoritarian bargain," the equivalent to "no taxation, no representation." Yet as we have seen, since the creation of the state, Saudi Arabians have demanded political participation, either within the Al Saud regime or in opposition to it, regardless of the state of the economy, so much so that responding to various political mobilizations in the twentieth century came to shape the Saudi state form. The people of Saudi Arabia have always wanted a say in political as well as economic, social, and cultural life. To think otherwise is at worst to reify regime narratives about Saudi Arabians not having political will or sensibilities and at best to be disconnected from everyday lived realities there.

Contemporary urban planning practices, such as those in Neom, offer a window into the regime's priorities and its disregard for popular will. For many, it is not clear how Neom differs from the financial and economic cities that Saudi Arabia planned during the reign of King Abdullah, some of which are still under construction.[31] Like Neom, these earlier megacities—in Riyadh, Rabigh, Jizan, or Medina—aimed to diversify and grow the economy while raising the standard of living for Saudis. But none has achieved these objectives. At the time, Saudi planners working on these projects predicted the failure of these cities, given their stated goals.[32] They still do today. Indeed, the planning of these financial and economic cities, as with so many other large-scale developments, has been scarred by corruption and ineptitude, a fact that is not lost on Saudi Arabians, not then, and not now. Such city planning has relied on the very same experts and consulting firms that the current crown prince commissions for all of his projects, and through which he promises to "salvage" these economic cities that "did not realize their potential."[33] As such, cities like Neom do not have the needs of the Saudi Arabian citizen in mind. They are driven by the rulers' legitimation politics, the profit motivations of the ultra-wealthy, and the requirements of global capital and cheap labor.

Unlike earlier megacities that Abdullah's regime sponsored, Neom has the added layer of being driven by an unpopular ruler who, facing domestic opposition, foreign-policy failures, and tenuous financial circumstances, must garner global support to ensure his own survival, both politically and financially. To increase investor confidence, Muhammad has promised that he will run state affairs differently. A week after announcing Neom, on November 4, 2017, he revealed an anticorruption campaign that in its first two days arrested princes, bureaucrats, military leaders, and business tycoons. Rival cousins such as Mit'ib ibn Abdullah and Muhammad ibn Nayif; Minister of Economy and Planning Adel Fakih; and heads of some of the wealthiest families, such as Bakr Binladin and Saleh Abdullah Kamel, were not spared. Muhammad used the media to broadcast these high-profile arrests in order to showcase his supposed commitment to fighting corruption—but also to scare the elites and the rest of the population into submission. Since then, the regime has quietly arrested thousands of Saudi Arabians in a campaign that has left most in the country terrorized.[34]

Saudi Arabians have long supported a crackdown on corruption. They have called for exactly that over the decades, and increasingly so during the reign of

King Abdullah. But many of the arrests that Muhammad has ordered have more to do with the centralization of his economic and political power and increasing his personal wealth than with rooting out corruption. Indeed, some business tycoons threatened to move more of their capital abroad only months before they were arrested. Having to deal with a struggling economy and a cash-strapped regime, the crown prince simply could not afford to allow further capital flight. He has deployed all means—legal, political, and coercive—to force these billionaires to give up significant portions of their wealth in return for their freedom.[35] At the same time, it is business as usual for many notoriously corrupt individuals and conglomerates, especially those that sided with the crown prince or turned a blind eye to his policies. So even as some Saudis celebrated the belated arrest of those who have pillaged the country's resources with great impunity, the corruption and nepotism of the current regime is not lost on them. While investors expressed concern about the viability of investing in such a volatile Saudi Arabia and the risk of meeting a fate like that of the country's once esteemed tycoons and investors, the crown prince was not worried. He was banking on the passage of time and a return to a "stable" state of affairs. He also knew well that the business community had no choice but to work with him if they were to maintain their financial interests in the kingdom.

Through a highly selective anticorruption campaign that targeted princes, bureaucrats, businessmen, religious scholars, and activists, Salman's regime accomplished several goals. It disempowered many of the economic elites and their Al Saud allies and expropriated their sources of income. Muhammad has shattered notions of consensus as well as the long-standing balance of power among the top ruling members of the monarchy, upending the traditional balance and cutting historically powerful branches of Al Saud down to size. While the latter may not have been able to prevent the crown prince from taking the throne if it were the king's wish, they could have presented many obstacles to the centralization of his power and the execution of the regime's national policies. After detaining several media moguls and investors, Muhammad privileged his immediate family's own media company and controlled the narrative coming out of Saudi Arabia. He also relied on Washington-based think tanks, lobbyists, and public relations firms to whitewash his crimes in Yemen and inside Saudi Arabia.[36] These globally portray him as a modernizer and reformer. His personal branding campaigns and tours in the United States and the United Kingdom in March 2018 were not even tarnished by Saudi Arabia's arrest of several renowned women's rights activists on the eve of and following the lifting of the ban on women driving in June 2018.[37] Even reports that some of these activists were tortured while in detention did not shake the image of the young prince worldwide.[38]

It was another act of Saudi brutality that unprecedentedly brought to the global forefront the violence and oppression that Muhammad unleashed on Saudi Arabians: the murder of journalist Jamal Khashoggi at the Saudi Arabian consulate in Istanbul on October 2, 2018. Khashoggi was a longtime Al Saud loyalist turned mild critic of the crown prince. His murder instilled fear among Saudi Arabians everywhere, not least because the negative attention it received globally did not translate to serious repercussions for the Saudi regime. Indeed, instilling a regime of terror will be a lasting legacy of Salman's Saudi Arabia. Not only are common practices such as advice, or *nasiha*, no longer tolerated, but the clerical class as a whole has also been overwhelmingly defeated and silenced, earning its members the moniker the "Sultan's clerics" (*'ulama' al-sultan*).[39] As for the Sahwa movement, many of its leaders were jailed, exiled, or co-opted. By May 2019, 'Aidh al-Qarni, a prominent Sahwa member, apologized on national television for all that the Sahwa stood for and for opposing the government. He proclaimed his support for the "moderate Islam" that the crown prince called for.[40] Salman's victory over the domestic opposition, and the religious sphere more broadly, was complete. Despite unprecedented global criticism of the Saudi regime, and Crown Prince Muhammad in particular, the world's political and economic elites lent the regime their unconditional support. If anything, many problematically view the regime's policies, especially the sidelining of religion and the religious bureaucrats, as a move in the right modernizing direction. Yet again, the political aspirations that Saudi Arabians have long fought for, and their dreams of leading better, more prosperous, and egalitarian lives, have been violently (if temporarily) crushed with great impunity and with almost unflinching and widespread global support. With the ancien régime fully purged and the opposition crushed, the field was clear for the regime to implement Salman's vision for Saudi Arabia on a national scale.

THE ARCHIVAL LANDSCAPE

As Salman and his son dominated the archival landscape and pacified the opposition, and the reconfiguration of religion in politics was complete, they accelerated the implementation of the post–Gulf War plan, which entered a new phase. The institutional rivalries, power fiefdoms, and private interests that had opposed, hindered, or capitalized on the archive wars that gripped the cultural and urban development fields since the 1990s were either eliminated or pacified. State archives and urban development authorities, as with all state institutions, came under Crown Prince Muhammad's unbridled control. The regime either created new institutions or restructured a handful of existing ones to oversee government functions and ensure that they all worked in tandem toward the same goals specified by Vision 2030. The attendant heightened centralization has stripped most institutions of their prerogatives, delegating all decision making power to select government bodies under the direct control of the crown prince, who primarily heeded the advice of foreign consulting firms.[41] The islands of sovereignty that marked twentieth-century Saudi power had become centralized under Muhammad's firm grasp.

Historical legitimation and economic diversification through archives, the built environment, and tourism became national priorities and received the political and financial support they lacked in the past. As king, Salman prioritized archive making and turned his attention to his long-held goal of establishing a national archive. He began with the National Center for Documents and Archives, located at the Council of Ministers compound.[42] The king ordered its relocation to the Royal Palace, where he resided, and changed its English name to the National Center for Archives and Records (NCAR).[43] He placed it under the supervision of none other than Fahd al-Semmari, the Darah's secretary-general, who was promoted to adviser to the king.[44] His regime then proceeded to consolidate its archival power, bringing all state archives, even those outside Riyadh, under the purview of the NCAR and issuing new archiving regulations to be universally executed.[45] During Abdullah's reign, the archival operation was primarily a spectacle for appropriating and centralizing documents under the guise of saving Arabia's material history. With Salman at the helm, the reconfigured national archive pursued the archival function to its logical end: it digitized those government records that were deemed "safe" and that did not counter state logics and made them available for researchers.[46] Al-Semmari finally received the backing he needed to pacify the institutional archive wars, oversee the development of the national archive, and continue the work of the Darah. He also announced the launch of several programs at the Darah to "modernize the field of history" in the kingdom.[47] The NCAR, with the creation of national digital archives that it prophesied, was central to Vision 2030, whose main goal is to streamline and modernize government functions; diversify the national economy; and strengthen national identity.

Having restructured the national archive and put it in the service of Vision 2030, Salman proceeded to pacify institutions that had stood in the way of his plans in the past, starting with the historically powerful Ministry of Finance. To ensure the execution of the capital-intensive Vision 2030, Salman moved the country's sovereign wealth fund, the Public Investment Fund (PIF), from the Ministry of Finance to the newly formed Council of Development and Economic Affairs (CEDA). The latter replaced the Supreme Economic Council. Placed under Crown Prince Muhammad's direct control, CEDA was responsible for all of Vision 2030's moving parts and would administer PIF with an eye to funding the vision's projects. Through CEDA and PIF, Muhammad oversaw all urban planning projects in Saudi Arabia. Those include ones in Riyadh, such as the heritage production projects. Several of them have since opened their doors, such as the Turaif District in Dir'iyya, which, according to al-Semmari, was an emotional moment for King Salman, who worked on the project for more than two decades.[48] They also included the remaking of the King Abdullah Financial District—which was subsumed into Vision 2030 in 2018—and Qiddiya, an $8 billion hub for entertainment, sports, and culture right outside of Riyadh.[49] The ADA, once Salman's prized institution, seems to have fallen by the wayside, with foreign consultancies and companies now responsible for all aspects of these development projects, from planning to execution.

Mecca, too, fell within the spectacular scope of Vision 2030, which would see the Grand Mosque undergo yet another expansion. On June 1, 2018, King Salman ordered the formation of the Royal Commission for Mecca City and Holy Sites, and a year later, the establishment of the Holy Sites Company for Development. Both operated under the umbrella of the PIF and fell under the direct control of the crown prince. With the Saudi Binladin Group defeated and conventional stakeholders marginalized, the two institutions aimed to centralize the redevelopment of Mecca and eschew the multiple rivalries that were a feature of the city's urban planning.[50] But the Holy Sites Company for Development also usurped all existing redevelopment projects around the Grand Mosque, to the chagrin of Saudi Arabian contractors. They had believed Vision 2030's promises of privatization and that the "Public Investment Fund will not compete with the private sector."⁵¹ They had hoped to benefit from these contracts and the $2.1 billion the city is expected to generate starting in 2030.⁵² By all accounts, Salman continued in Fahd and Abdullah's footsteps, paying little heed to (what remained of) the central district's material heritage, prioritizing profit and global construction trends above all else. While the hypercommodification of Mecca continued, with the stated goal of increasing the number of foreign visitors to Mecca from eight million to fifteen million per year, Salman's regime, unlike previous ones, did not rely on the traditional economic elites or attempt to strengthen ties with them through the development industry. His son, and the institutions directly under his control, directly managed the projects and reaped the financial benefits.

Salman's regime now had free rein in Mecca, whose few dissenting clerical voices were all but silenced. In fact, Mecca's clerics, like their counterparts elsewhere in the kingdom, were in the unabashed service of the king and his son. One can expect little resistance to the state's redevelopment plans, no less in an environment in which the once-independent position of imam of Mecca's Grand Mosque was mobilized in the service of the regime. In June 2018, Shaykh Abdulrahman al-Sudais unprecedentedly exalted the crown prince as a religious modernizer or "renewer" (*muhaddith* or *mujaddid*). In so doing, he "implicitly compar[ed] the crown prince to Caliph Umar," who was labeled as such by the Prophet Muhammad himself.⁵³ Mere months later, footage of Muhammad ibn Salman walking on top of the Kaaba—with al-Sudais and a few other companions—circulated on television and social media. No Saudi ruler had previously undertaken such an act, let alone been filmed during one. It is even believed that the prophet himself never climbed atop the Kaaba. This was, for Shaykh Abdulaziz (with whom I started this chapter) and so many others like him, the nail in the coffin of Islam in Saudi Arabia, one that would likely engender new opposition movements inside the kingdom.

With cultural and urban redevelopment well under way in Riyadh and Mecca, planning for other regions in the kingdom was brought in line with the national development plan during the last years of King Abdullah's reign and accelerated thereafter. Just as tourism was at the heart of the postwar plan, it was also pivotal to the success of Vision 2030. Muhammad thus gave the plan his undivided attention. Instead of supporting his brother Sultan, who headed Saudi Arabia's tourism and antiquities sector for almost two decades, Muhammad appropriated all the existing heritage sites as his own. In 2018, he replaced his brother with Ahmad Aqil al-Khatib as head of the Saudi Commission for Tourism and National Heritage. Muhammad then placed all cultural and heritage sites in the kingdom under the tutelage of the newly formed Ministry of Culture, headed by Prince Badr ibn Farhan Al-Saud.[54] The ministry's mission was to ensure that all cultural projects, which centered not just on heritage sites but on a diverse array of entertainment activities, were in line with Vision 2030. The country's new blueprint aimed to increase tourism spending by $18 billion from 2019 to 2020 alone. It would "dedicate 23 national transformation initiatives for the tourism sector" and "will see the increase in the number of festivals and events from 300 to 500 by 2020."[55]

Cultural and urban redevelopment reflects the material culture and built environment of Salman's Saudi Arabia, which enshrined his view of the past, present, and future. In these ways, space, and sites of secular heritage such as the archive broadly construed, became the regime's preferred battlegrounds. These battlegrounds constituted one register of violence upon which the regime operated. The regular erasure of historical voices, the enclosure of primary source records, and the destruction and reconstruction of spaces became the field for forging a collective Saudi Arabian identity, one that shapes and is constantly shaped by dynamics and various forms of profit and speculation in Saudi Arabia. Archivists, historians, clerics, planners, contractors, and other workers who had internally slowed down or created bottlenecks to archival consolidation since the 1990s were now either pacified or too intimidated to resist the state project. It remains to be seen whether they would fully comply with regime orders and whether Salman would force people, as well as government and private institutions, to relinquish all historical documents in their possession. It also remains to be seen whether the Aramco archive will succumb to the new power structure and be subsumed into the national archive now that the crown prince has, unprecedentedly for a member of the ruling family, begun to supervise the work of the oil company through the newly formed Supreme Council of the Saudi Arabian Oil Company. The archival landscape, both institutionally and spatially, has for the most part succumbed to Salman's decades-long national vision. With archives and the built environment conforming to the official historical narrative and revised national goals, the regime began to appropriate and repackage histories it once considered threatening. Al-Kairanawi and other South Asian religious scholars; Hijazi nationalists and literary critics like Muhammad Surur Sabban; and Arab nationalists, Abdullah al-Tariqi among them, were rebranded as national heroes.[56] It was a drawn-out and multitiered war that Salman seems to have won.

A MOST MODERN STATE

The material politics of the Saudi state and its expression in the archival and spatial configuration of official history are complex, multitiered, and multisited, as this book has shown. They include different generations of the ruling family, members of the religious establishment, Aramco employees, bureaucrats, experts, ordinary citizens, and cultural producers, located across Arabia and beyond. Each set of actors was motivated by diverse political, cultural, and economic logics, yet they all largely labored within the bounds of the regime's post–Gulf War agenda to reshape modern Saudi power, society, culture, and economy, with great consequences to power relations and social structures in Saudi Arabia. On the one hand, the regime employed the production of material history, as I have argued here, to engage, centralize, and pacify political opposition. On the other hand, the regime territorialized its own vision of the past to monumentalize Al Saud's history and diversify the economy at the expense of Arabia's other political, economic, religious, and historical formations. The tensions we encountered in the postwar project of remaking history and space reveal the fragility of authoritarian states, the multiplicity and plurality of state and regime, and the complexity and dynamism of modern power and how it manifests.

The regime's attempts at archival foreclosure—which reached into Saudi Arabia's state, corporate, and personal archives, as well as national archives in Egypt, the United States, and elsewhere—were central to the survival of the regime, which has based its monopoly over power and natural resources on its dubious historical claims. Eliding Arabia's histories from the permissible realm of discursive and material formations obscured political, social, and cultural life in the kingdom. After all, such pasts went against official regime representations of supposedly conservative and docile populations who supported the dictators that have ruled them and are also pacified by distributive wealth. In strictly policing and institutionalizing limits to knowledge production on Saudi Arabia, the state has shaped how we have come to know, and to not know, the place, further marginalizing the country within academic and popular analyses. Since September 11, 2001, these analyses have doubled down on viewing the country through the lens of religion, security, rentierism, and geopolitics. They continue to depict it as a hinterland without history, culture, and politics despite the place that Arabia has assumed in the global order. In doing so, they nurture the "desert Orientalism" that is prevalent in the Levant and North Africa.

In this book, I reveal the ways in which official history and its territorialization in the built environment were produced with political, economic, and religious interests and rivalries in mind and in the service of state formation. I do so in order to discern the ways in which frameworks of knowledge production, dissemination, and territorialization have not only obscured lived realities in Saudi Arabia but also contributed to their very production. Although projects of knowledge production are curated and constructed, they are marked by fissures and compromises and inevitably leave behind traces, fragments, and remains. These allow the narration of histories that are not sanctioned by the curators—as *Archive Wars* does—partial and selective as these histories ultimately are, to end with the quote that opened this book. At heart, unfolding how violence, struggle, and contestation—and their elision—are constitutive of history and history making reveals archive wars as central to transforming all territories, not just Saudia Arabia, into modern states.

Notes

PREFACE

1. *Okaz* (Saudi Arabia), September 6, 2004, emphasis mine.
2. Charles M. Sennott, "Saudi Schools Fuel Anti-US Anger," *Boston Globe*, March 4, 2002, http://archive.boston.com/news/packages/underattack/news/driving_a_wedge/part2.shtml; Steven Stalinsky, "Preliminary Overview—Saudi Arabia's Education System," Middle East Media and Research Institute (MEMRI), Special Report No. 12, December 20, 2002, https://www.memri.org; Vicky O'Hara, "Saudi Textbooks Still Teach Hate, Group Says," *National Public Radio*, May 24, 2006, https://www.npr.org/templates/story/story.php?storyId=5426633; and "ADL Analysis Finds Saudi School Textbooks Still Teach Anti-Semitic Incitement and Hatred," ADL, November 19, 2018, https://www.adl.org/news/press-releases/adl-analysis-finds-saudi-school-textbooks-still-teach-anti-semitic-incitement.
3. Record 49365, Royal Order, No. MB/1600/7, Presidency of Council of Ministers, December 14, 2004, Institute of Public Administration (IPA) Archives, Riyadh.
4. Madawi Al-Rasheed, *A History of Saudi Arabia* (London: Cambridge University Press, 2002); and Jörg Matthias Determann, *Historiography in Saudi Arabia: Globalization and the State in the Middle East* (London: I. B. Tauris, 2014).

INTRODUCTION

1. News of this incident circulated in Saudi Arabia's archive industry the next day, and Saudi Arabian and Egyptian document traders who bought some of these

documents confirmed the story. I traveled to Mecca and conducted interviews with Saudi Binladin Group site managers of the Grand Mosque Expansion Project (Mashru' Tawsi'at al-Haram) on January 17–25, 2011.

2. Yahya ibn Junaydh (director of the King Faisal Center for Research and Islamic Studies until 2016), interview with author, Riyadh, March 21, 2011; and Salih al-'Ubudi (archive and manuscripts director at the King Fahd National Library), interview with author, Riyadh, February 27, 2011.

3. Author interviews with archive managers in Riyadh, January 2010–June 2011. Also see "Darat al-malik Abdulaziz taktashif watha'iq wa makhtutat muzawarra" [The Darah discovers forged documents and manuscripts], *Watha'iq al-Khalij* (May 2008), 6.

4. Muhammad ibn Abd al-Wahhab was born in the Arabian town of al-'Uyayna in 1703. He moved to Dir'iyya—some forty kilometers to the southeast—in 1744, only after the town rejected the religious discourse he was preaching. He was thereafter welcomed by Al Saud (House of Saud) and took up residence in Dir'iyya.

5. Wahhabism is the Saudi variant of revivalist Islam and is concerned primarily with the purification of religious practice and the application of sharia. Although it draws on sources from the Hanbali school of law, Wahhabism is a product of the historical and political contexts of the Arabian Peninsula since the mid-eighteenth century. This orthodox Islamic tradition evolved in response to Al Saud's political power. While Wahhabism's followers refer to themselves as *al-muwahhidun* or *ahl al-tawhid* (monotheists), it has become common to refer to them as Wahhabis, a term I retain in this book. For a brief explanation of employing the term, see Guido Steinberg, *Religion und Staat in Saudi Arabien: Die wahhabitischen Gelehrten (1902–1953)* (Würzburg, Germany: Ergon, 2002), 28–32; Nabil Mouline, *The Clerics of Islam: Religious Authority and Political Power in Saudi Arabia*, trans. Ethan S. Rundell (New Haven, CT: Yale University Press, 2014), 8–11; and Michael Farquhar, *Circuits of Faith: Migration, Education, and the Wahhabi Mission* (Stanford, CA: Stanford University Press, 2017), 7.

6. Author interviews with the exhibition curators as well as several archivists at the Darah, Riyadh, January–February 2011.

7. Some Saudi Arabians who hailed from regions far beyond Mecca and who went there on pilgrimage sometimes shared their concerns and disillusionment with the nature of urban development in online forums. For an example, see Nazih al-Uthmani's blog post "Worship in Mecca between Spirituality and Capitalist Values," *Nazih al-Uthmani's Blog*, September 8, 2010, as well as the comments section, http://alothmany.me/blog/?p=207.

8. Gulf War refers to the mobilizations that underpinned the 1991 US-led war on Iraq, otherwise known as Operation Desert Shield (August 2, 1990–January 17, 1991) and Operation Desert Storm (January 17, 1991–February 28, 1991). The operations, which were in response to Iraq's invasion of Kuwait, involved the deployment of US troops inside Saudi Arabia and the setting up of a US military base there. For more on the war, see Andre Gunder Frank, "Third World War: A Political Economy of the Gulf War and the New World Order," *Third World Quarterly* 13, no. 2 (1992): 267–82.

9. See Pierre Bourdieu's *Outline of a Theory of Practice* (Cambridge: Cambridge University Press, 1977) and his *The Logic of Practice* (Stanford, CA: Stanford University Press, 1992).

10. Michel-Rolph Trouillot, *Silencing the Past: Power and the Production of History* (Boston: Beacon Press, 1995), 29.

11. Lisa Wedeen, *Ambiguities of Domination: Politics, Rhetoric, and Symbols in Contemporary Syria* (Chicago: University of Chicago Press, 1999); and Lina Khatib, *Image Politics in the Middle East: The Role of the Visual in Political Struggle* (New York: I. B. Tauris, 2012).

12. There has been an attempt to move away from studying documents and artifacts as "texts" and "representations," instead focusing on their materiality and the processes that they engender. See Bruno Latour, *Pandora's Hope: Essays on the Reality of Science Studies* (Cambridge, MA: Harvard University Press, 1999); "What Is Iconoclash: Or Is There a World beyond the Image Wars?" in *Iconoclash: Beyond the Image Wars in Science, Religion and Art*, ed. Bruno Latour and Peter Weibel (Cambridge, MA: MIT Press, 2002), 14–37; and Daniel Miller, ed., *Materiality* (Durham, NC: Duke University Press, 2005). As Matthew Hull points out, "Documents are not simply instruments of bureaucratic organization but rather are constitutive of bureaucratic rules, ideologies, knowledge, practices, subjectivities, objects, outcomes, and even the organizations themselves." It is the very materiality of documents that determines their lifeworlds and allows for the types of slippages that we see taking place, exemplified by the emergence of a black market in historical documents in Saudi Arabia. Matthew S. Hull, "Documents and Bureaucracy," *Annual Review of Anthropology* 41 (2012): 253.

13. Trouillot, *Silencing the Past*, 48–49. For recent debates and conversations about archives and historical production in Middle East studies, see Omnia El Shakry, "'History Without Documents': The Vexed Archives of Decolonization in the Middle East," *American Historical Review* 120, no. 3 (June 1, 2015): 920–34; and Seth Anziska, *Preventing Palestine: A Political History from Camp David to Oslo* (Princeton, NJ: Princeton University Press, 2018).

14. Ann Laura Stoler, *Along the Archival Grain: Epistemic Anxieties and Colonial Common Sense* (Princeton, NJ: Princeton University Press, 2009).

15. Michel Foucault, *The Archeology of Knowledge: And the Discourse of Language* (New York: Pantheon Books, 1972).

16. Chiara De Cesari, "Heritage Between Resistance and Government in Palestine," in "Forced Displacement and Refugees," special issue, *International Journal of Middle East Studies* 49, no. 4 (November 2017): 747–51. See also Bruno Latour, *Reassembling the Social: An Introduction to Actor-Network-Theory* (New York: Oxford University Press, 2007); Brian Larkin, "The Politics and Poetics of Infrastructure," *Annual Review of Anthropology* 42 (October 2013): 327–43; Timothy Mitchell, *Carbon Democracy: Political Power in the Age of Oil* (London: Verso, 2011); and Timothy Mitchell, *Rule of Experts: Egypt, Techno-Politics, Modernity* (Berkeley: University of California Press, 2002).

17. The French national archive is often held up as the exemplary modern archive, but it, too, is marred with the destruction of records. See Ralph Kingston, "The French Revolution and the Materiality of the Modern Archive," *Libraries and the Cultural Record* 46, no. 1 (2011): 1–25. In the United Kingdom, Operation Legacy, which took place between the 1950s and 1970s, entailed the purging of thousands of British imperial records and the secret hiding of many more. Ian Cobain, Owen Bowcott, and Richard Norton-Taylor, "Britain Destroyed Records of Colonial Crimes: Review Finds Thousands of Papers Detailing Shameful Acts Were Culled, While Others Were Kept Secret Illegally," *Guardian*, April 18, 2012. Also see Caroline Elkins, *Imperial Reckoning: The Untold Story of Britain's Gulag in Kenya* (New York: Holt Paperbacks, 2005). According to several archivists I spoke with at one of the United Kingdom's main state archives, the purging of "sensitive" records is not a thing of the past and has continued at the archive under the guise of "limited space" or "historically nonvaluable." Similar practices are also recorded in the United States, the most notorious of which is the documentation of Operation TPAJAX, the codename for the Central Intelligence Agency–led coup in Iran in 1953. See "CIA Confirms Role in 1953 Iran Coup," National Security Archive, August 19, 2013, https://nsarchive2.gwu.edu/NSAEBB/NSAEBB435/; James R. Jacobs, "Holes in History: The Dept of Interior Request to Destroy Records," *Free Government Information*, October 29, 2018, https://freegovinfo.info/node/13099; and Allya Sternstein, "CIA Plans to Destroy Some of Its Old Leak Files," *Daily Beast*, July 18, 2017, https://www.thedailybeast.com/cia-plans-to-destroy-some-of-its-old-leak-files.

18. Steffen Hertog, *Princes, Brokers, and Bureaucrats: Oil and the State in Saudi Arabia* (Ithaca, NY: Cornell University Press, 2010).

19. Political commemoration is common to all regimes. In "The French Revolution," Kingston notes how "the modern archive developed not as a result of the 'Restoration' or in the political reinvention of 'National Heritage' during the 1830s and 1840s but through the revolutionary administration's desire to document their own legacy" (18).

20. Rosie Bsheer, "A Counter-Revolutionary State: Popular Movements and the Making of Saudi Arabia," *Past and Present* 238, no. 1 (February 2018): 233–77; and Ziad Abu-Rish, "Conflict and Institution Building in Lebanon, 1946–1955" (PhD diss., University of California–Los Angeles, 2014).

21. David Scott, *Conscripts of Modernity: The Tragedy of Colonial Enlightenment* (Durham, NC: Duke University Press, 2004).

22. Muhammad Hasanayn Haykal, *Harb al-khalij: Awham al-quwwa wa-l-nasr* [The Gulf War: Illusions of power and triumph] (Cairo: Markaz al-Ahram li-l-tarjama w-al-nashr, 1992); Saadiyya Mufrih, "Al-Khalij lays naftan . . . wa-l-naft lays 'aran" [The Gulf is not oil . . . and oil is not a disgrace"], *Altaqreer*, May 4, 2015, via *Arabian Peninsula Blog*, on August 24, 2016, http://aljazeeraalarabiamodwana.blogspot.com/2016/08/blog-post_30.html; Khalid Al-Dakhil, "'Unsuriyyat 'al-qawmiyyin al-Arab' tijah al-jazeera al-Arabiyya" [The racism of "Arab Nationalists" toward the Arabian Peninsula], *Al-Hayat*, July 4, 2015, http://www.alhayat.com/article/819713/; and Badr al-Ibrahim, "Al-'unsuriyya bayn al-khalijiyyin wa baqiyat al-Arab" [Racism between Gulf citizens and other Arabs], *Al-Arabi al-Jadid*, August 22, 2016, https://www.alaraby.co.uk/opinion/2016/8/21/العنصرية-بين-الخليجيين-وبقية-العرب-1.

23. See, among others, Madawi Al-Rasheed, *Contesting the Saudi State: Islamic Voices from a New Generation* (New York: Cambridge University Press, 2007); Madawi Al-Rasheed and Robert Vitalis, eds., *Counter-Narratives: History, Contemporary Society and Politics in Saudi Arabia and Yemen* (New York: Palgrave, 2004); Robert Vitalis, *America's Kingdom: Mythmaking on the Saudi Oil Frontier* (Stanford, CA: Stanford University Press, 2007); Jörg Matthias Determann, *Historiography in Saudi Arabia: Globalization and the State in the Middle East* (London: I. B. Tauris, 2014); Ulrike Freitag, Malte Fuhrmann, Nora Lafi, and Florian Riedler, *The City in the Ottoman Empire: Migration and the Making of Urban Modernity* (New York: Routledge, 2011); Adam Hanieh, *Capitalism and Class in the Gulf Arab States* (New York: Palgrave Macmillan, 2011); Hertog, *Princes, Brokers, and Bureaucrats*; Toby C. Jones, *Desert Kingdom: How Oil and Water Forged Modern Saudi Arabia* (Cambridge, MA: Harvard University Press, 2010); Amelie Le Renard, *A Society of Young Women: Opportunities of Place, Power, and Reform in Saudi Arabia* (Stanford, CA: Stanford University, 2014); Pascal

Menoret, *Joyriding in Riyadh: Oil, Urbanism, and Road Revolt* (Cambridge: Cambridge University Press, 2014); Toby Matthiesen, *The Other Saudis: Shiism, Dissent and Sectarianism* (Cambridge: Cambridge University Press, 2015); Nadav Samin, *Of Sand or Soil: Genealogy and Tribal Belonging in Saudi Arabia* (Princeton, NJ: Princeton University Press, 2015); and Paul Aarts and Gerd Nonneman, eds., *Saudi Arabia in the Balance: Political Economy, Society, Foreign Affairs* (New York: New York University Press, 2005).

24. Sheila Carapico, "Arabia Incognita: An Invitation to Arabian Peninsula Studies," in Al-Rasheed and Vitalis, *Counter-Narratives*, 11–33; and Rosie Bsheer, "W(h)ither Arabian Peninsula Studies?" in *Handbook of Contemporary Middle East and North African History*, ed. Jens Hansen and Amal Ghazal (Oxford: Oxford University Press, 2017).

25. Nathalie Peutz, "Perspectives from the Margins of Arabia" (issue theme), in "Theorizing the Arabian Peninsula," ed. Rosie Bsheer and John Warner, *Jadmag* 1, no. 1 (Fall 2013): 26.

26. For an example of how Saudi kings have historically viewed the population as not ready for social or political reforms, see the transcripts of Barbara Walter's interview with late Saudi King Abdullah ibn Abdulaziz on October 14, 2005: "Transcript: Saudi King Abdullah Talks to Barbara Walters," ABC News, November 1, 2005, https://abcnews.go.com/2020/International/story?id=1214706&page=1&singlePage=true. See also Rosie Bsheer, "It's Not the Morality Police, Stupid," *Jadaliyya*, January 17, 2011, http://www.jadaliyya.com/Details/23621/It%E2%80%99s-Not-The-Morality-Police,-Stupid.

27. Rosie Bsheer, "A Counter-Revolutionary State: Popular Movements and the Making of Saudi Arabia," *Past and Present* 238, no. 1 (February 1, 2018): 233–77.

28. The archival record is replete with official instructions about, and approval of, such public relations campaigns. For some examples, refer to Record 22679, No. 806, Presidency of the Council of Ministers, December 30, 1969; Record 29829, No. 1725, Presidency of the Council of Ministers, October 14, 1974; and Record 37460, No. 238, Presidency of the Council of Ministers, July 31, 1979, which approves a payment of US$183,264 to *Fortune* magazine for the "investigative report it published on the kingdom." These records are all located in the Institute of Public Administration Archive, Riyadh. For a discussion of these issues, see Bsheer and Warner, "Theorizing the Arabian Peninsula."

29. Madawi Al-Rasheed, *A History of Saudi Arabia*, 2nd ed. (London: Cambridge University Press, 2010); David Commins, *The Wahhabi Mission and Saudi Arabia* (New York: I. B. Tauris, 2006); and Guido Steinberg, "The Wahhabi Ulama and the Saudi

State," in *Saudi Arabia in the Balance: Political Economy, Society, Foreign Affairs*, ed. Paul Aarts and Gerd Nonneman (New York: New York University Press, 2005), 11–34.

30. Reinhart Koselleck, *The Practice of Conceptual History: Timing History, Spacing Concepts* (Stanford, CA: Stanford University Press, 2002), 111–30.

31. Ernest Gellner, *Nations and Nationalism* (Ithaca, NY: Cornell University Press, 1983); and John A. Hall, ed., *States in History* (Oxford, UK: Basil Blackwell, 1986).

32. Talal Asad, *Genealogies of Religion: Discipline and Reasons of Power in Christianity and Islam* (Baltimore: Johns Hopkins University Press, 1993).

33. For more on the centrality of Saudi Arabian Wahhabism to petrocapitalism, see Mitchell, *Carbon Democracy*.

34. George S. Rentz, *The Birth of the Islamic Reform Movement in Saudi Arabia: Muhammad Ibn Abd al-Wahhab (1703/4–1792) and the Beginnings of Unitarian Empire in Arabia* (London: Arabian Publishing, 2004). Several of Abdulaziz ibn Saud's advisers had already produced hagiographies of the newly crowned king wherein they wrote him into history as the founder of the modern Saudi state, a hero whose political genius and military prowess enabled the conquering of the peninsula and "saving" it from the so-called age of ignorance (*jahiliyya*) that supposedly prevailed in Ottoman Arabia. See Ameen Rihani, *Tarikh Najd al-Hadith* [The modern history of Najd] (Beirut: Scientific Printing Press, 1928); Ameen Rihani, *Ibn Sa'oud of Arabia: His People and His Land* (London: Constable, 1928; London: Routledge, 2011); Hafız Wahbah, *Jazirat al-'Arab fi al-qarn al-'ishrin: Tabi'at Jazirat al-'Arab wa-halatuha al-ijtima'iyah al-hadirah* [The Arabian Peninsula in the twentieth century: The nature of the Arabian Peninsula and its present social state] (Cairo: Lajnat al-Ta'lif wa-al-Tarjamah wa-al-Nashr, 1935); and Fuad Hamza, *Al-bilad al-'Arabiyya al-Sa'udiyya* [Saudi Arabia] (Makkah: Matba'at Umm al-Qura, 1937).

35. The religious establishment historically comprised scholars, "religious ritual specialists" (*mutawwa'a*), the Ikhwan, and the *muhtasibun* (Salafi Wahhabi inspectors charged with maintaining public order, morality, health, cleanliness, and trade fairness and honesty). In early Islam, the *muhtasib* (pl. *muhtasibun*) or the inspector general of weights and measures, was in charge of policing urban markets and traders to prevent fraud and corruption, and also ensuring public morality, health, and cleanliness. See Al-Rasheed, *A History of Saudi Arabia*, 59–61; Caroline Stone, "The Muhtasib," *Aramco World Magazine* 28, no. 5 (September–October 1977), 22–25; and Michael Cook, *Commanding Right and Forbidding Wrong in Islamic Thought* (Oxford: Oxford University Press, 2000).

36. Abdulaziz al-Khidr, *Al-Saʻudiyya: Sirat dawla wamujtamaʻ, qiraʼa fi tajrubat thilth qarn min al-tahawulat al-fikriyya wa-l-siyasiyya wa-l-tanmawiyya* [Saudi Arabia: Biography of a state and society, a reading in a quarter-century experience of intellectual, political, and developmental transformations], 2nd ed. (Beirut: Arab Network for Research and Publications, 2011), 68–69.

37. Some scholars believe that Faisal adopted an Islamist tradition more common in Egypt, Syria, Morocco, India, and the Hijaz, and not the more conservative Wahhabism of Najd. Although such claims are convincing, especially given ideological struggles between Faisal and his uncle, Shaykh Muhammad ibn Ibrahim, I do not have the requisite evidence to make such an argument. For allusions to Faisal's Islamism, see Mouline, *Clerics of Islam*; and Farquhar, *Circuits of Faith*.

38. Hamad I. Salloom, *Education in Saudi Arabia*, 2nd ed. (Washington, DC: Saudi Arabian Cultural Mission to the United States of America, 1995), 6.

39. Madawi Al-Rasheed, *A Most Masculine State: Gender, Politics, and Religion in Saudi Arabia* (Cambridge: Cambridge University Press, 2013), 43–76.

40. Benedict Anderson, *Imagined Communities: Reflections on the Origin and Spread of Nationalism* (New York: Verso, 1983).

41. John S. Habib, *Ibn Saud's Warriors of Islam: The Ikhwan of Najd and Their Role in the Creation of the Saudi Kingdom, 1910–1930* (Leiden, The Netherlands: E. J. Brill, 1978).

42. Anthony Gorman, *Historians, State and Politics in Twentieth Century Egypt: Contesting the Nation.* (London: Routledge Curzon, 2003), 72.

43. This was, indeed, the first museum in Saudi Arabia, and not the National Museum that opened in Riyadh in 1999. Interestingly, the regime also announced the opening of a US$150 million national museum in Riyadh in 1978, but that project never materialized.

44. Author interviews in Riyadh with Ali al-Mughannam (historian, archeologist, Arriyadh Development Authority [ADA] consultant, and Dirʻiyya project manager) and with museologists and museum owners in the Eastern Province and in the Hijaz, March 2010–June 2011.

45. This claim is based on historical renovation proposals, including one by the renowned Egyptian architect Muhammad Kamal Ismail, that span the late 1960s and early 1970s and that King Faisal's regime rejected. Arriyadh Development Authority Archives, Riyadh; and author interview with Ali al-Mughannam (historian, archeologist, ADA consultant, and Dirʻiyya project manager), Riyadh, May 8, 2010.

46. Between 1966 and 1968 alone, Faisal's regime spent millions of dollars on public relations campaigns, which included newspaper and magazine articles as well

as films and books, most of which appeared in Arabic, English, and French, with some also in German. On May 2, 1966, the Presidency of the Council of Ministers Decision 1777, No. 12 (located at the Institute of Public Administration Archive, hereafter cited as IPA Archive, Riyadh), approved the publication of ninety thousand copies of *These Are Our Lands* [*Hadhihi Biladuna*], mainly for external consumption. The book did not appear within a concerted cultural policy or state effort to assert its ideal image of the Saudi state to its citizens. In 1988, a similar endeavor turned the book into a series of the same title, each detailing a specific region of Saudi Arabia. The book series project should be read within these attempts to highlight Arabia's diverse histories. In his capacity as president of Youth Welfare in Saudi Arabia, Faisal, the son of the late King Fahd, approved the proposal of several historians and intellectuals—including Muhammad al-Qash'ami, Hassan al-Huwaymil, and Salih al-Washmi—to commission locals to document the histories of their towns, resulting in the book series. See "Tahwil silsilat 'hadhihi biladuna' ila a'mal televisioniyya" [Turning 'These are our lands' series into a television production], *Al Watan*, September 2, 2010, https://www.alwatan.com.sa/article/60432. For a list of the book series, see "Silsilat hadhihi biladuna" [Hadhihi biladuna series], https://www.goodreads.com/series/179062.

47. Jon Mandaville, "The New Historians," *Aramco World Magazine* 31, no. 2 (March–April 1980).

48. Author interviews with historians, museologists, and archeologists who oversaw these cultural projects across Saudi Arabia, January 2010–June 2011. For some Wahhabi clerics, the recovery and preservation of artifacts and sites of material culture were common even though they contravened Wahhabi doctrine. The latter strictly forbids the monumentalization of symbolic material structures, seeing it as a mediated form of worship and an association with God and thus heretical. Those in the clerical establishment who supported this view regularly mobilized those in its pay to vandalize museums and archeological sites.

49. Finbar Flood, "Between Cult and Culture: Bamiyan, Islamic Iconoclasm and the Museum," *Art Bulletin* 84, no. 4 (2002): 641–59.

50. Mouline, *Clerics of Islam*, 149.

51. Ibid.

52. For a firsthand account of the rise of Islamist mobilizations in Saudi Arabia in 1974 leading to the takeover of the Grand Mosque in 1979, see Nassir al-Huzaymi, *Ayyam ma' Juhayman: Kuntu ma' "al-jama'a al-salafiyya al-muhtasiba"* [Days with Juhayman: I was with the "Society of Salafis" that commands right and forbids wrong] (Beirut: Al-Shabaka al-'Arabiyya li-l-abhath wa-l-nashr, 2011).

53. Shaykh Abdulaziz ibn Baz, Saudi Arabia's grand mufti from 1993 to 1999, was the "spiritual guide" of the group that took over the Grand Mosque, which Juhayman al-'Utaybi and others formed in the 1960s and that was later named al-Jama'a al-Salafiyya al-Muhtasiba. In 1977, the group split over ideological differences; the majority followed al-'Utaybi and thereafter became known as *ikhwan*. Except for the concept of the coming of the Mahdi (Messiah)—which al-'Utaybi incorporated into his discourse in 1978 although many of his companions did not believe in the concept—the group endorsed a strict Wahhabi reading of Islam, often relying on the works of hard-line Wahhabi scholars. Despite their defeat in 1979, the group's ideology informed future Islamists in the kingdom and abroad. See Thomas Hegghammer and Stéphane Lacroix, *The Meccan Rebellion: The Story of Juhayman al-'Utaybi Revisited* (Bristol, UK: Amal Press, 2011).

54. Toby C. Jones, "Rebellion on the Saudi Periphery: Modernity, Marginalization, and the Shi'a Uprising of 1979," *International Journal of Middle East Studies* 38 (2006): 213–33.

55. For the uprising in the Qatif, see Jones, *Desert Kingdom*, 177–216; and Matthiesen, *The Other Saudis*. For the takeover of the Grand Mosque in Mecca, see Yaroslav Trofimov, *Siege of Mecca: The Forgotten Uprising in Islam's Holiest Shrine* (New York: Penguin Books, 2008).

56. Hegghammer and Lacroix, *Meccan Rebellion*, 111.

57. For an in-depth, contemporaneous analysis of the ways in which the Saudi state imposed a media blackout and controlled the narrative of the events in 1979, and the effects this had on knowledge production and how both movements were reported in the Arab press, see Abu Dharr, "Ahdath al-Haram bayn al-haqa'iq wa-l-abatil" [The events of the Grand Mosque between truth and lies], *Sawt al-Tali'a* 22 (May 1980): 3–180, 187–200.

58. Although the Iranian Revolution mobilized many religious activists, both Sunni and Shi'i, throughout Asia, these were not derivative movements. As Toby C. Jones explains in *Desert Kingdom*, "the 1979 uprising [in Qatif] reflected the convergence of external factors with specifically local grievances and objectives" (186).

59. After the 1979 siege of Mecca, King Khalid received scores of letters from Saudi governors and heads of various municipalities as well as institutions such as the Ministry of Justice and the National Guard asking him to adopt stricter security and surveillance measures. Importantly, they requested that he empower the official religious establishment to "cleanse" the so-called extremist Islam that had led to the

1979 events from schools, universities, mosques, religious centers, and all the security apparatus. Letters accessed at the *King Khalid Exhibition* in Riyadh on May 27, 2010.

60. This support continued even after Khalid's death. In 1984, for example, the state announced that women could not accept jobs that required them to mix with men. Record 40035, No. 11651, Royal Decree, March 1, 1983, and Record 51554, No. 39/5/1/2526/3/B, circular, Ministry of Higher Education, May 6, 1984—both at the IPA Archive, Riyadh.

61. Madawi Al-Rasheed, "God, King and the Nation: The Rhetoric of Politics in Saudi Arabia in the 1990s," *Middle East Journal* 50, no. 3 (1996), 359–71; Al-Rasheed, *A Most Masculine State*; Asad, *Genealogies of Religion*, 200–238; and Bernard Haykel, "The Wahhabis and Radical Islamic Networks" (lecture in the series "Dimensions of Contemporary Islam," Hattiesburg, University of Southern Mississippi, February 5, 2007).

62. Abdullah Nasir al-Shihri, "Fi daw' kalam al-malik Fahd 'an waqi' al-iqtisad al-Sa'udi" [In light of King Fahd's statements on Saudi Arabia's economic reality], *Al-Hayat*, November 7, 1994; David E. Spiro, *The Hidden Hand of American Hegemony: Petrodollar Recycling and International Markets* (Ithaca, NY: Cornell University Press, 1999), 74–77; and Andrea Wong, "The Untold Story Behind Saudi Arabia's 41-Year U.S. Debt Secret," *Bloomberg*, May 31, 2016, https://www.bloomberg.com/news/features/2016-05-30/the-untold-story-behind-saudi-arabia-s-41-year-u-s-debt-secret.

63. Toby C. Jones, "Crude Ecology: Technology and the Politics of Dissent in Saudi Arabia," in *Entangled Geographies: Empire and Technopolitics in the Global Cold War*, ed. Gabrielle Hecht (Cambridge, MA: MIT Press, 2011), 209–230.

64. Mitchell, *Carbon Democracy*.

65. "620 milyar dollar khasa'ir harb al-khalij wa la arqam li-adhrar al-mada al-ba'id" [Gulf War results in 620 billion dollars and no figures for long-term damages], *Al-Hayat*, September 21, 1992; Madawi Al-Rasheed, *A History of Saudi Arabia*, 150–52; "Calculating the Cost of the Gulf War," *CQ Researcher* 1 (March 15, 1991): 145–55; and John E. Peters, *Out of Area or Out of Reach? European Military Support for Operations in Southwest Asia* (Santa Monica, CA: RAND, 1995).

66. Leonard Silk, "Economic Scene: The Broad Impact of the Gulf War," *New York Times*, August 16, 1991.

67. Eric Schmitt, "US to Sell Saudis $20 Billon in Arms; Weapons Deal Is Largest in History," *New York Times*, September 15, 1990, https://www.nytimes.com/1990/09/15/world/confrontation-gulf-us-sell-saudis-20-billion-arms-weapons-deal-largest-history.html.

68. Author interviews with high-ranking officials at the Ministry of Municipal and Rural Affairs and members of the board of directors of the Mecca Development Authority, Saudi Arabia, March 2010–June 2011.

69. "Al-mu'tamar al-Islami ajaza 'al-isti'ana' bi-quwwat ajnabiyya" [The World Muslim Congress condones "assistance" of foreign troops], *Al-Nahar*, September 14, 1990, American University of Beirut Archives. The internal critiques of and attacks against the Saudi monarchy were so sharp that the regime had one of the most powerful religious scholars and the future grand mufti (1993–1999), Abdulaziz ibn Baz, issue a fatwa legitimating the deployment of foreign troops to the kingdom. Ibn Baz was subsequently sharply criticized for this move, having called on all Gulf states in the 1940s to prohibit the employment of foreigners. See his fatwa "'Amal Saddam 'udwan athim wa munkar shani'" [Saddam's action is a sinful aggression and a heinous transgression], Official Website of Shaykh Bin Baz, https://binbaz.org.sa/old/30754. See also Abdeljalil Marhoun, "Afaaq al-dimuqratiya fi al-khalij wa-shibh al-jazira al-'Arabiyya" [Horizons of democracy in the Gulf and the Arabian Peninsula], *Shu'un Al-Awsat*, no. 13 (1992): 19–35; and Jarret Brachman, *Global Jihadism: Theory and Practice* (New York: Routledge, 2009), 27.

70. For a critical discussion of the petition, see Asad, *Genealogies of Religion*, 223–27.

71. Gwenn Okruhlik, "Rentier Wealth, Unruly Law, and the Rise of the Opposition: The Political Economy of Oil States," *Comparative Politics* 31, no. 3 (April 1999): 302.

72. The Sahwa Islamists bring together the politico-religious ideologies of the Muslim Brotherhood and Saudi Wahhabism. For more on the Islamist movement, see Turki al-Dakhil, *Salman al-'Odah min al sijn ila al-tanwir* [Salman al-'Odah from prison to enlightenment] (Dubai: Madarik, 2011); Al-Rasheed, *Contesting the Saudi State*; and Stéphane Lacroix, *Awakening Islam: The Politics of Religious Dissent in Saudi Arabia* (Cambridge, MA: Harvard University Press, 2011).

73. See Gregory Gause, "Oil and Political Mobilizations in Saudi Arabia," in *Saudi Arabia in Transition*, ed. Bernard Haykel, Thomas Hegghammer, and Stéphane Lacroix (New York: Cambridge University Press, 2016), 18–21.

74. Twelve of twenty Arab League states supported the US war on Iraq. That Yemen, which had a major labor force inside Saudi Arabia, and the Palestine Liberation Organization (PLO) were among those who did not was a major blow to Saudi Arabia. Not only did Saudi rulers support the PLO, but Palestine also played a significant role in Saudi socialization. The Palestinian cause took up a significant part of Saudi Arabia's

history textbooks from the 1950s and at least until 2014, when I last reviewed them. Record 59058, No. 114, Ministry of Education (*wizarat al-tarbiya wa-l-ta'lim*), July 22, 1954, IPA Archive, Riyadh.

75. Okruhlik, "Rentier Wealth, Unruly Law, and the Rise of the Opposition."

76. "Al-malik Fahd: Lan nuhidu 'an al-sharia wa-satakun hiya al-asas wa-l-qa'ida wa-l-muntalaq" [King Fahd: We will not diverge from sharia and it will be the foundation, basis, and starting point], *Al-Nahar*, March 7, 1991, American University of Beirut Archives.

77. Although the rulers pacified the Sahwa and the main threats it posed, they failed to crush the movement, which remains popular despite splintering into various ideologically driven groups.

78. Rahshe Aba-Namay, "Constitutional Reforms: A Systemization of Saudi Politics," *Journal of South Asian and Middle Eastern Studies* 16, no. 3 (Spring 1993): 43–88.

79. Madawi Al-Rasheed, "God, King and the Nation: The Rhetoric of Politics in Saudi Arabia in the 1990s." *Middle East Journal* 50, no. 3 (1996): 359–72; Al-Rasheed, *History of Saudi Arabia*, 172–76; Gwenn Okruhlik, "Networks of Dissent: Islamism and Reform in Saudi Arabia," *Current History* 101, no. 651 (January 2002): 22–29; and Jake Goldberg, "Saudi Arabia's Desert Storm and Winter Sandstorm," in *The Gulf Crisis and Its Global Aftermath*, ed. Gad Barzilai, Aharon Klieman, and Gil Shidlo (London: Routledge, 1993), 67–86. See also Aziz Abu-Hamad, *Empty Reforms: Saudi Arabia's New Basic Laws* (New York: Human Rights Watch, 1992).

80. For example, in 1984, King Fahd ibn Abdulaziz adopted the title of custodian of the two holy mosques—which Al Saud had appropriated from the Ottomans. See Bruce Masters, "Institutions of Ottoman Rule," in *The Arabs of the Ottoman Empire, 1516–1918: A Social and Cultural History* (Cambridge: Cambridge University Press, 2013), 48–72. But it was in 1993 that he reclaimed it as his official title and reasserted his commitment to protect the cities of Mecca and Medina. In the same vein in 1995, King Fahd established the Supreme Council of Islamic Affairs, made up of the most loyal ruling family members and their religious allies, in order to counter the increasingly challenging Council of Ulama, which refused to toe the regime line more times than the regime could tolerate. See Umar al-Malki, "Mi'dhalat al-mashru'iyya al-diniyya: al-inshiqaqat al-mutanasila min thuna'iyyat al-sulta" [The dilemma of religious legitimacy: Splits resulting from the duality of authority] *Al Hejaz*, n.d., http://www.alhejaz.org/qadaya/037604.htm.

81. William Safire, "The Split in the Saudi Royal Family," *New York Times*, September 12, 2002, https://www.nytimes.com/2002/09/12/opinion/the-split-in-the-saudi-royal-family.html.

82. See, for example, Al-Rasheed, "God, King and the Nation," 361.

83. *Tarikh al-Mamlakah al-'Arabiyya al-Sa'udiyya, 2005–2006* [History of the kingdom of Saudi Arabia, 2005–2006] (Kingdom of Saudi Arabia, Ministry of Education, 6th grade, 9th grade, 12th grade). For a recent example of how Saudi state media depicts the stagnancy and "backwardness" of Ottoman Arabia, see Salem al-Ahmadi, "Takmilat mashru' tawsi'at al-masjid al-nabawi wa mashari' tanmawiyya ukhra bi al-Madina al-Munawwara" [Continuation of expansion project of Prophet's Mosque and other development projects in Medina], *Al-Riyadh*, September 24, 2005, http://www.alriyadh.com/96067. Compare such official depictions to actual growth in Ottoman Medina; for example, Atef Alshehri, "Ottoman Spatial Organization of the Pre-modern City of Medina," *Architecture beyond Europe* 13 (2018): https://journals.openedition.org/abe/4341#entries.

84. Author interview with Thomas Ciolek, senior project manager on Dir'iyya for the Arriyadh Development Authority, Riyadh, March 10, 2010; author interviews with state historians and museologists, Riyadh, 2006–2011; and Arthur P. Clark, *A Kingdom Revealed: The Making of the King Abdulaziz Historical Centre* (unpublished report submitted to the Arriyadh Development Authority, December 30, 2002), ADA Archives, Riyadh.

85. Reinhart Koselleck, *Futures Past: On the Semantics of Historical Time* (Cambridge, MA: MIT Press, 1990).

86. Christian Lee Novetzke, "The Theographic and the Historiographic in an Indian Sacred Life Story," in *Time, History and the Religious Imaginary in South Asia*, ed. Anne Murphy (London: Routledge, 2011), 121.

87. Rosie Bsheer, "Making History, Remaking Space: Textbooks, Archives and Commemorative Spaces in Saudi Arabia" (PhD diss., Columbia University, 2014).

88. Rosie Bsheer, "How Mohammed bin Salman Has Transformed Saudi Arabia," *Nation*, May 21, 2018, https://www.thenation.com/article/how-mohammed-bin-salman-has-transformed-saudi-arabia/. For an example of the role of Salman ibn Abdulaziz in historical praxis, see Abdulaziz Jarallah, "Al-amir Salman yaktub tarikh al-Riyadh" [Prince Salman writes the history of Riyadh], *Al-Riyadh*, September 29, 2007, http://www.alriyadh.com/283306; and this interview with the Darah's Secretary General

Fahd al-Semmari: Ali Bluwi, "Darah: 40 Years of Recording History," *Arab News*, June 2, 2012. More recently, Salman was dubbed "al-malik al-mu'arrikh" [the historian king]: Khalid al-Tawil, "Salman bin Abdulaziz.. al-malik al-mu'arrikh" [Salman bin Abdulaziz: The historian king], *Sahifat Makkah*, March 14, 2016, https://www.google.com/amp/s/makkahnewspaper.com/ampArticle/135802.

89. The regime started considering the centennial celebration in 1993 but did not finalize it until 1996, when it was actually announced. Royal Decree No. 597, "King Fahd Declares Centennial Celebrations," 1996.

90. Academics and critics alike refer to the 1744 politico-religious contract as the marriage between politics and religion, or rather, between Al Saud and Al Abd al-Wahhab. They usually describe it as a union that enabled the emergence of the modern Saudi Arabian state. Madawi Al-Rasheed argues that the centennial's focus on Abdulaziz ibn Saud's conquest of Riyadh in 1902 "is bound to marginalize an important date in Islamists' historical imagination, that is the Wahhabi reform movement of 1744." Madawi Al-Rasheed, "The Capture of Riyadh Revisited: Shaping Historical Imagination in Saudi Arabia," in Al-Rasheed and Vitalis, *Counter-Narratives*, 183–200. See also Al-Rasheed, *A History of Saudi Arabia*, 182–210, on how Islamists opposed the centennial.

91. Oral history interviews between 2009 and 2014 with employees of the Arriyadh Development Authority, the Ministry of Municipal and Rural Affairs, and the Saudi Commission for Tourism and Antiquities.

92. Penelope Papailias, *Genres of Recollection: Archival Poetics in Modern Greece* (New York: Palgrave Macmillan, 2005), 20.

93. Interviews with employees at the Darah, the National Center for Documents and Archives, and the King Fahd National Library, Riyadh, 2009–2014.

94. For a similar example of the UK archives, see Cobain, Bowcott, and Norton-Taylor, "Britain Destroyed Records of Colonial Crimes."

95. The Ministry of Finance largely granted funds for the exploitation of historical sites in Riyadh alone, with the exception of some pre-Islamic sites that did not pose a threat to the regime's official history. Al-Hijr (Mada'in Salih) in the country's northwest is a prime example. Nominated as a World Heritage Site in 2008, Mada'in Salih underwent various excavations beginning in the 1960s. Saudi Arabia's Deputy Ministry of Antiquities and Museums has protected the site since 1972, which subsequently experienced minimal state intervention in the early 1980s. See Supreme

Commission for Tourism, Kingdom of Saudi Arabia, "Executive Summary: Al-Hijr Archeological Site (Madain Salih): Nomination Document for the Inscription on the UNESCO World Heritage List," January 2007, https://whc.unesco.org/en/documents/168942.

96. The institution was known as Arriyadh Development Authority, or ADA, until 2017. Since then, it has changed the spelling to Riyadh Development Authority, or RDA. Here, I maintain the original spelling and acronym.

97. Arriyadh Development Authority, "Form and Building Structure," in *Comprehensive Strategic Report for the City of Riyadh (2003)*, vol. 4 of 20, Metropolitan Development Strategy for Arriyadh (MEDSTAR), Report from the Arriyadh Development Authority, phase 1, 1997, p. 3.

98. Or "les lieux de memoires." See Pierre Nora, *Realms of Memory: The Construction of the French Past* (New York: Columbia University Press, 1992).

99. Author interviews with executives and project managers at the Saudi Commission for Tourism and Antiquities, Riyadh, 2010–2013; "The National Urban Heritage and Ways to Maintain, Develop and Invest in Tourism" (seminar at the King Abdulaziz Historical Center organized by the Saudi Commission for Tourism and Antiquity, the Ministry of Municipal and Rural Affairs, the Ministry of Education, the Arab Institute for Urban Development, and the Heritage Foundation, September 30–October 3, 2003); "The Role of Saudi Commission for Tourism and Antiquities in the Preservation and Development of Urban Heritage," First International Conference for Urban Heritage in the Islamic Countries (Riyadh: Saudi Commission for Tourism and Antiquities, May 23–28, 2010); and "General Strategy and Operational Plans," website of the Saudi Commission for Tourism and National Heritage, https://scth.gov.sa/en/AboutSCTA/Pages/General-Strategy-and-Operational-Plans.aspx.

100. In 2003, the antiquities sector was subsumed under the Supreme Commission for Tourism, which was renamed the Saudi Commission for Tourism and Antiquities (SCTA) in 2008 and the Saudi Commission for Tourism and National Heritage (SCTH) in 2015.

101. Trevor Boddy, "History's New Home in Riyadh," *Aramco World Magazine* 50, no. 5 (September–October 1999), 22–29.

102. Al-hay'a al-'amma li-al-siyaha wa-l-athar [Saudi Commission for Tourism and Antiquities, Kingdom of Saudi Arabia], *Al-'abath fi al-athar* [Tampering with antiquities], 2009; and *Buhuth nadwat al-watha'iq al-tarikhiyya fi al-Mamlaka al-'Arabiyya al-Sa'udiyya* [Symposium on historical documents in the Kingdom of Saudi Arabia], November 24–26, 1996 (Riyadh: Darat al-Malik Abdulaziz, 1997).

103. Oubai Shahbandar, "Riyadh: Heart of Arabian Heritage . . . Hub of Global Development," *Al-Arabiya*, August 22, 2016, http://english.alarabiya.net/en/views/news/middle-east/2016/08/22/Riyadh-Heart-of-Arabian-heritage-Hub-of-global-development.html; and "Travel and Tourism Economic Impact 2017 Saudi Arabia," *World Travel and Tourism Council*, March 2017, https://www.wttc.org/-/media/files/reports/economic-impact-research/archived/countries-2017/saudiarabia2017.pdf.

104. Gwenn Okruhlik argues, in "Struggles over History and Identity: 'Opening the Gates' of the Kingdom to Tourism," in Al-Rasheed and Vitalis, *Counter-Narratives*, 201–28, that the post-2001 tourism policy was aimed at international audiences. On the basis of oral history interviews I conducted between 2009 and 2014 with employees of the Arriyadh Development Authority and the Saudi Commission for Tourism and Antiquities, as well as pamphlets and records accessed at both institutions, I show that Saudi Arabian citizens were the main, short-term targets of the new local tourism policy. See also Clark, *A Kingdom Revealed*, 13.

105. See interview with Sultan ibn Salman Abdulaziz Al Saud, president of the Saudi Commission for Tourism and Antiquities, "SCTA President: Establish Companies for the Restoration and Maintenance of Urban Heritage Under the Leadership of National Cadres," website for the First International Conference for Urban Heritage in the Islamic Countries, May 23–28, 2010, http://www.islamicurbanheritage.org.sa/english/LatestNews.aspx?id=1.

106. Ibid.

107. For an example, see the language used to describe preservation projects in Riyadh and those elsewhere in the kingdom in "The Role of Saudi Commission for Tourism and Antiquities in the Preservation and Development of Urban Heritage."

108. Oral history interviews between 2009 and 2014 with employees of the Arriyadh Development Authority, Mecca Development Authority, the Ministry of Municipal and Rural Affairs, and the Saudi Commission for Tourism and Antiquities.

109. Ibid.

110. The Ottomans had conquered the Hijaz from the Egyptian Mamluks and incorporated it into their expanding empire in 1517. But they safeguarded its autonomy under its local Hashemite rulers, also known as Ashraf or nobles. Abdulaziz ibn Saud had allied with the British imperial forces against the Ottomans to extend his reign to other parts of the peninsula, subjugating, in the process, the main powers that had ruled these lands, namely the Ottoman intermediary Sharif Husayn ibn Ali, the Al Rashid clan, and al-Idrisi in 'Asir. The Ashraf's long rule in the Hijaz had left

a great material heritage that especially threatened the official historical narrative and the constructed claims on which it rested.

111. Hanieh, *Capitalism and Class in the Gulf Arab States*.

112. For work on the intersection of heritage practice and gentrification, see John Collins, *Revolt of the Saints: Memory and Redemption in the Twilight of Brazilian Racial Democracy* (Durham, NC: Duke University Press, 2015); and Neil Smith, *The New Urban Frontier: Gentrification and the Revanchist City* (London: Routledge, 1996).

113. Paul du Gay, ed., *Production of Culture/Cultures of Production* (Thousand Oaks, CA: Sage, 1997), shows how the production of cultural life is intimately tied to economic processes of production, circulation, and exchange. See also Immanuel Wallerstein, "The Bourgeois(ie) as Concept and Reality," *New Left Review* 1, no. 167 (January–February 1988): 91–106.

114. The Saudi regime pursued a policy of active neglect when it came to most historical and archeological sites outside of Riyadh and Mecca, especially those that date to the Portuguese and Ottoman eras, but others as well. Instead of being a target of demolition, most remained in ruins, at least until the mid-2010s, left to the vagaries of weather, time, and environmental and human degradation. See Rosie Bsheer, "Making History, Remaking Space."

115. Author interviews with historians, journalists, and prominent members of these communities who had been urging various state institutions to allow them to redevelop these sites.

116. Author interviews with historians, archeologists, project managers, and consultants working on the redevelopment of Dir'iyya, Riyadh, 2010–2014.

117. "The Role of Saudi Commission for Tourism and Antiquities in the Preservation and Development of Urban Heritage."

118. For a very different context in which both past- and future-oriented sites are employed as tools for legitimation, see the work of Kees Terlouw, "Iconic Site Development and Legitimating Policies: The Changing Role of Water in Dutch Identity Discourses," *Geoforum* 57 (2014): 30–39.

119. Jacques Derrida, *Archive Fever: A Freudian Impression* (Chicago: University of Chicago Press, 1996).

120. Papailias, *Genres of Recollection*, 20.

121. Yoav Di-Capua, *Gatekeepers of the Arab Past: Historians and History Writing in Twentieth-Century Egypt* (Berkeley: University of California Press, 2009), 10.

122. Henri Lefebvre, *The Production of Space* (Oxford, UK: Wiley-Blackwell, 1991).

123. Nadia Abu El-Haj, "Translating Truths: Nationalism, the Practice of Archaeology, and the Remaking of Past and Present in Contemporary Jerusalem," *American Ethnologist* 25, no. 2 (May 1998): 179.

124. Derrida, *Archive Fever*, 36.

125. Daniel R. Fusfeld, "The Rise of the Corporate State in America," *Journal of Economic Issues* 6, no. 1 (March 1972): 1–22. See also Micol Seigel, *Violence Work: State Power and the Limits of Police* (Durham, NC: Duke University Press, 2018).

126. Foucault, *Archeology of Knowledge*.

127. Antonio Gramsci, *Selections from the Prison Notebooks* (New York: International Publishers, 1971).

128. Ian Hacking, "Between Michel Foucault and Erving Goffman: Between Discourse in the Abstract and Face-to-Face Interaction," *Economy and Society* 33, no. 3 (2004): 277–302. Hacking notes that "Foucault gave us ways in which to understand what is said, can be said, what is possible, what is meaningful—as well as how it lies apart from the unthinkable and indecipherable. He gave us no idea of how, in everyday life, one comes to incorporate those possibilities and impossibilities as part of oneself. We have to go to Goffman to begin to think about that" (300).

129. Kirsten Weld, *Paper Cadavers: The Archives of Dictatorship in Guatemala* (Durham, NC: Duke University Press, 2014), 13.

130. Peter Galison, "Removing Knowledge," *Critical Inquiry* 31, no. 1 (Autumn 2004): 229–43; John Guillory, "The Memo and Modernity," *Critical Inquiry* 31, no. 1 (Autumn 2004): 108–32; Papailias, *Genres of Recollection*; and Stoler, *Along the Archival Grain*.

131. For more on the significance of Mecca to Islam, see Jonathan Berkey, *The Formation of Islam: Religion and Society in the Near East, 600–1800* (Cambridge University Press, 2003).

132. Ed Atwood, "Makkah Land Prices Hit $133,000 per Sq Metre," *Arabian Business*, February 18, 2010, https://www.arabianbusiness.com/makkah-land-prices-hit-133-000-per-sq-metre-report-40490.html. See also Savills World Research, "Monaco Residential Market," 2014, http://pdf.euro.savills.co.uk/monaco/spotlight-on-monaco-residential-markets-2014.pdf.

CHAPTER 1

1. Al-Kairanawi—also known as Kairanavi or al-Hindi—was an *allamah*, an honorary title given to the most esteemed scholars of Islamic thought, law, and philosophy, people who were also well versed in history and politics. Avril Ann Powell, "Maulana

Rahmat Allah Kairanawi and Muslim-Christian Controversy in India in the Mid-19th Century," *Journal of the Royal Asiatic Society of Great Britain and Ireland* 108, no. 1 (1976): 61–62.

2. Ibid.; and Siraj Husayn Fathi, "Al-Madrasa al-Sawlatiyya: Tarikh la yunsa" [The Sawlatiyya school: An unforgettable history], *al-Madina*, January 6, 2012, http://www.al-madina.com/node/381541.

3. "An Incredible Saudi-Indian Tale," *Saudi Gazette*, April 17, 2019, http://live.saudigazette.com.sa/article/563635/SAUDI-ARABIA/An-incredible-Saudi-Indian-tale-Eminent-Saudis-of-Indian-origin-evoke-nostalgic-memories; Muʻtasim billah Abdulrazzaq, "Al-qadaya fi qusas Muhammad Abdullah al-Malibari" [Issues in Muhammad Abdullah al-Malibari's stories], *Majalla al-Aasima* (Arabic University College, n.d.): 1–10; and Abdul Latif, "Al-ʻalaqat al-adabiyya wa-l-thaqafiyya bayn Malibar wa-l-bilad al-ʻArabiyya" [Literary and cultural relations between Malibar and Arab states], *Majalla al-Aasima* (Arabic University College) 9 (2017): 233–37.

4. Seema Alavi, *Muslim Cosmopolitanism in the Age of Empire* (Cambridge, MA: Harvard University Press, 2015); John Slight, *The British Empire and the Hajj, 1856–1956* (Cambridge, MA: Harvard University Press, 2015); and Lâle Can, *Spiritual Subjects: Central Asian Pilgrims and the Ottoman Hajj at the End of Empire* (Stanford, CA: Stanford University Press, 2020). For the influence of African ulama on Mecca and Medina, see Anne K. Bang, *Sufis and Scholars of the Sea: Family Networks in East Africa, 1860–1925* (London: Routledge Curzon, 2014); and Ahmed Chanfi, *West African Ulama and Salafism in Mecca and Medina: Jawab al-Ifriqi—The Response of the African* (Leiden: Brill, 2015).

5. Kemal Karpat, "The Transformation of the Ottoman State, 1789–1908," *International Journal of Middle East Studies* 3 (1972): 243–81; Selim Deringil, *The Well-Protected Domains: Ideology and Legitimacy in the Late Ottoman Empire, 1876–1909* (London: I. B. Tauris, 1998); and M. Şükrü Hanioğlu, *A Brief History of the Late Ottoman Empire* (Princeton, NJ: Princeton University Press, 2008).

6. Frederick F. Anscombe, *The Ottoman Gulf: The Creation of Kuwait, Saudi Arabia and Qatar* (New York: Columbia University Press, 1997); and Dina Rizk Khoury, *State and Provincial Society in the Ottoman Empire: Mosul, 1540–1834* (Cambridge: Cambridge University Press, 1997).

7. Mostafa Minawi, *The Ottoman Scramble for Africa: Empire and Diplomacy in the Sahara and the Hijaz* (Stanford, CA: Stanford University Press, 2016).

8. William Ochsenwald, "Ottoman Arabia and the Holy Hejaz, 1516–1918," in "Understanding Transformations in the Arabian Peninsula," special edition, *Journal of Global Initiatives: Policy, Pedagogy, Perspectives* 10, no. 1 (2016): 29.

9. On the Nahda, and cultural and social developments in general, and their connection to the Tanzimat, see Stephen Sheehi, *Foundations of Modern Arab Identity* (Gainesville: University Press of Florida, 2004); and Ussama Makdisi, *The Culture of Sectarianism: Community, History, and Violence in Nineteenth-Century Ottoman Lebanon* (Berkeley: University of California Press, 2000).

10. For the ways in which al-Kairanawi and his followers contributed to the Islamic modernism and reformism central to the Nahda, see Alavi, *Muslim Cosmopolitanism in the Age of Empire*.

11. Suhaila al-Rimali, *Al-ittijahat al-fikriyya li-l-thawra al-'Arabiyya al kubra: Min khilal jaridat al-Qibla* [Ideological directions of the Great Arab Revolt: Through *al-Qibla* newspaper] (Amman: Lajnat Tarikh al-Urdun, 1992); and Ahmad al-Siba'i, *Ta'rikh Makkah: Dirasat fi al-siyasa wa-l-'ilm wa-l-ijtima' wa-l-'umran* [Historicizing Mecca: Studies in politics, knowledge, society, and architecture] (Mecca: Al-Safa Press, 1999). *Ta'rikh Makkah* is largely based on oral history interviews, Ottoman and Meccan documents, and the author's conversations with other historians of Mecca. Historian and literary writer al-Siba'i made several corrections to the book in its eight editions, but he died before he was able to correct all the errors. Ahmad Abdulghafur 'Attar and Abdulquddus al-Ansari noted many of these mistakes in *al-Bilad al-Sa'udiyya* and *al-Manhal*, respectively.

12. In the nineteenth-century colonized world, education was a site of political contestation. Colonial powers tried to limit the development of schools in their colonies. At the very least, they tried to control the curriculum being taught so as to prevent the politicization of students as well as the nurturing of anticolonial sentiments. Frantz Fanon, *The Wretched of the Earth* (New York: Grove Press, 1963); Bernard S. Cohn, *Colonialism and Its Forms of Knowledge: The British in India* (Princeton, NJ: Princeton University Press, 1996); Nicholas Dirks, *Castes of Mind: Colonialism and the Making of Modern India* (Princeton: Princeton University Press, 2001); and Timothy Mitchell, *Colonizing Egypt* (Berkeley: University of California Press, 1991).

13. For the purposes of this book, I highlight only the influence of Mecca-based Indian reformists on those hailing from the Arabian Peninsula. For the ways in which they influenced thinkers and scholars across Asia, Africa, and beyond, see Alavi, *Muslim Cosmopolitanism in the Age of Empire*.

14. William Ochsenwald, *Religion, Society, and the State in Arabia: The Hijaz Under Ottoman Control, 1840–1908* (Columbus: Ohio State University Press, 1984).

15. Al-Sibaʻi, *Taʾrikh Makkah*, 559.

16. Francis R. Bradley, "Islamic Reform, the Family, and Knowledge Networks Linking Mecca to Southeast Asia in the Nineteenth Century," *Journal of Asian Studies* 73, no. 1 (February 2014): 89–111.

17. Ibid.

18. In 2010, Mecca governor Prince Khalid ibn Faisal called for Arabizing the names of streets, commercial stores, and halls in Mecca in a move that was hailed by many intellectuals in Saudi Arabia. Muhammad Said al-Zahrani, "Taʻrib al-asmaʾ taʾkid li-irtibat al-insan bi-thaqafatih wa-l-hifadh ʻala hawiyyatih" [Arabizing names evinces man's attachment to his culture and safeguarding his identity], *Okaz*, October 10, 2010, https://www.okaz.com.sa/article/358104.

19. Achille Mbembe, "The Power of the Archive and Its Limits," in *Refiguring the Archive*, ed. Carolyn Hamilton, Verne Harris, Jane Taylor, Michele Pickover, Graeme Reid, and Razia Saleh (Dordrecht, The Netherlands: Kluwer, 2002), 23.

20. Talal Asad, "Conscripts of Western Civilization," in *Dialectical Anthropology: Essays in Honor of Stanley Diamond*, vol. 1 of *Civilization in Crisis*, ed. Stanley Diamond and Christine Gailey (Gainesville: University Press of Florida, 1992), 337.

21. David Scott, "Colonial Governmentality," *Social Text* 43 (1995): 21–49.

22. John Willis writes about the centrality of Mecca in the global Muslim imagination in the late Ottoman Empire and of the interwar universalist moment as one in which Muslim scholars worldwide saw Mecca as a possible political counter to European empire and the European state system in "Burying Muhammad Ali Jauhar: The Life and Death of the Meccan Republic," (unpublished manuscript, 2019), PDF file.

23. Alavi, *Muslim Cosmopolitanism in the Age of Empire*, 31. See also Abdullah ibn Abdulrahman ibn Salih Al Bassam, *Ulama Najd khilal thamaniyat qurun* [Religious scholars of Najd over eight centuries] (Riyadh: Dar al-ʻAsima, 1999); and Ibrahim ibn Abdullah al-Mudayhish, "Min ʻulamaʾ Najd al-ladheen rahalu ila al-hind li-talab al-ʻilm" [Religious scholars of Najd who went to India for education], *alukah*, April 13, 2013, https://www.alukah.net/culture/0/52987/.

24. "Muhammad Tahir al-Dabbagh.. Abraz muʾassisi al-haraka al-taʻlimiyya fi al-mamlaka" [Muhammad Tahir al-Dabbagh: Most prominent founder of the educational movement in the kingdom], *Al-Riyadh*, August 22, 2014, http://www.alriyadh

.com/962895. See also Mai Yamani, *Cradle of Islam: The Hejaz and the Quest of an Arabian Identity* (London: I. B. Tauris, 2004); and Ochsenwald, *Religion, Society, and the State in Arabia.*

25. Gary Wilder, "Untimely Vision: Aimé Césaire, Decolonization, Utopia," *Public Culture* 21, no. 1 (2009): 104.

26. Shaykh Ahmad ibn Zayni Dahlan wrote about major events in the region. In *Fitnat al-Wahabiyya*, he wrote about the French occupation of Egypt in 1798, the Wahhabi occupation of the Hijaz from 1803 to 1811, and the dangers of the new religious movement.

27. Fathi, "Al-Madrassa al-Sawlatiyya."

28. Pfander was in Istanbul in 1863 conducting missionary work and regularly talked about the previous decade's debate, which is most likely how Sultan Abdulaziz had learned of al-Kairanawi and asked the ruler of Mecca, Sharif Abdullah ibn Awn, to arrange for a meeting. See Powell, "Maulana Rahmat Allah Kairanawi."

29. Al-Siba'i, *Ta'rikh Makkah*, 466.

30. Ibid., 580.

31. Ahmad 'Amir, "Al-Sawlatiyya fi al-Ka'kiyya ba'd 100 'amm fi al-Khandarisa" [Al-Sawlatiyya moves to al-Ka'kiyya after one hundred years in al-Khandarissa], *Makkawi* website, July 2010, http://forum.makkawi.com/showthread.php?t=87416. The building that housed al-Sawlatiyya school for one hundred years, located in the Khandarisa neighborhood of Mecca's Bab al-Hara, was demolished on April 27, 2010, to make way for a megaproject north of the Grand Mosque.

32. Wa'il al-Lahhibi, "Al-Madrasa al-Sawlatiyya bi Makkah aqdam al-madaris al-nizamiyya fi al-Jazira al-'Arabiyya" [Al-Sawlatiyya School in Mecca, one of the oldest regular schools in the Arabian Peninsula], *Al-Riyadh*, March 10, 2008, http://www.alriyadh.com/2008/03/10/article324539.html.

33. Al-Siba'i, *Ta'rikh Makkah*, 581.

34. Ibid.

35. Powell, "Maulana Rahmat Allah Kairanawi," 63.

36. The Ottomans curtailed the growth of mass printing technologies until the nineteenth century. Ottoman rulers (following Europe's Protestant Reformation) feared that uncontrolled mass knowledge production would infringe on the sultan's legitimacy and ability to rule and collect taxes. The sultan allowed mass printing, under the tight control of the state, only after the notables (*a'yan*) offered legitimating services to the sultan, replacing the religious scholars of the eighteenth

century. In the nineteenth century, the Ottoman government relaxed measures of control, using the printing press as an alternative mode of establishing legitimacy and a tool to shape public opinion. Ahmad ibn Zayni Dahlan first oversaw the establishment and management of al-Amiriyya Press. Under Al Saud, its name was changed to Umm al-Qura Press. See Metin M. Coşgel, Thomas J. Miceli, and Jared Rubin, "The Political Economy of Mass Printing: Legitimacy, Revolt, and Technological Change in the Ottoman Empire," *Journal of Comparative Economics* 40, no. 3 (August 2012): 375–78.

37. Michael Laffan, *The Makings of Indonesian Islam: Orientalism and the Narration of a Sufi Past* (Princeton, NJ: Princeton University Press, 2011), 60–63; Alavi, *Muslim Cosmopolitanism in the Age of Empire*; Bang, *Sufis and Scholars of the Sea*; Ahmed Chanfi, *West African Ulama and Salafism in Mecca and Medina*; and Bradley, "Islamic Reform, the Family, and Knowledge Networks."

38. William L. Ochsenwald, "Ottoman Subsidies to the Hijaz, 1877–1886," *International Journal of Middle East Studies* 6, no. 3 (July 1975): 300.

39. The amir did this not necessarily because he opposed constitutional rights, for he was known to be a liberal supporter of constitutionalism, but because he feared being toppled and losing power. See Randall Baker, *King Hussein and the Kingdom of Hejaz* (New York: Oleander Press, 1979), 14–16; and al-Siba'i, *Ta'rikh Makkah*, 581.

40. "Marhaban bi-'amid al-Falah" [Welcome to the dean of al-Falah], *al-Adwa'*, November 18, 1958, 1, Prince Salman Library at the King Saud University, Riyadh.

41. Muhammad Salih Nasif started the daily *Barid al-Hijaz* in 1924 during Hashemite rule. Under its editor Abdulwahhab 'Ashshi, its name was changed to *Sawt al-Hijaz* upon the formation of the Saudi state in 1932.

42. Abdulhamid Abdulmajid Hakim, *Nizam al-ta'lim wa siyasatuh* [The educational system and its policies] (Cairo: Itrak Press, 2012). For the Alireza family's connections to India, see Siraj Wahab, "The Saudi Businessman Who Made India His Home," *Arab News*, February 20, 2019.

43. William L. Ochsenwald, "Arab Nationalism in the Hijaz," in *The Origins of Arab Nationalism*, ed. Rashid Khalidi, Lisa Anderson, Muhammad Muslih, and Reeva S. Simon (New York: Columbia University Press, 1991), 189–203. The borders of this Arab Kingdom are a subject of contention, especially as it pertains to the place of historic Palestine in it. See Eugene Rogan, *The Fall of the Ottomans: The Great War in the Middle East* (New York: Basic Books, 2015), 275–310.

44. Al-Siba'i, *Ta'rikh Makkah*, 559.

45. Baker, *King Hussein*, 14–16.

46. Al-Sibaʻi, *Taʾrikh Makkah*, 567.

47. After the CUP took over government in 1908, the party decided to impose a tax on burials. The returns went to the upkeep of local cemeteries. The people of Mecca, accustomed to receiving Ottoman financial tributes as opposed to paying them, revolted against the CUP government and their Ashraf intermediaries. After violence led to many deaths, the imperial rulers removed Sharif Ali and appointed Abdullah ibn Muhammad ibn Awn instead, but he died soon after. The CUP government then wanted to appoint the second in line, Ali Haydar, who had long presented himself as a liberal and supporter of constitutionalism. The old guard, however, feared Ali and thus chose, successfully, the more conservative Sharif Husayn ibn Ali, who opposed popular political participation and constitutionalism, and had been in forced exile in Constantinople for fifteen years. See Baker, *King Hussein*, 14.

48. Ibid., 20.

49. "Hal tuwjad fi al-Mamlaka al-ʻArabiyya nahda haqiqiyya" [Is there a true Nahda in the Arabian Kingdom?], *Sawt al-Hijaz*, no. 89, December 25, 1933, 1.

50. Ahmad ibn Zayni Dahlan first oversaw the establishment and management of al-Amiriyya Press. Under Al Saud, its name was changed to Umm al-Qura Press.

51. Al-Sibaʻi, *Taʾrikh Makkah*, 556. On the CUP reorganization and restoration of law and order, see Hanioğlu, *Brief History*, 149.

52. Hasan Kayalı, *Arabs and Young Turks: Ottomanism, Arabism, and Islamism in the Ottoman, 1908–1918* (Los Angeles: University of California Press, 1997), 152–53.

53. Al-Sibaʻi, *Taʾrikh Makkah*, 556. William Ochsenwald argues that Sharif Husayn shut it down because its ethnically Turkish owners were "sympathetic to the CUP," but local sources claim otherwise. Ochsenwald, "Arab Nationalism in the Hijaz," 197.

54. The other newspapers, which emerged and shut down between 1908 and 1916, were *al-Islah al-Hijazi* (a weekly newspaper published in May 1909 by a private printing press in Jeddah), *Safaʾ al-Hijaz* (Purity of the Hijaz; published in August 1909); *al-Raqib* (The observer; published in Medina), and *al-Madina al-Munawwara* (The illuminated Medina; published in late 1909). Both Medina-based newspapers were written by hand because of a lack of printing technology in that city. For more details, see Muhammad Shamikh, *Al-Sahafa fi al-Hijaz: Dirasa wa nusus* [The press in the Hijaz, 1908–1941: Study and texts] (Beirut: Dar al-Amana, 1971).

55. Abdulaziz ibn Saud shut it down upon conquering the Hijaz in 1924–1925.

56. Ochsenwald, *Religion, Society, and the State in Arabia*.

57. For a detailed biography, see Muhammad Zahid Abu Ghidda, "Khayr al-Din al-Zirikli," *Rabitat al-'Ulama' al-Suriyyin*, May 5, 2013, http://islamsyria.com/index.php?/site/show_cvs/345.

58. Muhammad Shamikh, *Al-Sahafa fi al-Hijaz*, 437–38.

59. For transformations in political life under the CUP and the committee's increasing Turkification policies, see Hanioğlu, *Brief History*, 156–67. While this chapter focuses on the Hijaz, Najd witnessed its own intellectual and cultural growth. As Guido Steinberg notes, merchants played a significant role in the transmission of knowledge in central Arabia: "It is intriguing that this development [the majalis of merchants] coincided not only with an intensification of foreign trade, but also with the first massive influx of printed books in Central Arabia. For example, Charles Doughty in 1877 visited a local notable in 'Unaiza, Abdullah al-Khunaini. There he saw the first volume of Butrus al-Bustani's encyclopedia, which had only appeared in 1876. At that time, several young merchants read this book, and furthermore deal with genealogy, history, and poetry and spoke foreign languages such as English or Hindi. Whenever possible, they read newspapers from Beirut and Cairo." Guido Steinberg, "Ecology, Knowledge, and Trade in Central Arabia," in *Counter-Narratives: History, Contemporary Society and Politics in Saudi Arabia and Yemen*, ed. Madawi Al-Rasheed and Robert Vitalis (New York: Palgrave, 2004), 97.

60. Husayn Muhammad Nasif's *Madi al-Hijaz wa hadiruh* [Hijaz's past and its present] (Cairo, 1931), for example, references Rashid Rida, Khayr al-Din al-Zirikli, and Shakib Arslan, among others. See also Saad al-Surayhi, *Idiologia al-sahra': Afaq al-tajdid wa su'al al-hawiiya al-mu'alaqqa* [Desert ideology: Horizons of renewal and the question of suspended identity] (Beirut: Dar Jadawil, 2015).

61. "Khawatir 'Awwad athar jadalan qabla 80 'amman wa sadah mustamiran" ['Awwad's *Authorized Reflections* stirred controversy 80 years ago and its echoes persist], *al-Watan*, April 4, 2012, http://www.alwatan.com.sa/Dialogue/News_Detail.aspx?ArticleID=97401&CategoryID=4.

62. Ochsenwald, "Arab Nationalism in the Hijaz."

63. Mary C. Wilson, "The Hashemites, the Arab Revolt, and Arab Nationalism," *The Origins of Arab Nationalism*, ed. Rashid Khalidi, Lisa Anderson, Muhammad Muslih, and Reeva S. Simon (New York: Columbia University Press, 1991), 204–6. Acting at the request of Arab nationalist secret societies, Sharif Husayn, in his correspondence with McMahon, called for Arab independence in Syria, Palestine, and Iraq. The British, however, recognized him as king of the Hijaz.

64. Mahmoud Abdul-Ghani Sabbagh, "Modernity in Makkah: History at a Glance," *Arab News*, March 3, 2010, http://www.arabnews.com/node/338655. For the concept of the imagined community, see Benedict Anderson, *Imagined Communities: Reflections on the Origin and Spread of Nationalism* (New York: Verso, 1991).

65. Muhammad Hassan 'Awwad, *Khawatir musarraha* [Authorized reflections] (Cairo: Arab Press, 1926). For a discussion of his accomplishments and role in the Arab Nahda, see Ali al-Dumaini, "Al-sawt.. wa-l-ajras ufuq al-hadatha min 'al-'Awwad' ila 'al-Ali'" [The voice and bells are horizons of modernity from "al-'Awwad" to "al-Ali"], *Al-Faisal Magazine*, May 8, 2016, 74–81. For a discussion of the role of Hijazi intellectuals in the Arab Nahda, see Ahmad Abubakr Ibrahim, *Al-Adab al-Hijazi fi al-*Nahda *al-haditha* [Hijazi literature in the modern Nahda] (Cairo: Matba'at Nahdat Masr, 1948).

66. Khayr al-Din Zirikli, *Ma ra'ayt wa ma sami't min Dimashq ila Makkah, 1929* [What I saw and what I heard from Damascus to Mecca, 1929] (Beirut: al-Mu'assassa al-'Arabiyya li-l-Dirasat wa-l-Nashr, 2009).

67. European consulates in Jeddah regularly filed reports expressing concern about extensive communist activities and mobilizations in Jeddah and Mecca. A letter from the French minister of interior warned the French consul general in Jeddah that communist leaders in Jeddah and Mecca were about to hold a propaganda campaign targeting pilgrims. Record 19775, French Collection, File 103, No. 316, October 1, 1925. Darah Archives. A Dutch report warned about three meetings that communists held in Mecca, one attended by sixty members and another at which anti–Al Saud plans were discussed. Record 28940, Dutch Collection, File 102, Report 3296, August 30, 1927, Darah Archives, Riyadh.

68. James Onley, *The Arabian Frontier of the British Raj: Merchants, Rulers, and the British in the Nineteenth-Century Gulf* (Oxford: Oxford University Press, 2007); Mehrdad R. Izady, "The Gulf's Ethnic Diversity: An Evolutionary History," in *Security in the Persian Gulf: Origins, Obstacles, and the Search for Consensus*, ed. Gary Sick and Lawrence Potter (New York: Palgrave Macmillan, 2002), 69; John Willis, "Making Yemen Indian: Rewriting the Boundaries of Imperial Arabia," *International Journal of Middle East Studies* 41, no. 1 (2009): 23–38; and Anscombe, *Ottoman Gulf*.

69. Salman al-Hajji, "Al-Shaykh Salih ibn Muhammad al-Sultan wa muharabat al-fikr al-isti'mari, 1924–2010" [Shaykh Salih ibn Muhammad al-Sultan and fighting colonial ideology, 1924–2010], *al-Waha*, no. 60 (Winter 2010): 100.

70. Haytham Muhammad al-Jishi, "Al-Imam Hassan Ali al-Badr . . . al-Shaykh al-mujahid" [Imam Ali al-Badr . . . the Fighter Shaykh], *Rasid*, September 17, 2005.

71. For life histories of the most notable ulama, scholars, and poets from Qatif and al-Ahsa as well as of those who resided there for a significant part of their lives, see Muhammad Saʿid al-Muslim, *Sahil al-dahab al-aswad: Dirasa tarikhiyya insaniyya li-mantiqat al-Khalij al-ʿArabi* [Black Gold Coast: Historical study of the Arab Gulf region], 2nd ed. (Beirut: Dar Maktabat al-Hayat, 1960), 283–307. Guido Steinberg, a writer of cultural and intellectual exchange between Najd and India, points out that "any clear-cut differentiation between economic and cultural dimensions would obscure these interrelations," in Steinberg, "Ecology, Knowledge, and Trade in Central Arabia," in Al-Rasheed and Vitalis, *Counter-Narratives*, 95.

72. Yaʿqub Y. Al-Ghunaym, ed., *Tarikh al-taʿlim fi dawlat al-Kuwayt: Dirasa tawthiqiyya* [The history of education in the State of Kuwait: A survey], 6 vols. (Kuwait: Markaz al-Buhuth wa-l-Dirasat al-Kuwaytiyya, 2002), 99–100. Al-Ahsa, al-Qatif, and the island of Bahrain historically made up a regional unit known as Bahrain. Many of al-Badr's coreligionist ulama opposed Al Saud as well, but unlike him, they were not prepared to take up arms against the invading army.

73. The school was named after its patron and Kuwait's ruler, Shaykh Nasir ibn Mubarak al-Sabah. Yusuf ibn Isa al-Qinaʿi (its first principal) and Yassin al-Tabatabaʾi, however, initiated and followed through with the idea. The schools had many teachers, including Hafız Wahba, the Egyptian-born teacher who was exiled by the British and later became Saudi King Abdulaziz's political adviser and, in 1930, ambassador to England.

74. Abdulaziz al-Rushayd, *Tarikh al-Kuwait* [History of Kuwait], rev. ed. (Beirut: Dar Maktabat al-Hayat, 1978), 325; and Yusuf ibn Isa al-Qinaʿi, *Safahat min tarikh al-Kuwait* [Pages from the history of Kuwait], 4th ed. (Kuwait: Matbaʿat hukumat al-Kuwait, 1968).

75. Al-Rushayd, *Tarikh al-Kuwait*, 353. For Rashid Rida's role in the debates on the Islamic caliphate, see John Willis, "Debating the Caliphate: Islam and Nation in the Work of Rashid Rida and Abul Kalam Azad," *International History Review* 32, no. 4 (2010): 711–32.

76. Al-Rushayd, *Tarikh al-kuwait*, 325. *Al-Qibla* and *al-Hijaz* newspapers, as well as Rashid Rida's *al-Manar*, provide ample examples of intellectual, political, and literary connections between Ottoman Arabia and the rest of the empire and South Asia. Also see Nasif, *Madi al-hijaz wa hadiruh* [Hijaz's past and its present]; and Zirikli, *Ma raʾayt wa ma samiʿt min Dimashq ila Makkah, 1929* [What I saw and what I heard from Damascus to Mecca, 1929].

77. Founders of the Hijaz National Party were Muhammad al-Tawil, Muhammad Tahir Dabbagh (secretary of party), Qassim Zaynal (treasurer), Sulayman Qabil (Jeddah mayor), Abdullah Rida (district governor of Jeddah), Salih Shatta, Muhammad Salih Nasif, Abd al-Ra'uf al-Sabban (Meccan notable), Mahmud Shalhub (Meccan notable), Sharaf ibn Rajih (Meccan sharif), Ali Salama, and Majid Kurdi (Meccan notable). See Nasif, *Madi al-Hijaz*, 133–34.

78. Speech of general secretary of the Hijaz National Party, Tahir al-Dabbagh, after the enthronement of King Husayn and the party's correspondence with him on October 4, 1924. In al-Siba'i, *Ta'rikh Makkah*, 632–35; and Nasif, *Madi al-Hijaz*, 130–41.

79. Al-Siba'i, *Ta'rikh Makkah*, 635–36.

80. Abdulaziz ibn Saud, "Balagh 'an mustaqbal al Hijaz" [An announcement on the future of the Hijaz], in Abdulaziz ibn Muhammad al-Fahd al-Issa, *Arshif Mamlakat al-Hijaz wa saltanat Najd wa Mulhaqatiha: min 1343h until 1346h* [The archive of the Kingdom of Hijaz and Sultanate of Najd and Its Dependencies: From 1924 until 1928] (Beirut: Jadawil, 2013), 116.

81. *Barid al-Hijaz* started publishing in 1924 under its editor Muhammad Salih Nasif. According to Abdulrahman S. Shobaili, "It also published the official communiqués, official town notices, regulations and royal declaration. The newspaper also gave some coverage to world news and printed a number of interesting articles dealing with the important topic of the 'Caliphate' which had been adopted by King Hossein of Al Hijaz. The paper also carried a number of items quoted from contemporary Egyptian papers notably *Al Muquattam*." See Abdulrahman S. Shobaili, "An Historical and Analytical Study of Broadcasting and Press in Saudi Arabia" (PhD diss., Ohio State University, 1971), 51.

82. Ali al-Wardi, *Qissat al-Ashraf wa Ibn Sa'ud* [The story of the Ashraf and Ibn Saud] (London: Alwarrak, 2007), 248–49. *Umm al-Qura*, under its editor Yusuf Yassin, became the official gazette of Abdulaziz ibn Saud's government of the Hijaz and Najd and Its Dependencies and starting in 1932, of the Kingdom of Saudi Arabia as well. *Umm al-Qura* published royal decrees, treaties, regulations, government and court decisions, and other relevant official material.

83. For details of the Saudi-Wahhabi conquest of the Hijaz, see al-Wardi, *Qissat al-Ashraf*.

84. "General Announcement" and "Notice from the Royal Court," in al-Issa, *Arshif Mamlakat al-Hija* [Archive of the Kingdom of Hijaz], 146, 163.

85. Sabbagh, "Modernity in Makkah," 3.

86. 'Awwad wrote the introduction of Husayn Muhammad Nasif's 1931 *Madi al-hijaz wa hadiruh*.

87. 'Awwad, *Khawatir Musarraha*.

88. Ibid., 4.

89. Ibid.

90. In addition to the Arabian authors already listed, see Muhsin Giyadh 'Ujayl, *Sulaiman bin Salih al-Dakhil al-Najdi: al-sahafi, al-siyasi, al-mu'arrikh* [Sulaiman bin Salih al-Dakhil al-Najdi: The journalist, the politician, and the historian] (Beirut: Dar al-Arabiyya lilmawsu'at, 2002); Mansur al-Assaf, "Sulaiman al-Dakhil.. awwal sahafi siyasi fi Najd" [Sulaiman al-Dakhil: The first political journalist in Najd], *Al-Riyadh*, November 25, 2016, http://www.alriyadh.com/1550265#; and Mirza al-Khuwayldi, "Khalid al-Faraj.. Sirat rajul jassada hilm al-wihda bayn al-khalijayn" [Khalid al-Faraj: A man who embodied the dream of unification of the two gulfs], *Al-Sharq al-Awsat*, September 27, 2014, https://aawsat.com/home/article/189746.

91. Sheehi, *Foundations of Modern Arab Identity*; Elizabeth Suzanne Kassab, *Contemporary Arab Thought: Cultural Critique in Comparative Perspective* (New York: Columbia University Press, 2010); Dyala Hamzah, ed., *The Making of the Arab Intellectual: Empire, Public Sphere and the Colonial Coordinates of Selfhood* (New York: Routledge, 2013); Ilham Khuri-Makdisi, *The Eastern Mediterranean and the Making of Global Radicalism, 1860–1914* (Berkeley: University of California Press, 2010); Jens Hanssen and Max Weiss, *Arabic Thought beyond the Liberal Age: Towards an Intellectual History of the Nahda* (Cambridge: Cambridge University Press, 2016); Jens Hanssen and Max Weiss, *Arabic Thought against the Authoritarian Age: Towards an Intellectual History of the Present* (Cambridge: Cambridge University Press, 2018); and Tarek El-Ariss, ed., *The Arab Renaissance: A Bilingual Anthology of the Nahda* (New York: Modern Language Association of America, 2018).

92. Hamzah, *The Making of the Arab Intellectual*.

93. Malik Dahlan, *The Hijaz: The First Islamic State* (London: Hurst, 2017), 120–122.

94. Priya Satia, *Spies in Arabia: The Great War and the Cultural Foundations of Britain's Covert Empire in the Middle East* (Oxford: Oxford University Press, 2008).

95. Steinberg, "Ecology, Knowledge, and Trade in Central Arabia."

96. Basheer M. Nafi, "A Teacher of Ibn Abd al-Wahhab: Muhammad Hayat al-Sindi and the Revival of Ashab al-Hadith's Methodology," *Islamic Law and Society* 13, no. 2

(2006): 208; and Natana J. Delong-Bas, *Wahhabi Islam: From Revival and Reform to Global Jihad* (Oxford: Oxford University Press, 2008).

97. This narration is based on interviews with Saudi state historians in Riyadh in March–June 2011, in which they referred to this narrative as the "real" one that would never make it into the exhibition and museum displays they were overseeing.

98. Hanioğlu, *A Brief History*, 12.

99. Muhammad Shams, "'Ulama' al-Hijaz yunashidun al-sultan al-'Uthmani al-tadakhul" [Hijazi ulama plea with Ottoman Sultan to intervene], *al-Hijaz* website, http://www.alhejaz.org/tarekh/0910901.htm; Khaled Fahmy, *All the Pasha's Men: Mehmed Ali, His Army and the Making of Modern Egypt* (Cairo: American University in Cairo Press, 2002); and al-Muslim, *Sahil al-dahab al-aswad* [Black Gold Coast], 181.

100. Al Saud's eighteenth- and nineteenth-century political formations were not modern "states." But in the second half of the twentieth century, official Saudi discourse began to refer to them as such in order to produce the modern Saudi state—referred to as the "third Saudi state" in this new rendering—as the teleological continuation of the earlier ones.

101. The northwestern Persian Gulf coast was historically diverse and culturally, economically, and politically influenced by Persian, and to a much lesser extent Portuguese, empires before the Ottomans managed to defeat the Portuguese in the region in the mid-sixteenth century. Until Al Saud conquered the region for the last time in 1913, local and Ottoman forces struggled over power there, and the region became a site of Ottoman-British rivalry. The Great Game—during which Russian encroachment into Persia and its influence in Afghanistan increased—threatened Britain's access to India, thus increasing the importance of the Persian Gulf for British imperial power. In the 1880s, the Ottoman imperial center reacted by reorganizing the government and reining in such "peripheries" as the western Gulf coast. These efforts were a financial strain for the Ottomans, yet they failed to compete with British forces in controlling the coastal regions of the Gulf. See Robert Vitalis, *America's Kingdom: Mythmaking on the Saudi Oil Frontier* (Stanford, CA: Stanford University Press, 2007); and Anscombe, *The Ottoman Gulf*.

102. Askar H. Al-Enazy, *The Creation of Saudi Arabia: Ibn Saud and British Imperial Policy, 1914–1927* (New York: Routledge, 2010). See also Satia, *Spies in Arabia*. Some scholars argue that Muhammad ibn Abd al-Wahhab had introduced the concept of the state to Wahhabi political theology and to Al Saud's political ideology. Khalid

Aldakhil, *Al-Wahhabiyya bayn al-shirk wa tasaddu' al-qabila* [Wahhabism between idolatry and fragmentation of the tribe] (Beirut: Al-Shabaka al-Arabiyya li-l-abhath wa-l-nashr, 2013). But to do so is to read history in teleological fashion and to project the meaning of the modern twentieth-century state onto the eighteenth century.

103. The geographic territory that Abdulaziz ruled between 1926 and 1932 is regularly referred to as the Kingdom of Hijaz and Sultanate of Nejd and Its Dependencies, but the constitution that his regime issued was titled "Al-ta'limat al-asasiyya li-l-Mamlaka al-Hijaziyya" [The basic laws of the Kingdom of Hijaz], Mecca, September 4, 1926, Arabian Peninsula Collection, American University of Beirut Archives. This is because the sultanate was changed to a kingdom on April 2, 1927. "Faisal Announces Changing the Sultanate of Najd and Its Dependencies to the Kingdom of Najd and Its Dependencies," *Umm al-Qura*, no. 121, April 2, 1927.

104. Asian pilgrims to some of Iraq's wealthiest regions, Najaf and Karbala, were known to bring rare and expensive gifts and money with them to leave at the tombs of Ali ibn abi Talib and Husayn ibn Ali.

105. For a detailed description of Wahhabism and religious shrines, see Hanioğlu, *Brief History*.

106. British-supplied arms and favorable geopolitics enabled Abdulaziz ibn Saud to defeat his many rivals in the east, west, and central regions. The Ikhwan fighting force, also known as Soldiers of Unitarianism (Jund al-Tawhid), had accepted the British-Saudi alliance, and they, too, were instrumental in conquering and securing the territories that later made up the Saudi state. With the emergence of Iraq and Transjordan as modern states that were under the British Mandate, and Kuwait, Qatar, and Bahrain as British protectorates, the imperial power pressured Abdulaziz ibn Saud to respect the new territorial boundaries. While the Saudi regime—bureaucrats and ulama alike—finally accepted the necessity of delineating and respecting borders, especially to safeguard the new extraction economy, the Ikhwan refused to acquiesce to that. See Madawi Al-Rasheed, *History of Saudi Arabia* (London: Cambridge University Press, 2010), 47, 50–62.

107. The British, through Percy Cox, signed the 1915 Qatif Treaty (or the Darin Treaty) in which they favored the chieftaincy of Abdulaziz ibn Saud over Qatif, al-Ahsa, and Najd and guaranteed hereditary succession to his dynasty in return for loyalty to Britain alone. The 1927 Jeddah Treaty replaced the first treaty and recognized the Kingdom of Hijaz and Najd and Its Dependencies as a sovereign state. Through arms and financial provisions, the British thus enabled Al Saud to prevail—even against

the British-allied Hashemite regime in the Hijaz. For more on the support that the British and others provided Abdulaziz ibn Saud to build a regular army, see Record 14773, Dutch Collection, File 102, Report No. 180, original No. 1578, July 7, 1929, Darah Archives, Riyadh.

108. To gauge the extent to which British intelligence was instrumental to the survival of the Al Saud regime and the newly formed Saudi state, see Coll 6/52, "Saudi Arabia: Anti-Saudi Activities of Sayed Mohamed Tahir al Dabbagh," British Library: India Office Records and Private Papers, IOR/L/PS/12/2119, *Qatar Digital Library,* https://www.qdl.qa/archive/81055/vdc_100000000555.0x000291.

109. Quoted in Ameen Rihani, *Ibn Sa'oud of Arabia* (London: Routledge, 2011), 214. Rihani, an astute observer of 1920s politics in the peninsula, was a confidant and admirer of Abdulaziz ibn Saud. Rihani's book was originally published in London by Constable in 1928.

110. Al-Rasheed, *History of Saudi Arabia,* 59–61.

111. "Instructions: Regulations of the Committees for the Promotion of Virtue and the Prevention of Vice, August 17, 1927," in al-Issa, *Arshif Mamlakat al-Hijaz* [The archive of the Kingdom of Hijaz], 316. In early Islam, the *muhtasib* (pl. *muhtasibun*), or the inspector general of weights and measures, was in charge of policing urban markets and traders to prevent fraud and corruption, and also ensuring public morality, health, and cleanliness. See Caroline Stone, "The Muhtasib," *Saudi Aramco World,* September–October 1977, http://www.saudiaramcoworld.com/issue/197705/the.muhtasib.htm; and Michael Cook, *Commanding Right and Forbidding Wrong in Islamic Thought* (Oxford: Oxford University Press, 2000).

112. Ibrahim al-Rashid, ed., *The Unification of Central Arabia under Ibn Saud, 1909–1925,* vol. 1 of *Documents on the History of Saudi Arabia* (Salisbury, NC: Documentary Publications, 1976), 128.

113. Ministry of Education, Kingdom of Saudi Arabia, *Tarikh al-Mamlakah al-'Arabiyya al-Sa'udiyya, 2005–2006* [History of the Kingdom of Saudi Arabia, 2005–2006] (6th grade, 9th grade, 12th grade). See also Emine Ö. Evered, "Rereading Ottoman Accounts of Wahhabism as Alternative Narratives: Ahmed Cevdet Paşa's Historical Survey of the Movement," *Comparative Studies of South Asia, Africa and the Middle East,* 32, no. 3 (2012): 622–32.

114. Ali Baqir al-'Awwami, "Al-Haraka al-wataniyya sharq al-Sa'udiyya, 1953–1973" [The nationalist movement in eastern Saudi Arabia, 1953–1973] (unpublished manuscript, al-Qatif, 2011), PDF files, 1:306; and Al-Rasheed, *History of Saudi Arabia.*

115. As the capital of the Hashemite state, Mecca had more developed bureaucratic and human resources, and under the Saudi regime it remained the administrative capital until the regime was ready to develop Riyadh and build state institutions there.

116. Sultan Alamer, "Beyond Sectarianism and Ideology: Regionalism and Collective Political Action in Saudi Arabia," in *Salman's Legacy*, ed. Madawi Al-Rasheed (London: Hurst, 2018), 114.

117. For a detailed account of the development of Saudi historiography, see Jörg Matthias Determann, *Historiography in Saudi Arabia: Globalization and the State in the Middle East* (London: I. B. Tauris, 2014).

118. Rosie Bsheer, "A Counter-Revolutionary State: Popular Movements and the Making of Saudi Arabia," *Past and Present* 238, no. 1 (February 2018): 233–77.

119. Al-Rasheed, *History of Saudi Arabia*.

120. These include an Arab state under the Ashraf of Mecca, a separate Hijazi state, a southern region joining the state of Yemen, and various ideas about territorial formations in the east. See Al-Rasheed and Vitalis, *Counter-Narratives*; Ochsenwald, *Religion, Society, and the State in Arabi*; Dahlan, *The Hijaz*; Tariq Moraiwed Tell, *The Social and Economic Origins of Monarchy in Jordan* (New York: Palgrave Macmillan, 2013); and John Willis, *Unmaking North and South: Cartographies of the Yemeni Past* (London: Hurst, 2012).

121. "Relations with Transjordan, May–November 1932: The Rebellion of Ibn Rifada," 2 June 1932, FO, in Records of Saudi Arabia, 1932–34, 52–54, 67, Coll 6/52, "Saudi Arabia: Anti-Saudi Activities of Sayed Mohamed Tahir al Dabbagh"; and al-'Awwami, "Al-haraka al-wataniyya."

122. Sultan Alamer, ed., *Fi tarikh al-'uruba: qira'at naqdiyya fi hawamish al-zaman wa al-makan* [On the history of Arab nationalism: Critical readings on the margins of time and space] (Beirut: Jusur li-l-tarjama wa-al-nashr, 2016).

123. Srirupa Roy, *Beyond Belief: India and the Politics of Postcolonial Nationalism* (Durham, NC: Duke University Press, 2007).

124. Reports from European embassies in Jeddah that I accessed at the Darah regularly alerted their home governments of social unrest and political discontent in Saudi Arabia. For an example, see this German report, which details attempts to overthrow Al Saud from power and notes that "the people of Hejaz are not satisfied with the rule of King Ibn Saud." Report from the archive of Foreign Ministry–Bonn, July 1, 1938, Record 23744, File 101, No. 2580, German Collection, Darah, Riyadh. For

a detailed discussion of the various attempts to overthrow or oppose Al Saud, see Bsheer, "A Counter-Revolutionary State."

125. Madawi Al-Rasheed, *A Most Masculine State: Gender, Politics, Religion in Saudi Arabia* (Cambridge: Cambridge University Press, 2013).

126. Between 1930 and 1940, only nine thousand pilgrims had traveled to Mecca, down from one hundred thousand only a decade before. See Ahmad Adnan, *Al-Sajin 32: Ahlam Muhammad Sa'id Tayyib wa haza'imoh* [Prisoner 32: The dreams of Muhammad Sa'id Tayyib and his defeats], 2nd ed. (al-Dar al-Bayda', Morocco: al-Markaz al-Thaqafi al-'Arabi, 2011), 19.

127. The Standard Oil Company of California (SOCAL) signed the oil agreement with Saudi Arabia in 1933, but after three years of SOCAL's unsuccessfully searching for oil, Texas Oil Company (Texaco) purchased 50 percent of the concession. In 1945, California-Arabian Standard Oil Company (CASOC) changed its name to Arabian American Oil Company (Aramco). In 1948, Standard Oil of New Jersey purchased 30 percent of the oil company and later Socony Vacuum purchased 10 percent. Both were shareholders in the Iraq Petroleum Company.

128. Walid Khadduri, ed., *Abdullah al-Tariqi: al-A'mal al-kamila* [Abdullah al-Tariqi: Complete works], 2nd ed. (Beirut: Markaz Dirasat al-Wihda al-'Arabiyya, 2005), 30, 126. In the aftermath of the Arab defeat in the 1967 Arab-Israeli War, former minister of oil Abdullah al-Tariqi lamented that "we all know that the oil companies are of a political in addition to an economic and commercial nature, and that they amount to governments in the Arab regions in which they operate, and their regulations ensure they operate as independent governments with sovereignty.... They [oil companies] deal with local government on equal footing and they hold an amount of actual power that enable them to act as if they were the only authority in the country." See also Vitalis, *America's Kingdom*.

129. Memorandum from Nabih Amin Faris, Princeton University, to the White House, October 24, 1941, President's Secretary's File, Saudi Arabia, 1933–1945 (1941), Franklin D. Roosevelt Presidential Library and Museum, Hyde Park, NY.

130. Memorandum by the State Department, from Secretary Cordell Hull to President Franklin D. Roosevelt, April 21, 1941, 3, Franklin D. Roosevelt Presidential Library and Museum, Hyde Park, NY, President's Secretary's File, Saudi Arabia, 1933–1945 (1941).

131. In a letter dated May 17, 1941, H. A. Stuart, rear admiral of the US Navy and director of Naval Petroleum Reserves, wrote the secretary of the navy clarifying that

the quality of Saudi oil was not suitable for use for navy purposes and did not meet the requirements set out by US Navy specifications. As such, it was inadvisable to use Saudi oil for either naval vessels or airplanes, more so because it would also "cause serious discomfort—if not more harmful effects—to anti-aircraft personnel." Harry L. Hopkins, one of President Roosevelt's closest advisers, supported the idea of the "shipment of food directly under the Lend-Lease Bill," pointing out, however, that "just how we could call that outfit a 'democracy' I don't know." Memorandum from H. A. Stuart, director of Naval Petroleum Reserves, Secretary of the Navy, Navy Department, Washington, May 17, 1941, President's Secretary's File, Saudi Arabia, 1933–1945 (1941), Franklin D. Roosevelt Presidential Library and Museum, Hyde Park, NY.

132. Nate Herring, "A Lasting Legacy: The Dhahran Airfield and Civil Air Terminal," Public Affairs Office, May 23, 2014, US Army Corps of Engineers; and Timothy Mitchell, *Carbon Democracy: Political Power in the Age of Oil* (London: Verso, 2011), 208.

133. Correspondence between King Abdulaziz ibn Saud and President Franklin D. Roosevelt, March 10–April 15, 1945, Fawzan al-Sabiq Collection, Folder 5, number 400, Darah Archives, Riyadh.

134. Al-Rashid, *Documents on the History of Saudi Arabia*, 1:135.

135. See letter from King Abdulaziz ibn Saud to President Franklin D. Roosevelt, March 10, 1945, No. 45/1/4/26, Institute of Public Administration Archive (hereafter cited as IPA Archive), Riyadh. For a detailed account of the multisited, decades-long struggle between British and US imperial powers over the postwar control of oil, see Mitchell, *Carbon Democracy*, 113–27.

136. Aramco had also contributed to the war economy by importing goods and food into the country, transporting thousands of tons of nutritional goods to Riyadh in 1944. See Abdulrahman Abdullah al-Ahmari, "Dawr Sharikat al-Zayt al-'Arabiyya al-Amrikiyya fi tanmiyat al-Mantaqa al-Sharqiyya min al-Mamlaka al-'Arabiyya al-Sa'udiyya, 1944–1964" [The role of the Arabian American Oil Company in developing the Eastern Province of Saudi Arabia, 1944–1964] (PhD diss., King Saud University, 2007), 141.

137. In 1947, J. Rives Childs, the US consular official in Saudi Arabia, complained to the US secretary of state that Aramco continued to assume government functions, despite previous complaints by US officials at the Jeddah Legation. Childs warned: "I would not make so much of this instance were it not that over a long period of time this irregular assumption of diplomatic functions by the company shows no signs of abatement and unless checked, it is likely in my opinion to provoke difficulties for us in the transaction of government business, as it has in the past. It is also likely to create confusion in the minds of Saudi Arabian officials as to whether ARAMCO or

representatives of the United States Government in Saudi Arabia are the mouthpieces of the American government." J. Rives Childs, "Irregular Assumption by ARAMCO of Diplomatic Functions," February 13, 1947, in al-Rashid, *Saudi Arabia Enters the Modern World: Secret U.S. Documents on the Emergence of the Kingdom of Saudi Arabia as a World Power, 1936–1949*, vol. 1 of *Documents on the History of Saudi Arabia* (Salisbury, NC: Documentary Publications, 1980), 64–65.

138. The same was true of oil companies in Latin America and elsewhere. See Miguel Tinker Salas, *The Enduring Legacy: Oil, Culture, and Society in Venezuela* (Durham, NC: Duke University Press, 2009).

139. For the CIA's role in Saudi and Arab affairs more generally, see Irene L. Gendzier, "Oil, Politics and US Intervention," in *A Revolutionary Year: the Middle East in 1958*, ed. Wm. Roger Louis and Roger Owen (New York: I. B. Tauris, 2002), 101–42; Khadduri, *Abdullah al-Tariqi*, 350–53; Douglas Little, "Pipeline Politics: America, TAPLINE and the Arabs," *Business History Review* 64, no. 2 (Summer 1990): 255–85; Fawwaz Traboulsi, *A History of Modern Lebanon* (New York: Pluto Press, 2007); Vitalis, *America's Kingdom*; Salim Wakim, *Al-Malik Sa'ud: Mu'assis al-dawla al-Sa'udiyya al-haditha* [King Sa'ud: Founder of the modern Saudi state] (Beirut: Dar al-Saqi, 1966); and Hugh Wilford, *America's Great Game: The CIA's Secret Arabists and the Shaping of the Modern Middle East* (New York: Basic Books, 2013).

140. Aramco officials claimed that they paid for local donations and contributions from Aramco's budget and not that of the Saudi government. However, scholars like Abdulrahman al-Ahmari who have perused Aramco's archival documents in Dhahran and Riyadh were not able to prove such claims. Al-Ahmari also states that Aramco even spent more in donations abroad than it did in Saudi Arabia. Al-Ahmari, "Dawr Sharikat al-Zayt al-'Arabiyya al-Amrikiyya," 78, 85.

141. Ibid., 149; and *Al-zayt yusahhil subul al-raqi* [Oil facilitates progress] (Dhahran: Da'irat al-'alakat al-'amma fi al-Sharq al-Awsat, sharikat al-zayt al-'Arabiyya al-Amrikiyya, 1950), 17.

142. Royal Decree No. 30/4/1/1046, April 20, 1952, IPA Archive, Riyadh.

143. Micol Seigel, *Violence Work: State Power and the Limits of Police* (Durham, NC: Duke University Press, 2018); and Betsy Beasley, "Service Learning: Oil, International Education, and Texas's Corporate Cold War," *Diplomatic History* 42, no. 2 (2018), 177–203.

144. This was still a time in which those wanted by the security regime simply went to a different city to escape prosecution, imprisonment, or punishment, and often sought pardon from the king.

145. In 1954, the Saudi regime asked Aramco to draw up comprehensive maps of the country, which it completed in both Arabic and English in 1963. See al-Ahmari, "Dawr Sharikat al-Zayt al-'Arabiyya al-Amrikiyya," 349.

146. Bsheer, "A Counter-Revolutionary State."

147. Islamist groups such as the Organization of Islamic Revolution in the Arabian Peninsula (Munazamat al-Thawra al-Islamiyya fi al-Jazira al-Arabiyya), Liberation of the Peninsula (Hizb Tahrir al-Jazira), the Da'wah Society (Jam'iyyat al-Da'wa), and the Muslim Brotherhood (al-Ikhwan al-Muslimin) were formed in the 1950s and 1960s. As with the Saudi leftists, their histories have also been excised from the record because they used political religion to challenge the Saudi monarchy. See Abdulaziz al-Khidr, *Al-Saudiyya: Sirat dawla wamujtama', qira'a fi tajrubat thilth qarn min al-tahawulat al-fikriyya wa-l-siyasiyya wa-l-tanmawiyya* [Saudi Arabia: Biography of a state and society, a reading in a quarter-century experience of intellectual, political and developmental transformations], 2nd ed. (Beirut: Arab Network for Research and Publications, 2011), 829.

148. Royal Decree No. 37, December 22, 1960, in *Umm al-Qura*, 23 December 23, 1960, IPA Archive, Riyadh; "Al-nizam al-asasi, 1959–1960" [The basic law], *al-Jaridah*, December 27, 1960; and "Alnizam al-asasi, 1959–1960" [The basic law], King Saud's personal library, Jeddah.

149. "Bayan 'an siyasat al-hukuma al-dakhiliyya wa alkharijiyya" [Statement on the government's internal and foreign policies], *Umm al-Qura*, December 30, 1960, IPA Archive, Riyadh.

150. Abdel Razzaq Takriti, *Monsoon Revolution: Republicans, Sultans, and Empires in Oman, 1965–1976* (Oxford: Oxford University Press, 2016), 53.

151. Letter from King Faisal ibn Abdulaziz to US president Lyndon Johnson (month and day unclear, 1966), Arabian Peninsula Collection, American University of Beirut Archives. See also "Attacks on Saudi Arabia in the Lebanese Press," Khalil Itani (Lebanese ambassador to Saudi Arabia) to Lebanese Foreign Minister, No. 77/February 25, 1968, Abdullah Yafi Collection, American University of Beirut Archives.

152. See *Saudi Arabia: A Disruptive Force in Western–Arab Relations*, [US] Department of State Intelligence Report No. 7144, Prepared by the Division of Research for the Near East, South Asia, and Africa, January 18, 1956, in OSS/State Department, *Intelligence and Research Reports, pt. XII, The Middle East, 1950–1961 Supplement*, ed. Paul Kesaris (Washington, DC, 1979); and Rosie Bsheer, "A Counter-Revolutionary State." I found very few documents in Riyadh's archives on the arrests of the 1960s, but for an example, see Record 17102, No. 342, Presidency of the Council of Ministers, July 14, 1965, IPA Archive, Riyadh.

153. Vitalis, *America's Kingdom*; and Rosie Bsheer, review of *Politics and Society in Saudi Arabia: The Crucial Years of Development, 1960–1982*, by Sarah Yizraeli, *International Journal of Middle East Studies* 46, no. 2 (May 2014): 412–14.

154. Sarah Yizraeli, *Politics and Society in Saudi Arabia, 1960–1982* (New York: Columbia University Press, 2012).

155. Toby Jones, *Desert Kingdom: How Oil and Water Forged Modern Saudi Arabia* (Cambridge, MA: Harvard University Press, 2010); and David S. Painter, "Oil and the American Century," in "Oil in American History," special issue, *Journal of American History* 99, no. 1 (June 2012): 24. For a firsthand account of how Aramco did so, see Al-'Awwami, "Al-Haraka al-wataniyya," 1:211, 329.

156. Khadduri, *Abdullah al-Tariqi*, 350–53.

157. Madawi Al-Rasheed, *Transnational Connections and the Arab Gulf* (London: Routledge, 2005); and Nathalie Peutz, "Perspectives from the Margins of Arabia" (issue theme), in Rosie Bsheer and John Warner, eds., "Theorizing the Arabian Peninsula," *Jadmag* 1, no. 1 (Fall 2013): 24.

158. Vitalis, *America's Kingdom*, 154; Bsheer, review of *Politics and Society in Saudi Arabia*; and Rosie Bsheer, "Making History, Remaking Space: Textbooks, Archives and Commemorative Spaces in Saudi Arabia" (PhD diss., Columbia University, 2014). See, for example, the 1958 Aramco/Standard Oil Company of California film, *Desert Venture*, http://archive.org/details/DesertVe1958 and http://archive.org/details/DesertVe1958_2. Public relations films continued to propagate Aramco's role in civilizing the Saudi Arabians until ruling members of the Al Saud family actually saw one on a trip to New York City and were appalled by the role they were made to play as uncivilized and in need of US development. They demanded that Aramco halt the production and dissemination of all such films.

159. Sheila Carapico, "Arabia Incognita: An Invitation to Arabian Peninsula Studies," in Al-Rasheed and Vitalis, *Counter-Narratives*, 11–33.

160. David Scott, *Conscripts of Modernity: The Tragedy of Colonial Enlightenment* (Durham, NC: Duke University Press, 2004), 56.

CHAPTER 2

1. Ali ibn Ahmad ibn Lawand al-Burayki is the Ottoman governor who built Qasr Ibrahim. A later governor, Ibrahim ibn 'Ufaysan, is said to have renovated it in 1802. See Muhammad Buhamida, "'Hayy al-Qut' markaz al-Ahsa' bayna raw'at al-madi wa qaswat al-hadir" ["Al-Qut neighborhood," the center of al-Ahsa, between the splendor of the past and ruthlessness of the present], *al-Sharq al-Awsat*, August 30, 2012.

2. At the time, the ministry was still known as Wizarat al-Maʿarif (Ministry of Knowledge), not by its later name, Wizarat al-Tarbiyya wa-l-Taʿlim (Ministry of Education). The ministry oversaw the Darah from its establishment in 1972 until 1996.

3. Yahya ibn Junayd, interview with author, Riyadh, March 21, 2011. At the time of the interview, Ibn Junaydh was secretary-general of the King Faisal Center for Research and Islamic Studies. At the time of writing, he is the head of the Saudi Center for Research and Intercommunication, a position he assumed in 2018.

4. Mutlaq al-Buluwi, *Al-wujud al-uthmani fi shamal al-jazira al-Arabiyya, 1908–1923* [The Ottoman presence in the northern parts of the Arabian Peninsula, 1908–1923] (Beirut: Jadawel, 2011), 48–55.

5. Rosie Bsheer, "A Counter-Revolutionary State: Popular Movements and the Making of Saudi Arabia," *Past and Present* 238, no. 1 (February 1, 2018): 233–77.

6. Benedict Anderson, *Imagined Communities: Reflections on the Origin and Spread of Nationalism* (New York: Verso, 1983).

7. Anthony Gorman, *Historians, State and Politics in Twentieth Century Egypt: Contesting the Nation* (London: Routledge Curzon, 2003), 72.

8. Rosie Bsheer, "Teaching the Nation: State and Citizen in Saudi Arabian History Textbooks" (master's thesis, Columbia University, 2006).

9. Ann Laura Stoler, "Colonial Archives and the Arts of Governance," *Archival Science* 2, nos. 1–2 (2002): 90.

10. Kirsten Weld, *Paper Cadavers: The Archives of Dictatorship in Guatemala* (Durham, NC: Duke University Press, 2014); Shay Hazkani, "Catastrophic Thinking: Did Ben-Gurion Try to Rewrite History," *Haaretz*, May 16, 2013, https://www.haaretz.com/.premium-ben-gurion-grasped-the-nakba-s-importance-1.5243033; Musa Budeiri, "Controlling the Archive: Captured Jordanian Security Files in the Israeli State Archives," *Jerusalem Quarterly* 66 (2016): 87–98; Hagar Shezaf, "Burying the Nakba: How Israel Systematically Hides Evidence of 1948 Expulsion of Arabs," *Haaretz*, July 4, 2019, https://www.haaretz.com/israel-news/.premium.MAGAZINE-how-israel-systematically-hides-evidence-of-1948-expulsion-of-arabs-1.7435103; "Britain Destroyed Records of Colonial Crimes," *Guardian*, April 18, 2012; and Ralph Kingston, "The French Revolution and the Materiality of the Modern Archive," *Libraries and the Cultural Record* 46, no. 1 (2011): 1–25. This is also true of the US government, whether under presidents Donald Trump, Barack Obama, or others. See "Obama Admin Spent $36M on Lawsuits to Keep Info Secret," *CBS News*, March 14, 2017, https://www.cbsnews.com/news/obama-administration-spent-36m-on-records-lawsuits-last-year/; and "De-

mocracy Forward Sues Trump Administration for Unlawfully Withholding Documents on Efforts to Secure Saudi Nuclear Deal" (press release), *Democracy Forward*, February 28, 2019, https://democracyforward.org/press/democracy-forward-sues-trump-administration-for-unlawfully-withholding-documents-on-efforts-to-secure-saudi-nuclear-deal/.

11. Philip Abrams, "Notes on the Difficulty of Studying the State," *Journal of Historical Sociology* 1, no. 1 (March 1988): 58–89; Timothy Mitchell, "The Limits of the State: Beyond Statist Approaches and Their Critics," *American Political Science Review* 85, no. 1 (March 1991): 77–96; and James C. Scott, *Seeing Like a State: How Certain Schemes to Improve the Human Condition Have Failed* (New Haven, CT: Yale University Press, 1998).

12. Michel-Rolph Trouillot, *Silencing the Past: Power and the Production of History* (Boston: Beacon Press, 1995); Michel de Certeau, *The Writing of History* (New York: Columbia University Press, 1992); Penelope Papailias, *Genres of Recollection: Archival Poetics in Modern Greece* (New York: Palgrave Macmillan, 2005); and Ann Laura Stoler, *Along the Archival Grain: Epistemic Anxieties and Colonial Common Sense* (Princeton, NJ: Princeton University Press, 2009).

13. According to a Darah manager, who referred to Aramco as the Saudi government's "executive branch" (*al-jihaz al-tanfizi*), a few former Aramco executives agreed to share with the Darah some of the records they had kept in their personal possession. Some children of former Aramco executives formed a group called "Aramco Brats," which donated some records to the Darah as well. The government later hosted eighteen members in the Eastern Province to show its gratitude for their being "friends of Saudi Arabia."

14. Bsheer, "A Counter-Revolutionary State."

15. Ali Baqir al-Awwami, "Al-Haraka al-wataniyya sharq al-Saudiyya, 1953–1973" [The nationalist movement in eastern Saudi Arabia, 1953–1973], 2 vols. (unpublished manuscript, al-Qatif, 2011), PDF; Ali al-Dumayni, *Zaman li-l-sijn . . . azmina li-l-hurriyya* [A time for prison . . . times for freedom] (Beirut: Dar al-Kunuz, 2004); Turki al-Hamad, *Al-karadib* [The prison cells] (Beirut: Dar al-Saqi, 1998); Bsheer, "A Counter-Revolutionary State"; and author interviews with former Saudi Arabian political prisoners, Saudi Arabia, Lebanon, France, and the United States, 2007–2012.

16. As a regime propaganda tool, Sawt al-Arab, or the Voice of the Arabs, broadcast the opinions of Nasser's revolutionary regime throughout the Arab world. It also broadcast the ideals and music of secular Arab nationalism, shaping generations of Arab nationalists. Laura M. James, "Whose Voice? Nasser, the Arabs, and 'Sawt al-Arab'

Radio," *Transnational Broadcasting Studies* 16 (2006): https://www.arabmediasociety.com/whose-voice-nasser-the-arabs-and-sawt-al-arab-radio/.

17. Vernon Bogdanor, "The Monarchy and the Constitution," *Parliamentary Affairs* 49, no. 3 (July 1, 1996): 407–22.

18. Bsheer, "A Counter-Revolutionary State."

19. Interestingly, a project of historiographical revisionism was taking place at the same time in Nasserist Egypt. See Yoav Di-Capua, *Gatekeepers of the Arab Past: Historians and History Writing in Twentieth-Century Egypt* (Berkeley: University of California Press, 2009), 285–86.

20. Record 17955, No. 180, June 10, 1966, Presidency of the Council of Ministers, Institute of Public Administration Archive (hereafter cited as IPA Archive), Riyadh, on the US-Saudi agreement to build two television stations in Riyadh and Jeddah.

21. Bsheer, "A Counter-Revolutionary State."

22. "Bayan min wizarat al-i'lam" [Declaration from the Ministry of Information], *Okaz*, November 11, 1963.

23. Abdulfattah Abu Mudin, *Watilka alayyam* [Those were the days] (Jeddah: Dar Kunuz al-Ma'rifa, 1985). For more on the history of the press in Saudi Arabia, see Uthman Hafız, *Tatawur al-sahafa fi al-Mamlaka al-Arabiyya al-Saudiyya* [The development of the press in the Kingdom of Saudi Arabia] (Jeddah: Sharikat al-Madina li-l-Tiba'a wa-l-Nashr, 1989).

24. Mahmood Sabbagh, "1963: Qarar ta'mim al-suhuf.. madha jara?" [1963: The decision to "nationalize" newspapers: What happened?], *mahsabbagh* (blog), https://mahsabbagh.net/2011/05/15/ksa1963/.

25. King Faisal ibn Abdulaziz to US President Lyndon Johnson (month and day unclear, 1966), Arabian Peninsula Papers, American University of Beirut Archives. See also Khalil Itani (Lebanese ambassador to Saudi Arabia) to the Lebanese foreign minister, "Attacks on Saudi Arabia in the Lebanese Press," No. 77/February 25, 1968, Abdullah Yafi Collection, American University of Beirut Archives. In 1957, the Saudi regime spent US$1.4 million on broadcasting services, or 0.5 percent of the $310 million state budget. In 1968–69 alone, spending increased to more than $22 million, or 1.8 percent of the $1.25 billion budget. See Saudi Arabian Monetary Agency, "Saudi Arabia: Budget for the Year 1388–9 A.H" (report), September 25, 1968, Jeddah, IPA Archive, Riyadh.

26. The Saudi regime had already used historical documents in its possession to assert its territorial claims in border disputes with Yemen in 1934 and with Muscat and Abu Dhabi in 1955.

27. For an excellent account of the formation of the 'Abdin archive in Egypt, see Di-Capua, *Gatekeepers of the Arab Past*, 91–140.

28. Achille Mbembe, "The Power of the Archive and Its Limits," in *Refiguring the Archive*, eds. Carolyn Hamilton, Verne Harris, Michèle Pickover, Graeme Reid, Jane Taylor, and Razia Saleh (Dordrecht, The Netherlands: Kluwer, 2002).

29. Decision of the High Committee for Administrative Reform No. 10 of August 8, 1966, approved by Royal Decree No. 9710, August 14, 1966, IPA Archive, Riyadh.

30. The archives of the Ministry of Finance and National Economy were established per Ministerial Resolution No. 182, March 22, 1947, IPA Archive, Riyadh.

31. See Huda al-Abd al-Ali, "Al-watha'iq al-tarikhiyya fi al-Mamlaka al-'Arabiyya al-Sa'udiyya: Dirasa mashiyya taqyimiyya" [Historical documents in the Kingdom of Saudi Arabia: An evaluative assessment] (PhD diss., Riyadh Women's University, 2007), 21. The Central Archives hold 25,000 files (*sijill*), in addition to 40,000 medium-sized cardboard boxes, each holding a hundred documents; 2,000 bags full of approximately 1,300 documents each; approximately 1,000 metal cases with 1,000 records each; 500 envelopes with 150 documents each; and finally, approximately 6,000 personnel files. See Sayyid Hasaballah Muhammad al-Ghazali, *Al-Mahfuzat fi al-ajhiza al-hukumiyya, dirasa maydaniyya 'an al-mahfuzat fi al-Mamlaka al-'Arabiyya al-Sa'udiyya* [Archives in government institutions: A practical survey on archives in the Kingdom of Saudi Arabia] (Riyadh: n.p., 1982), 93.

32. Malcolm H. Kerr first coined the term in *The Arab Cold War: Gamal 'Abd al-Nasir and His Rivals, 1958–1970* (Oxford: Oxford University Press, 1965). Denoting the power struggle between Arab nationalist republics and Arab monarchies, the "Arab Cold War" spanned the mid-1950s until Nasser's death in 1970, and largely played out throughout the 1962 Yemen Civil War.

33. For more on "bureaucratic fiefdoms" in Saudi Arabia, see Steffen Hertog, *Princes, Brokers, and Bureaucrats: Oil and the State in Saudi Arabia* (Ithaca, NY: Cornell University Press, 2010).

34. Author interviews with former bureaucrats in Faisal's regime, as well as senior members of the contemporary archiving regime, Riyadh, 2009–2010.

35. Author interviews with two members of the Saudi Arabian delegation that negotiated these protocols with the Egyptian government, Riyadh, March 2, 2011.

36. Timothy Mitchell, "Society, Economy, and the State Effect," in *The Anthropology of the State*, ed. Aradhana Sharma (Malden, MA: Blackwell, 2006), 169–186.

37. Shaykh Hassan ibn Abdullah Al Al-Shaykh graduated from Sharia College in Mecca in 1953 and became a member in the Presidency of Judges in the Hijaz. When

the judiciary in the country was unified, he became vice president of the Presidency of Judges, which at the time was under the powerful Shaykh Muhammad ibn Ibrahim Al al-Shaykh. He held several other prominent positions, including minister of education (1963–1966), minister of health (1966–1970), and minister of higher education (1975–1987). See Abdulrahman al-Shubayli, "Hassan bin Abdullah Al Al-Shaykh. thalathun ʿaman min al-rahil" [Hassan bin Abdullah Al Al-Shaykh: Thirty years later], *Al-Sharq al-Awsat*, May 22, 2016; and "The Page of the Meccan Scholar: Hassan bin Abdullah Al Al-Shaykh," web page of Hassan bin Abdullah Al Al-Shaykh, https://makkahscholars.org/scholar/80.

38. Royal Decree No. 45/m, September 13, 1972, IPA Archive, Riyadh.

39. Khawla bint Muhammad ibn Saad al-Shuwayʿer, *Marakiz hafdh al-wathaʾiq fi al-Riyadh: Dirasa li-ʿadad minha* [Archives in Riyadh: A selective study] (Riyadh: King Fahd National Library, 2004), 93.

40. President of the Office of Council of Ministers to the Ministry of Education, October 1, 1974, Ministerial Order No. 28087, IPA Archive, Riyadh.

41. Royal Decree No. 5/12608, May 5, 1976, IPA Archive, Riyadh.

42. Darat al-Malik Abdulaziz, "Tajrubat al-Markaz al-Watani li-l-Wathaʾiq wa-l-Mahfuzat bi al-Darah" [The experience of the National Center for Documents and Archives at the Darah], in *Nadwat tawthiq al-maʿlumat al-idariyya* [Symposium on archiving administrative information] (Riyadh: Institute of Public Administration, 1989), 145.

43. Minister of Defense and Aviation to the Council of Ministers, January 22, 1979, letter no. 2/9/1/1038, IPA Archive, Riyadh.

44. Fahd ibn Ibrahim al-ʿAskar, "Idarat al-wathaʾiq al-tarikhiyya wa tatbiqatiha fi al-Mamlaka al-Saʿudiyya al-ʿArabiyya" [The management of historical documents and their application in Saudi Arabia], in *Buhuth nadwat al-wathaʾiq al-tarikhiyya fi al-Mamlaka al-ʿArabiyya al-Saʿudiyya. November 24–26, 1996* [Symposium on historical documents in the Kingdom of Saudi Arabia] (Riyadh: Darat al-Malik Abdulaziz, 1997), 68.

45. Council of Minsters Decree No. 958, June 13, 1976, IPA Archive, Riyadh.

46. President of the General Auditing Bureau to the minister of Finance and National Economy, February 20, 1980, letter no. 6693/4, IPA Archive, Riyadh.

47. Royal Decree No. 92, March 31, 1961, IPA Archive, Riyadh.

48. Council of Ministers Order No. 1, April 26, 1983, IPA Archive, Riyadh.

49. Article 4 of Royal Decree No. M/55, September 5, 1988, IPA Archive, Riyadh. The naming of the center indicates a difference in the type of records to be archived

and how they are to be dealt with. "Documents" refer to government-generated records that are still needed as reference for daily government functions, whereas "archives" refer to these government-generated records that are no longer needed for administrative purposes and contain historical value only. The author has copies of all the regulations of the National Center for Documents and Archives, which were hosted on its former website at http://www.ncda.gov.sa/detail.asp?InServiceID=1&intemplatekey =MainPage. However, since Salman assumed power in 2015, the center's English name has been changed to the National Center for Archives and Records (NCAR), and its URL address changed to http://ncar.gov.sa/Home/Index. It is not clear when exactly the location was also moved from the Council of Ministers to the Royal Palace.

50. Article 2 of Royal Decree No. M/55, September 5, 1988, IPA Archive, Riyadh. The aim of incorporating the national archive into the Council of Ministers was to give it the status and support needed for other ministries to cooperate with it and deposit their records there.

51. Aramco introduced gated communities to the Eastern Province of Saudi Arabia in the 1930s in order to afford the company's US and other non-Arab citizens freedom from Saudi Arabia's laws. The compound phenomenon, however, was popularized among Saudis in 1950, when then crown prince Saud ibn Abdulaziz built the first concrete residence for his family west of what is now Old Riyadh. Enclosed by high walls, the royal complex consisted of several palaces, villas, buildings, and gardens, with two guarded gates. As most members of the ruling family moved out of Old Riyadh's traditional mud houses toward the end of the 1950s, they adopted the same housing model. The ruling and economic elites followed suit. The enclosed compound became a marker of socioeconomic standing, and it was also an exceptional enclave, where the law of the land did not apply. The walls acted as barriers from the strict morality codes that the Committee for the Promotion of Virtue and the Prevention of Vice enforced in public life. Today, the majority of expatriate laborers who can afford to do so live in enclosed, guarded compounds throughout Saudi Arabia. Many government buildings are also located in such clusters within similar compounds.

52. Article 5 of Royal Decree No. M/55, September 5, 1988, IPA Archive, Riyadh.

53. Khudran al-Damuk (vice president of the National Center for Documents and Archives), interview with author, Riyadh, May 5, 2011.

54. Article 10 of Royal Decree No. 7/1379/m, "General Bylaws for Documents," December 15, 1995, IPA Archive, Riyadh.

55. Of the National Center's sixty employees, the majority had undergraduate degrees in law, literature, or arts from Riyadh's universities or the Institute of Public

Administration. Those who work in the center's small Department of Preservation and Sterilization received their training at the King Faisal Center for Research and Islamic Studies.

56. Jennifer Mulligan, "'What Is an Archive?' in the History of Modern France," in *Archive Stories: Facts, Fictions, and the Writing of History*, ed. Antoinette Burton (Durham, NC: Duke University Press, 2005), 163.

57. Kiren Aziz Chaudhry, *The Price of Wealth: Economics and Institutions in the Middle East* (Ithaca, NY: Cornell University Press, 1997), 81.

58. Interview with author in Riyadh, May 15, 2010.

59. Papailias, *Genres of Recollection*, 11.

60. Mbembe, "The Power of the Archive and Its Limits."

61. This conclusion is based on dozens of interviews conducted from 2009 to 2011 with managers, archivists, and employees in the archiving industry in Saudi Arabia and with two archivists involved in assessing the state of documents at the major archives in Riyadh.

62. Secondary sources have sufficiently shown how successive Saudi regimes have sought to hide the role that the British and US governments have played in propping up the Al Saud monarchy. See Madawi Al-Rasheed, *A History of Saudi Arabia* (London: Cambridge University Press, 2002). Indeed, decision makers I worked with in the archiving industry made it clear that these were some of the "red lines" that they needed to be vigilant about.

63. The IPA and KFNL were not the only institutions that collected primary sourced documents on Saudi Arabia. The King Abdulaziz Public Library, for instance, purchased records on Arabia from the Ottoman archives in Turkey and, much later on, the George Rentz collection from Qatar. Other libraries housed in the country's many universities also hold significant collections on Saudi Arabia. But their archiving efforts began only following those of the KFNL in the 1980s and did not become a significant part of their mission statements until the late 2000s.

64. Royal Decree No. 92 of March 31, 1961, and Royal Decree No. 93 of April 10, 1961, IPA Archive, Riyadh.

65. The Ministry of Finance and National Economy was restructured on April 30, 2003, with the office of finance becoming independent and that of economy joining the Ministry of Planning instead, to form the Ministry of Economy and Planning.

66. Institute of Public Administration, "Tajrubat Markaz al-Watha'iq fi Ma'had al-Idara al-'Amma" [The experience of the National Center for Documents at the

Institute of Public Administration], in *Nadwat tawthiq al-ma'lumat al-idariyya"* [Symposium on archiving administrative information] (Riyadh: Institute of Public Administration, 1989), 154.

67. "Documentation and Library," Institute of Public Administration, Riyadh, 1963, http://www.ipa.edu.sa/EN/DocumentingAndLibrary/Pages/ALibrary.aspx.

68. Ibid., 158.

69. IPA Administrative Decision no. 86, 28/1/1400 (December 16, 1979), IPA Archive, Riyadh. See al-'Askar, "Idarat al-watha'iq al-tarikhiyya," 80–82.

70. Decision No. 556 by the Institute for Public Administration General Manager, October 23, 1991, IPA Archive, Riyadh.

71. Record 56738, No. 230, Speech, Riyadh Principality, September 8, 1987, IPA Archive, Riyadh. The Council of Ministers, and subsequently the Royal Court, approved the system of KFNL. Record 44569, No. 80, Presidency of the Council of Ministers, December 5, 1989; and Record 44579, No. 9/M, Royal Decree, December 12, 1989, IPA Archive, Riyadh.

72. Yahya ibn Junayd, interview with author, King Faisal Center for Research and Islamic Studies, Riyadh, March 21, 2011.

73. Mbembe, "The Power of the Archive and Its Limits."

74. Stoler, *Along the Archival Grain*; and Antoinette Burton, ed., *Archive Stories: Facts, Fictions, and the Writing of History* (Durham, NC: Duke University Press, 2005).

75. Francis X. Blouin Jr. and William G. Rosenberg, eds., *Archives, Documentation, and Institutions of Social Memory: Essays from the Sawyer Seminar* (Ann Arbor: University of Michigan Press, 2007). On the archive as a mode of knowledge production and record making, see Jacques Derrida, *Archive Fever: A Freudian Impression* (Chicago: University of Chicago Press, 1996); Roberto González Echevarria, *Myth and the Archive: A Theory of Latin American Narrative*, 2nd ed. (Durham, NC: Duke University Press, 1998); Michel Foucault, *The Archeology of Knowledge: And the Discourse of Language* (New York: Pantheon Books, 1972); Peter Galison, "Removing Knowledge," *Critical Inquiry* 31, no. 1 (Autumn 2004): 229–43; John Guillory, "The Memo and Modernity," *Critical Inquiry* 31, no. 1 (Autumn 2004): 108–32; Miles Ogborn, *Indian Ink: Script and Print in the Making of the English East India Company* (Chicago: University of Chicago Press, 2007); Papailias, *Genres of Recollection*; Elizabeth Povinelli, *The Cunning of Recognition: Indigenous Alterities and the Making of Australian Multiculturalism* (Durham, NC: Duke University Press, 2002); and Stoler, *Along the Archival Grain*.

76. Ibn Junayd, interview.

77. The word often used to refer to this gender exceptionalism is *khususiyyat al-mujtamaʿ*, which refers to both the specificity and the privacy of Saudi society.

CHAPTER 3

1. *Mashruʿ masih al-masadir al-tarikhiyya al-wataniyya: al-marhala al-uwla, 1996–1997* [The project of surveying national historical sources: Phase 1, 1996–1997] (Riyadh: Darat al-malik Abdulaziz, 1999). See also Fahd al-Semmari, "Al-watha'iq al-tarikhiyya al-wataniyya wa-l-ihtimam al-matlub" [National historical documents and the required attention], in *Buhuth nadwat al-watha'iq al-tarikhiyya* [Symposium on historical documents in the Kingdom of Saudi Arabia], November 24–26, 1996 (Riyadh: Darat al-Malik Abdulaziz, 1997), 33.

2. The Darah's board of directors approved the first survey in its meeting of May 1996 and the second on November 18, 1998. "Annual Financial Report 1997–1998," Darat al-Malik Abdulaziz, 11–12, Institute of Public Administration Archives (hereafter cited as IPA Archives), Riyadh. See also Fahd al-Semmari, "King Abdulaziz Foundation for Research and Archives," *Middle East Studies Association Bulletin* 35, no. 1 (Summer 2001): 45–46.

3. Author interview with Darah employees, Riyadh, April 2010–March 2011.

4. Darah laboratory technicians and employees at the Darah's Markaz al-Tarmim wa-l-Muhafadha ʿala al-Mawwad al-Tarikhiyya (Center for Restoration and Preservation of Historical Material, now called the King Salman Center for Restoration and Preservation of Historical Material), interviews with author, Riyadh, April 20, 2011.

5. Employee at the Darah's Center for Restoration and Preservation of Historical Materials, interview with author, Riyadh, April 20, 2011.

6. Bruno Latour, *The Pasteurization of France* (Cambridge, MA: Harvard University Press, 1993); Nicholas Dirks, *Colonialism and Culture* (Ann Arbor: Michigan University Press, 1992); and Steven Shapin and Simon Schaffer, *Leviathan and the Air-Pump: Hobbes, Boyle, and the Experimental Life* (Princeton, NJ: Princeton University Press, 1985), 332.

7. Ian Hacking, "How Should We Do the History of Statistics," in *The Foucault Effect: Studies in Governmentality*, ed. Graham Burchell (Chicago: Chicago University Press, 1991), 181–196.

8. In an opening statement at the King Fahd Historical Symposium at the Darah on April 1, 2015—mere months after ascending the throne—Salman described Fahd

as his "second father" who had raised him since childhood. Badr al-Kharif wa Bandar al-Shrayda, "Al-Malik Salman: Fahd bin Abdulaziz walidi al-thani.. tarabaytu tahta dhilih wa ri'ayatih" [King Salman: Fahd bin Abdulaziz is my second father: I was raised under his shadow and care], *Al-Sharq al-Awsat*, April 1, 2015.

9. Jacques Derrida, *Archive Fever: A Freudian Impression* (Chicago: University of Chicago, 1996).

10. Fahd al-Semmari, "Darah: 40 Years of Recording History," *Arab News*, June 2, 2012, http://www.arabnews.com/darah-40-years-recording-history.

11. Author interview with one of the Darah's many managers, Riyadh, April 14, 2010.

12. Fahd al-Semmari, the Darah's secretary-general—and since 2015, general supervisor of the National Center for Documents and Archives and the adviser to King Salman's Royal Court—admitted that weakness and failure still mark the archiving process in Saudi Arabia. Abdulhakim Shar, "Al-Semmari ya'tarif bi-wujud qusur wa-naqs fi hafdh al-watha'iq al-wataniyya" [Al-Semmari admits to failure of and shortage in preserving historical records], *Sabq*, December 15, 2015, https://sabq.org/KROgde.

13. Saul Bloom, *Hidden Casualties: Environmental, Health, and Political Consequences of the Persian Gulf War* (Berkeley, CA: North Atlantic Books; San Francisco, CA: ARC/Arms Control Research Center, 1994); and Arthur H. Westing, *Pioneer on the Environmental Impact of War* (London: Springer, 2013).

14. Gwenn Okruhlik, "Rentier Wealth, Unruly Law, and the Rise of the Opposition: The Political Economy of Oil States," *Comparative Politics* 31, no. 3 (April 1999): 302.

15. See the introduction of this book for a more detailed discussion of the Sahwa movement and how religion came to constitute a threat to the regime following the 1991 Gulf War.

16. This figure relies on various budgets for the development of historical sites that I perused at the archives of the Arriyadh Development Authority (hereafter cited as ADA Archives) as well as interviews with project managers there, the last series of which took place in June 2011. This was several years before most of the projects under study were even completed. Without exception, each interview indicated that even by then, the ADA was over budget on many of its projects.

17. Ann Laura Stoler, "Colonial Archives and the Arts of Governance," *Archival Science* 2 (2002): 87–109; and Elizabeth A. Povinelli, *The Cunning of Recognition: Indigenous Alterities and the Making of Australian Multiculturalism* (Durham, NC: Duke University Press, 2002).

18. For a similar example of the politicization of archives, see Houda ben Hamouda, "L'accès aux fonds contemporains des archives nationales de Tunisie: Un état des lieux" [Access to contemporary holdings of the National Archives of Tunisia: An inventory], in "Besoins d'histoire: Historiographies et régimes d'historicité au Maghreb à l'aune des révolutions arabes," special issue, *L'Année du Maghreb* 10 (2014): 41–48.

19. The regime started considering the centennial celebration in 1993, but it did not agree on or announce it until 1996. Royal Decree No. 597, "King Fahd Declares Centennial Celebrations," 1996, IPA Archives, Riyadh.

20. Madawi Al-Rasheed, "Political Legitimacy and the Production of History: The Case of Saudi Arabia," in *New Frontiers in Middle East Security*, ed. Lenore G. Martin (New York: St. Martin's Press, 1999), 25–46.

21. Royal Decree No. 11552, Record 10845, dated July 4, 1950, on the importance of celebrating the fiftieth anniversary of King Abdulaziz's conquest of Riyadh, IPA Archives, Riyadh.

22. Royal Decree No. 597, "King Fahd Declares Centennial Celebrations," 1996, IPA Archives.

23. The Governance Palace is a complex of palaces that Abdulaziz commissioned in 1936 outside Riyadh's city walls to house his family. They moved there in 1937.

24. Arthur P. Clark, "A Kingdom Revealed: The Making of the King Abdulaziz Historical Centre" (final draft submitted to the Arriyadh Development Authority, December 30, 2002), 15, ADA Archives. According to Clark's report, "The TOR also asked designers to focus their thinking on what the project might mean for future development in the heart of the city. They were directed to develop a '50-Year Vision' for the area, with a view to phased development of that vision."

25. "The King Abdulaziz Historical Center," Arriyadh Development Authority Project Description, 1999, ADA Archives.

26. Since the advent of subaltern studies in 1982, postcolonial critics have theorized the colonial and postcolonial archive and the kinds of histories one is able to produce based on these sources. Writing the national histories of most formerly colonized states, these critiques note, has entailed reliance on foreign, often imperial or colonial, sources. The Saudi regime prides itself on not having been colonized or fallen under imperial rule, as was the fate of all its neighbors. Yet its reliance on foreign sources for the writing of its own history reveals the extent to which Saudi Arabia was entrenched in imperial and global systems of dominance.

27. Khalid al-Nasir (director of Darah archives and library), interview with author, Riyadh, April 14, 2010.

28. Ibid. The Darah translated many of the Ottoman documents it had acquired into Arabic, but by 2011, it availed only Arabic summaries of the actual topics to researchers, and even then, there were many discrepancies in the translation.

29. Darat al-Malik Abdulaziz, "Tajrubat al-Markaz al-Watani li-l-Watha'iq wa-l-Mahfuzat bi al-Darah" [The experience of the National Center for Documents and Archives at the Darah], in *Nadwat tawthiq al-ma'lumat al-idariyya* [Symposium on archiving administrative information] (Riyadh: Institute of Public Administration, 1989), 145, IPA Central Library.

30. Fahd al-Semmari, interview with author, Riyadh, April 17, 2011.

31. Al-Semmari, "King Abdulaziz Foundation for Research and Archives," 45–46.

32. *Darat al-Malik Abdulaziz: Wa masirat 'ishrin 'aman 1972–1992* [King Abdulaziz Research Center: A twenty-year journey, 1972–1992] (Riyadh: Darat al-Malik Abdulaziz, 1992).

33. Al-Semmari, "Al-watha'iq al-tarikhiyya al-wataniyya," 24, 38. For a more recent example, see Shar, "Al-Semmari Admits to Failure of and Shortage in Preserving Historical Records."

34. "Annual Financial Report 1997–1998," Darat al-Malik Abdulaziz, 48, IPA Archives, Riyadh.

35. The stated number of employees in 2009 at Saudi Arabia's National Center for Documents and Archives was sixty. According to Yahya ibn Junayd—former head of operations at the King Fahd National Library—other archive managers in Riyadh, and employees at the National Center, the number of employees at the national archive fell remarkably short of this stated number. Their figures varied between fifteen and thirty-five employees.

36. Fahd al-Semmari, "Kalimat al-mushrif 'ala darat al-malik Abdulaziz" [The address of the Darah's supervisor], in *Buhuth nadwat al-watha'iq al-tarikhiyya* [Symposium on historical documents in the Kingdom of Saudi Arabia], November 24–26, 1996 (Riyadh: Darat al-Malik Abdulaziz, 1997), 23–24.

37. Al-Nasir, interview.

38. Prince Salman ibn Abdulaziz, "Kalimat sahib al sumuw al-malaki al-Amir Salman ibn Abdulaziz" [Keynote speech of His Royal Highness Prince Salman ibn Abdulaziz], in *Buhuth nadwat al-watha'iq al-tarikhiyya* [Symposium on historical

documents in the Kingdom of Saudi Arabia], November 24–26, 1996 (Riyadh: Darat al-Malik Abdulaziz, 1997), 9–11.

39. In 1967, King Faisal went as far as changing the name of King Saud University to Riyadh University, a decision that King Khalid undid in 1981.

40. Fahda bint Saud ibn Abdulaziz Al Saud, "Al-Malik Saud wa dawrahu fi ta'sis al-mamlaka" [King Saud and his role in the establishment of the kingdom] (paper presented at the King Saud historical workshop at the King Abdulaziz Historical Center, Riyadh, 1999).

41. Scholars of Arabia often attribute the Ten-Point Program to Faisal's reformist politics, when the archival record shows that Faisal's regime actually prevented the implementation of many so-called reformist projects, including the constitution that Saud had signed into law.

42. Fahda bint Saud ibn Abdulaziz Al Saud (daughter of King Saud), interview with author, Jeddah, June 5, 2011.

43. Fahda bint Saud ibn Abdulaziz, *King Saud* (Riyadh: The King Saud Library, 2006).

44. *Al-Malik Saud bin Abdulaziz Al Saud: Buhuth wa dirasat* [King Saud ibn Abdulaziz Al Saud: Research and studies], 5 vols. (Riyadh: Darat al-Malik Abdulaziz, 2006).

45. The constitution that Saud's regime was going to adopt was based on the one that the Free Princes had commissioned Egyptian lawyers to begin drafting in 1959, and that Saud announced on Radio Mecca on December 25, 1960. It was also published as "Al-nidham al-asasi" [The basic law], *Al-Jaridah*, December 27, 1960.

46. Descendants of King Faisal, interviews with author, 2009–2011.

47. Fahda bint Saud ibn Abdulaziz Al Saud, interview with author, Jeddah, June 5, 2011. For more on social and political life in mid-twentieth-century Saudi Arabia, and the role of King Saud therein, see Rosie Bsheer, "A Counter-Revolutionary State: Popular Movements and the Making of Saudi Arabia," *Past and Present* 238, no. 1 (February 1, 2018): 233–77.

48. King Saud Library official website, https://thekingsaudlibrary.org/en/ (formerly www.kingsaud.net/english). See also Nura al-Huwayti, "Al-Amira Fahda bint Saud: Nahnu na'malu 'ala bina' markaz lihafdh tarikh al-malik Saud" [Princess Fahda bint Saud: 'We are working on building an institution to preserve the history of King Saud'], *al-Riyadh*, November 18, 2006.

49. Al-Semmari, "Al-watha'iq al-tarikhiyya al-wataniyya," 39–40.

50. Ibid., 40.

51. Michel-Rolph Trouillot, *Silencing the Past: Power and the Production of History* (Boston: Beacon Press, 1995).

52. Although Salman could use his personal power and coercion to ensure that the Darah was the most powerful archiving institution in the country, for most of his tenure in office, he did not have the unbridled power to surpass the Council of Ministers and elevate the Darah into a national archive, supposing that he did indeed want to. As Salman assumed his first ministerial post in 2011 and became crown prince in 2012 and king in 2015, those in the archiving industry expected the Darah's place in archival consolidation to be bolstered greatly.

53. The few documents that the Darah managed to procure on the history of oil in Saudi Arabia incriminated Al Saud in collaborating with the British and US governments. They are currently inaccessible and will probably remain so.

54. "Archives," King Abdulaziz Center for World Culture website, http://en.kingabdulazizcenter.com/explore/center-facilities/archives#.Uy7jgNyob1o. Readers can access the cultural center's new website for more information, at https://www.ithra.com/ar/.

55. Tariq Al-Sh'aifan (public relations director at Saudi Aramco), interview with author, Dhahran, February 27, 2010.

56. In the ten years it took to construct the center, which opened its doors to the public in 2018, the center underwent major transformations that reflected the country's changing political landscape and Salman's rise to power. Not only was its name changed to the King Abdulaziz Center for World Culture, or Ithra, but there was no evidence, at the time of this writing, that the hundred-thousand-square-meter space would still include an archive.

57. Author interviews (2009–2012) with several historians, archivists, archeologists, architects, and journalists who worked in different sectors of the postwar cultural redevelopment projects in Riyadh, Dhahran, Qatif, Medina, and Mecca.

58. Author interview with Saudi Arabian journalist, Riyadh, March 2010.

59. Author interview with Saudi Arabian activist, Medina, June 2011.

60. The author conducted over twenty-two oral history interviews with employees of Riyadh's state archives, 2009–2012.

61. Al-hay'a al-'amma li-al-siyaha wa-l-athar [Saudi Commission for Tourism and Antiquities, Kingdom of Saudi Arabia], *Al-'abath fi al-athar* [Tampering with antiquities], 2009.

62. In the first phase of the national project, the Darah acquired only 33,150 records in total. Of these, 11,000 were from Mecca, 8,000 from the northwestern city of Tabuk, and 7,500 from Riyadh. *Mashruʿ masih al-masadir al-tarikhiyya al-wataniyya: al-marhala al-uwla, 1996–1997* [The project of surveying national historical sources: Phase 1, 1996–1997] (Riyadh: Darat al-Malik Abdulaziz, 1999), 31. According to Fahd al-Semmari ("Al-wathaʾiq al-tarikhiyya al-wataniyya," 33), the Darah managed to record 284 oral history interviews with those who witnessed the reign of Abdulaziz for its Oral History Center, which was established in 1996. See also al-Semmari, "King Abdulaziz Foundation for Research and Archives."

63. Interviews with families who had donated their records to the Darah as well as archivists and other Darah employees.

64. The Darah also translated historical source material from foreign languages and embarked on an oral history project (in 1996) with those who had fought with King Abdulaziz ibn Saud during his wars of conquest (1902–1932) in order to record their narrations of Abdulaziz's historical accomplishments.

65. Those who donate historical documents to the Darah are honored by Prince Salman at his office in the presence of the country's media by way of encouraging others to do the same. For examples, see "Wazir al-difaʿ yatasallam wathaʾiq tarikihiyya li-murasalat al-malik Abdulaziz" [Secretary of Defense receives historical documents of King Abdulaziz's correspondences], *al-Riyadh*, March 18, 2012, http://www.alriyadh .com/2012/03/18/article719451.html; and "Prince Salman bin Abdulaziz Takes Personal Delivery of All Manuscripts and Documents from Members of the Public," ADA, January 11, 2011, http://www.arriyadh.com/Eng/Content/getdocument.aspx?f=/openshare /Eng/Content/-No-conflict-over-the-collection-of-.doc_cvt.htm.

66. Huda Al-Abd al-Ali, "Al-wathaʾiq al-tarikhiyya fi al-Mamlaka al-ʿArabiyya al-Saʿudiyya: Dirasa mashiyya taqyimiyya" [Historical documents in the Kingdom of Saudi Arabia: An evaluative assessment] (PhD diss., Riyadh Women's University, 2007).

67. Employee at the Darah's Center for Restoration and Preservation of Historical Materials, interview with author, Riyadh, April 20, 2011. For more on the center, see Nayif Kariri, "Markaz al-Tarmim wa-l-Muhafaza ʿala al-Mawwad al-Tarikhiyya bi Darat al-Malik Abdulaziz ... ʿamal muʾassasi li-hafz al-turath" [Center for Restoration and Preservation of Historical Materials at the Darah of King Abdulaziz ... Institutional work to preserve heritage], *al-Madina*, March 30, 2011, http://www.al-madina .com/node/296032.

68. This anxiety extended to the King Faisal Center for Research and Islamic Studies. Its chairman, Prince Turki al-Faisal, a former ambassador to the United States

and son of the late King Faisal, ordered the cancellation of the center's annual international manuscript exhibition in 2011, fearing that his uncle Prince Salman would force the center to surrender any number of its manuscripts to the Darah if they became known publicly. The relationship between the Darah and the King Faisal Center for Research and Islamic Studies is especially fraught with mistrust and hostility. King Faisal's descendants claim that the Darah's managers are marginalizing King Faisal from Saudi Arabian history and undermining his modernizing accomplishments, and that the Darah is instead unfairly bringing King Saud into the historical narrative.

69. Ali Saad al-Qahtani, "Al-Samira'i: hunak wathiqa muzawwarra biy'at bi 30 malyon dollar" [Al-Samira'i: A forged document sold for $30 million], *Al-Jazirah*, no. 11499, March 23, 2004, http://www.al-jazirah.com/2004/20040323/cu1.htm. See Fa'iz ibn Musa al-Harbi, "Turuk kashf al-tazwir fi al-watha'iq al-mahaliyya" [Authenticating local documents], in *Sijjil dawrat al-watha'iq al-mahaliyya,* April 3, 2009 [Proceedings of training course on local documents], ed. Abdullah ibn Abdulrahman al-Abduljabbar et al. (Riyadh: King Saud University, 2010), 213–31.

70. M. D. Rasooldeen, "Shura Approves New Anti-Forgery Law," *Arab News*, January 10, 2011.

71. Interviews conducted in 2010–2011 with ADA project managers, architects, and historians involved in the planning and supervision of the centennial celebrations. This assessment is also based on the annual budgets of the King Abdulaziz Historical Center and the renovation of Dir'iyya. See "The Historic Addiriyyah Redevelopment Program: Cost Estimation Report, September 2000" (Arriyadh Development Authority), ADA Archives.

72. Yahya ibn Junayd, interview with author, Riyadh, March 21, 2011. At the time of the interview, Ibn Junaydh was secretary-general of the King Faisal Center for Research and Islamic Studies. At the time of writing, he was the head of the Saudi Center for Research and Intercommunication; and Abdulaziz al-Rajhi (archive director at the King Fahd National Library), interview with author, Riyadh, March 21, 2011.

73. The last two decades of the Darah's awareness campaigns had made the importance of such documents clear to all, including the country's sizable foreign labor force.

74. "No Conflict over the Collection of Historical Manuscripts," Fahd al-Semmari interview with *Saudi Gazette*, January 11, 2011.

75. Dominick LaCapra, *History in Transit: Experience, Identity, Critical Theory* (Ithaca, NY: Cornell University Press, 2004), 17.

76. A random sample of the Darah's publications includes *Limadha ahbabtu ibn Saud* [Why I loved ibn Saud], by Muhammad Amin al-Tamimi; *King Ibn Saud and the*

Arabian Peninsula, by D. Van Drmolin; *Al-rahalat al-malakiyya: rahalat jalalat al-malik Abdulaziz ila Makkah al-Mukarrama wa-l-Madina al-Munawwara wa-l-Riyadh* [The royal travels: The travels of His Majesty King Abdulaziz to Mecca, Medina and Riyadh] by Yusuf Yasin; *Al-malik Abdulaziz fi al-sahafa al-'Arabiyya* [King Abdulaziz in the Arab press] by Nasir al-Juheimi; and *Al-malik Abdulaziz: ru'a wa-dirasat tarikhiyya* [*King Abdulaziz: Historical visions and studies*] by the Darah's secretary-general Fahd al-Semmari and Nasir al-Juhaymi.

77. In 1998 alone, the Darah donated 7,500 copies of its various publications, according to the "Annual Financial Report 1997–1998," 18.

78. The Standing Committee for Scholarly Research and Issuing Fatwas also issued Fatwa No. 23194, dated May 31, 2005, for the transfer of rare manuscripts from private libraries and individuals to the Darah. "Rare Manuscripts Exhibitions Set to Attract Scholars," *Saudi Gazette*, January 5, 2011.

79. Many of the documents at the Mecca archives, the oldest in the kingdom, were ignored and stolen, and remain scattered across Saudi Arabia to this day.

80. Ibn Junayd, interview.

81. "Al-markaz al-watani li-al-watha'iq wa-l-mahfuzat fi al-Sa'udiyya" [The National Center for Documents and Archives in Saudi Arabia], *al-Yasir* (blog), June 4, 2008, http://alyaseer.net/vb/archive/index.php?t-11193.html.

82. Khudran al-Damuk (vice president of the National Center for Documents and Archives), interview with author, Riyadh, May 5, 2011.

83. Derrida, *Archive Fever*, 36.

84. "Annual Financial Report 1997–1998," 18.

85. Al-Abd al-Ali, "Al-watha'iq al-tarikhiyya."

86. Michel Foucault, *The Archeology of Knowledge: And the Discourse of Language* (New York: Pantheon Books, 1972), 128.

87. Wendy Brown, *States of Injury: Power and Freedom in Late Modernity* (Princeton, NJ: Princeton University Press, 1995), 27–28.

88. Vision 2030 website, https://vision2030.gov.sa/en.

CHAPTER 4

1. "City of Riyadh Planning Scheme," memorandum from the urban management planner to Medstar Team, October 21, 2001, 7, Arriyadh Development Authority Archives (hereafter cited as ADA Archives), Riyadh.

2. Shaped by its founder Harland Bartholomew, formerly with the US Army Corps of Engineers and once known as the "dean of city planners," the planning agency was notorious for the wholesale destruction of urban neighborhoods and distressed buildings and replacing them with highways and parking lots. Harry Kollatz Jr., "A Man with a Plan," *Richmond Magazine*, August 14, 2017, https://richmondmagazine.com/news/richmond-history/city-planner-harland-bartholomew/.

3. Arriyadh Development Authority, "Form and Building Structure," in *Comprehensive Strategic Report for the City of Riyadh (2003)*, vol. 4 of 20, Metropolitan Development Strategy for Arriyadh (MEDSTAR), Report from the Arriyadh Development Authority, phase 1, 1997, 3; and "City of Riyadh Planning Scheme," memorandum from the urban management planner to Medstar Team, October 21, 2001, 7. Both at the ADA Archives, Riyadh. It must be noted here that as Salman ascended the throne in 2015, his regime overhauled state institutions along with their corporate branding. The names of many organizations as well as their website domains changed, rendering previous web addresses and the information they hosted inaccessible. The name of the High Commission for the Development of Arriyadh, one of the main actors in this chapter, was changed to the Royal Commission for Riyadh City. The regime also intervened in the information that these organizations had published in the past, manipulating their online versions to conform to the politics of the new regime. A case in point here is MEDSTAR and other planning documents on Riyadh; in physical form (in the possession of the author), they regularly contradict the versions available online at the time of this writing. This has complicated research on the kingdom, making future scholarly work that much more difficult.

4. Arriyadh Development Authority, "Form and Building Structure."

5. "Future Vision," in *Brief Summary of the Comprehensive Strategic Plan*, ADA, 2003, 9–10, ADA Archives, Riyadh.

6. "Strategies and Plans," in *Brief Summary of the Comprehensive Strategic Plan*, ADA, 2003, 16–18, ADA Archives, Riyadh.

7. The recreational aspect of these sites especially countered official Wahhabi thought. See Salih ibn Fawzan al-Fawzan, "Hikm ihya' al-athar wa-l-'inaya bi-umur al-jahiliyya wa shakhsiyatiha" [Ruling on the preservation of antiquities and caring for pre-Islamic matters and its personalities], official website of Shaykh Salih ibn Fawzan al-Fawzan, February 27, 2012, https://www.alfawzan.af.org.sa/en/node/13938; and Abdulaziz ibn Baz, "Hikm al-safar li-ru'yat al-athar al-islamiyya" [Ruling on traveling

to see Islamic antiquities], Imam Ibn Baz Official Website, n.d., https://binbaz.org.sa
/fatwas/22921/%D8%AD%D9%83%D9%85-%D8%A7%D9%84%D8%B3%D9%81
%D8%B1-%D9%84%D8%B1%D9%88%D9%8A%D8%A9-%D8%A7%D9%84%D8
%A7%D8%AB%D8%A7%D8%B1-%D8%A7%D9%84%D8%A7%D8%B3%D9%84
%D8%A7%D9%85%D9%8A%D8%A9.

8. For an example, see the section "Tourism Overview" in "Sustaining Growth: Innovative Strategies Are Being Employed to Improve Offerings," in Oxford Business Group, *The Report: Saudi Arabia 2014* (London: Oxford Business Group), 326–36.

9. "Strategies and Plans," 16.

10. Bruno Latour, *The Pasteurization of France* (Cambridge, MA: Harvard University Press, 1993); and Nicolas Dirks, *Colonialism and Culture* (Ann Arbor: University of Michigan Press, 1992).

11. Chiara De Cesari, "Heritage Between Resistance and Government in Palestine," in "Forced Displacement and Refugees," special issue, *International Journal of Middle East Studies* 49, no. 4 (November 2017): 747–51. See also Deen Sharp, "The Urbanization of Power and the Struggle for the City," *MERIP* 287 (Summer 2018).

12. "Metropolitan Development Strategy for Arriyadh MEDSTAR," High Commission for the Development of Arriyadh City, ADA Archives, Riyadh.

13. Upon assuming the throne in 2005, Abdullah ordered the construction of several new financial, economic, and industrial cities across Saudi Arabia. In Riyadh, he would establish the King Abdullah Financial District (KAFD), with the Saudi Binladin Group as the major developer. Unlike other construction projects in Riyadh, KAFD did not fall under the purview of Salman's ADA.

14. As scholars have shown, sites of memorialization have lives of their own that often contradict their makers' intentions. See, e.g., James Edward Young, *The Texture of Memory: Holocaust Memorials and Meaning* (New Haven, CT: Yale University Press, 1994).

15. State planners in Riyadh unanimously agree that Dr. Muhammad ibn Abdulaziz Al-Shaykh was largely responsible for the implementation of the regime's official historic preservation projects. Al-Shaykh was the minister of municipal and rural affairs (1992–1996), a former member of the High Commission for the Development of Arriyadh, and the former president of the ADA. He was fired from his position at the ADA in 2003 after he refused to illegally grant one of the sons of Prince Salman ibn Abdulaziz land in Riyadh that legally belonged to a Saudi Arabian citizen.

16. Carl von Clausewitz, *On War* (Princeton, NJ: Princeton University Press, 1989).

17. Pierre Nora, "Between Memory and History: Les Lieux de Memoires," in "Memory and Counter-Memory," special issue, *Representations* 26 (1989): 7–24.

18. Governance Palace (Qasr al-Hukm) and Justice Palace (Qasr al-'Adl) are often used interchangeably.

19. Riyadh's heritage and historical tourism industry is expected to generate 1.1 million jobs by 2025, according to "Contextual Analysis," Master Plan, chap. 3: "Lord Cultural Resources," September 15, 2008, ADA Archives, Riyadh.

20. Author interviews in Riyadh 2009–2011 with project managers and the deputy director of the Saudi Commission for Tourism and Antiquities (SCTA), now renamed the Saudi Commission for Tourism and National Heritage. For a comprehensive analysis of the emerging national tourism industry and its projected potential between 2000 and 2020, see the Supreme Commission for Tourism, "National Tourism Development Project in the Kingdom of Saudi Arabia, Phase 1: General Strategy," 2000–2002, ADA Archives, Riyadh. For more on tourism development plans during Salman's reign, see "General Strategy and Operational Plans," website of the Saudi Commission for Tourism and National Heritage, at https://scth.gov.sa/en/AboutSCTA/Pages/General-Strategy-and-Operational-Plans.aspx.

21. "Strategy for Public Spaces," *Comprehensive Strategic Report for the City of Riyadh, May 2002 (2001)*, ADA, 68; and Abdullah al-Rukban (ADA engineer), interview with author, Riyadh, May 17, 2010. MEDSTAR's architects had predicted that revenues from international tourism would significantly contribute to the Saudi economy in decades to come. Developing the international tourism sector was therefore a crucial part of their long-term plan for the city. Already in 2014, revenues from international tourism were expected to almost double by 2024, to reach $35 billion. *The Report: Saudi Arabia 2014*, 7.

22. The distribution of resources across space discloses unequal relations of power in both social and material forms. The uneven development of urban spaces, for instance, is an endemic feature of modern capitalist economies in which states, businesses, and individuals attempt investment in new areas as a spatial fix for fledgling markets. David Harvey, *The New Imperialism* (Oxford: Oxford University Press, 2003).

23. Immanuel Wallerstein, "The Bourgeois(ie) as Concept and Reality," *New Left Review* 1, no. 167 (January–February 1988): 101; Isam Al-Khafaji, *Tormented Births: Passages to Modernity in Europe and the Middle East* (London: I. B. Tauris, 2004); and Giacomo Luciani, "From Private Sector to National Bourgeoisie: Saudi Arabian

Business," in *Saudi Arabia in the Balance: Political Economy, Society, Foreign Affairs*, ed. Paul Aarts and Gerd Nonneman (New York: New York University Press, 2005), 144–84.

24. Paul du Gay, ed., *Production of Culture/Cultures of Production* (Thousand Oaks, CA: Sage, 1997) shows how the production of cultural life is intimately tied to economic processes of production, circulation, and exchange. Also see G. J. Ashworth and J. E. Tunbridge, "Old Cities, New Pasts: Heritage Planning in Selected Cities of Central Europe," in "Post-Socialist Urban Transition in Eastern and Central Europe," special issue, *GeoJournal* 49, no. 1 (1999): 105–16.

25. See the different views on the matter by former mufti Abdulaziz ibn Baz (1993–1999) and member of the Council of Senior Scholars Abdulwahhab Ibrahim Abu Sulayman (1994–present): Shaykh Abdulaziz ibn Abdullah ibn Baz, "Al-radd 'ala Salih Muhammad Jamal" [The response to Salih Muhammad Jamal], official website of Imam Ibn Baz, n.d., https://binbaz.org.sa/articles/38/%D8%A7%D9%84%D8%B1%D8%AF-%D8%B9%D9%84%D9%89-%D8%B5%D8%A7%D9%84%D8%AD-%D9%85%D8%AD%D9%85%D8%AF-%D8%AC%D9%85%D8%A7%D9%84; and Abdulwahhab Ibrahim Abu Sulayman, *Al-amakin al-ma'thura al-mutawatira fi Makkah al-Mukarramah* [Islamic historical places in the Holy City of Makkah Al-Mukarramah], (London: Mu'asasat al-Firqan li-l-Turath al-Islami, 2010). For a longer discussion of different views, see Fahd ibn Saad Aba Hussein, "Asnam al-mushrikin.. hel satuhma bi'ism al-athar?" [Statues of unbelievers: Will they be protected in the name of antiquities?], February 20, 2010, https://www.alukah.net/sharia/0/9655/#ixzz2z8nD7oJq. For a different view from within the Wahhabi establishment, see "Ma sihhat al-jara'im al-Wahhabiyya fi haq al-athar al-nabawiyya?" [How true are Wahhabi crimes against sites related to the Prophet?], alaathar.com, https://alaathar.com/?p=658; and Abdulwahhab al-Faisal and Ahmad Rafed, "Izalat al-amakin al-ta'rikhiyya fi Makkah wa-al-Madina mahu li-ta'rikh al-umma" [The removal of historical sites in Mecca and Medina is an erasure of the nation's history], *Al-Madina*, June 4, 2010, https://www.al-madina.com/article/8348.

26. See, for example, how Salih ibn Fawzan al-Fawzan (member of the Council of Senior Scholars) explains the need to neglect and not preserve antiquities, and how investing in, and commercializing, historical sites goes against religion. "Hikm ihya' al-athar wa-l-'inaya bi-umur al-jahiliyya wa shakhsiyatiha" [Ruling on the preservation of antiquities and caring for pre-Islamic matters and its personalities], official website of Shaykh Salih ibn Fawzan al-Fawzan, February 27, 2012, https://www.alfawzan.af.org.sa/en/node/13938.

27. Author interviews with employees at the National Museum as well as the Arriyadh Development Authority, Riyadh, 2010–2011.

28. So alarming was the damage inflicted upon historical sites that in 1980, the Council of Ministers approved a petition by the minister of culture and the president of the High Commission for Antiquities that called on responsible government institutions to maintain historical sites and old neighborhoods and stop destroying them. Record 38495, No. 25, Presidency of the Council of Ministers, December 23, 1980, Institute of Public Administration Archives (hereafter cited as IPA Archives), Riyadh.

29. I have already cited several of these instances throughout the book. For more examples, see Sultan ibn Salman's opening statement and other parts of Al-hay'a al-'amma li-al-siyaha wa-l-athar [Saudi Commission for Tourism and Antiquities, Kingdom of Saudi Arabia], *Al-'abath fi al-athar* [Tampering with antiquities], 2009; and Salman ibn Abdulaziz and Fahd al-Semmari's two statements in *Buhuth nadwat al-watha'iq altarikhiyya fi al-Mamlaka al-'Arabiyya al-Sa'udiyya* [Symposium on historical documents in the Kingdom of Saudi Arabia], November 24–26, 1996 (Riyadh: Darat al-Malik Abdulaziz, 1997).

30. Saudi Arabia's first two development plans, covering the 1970s, emphasized infrastructure. According to "Business Outlook Abroad: Current Reports from the Foreign Service," *Business America* 5, no. 13 (June 28, 1982): 18, "The results were impressive—the total length of paved highways tripled, power generation increased by a multiple of 28, and the capacity of the seaports grew tenfold. For the third plan (1980–85), the emphasis changed. Spending on infrastructure declined, but it rose markedly on education, health, and social services."

31. Paul Bonnenfant, "Real Estate and Political Power in 1970s Riyadh," trans. Diantha Guessous and Pascal Menoret, *City* 18, no. 6 (1982): 708–22.

32. The Saudi Arabian press has published several articles since 2010 on religious leaders in the country visiting historical sites and praising the state's efforts. It is increasingly evident that these leaders' public support started only after most historical sites in Mecca were already destroyed. The following article critiques religious leaders' praise of historical sites and calls on the SCTA—SCT until 2008—to look at the prophet's material history: Fa'iz ibn Salih Jamal, "Al-Shaykhan wa-l-athar.. tahawwul mahmud wa-fi'il matlub" [The two shaykhs and antiquities: A welcome transformation and required actions], *Maccawi*, February 16, 2013, http://www.makkawi.com /Liberary/Articles/ItemDetails.aspx?ID=1859.

33. Madawi Al-Rasheed, *A History of Saudi Arabia* (London: Cambridge University Press, 2002); Khaled Fahmy, *All the Pasha's Men: Mehmed Ali, His Army and the Making of Modern Egypt* (Cairo: American University in Cairo Press, 2000); and Frederick F. Anscombe, *The Ottoman Gulf: The Creation of Kuwait, Saudi Arabia and Qatar* (New York: Columbia University Press, 1997).

34. Record 31444, Ottoman Collection, File 104/14/7, No. 38, January 29, 1905. Original number 105/76; and Record 34330, Ottoman Collection, File 104/4/5, No. 28, November 21, 1915. Original number 17447-421. Both at the IPA Archives, Riyadh.

35. Foreign consulates in Jeddah regularly wrote reports on Abdulaziz ibn Saud and his relationship with other states, including the British, even after World War I. For an example, see report on the relationship between the British, amir of Kuwait, and Ibn Saud and neighboring states. Record 13025, German Collection, File 101, No. 517, August 29, 1939, Darah, Riyadh.

36. Abdulrahman Moghis Qhtani and Adel Nasser Al Fassam, "Development Strategy for Arriyadh, Saudi Arabia," *Geospatial World*, October 31, 2011, https://www.geospatialworld.net/article/development-strategy-for-arriyadh-saudi-arabia/.

37. Barry Reynolds, "A Walk Through History," *Saudi Aramco World* 30, no. 2 (March–April 1979), http://www.saudiaramcoworld.com/issue/197902/a.walk.through.history.htm.

38. "Atturaif District of Addiriyah, Operations Master Plan," Lord Cultural Resource, September 2008, ADA Archives, Riyadh.

39. Saleh al-Hathloul, "Riyadh Architecture in One Hundred Years: An Essay on a Public Lecture Presented at Darat al-Funun, Amman on April 21, 2002" (Amman: Center for the Study of the Built Environment, 2003), 2.

40. According to Arthur P. Clark, Abdulaziz's sister, Princess Nora, "had pioneered the way when she built her palace outside the city proper in the early 1930s," and the others followed in her footsteps. Arthur P. Clark, "A Kingdom Revealed: The Making of the King Abdulaziz Historical Centre" (final draft submitted to the Arriyadh Development Authority, December 30, 2002), ADA Archives, Riyadh.

41. Ibid.

42. *Qasr al Hukm District Development Program: Phase 2* (Riyadh, Arriyadh Development Authority, 1992), 8, ADA Archives, Riyadh.

43. According to the basic rules of the Kingdom of the Hijaz, issued in 1926, Mecca was to be the capital. It remained the administrative capital throughout Abdulaziz ibn Saud's reign because it was more institutionally developed than Riyadh. As the

capital of the Hashemite state, Mecca had more developed bureaucratic and human resources. Jeddah was the headquarters of diplomatic representation, and Taif was the summer capital of the state. After Abdulaziz passed away, King Saud ordered the Council of Ministers and the headquarters of the ministries and government buildings to move to Riyadh in 1956, with secondary branches of the above-mentioned institutions established in Jeddah.

44. Faisal A. Al-Mubarak, "Urban Growth Boundary Policy and Residential Suburbanization: Riyadh, Saudi Arabia," *Habitat International* 28 (2004): 589.

45. Ibid.

46. Rosie Bsheer, "A Counter-Revolutionary State: Popular Movements and the Making of Saudi Arabia," *Past and Present* 238, no. 1 (February 1, 2018): 233–77.

47. Al-Hathloul, "Riyadh Architecture in One Hundred Years," 4–5; and Saleh al-Hathloul, "Riyadh Development Plans in the Past Fifty Years (1967–2016)," *Current Urban Studies* 5 (2017): 97–120.

48. Bonnenfant, "Real Estate"; Deborah Antoinette Middleton, "Growth and Expansion in Post-War Urban Design Strategies: C. A. Doxiadis and the First Strategic Plan for Riyadh Saudi Arabia (1968–1972)" (PhD diss., Georgia Institute of Technology, December 2009); Pascal Menoret, *Joyriding in Riyadh: Oil, Urbanism, and Road Revolt* (Cambridge: Cambridge University Press, 2014); and al-Hathloul, "Riyadh Development Plans in the Past Fifty Years (1967–2016)."

49. Hashim Sarkis, *Circa 1958: Lebanon in the Pictures and Plans of Constantinos Doxiadis* (Beirut: Editions Dar An-Nahar, 2003); and Panayiota Pyla, "Back to the Future: Doxiadis's Plans for Baghdad," *Journal of Planning History* 7, no. 1 (2008): 3–19; Matthew Hull, *Government of Paper: The Materiality of Bureaucracy in Urban Pakistan* (Berkeley: University of California Press, 2012).

50. Michelle Provoost, "New Towns on the Cold War Frontier: How Modern Urban Planning Was Exported as an Instrument in the Battle for the Developing World," *Eurozine*, June 28, 2006, http://www.eurozine.com/new-towns-on-the-cold-war-frontier-4/?pdf.

51. Lord Consulting Services, "Security Strategy and Guideline Report," Atturaif Operations Master Plan, 2004, ADA Archives, Riyadh; and author interview with members of the security planning team at the ADA, Riyadh, March 2, 2011.

52. Saleh al-Hathloul (former deputy minister of town planning), interview with author, Riyadh, March 28, 2010; and ADA state planners, interviews with author, Riyadh, 2010–2011.

53. For more on this, see Alaa Alrawaibah, "Archeological Site Management in the Kingdom of Saudi Arabia: Protection or Isolation," in *Cultural Heritage in the Arabian Peninsula*, ed. Karen Exell and Trinidad Rico (New York: Routledge, 2016), 143–56.

54. For more on the history of archeology in Saudi Arabia, see Saad A. al-Rashid, "The Development of Archeology in Saudi Arabia," in *Papers from the Thirty-Eighth Meeting of the Seminar for Arabian Studies Held in London, 22–24 July 2004*, vol. 35 of *Proceedings of the Seminar for Arabian Studies* (Oxford: Archaeopress, 2005), 207–14.

55. Council of Ministers Resolution No. 717, June 20, 1974, IPA Archives, Riyadh.

56. MOMRA was established according to Council of Ministers Resolution No. A/266 (September 14, 1975) and was approved a month later by Royal Decree on October 13, 1975 (IPA Archives, Riyadh). Saudi Arabia's municipal system dates to 1937, when the regime of the newly established state issued a royal decree, No. 8723, that heralded government intervention in urban development, specifically in Mecca and Medina, for the purposes of serving Muslim pilgrims there. The decree was updated twice, once in 1941 and again in 1976 (Royal Decree No. 5). The three decrees, despite their limitations, still constitute the backbone of municipal planning and management in Saudi Arabia.

57. Since its creation, MOMRA has had several ministers, including Prince Majid ibn Abdulaziz (1975–1979) and Prince Mit'ib ibn Abdulaziz (1979–1982 and 2003–2009). The latter's son, Mansur, ran the ministry from 2009 to 2014, when Abdullatif ibn Abdulmalik Al al-Shaykh took over.

58. MOMRA's primary functions include city and town planning, and the development and maintenance of the basic infrastructure, such as roads and sanitation. Its goals are to design and update the national spatial strategy, foster capacity development among the different municipalities, and support the implementation of regional urban plans within the parameters of the national spatial strategy. For more on MOMRA's history, see MOMRA's website, "Nabza 'an al-wizara" [Overview of the ministry], http://www.momra.gov.sa/About/About.aspx.

59. Wallerstein, "Bourgeois(ie) as Concept and Reality," 103.

60. MOMRA corruption became a topic of national discussion in 2009, when the city of Jeddah flooded after a rainstorm. Jeddah's sewage and drainage infrastructure had cost billions of riyals over the previous three decades. Yet in the aftermath of the floods, it became apparent that no such infrastructure had been built, despite its existence on paper. The floods led to the death of 120 Saudi Arabians and the loss of hundreds of homes. For more on the failure of the Jeddah sewage system, see Ali

al-Ahmed, "Jeddah Flood Deaths Shame Saudi Royals," *Guardian*, December 3, 2009, http://www.guardian.co.uk/commentisfree/2009/dec/03/jeddah-floods-sewage-al-saud.

61. Council of Ministers Resolution No. 221, 13 June 1983, ADA Archives, Riyadh.

62. Ibid.

63. Al-Mubarak, "Urban Growth Boundary Policy," 569.

64. Al-Hathloul, interview with author.

65. The early redevelopment of Medina in the 1970s was a joint effort of its then prince Abdulmuhsin ibn Abdulaziz and his powerful half brother Majid ibn Abdulaziz, MOMRA's first minister and prince of Mecca Region from 1980 to 1999.

66. The exception was such oil cities as Dammam, Khubar, and Dhahran, which Aramco and its US planners developed in the 1940s and 1950s. For the consequences of centralized planning in Riyadh, see Shaibu Bala Garba, "Managing Urban Growth and Development in the Riyadh Metropolitan Area, Saudi Arabia," *Habitat International* 28, no. 4 (December 2004): 593–608.

67. In the first two decades after the Saudi state was formed in 1932, Saudi Arabia did not have a fiscal system. The rulers at the time allocated Mecca Province and Riyadh Province the same budget. With the transfer of the administrative capital from Mecca to Riyadh in 1956, King Saud's regime instituted a fiscal system. It also diverted the majority of state resources to the capital, and restricted and policed what other cities received. Within the three regions (Najd, Hijaz, and Eastern Province), therefore, some provinces received more state attention while others were neglected and underdeveloped. Other regions in the northern and southern parts of the kingdom were also completely neglected and almost severed from the Saudi national imaginary. This analysis is based on a review of available financial records since the 1920s (with Al Saud's wars of conquest), from various sources: "Al-hisabat al-maliyya" [Financial accounts], "Al-shu'un al-tijariyya" [Economic affairs], and "Al-khadamat al-'amma" [General services], all in Al-watha'iq al-wataniyya [National records], Darah, Riyadh; and Al-muwazana al-'amma li-l-Mamlaka al-Arabiyya al-Sa'udiyya, *Umm al-Qura* (various years starting from 1930).

68. Bonnenfant, "Real Estate."

69. Record 29244, No. 1123, Presidency of Council of Ministers (September 11, 1974), 2, IPA Archives, Riyadh.

70. Al-Mubarak, "Urban Growth Boundary Policy," 582; and Abdulrahman Moghis Qhtani and Adel Nasser Al Fassam, "Development Strategy for Riyadh," *Geospatial*

World, October 31, 2011, https://www.geospatialworld.net/article/development-strategy-for-arriyadh-saudi-arabia/.

71. Al-Mubarak, "Urban Growth Boundary Policy," 582. For a study on the politicization of space in Riyadh, see Menoret, *Joyriding in Riyadh*.

72. Al-Mubarak, "Urban Growth Boundary Policy," 579.

73. Ali Shuaibi and Saleh al-Hathloul, "The Justice Palace District, Riyadh," in *Continuity and Change: Design Strategies for Large-Scale Urban Development*, ed. Margaret Bentley Sevcenko (Cambridge, MA: Aga Khan Program for Islamic Architecture at Harvard and MIT, 1984), 38.

74. Many government officials I interviewed confirmed that Salman often reiterated such statements in meetings when questions of transparency, democratization, and legitimacy were raised in public. In many public lectures I watched on Saudi television in 2010 and 2011, Salman regularly referred to the so-called first and second Saudi states, and to the third state that "we inherited from Abdulaziz." See also Fahd ibn Mutlaq al-Utaybi, "Salman bin Abdulaziz.. Al-malik al-mu'arrikh" [Salman bin Abdulaziz: The historian king], *Al-Riyadh*, January 3, 2018.

75. In 1902, Abdulaziz ibn Saud ambushed his Al Rashid rivals at Masmak Fortress in Riyadh, captured it, and thereafter conquered the whole town. The fortress was the main landmark in Riyadh, and in national education, long before the new wave of memorialization began.

76. Metropolitan Development Strategy for Arriyadh (MEDSTAR), Report from the Arriyadh Development Authority, phase 1, 1997, ADA Archives, Riyadh.

77. Abdullah al-Rukban (engineer and Dir'iyya project manager), interview with author, Riyadh, May 17, 2010. See also "Future Vision," *Brief Summary of the Comprehensive Strategic Plan*, ADA, 2003, 9–10, ADA Archives, Riyadh.

78. "King Abdulaziz Historical Center," High Commission for the Development of Arriyadh website, http://www.ada.gov.sa/ADA_e/DocumentShow_e/?url=/res/ADA/En/Projects/KAHC/index.htm.

79. International Energy Agency, "Short-Term Energy Outlook, Imported Crude Oil Prices," January 2020, https://www.eia.gov/outlooks/steo/realprices/; and "Energy Production and Prices," *Organisation for Economic Co-operation and Development Factbook 2007*, https://www.oecd.org/about/publishing/38413051.pdf. Crude oil prices had already plummeted as a result of the Iraq-Iran War (1980–1988), reaching $21 per barrel in 1986. The 1991 Gulf War had therefore taken place after over a decade of collapsing oil prices, which by 1995 were barely starting to recover. The 1997 Asian

economic crisis then reduced the price of oil to levels not seen since before 1973 and limited productive investment opportunities around the globe.

80. "The Historic Addiriyyah Redevelopment Program: Cost Estimation Report, September 2000" (Arriyadh Development Authority) estimates that the price of renovating the historical buildings alone, without any of the costlier infrastructural and telecommunications plans, would amount to $37 million. In 2010, project managers, however, explained that they had long exceeded the allotted budget. Located in the ADA Archives, Riyadh.

81. Series of interviews with high-ranking ADA executives in Riyadh in 2010–2012.

82. Royal Decree No. 528/m, October 8, 1998, Darah, Riyadh.

83. Ali al-Mughannam (historian, archeologist, ADA consultant, and Dir'iyya project manager), interview with author, Riyadh, May 8, 2010.

84. Al-Hathloul, interview.

85. M. Th. Houtsma et al., eds., *First Encyclopedia of Islam, 1913–1936* (Leiden, Netherlands: E. J. Brill, 1993), 1100; Soraya Altorki and Donald P. Cole, *Arabian Oasis City: The Transformation of 'Unayzah* (Austin: University of Texas Press, 1989), 37–39; and Shuaibi and al-Hathloul, "Justice Palace District, Riyadh."

86. Shuaibi and al-Hathloul, "Justice Palace District, Riyadh," 42; and al-Mughannam, interview.

87. "Nidham naz' mulkiyyat al-'iqarat li-l-manfa'a al-'amma wa wad' al-yad al-mu'aqqat 'ala al-'ikar," Ta'mim min ra'ees diwan ri'asat majlis al-wuzara' al-barqi no. 8/b/12662 of 17/3/1424 (May 18, 2003) ["Regulations for expropriating real estate for public use and the temporary confiscation of property," proclamation from the head of the office of Interior Ministry No. 8/b/12662 of 17/3/1424], IPA Archives, Riyadh.

88. Saudi Council of Ministers issued Resolution No. (9), April 16, 2000. Also see Supreme Commission for Tourism, "National Tourism Development Project in the Kingdom of Saudi Arabia."

89. "Al-Amir Salman: Mawaqi'una al-turathiyya tatatallab minna al-'inaya hatta yastalhim minha al-shabab tarikh biladihum" [Prince Salman: Our heritage spaces require our care so they inspire our youths to understand their country's history], *al-Riyadh*, December 8, 2011, http://www.alriyadh.com/2011/12/08/article689643.html.

90. Rosie Bsheer, "Heritage as War," in "Forced Displacement and Refugees," special issue, *International Journal of Middle East Studies* 49, no. 4 (November 2017), 729–34.

91. ADA urban planners, interviews with author, Riyadh, January 2010 and May 2011; and Happold Consulting Services employees, interviews with author, Riyadh, April 12, 2010.

92. Author interviews in Riyadh, 2010–2012, with high-ranking executives and project managers at the ADA, all of whom reiterated the importance of the centennial and the unprecedented support they received for it.

93. For an urban planning perspective on MEDSTAR, see Al-Hathloul, "Riyadh Development Plans in the Past Fifty Years (1967–2016)."

94. Abdulrahman ibn Mohammed Alangari, "Mantiqat Qasr Alhukm: A Twentieth-Century Development," in *Al-Mamlaka al-'Arabiyya al-Sa'udiyya fi mi'at 'am: buhouth wa dirasat* [The Kingdom of Saudi Arabia in one hundred years: Research and studies], (Riyadh: Darat al-Malik Abdulaziz, 2007), 5:482, 511.

95. Archie Walls, with Rasem Badran Associates and Omrania and Associates, "Restoration of Qasr al-Murabba, Darat al-Malik Abdulaziz, Saudi National Museum" (report for Arriyadh Development Authority, November 1996), PDF file, Ref: 1030/AWD, ADA Archives, Riyadh.

96. Qasr al Hukm District Development Program: Phase Two (Riyadh: Arriyadh Development Authority, 1992), 36, ADA Archives, Riyadh.

97. Alangari, "Mantiqat Qasr Alhukm," 482.

98. "Qasr al Hukm District," Arriyadh Development Authority website, http://www.arriyadh.com/Eng/Tourism/Left/Musems/getdocument.aspx?f=/openshare/Eng/Tourism/Left/Musems/Qasr-Al-Hokm-District.doc_cvt.htm.

99. "Urban Design Failure" and "Elements of KAAHC," in ADA internal reports on the design and construction of the King Abdulaziz Historical Center, ADA Archives, Riyadh.

100. Ibid.

101. See the report by project consultant Arthur P. Clark, "A Kingdom Revealed: The Making of the King Abdulaziz Historical Center" (final draft submitted to the Arriyadh Development Authority, December 30, 2002), ADA Archives, Riyadh.

102. Al-Mughannam, interview.

103. Al-Rashid, "The Development of Archeology in Saudi Arabia."

104. Clark, "A Kingdom Revealed."

105. See Trevor Boddy, "History's New Home in Riyadh," *Saudi Aramco World* 50, no. 5 (September–October 1999), http://www.saudiaramcoworld.com/issue/199905/history.s.new.home.in.riyadh.htm; and "Al-khutta al-tanfiziyya al-khamsiyya li-

al-mathaf al-watani" [The five-year executive plan for the National Museum], High Commission for the Development of Riyadh City, 2012, National Museum Archives, Riyadh.

106. In covering the first temporary exhibition hosted at the mansion in 2019, Saudi newspapers collectively described the Red Palace as a relic of the 1940s that Abdulaziz ibn Saud commissioned for his son, Saud. Planning records in my possession indicate that the palace was built in the 1950s under orders from Saud himself.

107. Fahda bint Saud ibn Abdulaziz Al Saud (daughter of King Saud), interview with author, Jeddah, June 5, 2011.

108. Khalid al-Hazzani (engineer and Red Palace project manager), interview with author, Riyadh, April 12, 2010.

109. For more on the preservation of adobe architecture in Saudi Arabia, see William Facey, *Back to Earth: Adobe Building in Saudi Arabia* (Riyadh: Al-Turath, 2015).

110. "The Historic Addiriyyah Redevelopment Program: Cost Estimation Report, September 2000" (Arriyadh Development Authority), ADA Archives, Riyadh.

111. "Manhajiyat al-ta'amol ma' hayy al-Turaif" [Approach to dealing with al-Turaif District], Historic Diriya Redevelopment Program, ADA Archives, Riyadh.

112. Saudi Arabia's Antiquities Act was passed by Royal Decree No. 26/M of March 1972, IPA Archives, Riyadh.

113. Al-Rukban, interview.

114. Hatoon al-Fassi (historian and women's rights activist) interview with author, Riyadh, April 1, 2010.

115. Royal Decree No. 528/m, October 8, 1998, IPA Archives, Riyadh.

116. "Historical Addir'iyah Development Program," Arriyadh Development Authority website, http://www.arriyadh.com/Eng/ADA/Left/DevProj/getdocument.aspx?f=/openshare/Eng/ADA/Left/DevProj/AddiriyaEn093.doc_cvt.htm.

117. Agency for City Planning at the Ministry of Municipal and Rural Affairs, *Al-Turath al-'umrani fi al-Mamlaka al-'Arabiyya al-Sa'udiyya* [Architectural heritage in the Kingdom of Saudi Arabia] (Riyadh: Ministry of Municipal and Rural Affairs, 2002), 46–47.

118. Al-Rukban, interview. Author also has all ADA planning documents and consultant reports on Atturaif District since 1988.

119. Canadian company Lord Cultural Resources, which provided exhibit design and museology services to the National Museum in Riyadh, won the competition to design the internal exhibition spaces of al-Turaif District and all museological aspects;

Australian ASG was responsible for the site's other museums. The economic aspect was equally important for the regime. After the project's vision and initial planning phase were completed, the ADA hired a Spanish consultant to develop al-Turaif District for investment and economic purposes.

120. Al-Mughannam, interview.

121. Thomas Cielek (ADA planner and architect), interview with author, Riyadh, May 17, 2010.

122. I attended these and other meetings pertaining to the Dirʿiyya Redevelopment Program at the ADA in Riyadh, 2010.

123. UNESCO World Heritage Committee, "At-Turaif District in ad-Dirʿiyah (Saudi Arabia) No. 1329," in *2010 Evaluations of Cultural Properties* (report for the 34th Ordinary Session of the World Heritage Convention, July 25–August 3, 2010, Brazil) (Paris: Secrétariat ICOMOS International, 009), 84, http://whc.unesco.org/archive/2010/whc10-34com-inf.8B1e.pdf.

124. Ibid., 83–84.

125. Members of the Dirʿiyya Redevelopment Program team, interviews with author, Riyadh and Dirʿiyya, May 16–19, 2010.

126. The ADA commissioned a complete and thorough aerial laser scan and survey of Dirʿiyya, which Dafos in Holland and ATM3D in France conducted.

127. "Historical Addiriyah," Projects, Arriyadh Development Authority website, http://www.ada.gov.sa/ADA_e/DocumentShow_e/?url=/res/ADA/En/Projects/Addiriyah/index.html.

128. The addition of the Sheikh Mohammad Bin Abdulwahhab Cultural Foundation is likely a reaction to local critiques of the sidelining of religious history as well as the opening of the mosque's namesake in Qatar in 2011.

129. UNESCO World Heritage Committee, "Cultural Properties—At-Turaif District in ad-Dirʿiyah (Saudi Arabia)," in *Report of the Decisions Adopted by the World Heritage Committee at Its 34th Session (Brasilia, 2010)* (Convention Concerning the Protection of the World Cultural and Natural Heritage, Paris, 2010), http://whc.unesco.org/en/decisions/3994.

130. "City of Riyadh Planning Scheme," memorandum from the urban management planner to Medstar Team, October 21, 2001, 7.

131. See the official website of Vision 2030, at https://vision2030.gov.sa/en/node.

132. Ad Diriyah Formula E website, at https://diriyah-eprix.com/en/.

133. Mandana Limbert, *In the Time of Oil: Piety, Memory, and Social Life in an Omani Town* (Stanford, CA: Stanford University Press, 2010); and Nathalie Peutz, *Is-*

lands of Heritage: Conservation and Transformation in Yemen (Stanford, CA: Stanford University Press, 2018).

134. Henri Lefebvre, *The Production of Space* (Oxford: Wiley-Blackwell, 1991). See also Timothy Mitchell, "The World as Exhibition," *Comparative Studies in Society and History* 31, no. 2 (1989): 217–36.

135. Michel-Rolph Trouillot, *Silencing the Past: Power and the Production of History* (Boston: Beacon Press, 1995), 5.

CHAPTER 5

1. Central Mecca has twelve historic neighborhoods: al-Misfala, al-Muʻabida, al-Naqa, al-Qarara, al-Qashashiyya, al-Shamiyya, al-Shubayka, al-Sulaymaniyya, Harat al-Bab, Jiyad, Jurul, Shaʻb ʻAmir, and Suq al-Layl, which is one of oldest neighborhoods in Mecca and the site of the Prophet's birth. See "Athar Mecca al-nabawiyya wa-l-tarikhiyya: Al-Mawlid al-nabawi" [The Prophet's sites and historical sites in Mecca: Birth of the prophet], *Maccawi*, http://www.makkawi.com/Articles/Show.aspx?ID=815. These neighborhoods are being replaced by the following development megaprojects: the Development of King Abdul Aziz Endowment Project, Jabal Omar Development Project, Al Shamiyya Development Project, Jabal Khandama Development, Jabal al-Kaʻba, Ajyad Hospital, and the western entrance to Mecca.

2. Ministry of Education, Kingdom of Saudi Arabia, *Tarikh al-Mamlaka al-ʻArabiyya al-Saʻudiyya* [History of the Kingdom of Saudi Arabia] (Riyadh: Ministry of Education, 2005–2006), sixth, ninth, and twelfth grades. For a recent example of how Saudi state media depict the stagnancy and "backwardness" of Ottoman Arabia, see Salem al-Ahmadi, "Takmilat mashruʻ tawsiʻat al-masjid al-nabawi wa mashariʻ tanmawiyya ukhra bi al-Madina al-Munawwara" [Continuation of expansion project of Prophet's Mosque and other development projects in Medina], *al-Riyadh*, September 24, 2005, http://www.alriyadh.com/96067.

3. See "Heritage in Context" in Chapter 4 for a more detailed discussion of the various debates on memorialization practices in Wahhabi thought and how they affect religious and historical sites.

4. Some of the same members who served on the boards of Arriyadh Development Authority and the High Commission for the Development of Dirʻiyya were employed by the Mecca Development Authority and MOMRA, at times also consulting for the big construction firms responsible for redeveloping Mecca.

5. In 2018, planners predicted that in coming years the city would host twenty million visitors a year, with eight million visiting at once during the pilgrimage. Muna al-

Manjumi, "Al-mamlaka tu'akkid bi 'hay'at tatwir Makkah wa-l-masha'ir': Khidmat duyuf al-rahman al-hadaf al-asma" [The kingdom confirms through the "Mecca and Masha'ir Development Authority": Serving pilgrims is the prime goal], *Al-Hayat*, June 3, 2018.

6. See this article in a state-owned newspaper, *Al-Sharq al-Awsat*, calling on Mecca to deliver entertainment opportunities so it can compete with cities like Dubai and Paris for tourism: Abdulrahman al-Rashid, "Hel yumkin tatwir Makkah?" [Can Mecca be developed?], *Al-Sharq al-Awsat*, no. 14433, June 4, 2018. For a study of pilgrimage revenues and the developing tourism sector in Mecca, see Said M. Ladki and Rayan A. Mazeh, "Comparative Pricing Analysis of Mecca's Religious Tourism," *International Journal of Religious Tourism and Pilgrimage* 5, no. 1 (2017): 20–28.

7. Michelle Buckley and Adam Hanieh, "Diversification by Urbanization: Tracing the Property-Finance Nexus in Dubai and the Gulf," *International Journal of Urban and Regional Research* 18, no. 1 (2013): 155–75.

8. Nils E. Lind, Confidential, Department of State, Office of Chief, 890F.00/11-10945, November 10, 1945, in Ibrahim al-Rashid, ed., *Documents on the History of Saudi Arabia*, vol. 1, *Saudi Arabia Enters the Modern World: Secret U.S. Documents on the Emergence of the Kingdom of Saudi Arabia as a World Power, 1936–1949* (Salisbury, NC: Documentary Publications, 1980), 11.

9. Other notable families include Ali Riza, Olayan, Qusaybi, Al Fawzan, Khashuqji, and Bin Mahfuz, but none would acquire the wealth and power that the Binladins achieved.

10. Muhammad Binladin had his own network of Hadrami moneylenders, such as Salim ibn Mahfuz.

11. Royal Decree No. 2265/138/1/21, July 23, 1955, Institute of Public Administration Archives (hereafter cited as IPA Archives), Riyadh; and Steve Coll, *The Bin Ladens: An Arabian Family in the American Century* (London: Penguin Books, 2008), 51, 64.

12. The Saudi Binladin Group is one of the largest construction companies in the world, and Al Saud ranks among the world's wealthiest families.

13. Malcolm H. Kerr, *The Arab Cold War: Gamal 'Abd al-Nasir and His Rivals, 1958–1970* (Oxford: Oxford University Press, 1971). For more recent literature, see Salim Yaqub, *Containing Arab Nationalism: The Eisenhower Doctrine and the Middle East* (Chapel Hill: University of North Carolina Press, 2004); Rashid Khalidi, *Sowing Crisis: The Cold War and American Dominance in the Middle East* (Boston: Beacon Press, 2009); and Abdel Razzaq Takriti, *Monsoon Revolution: Republicans, Sultans, and Empires in Oman, 1965–1976* (Oxford: Oxford University Press, 2016).

14. Saudi Binladin Group, footage of construction work on roads connecting Jeddah to Mecca and Medina and their surroundings, as far south as the 'Asir Region, DVD, Saudi Binladin Archives, Jeddah.

15. It is not clear how early the SBG started investing in the petroleum and petrochemical industry, but these investments, which the Saudi regime secured for the company, made the SBG one of the richest development companies in the world.

16. Record 25294, No. 1109, Presidency of the Council of Ministers, September 25, 1973, a request by the minister of interior to allow the firm to keep working on development plans for the major cities in the Hijaz, IPA Archives.

17. By 1981, the Hajj Research Center became an official state institution. It was first affiliated with King Abdulaziz University in Jeddah and, by 1982, with Umm al-Qura University in Mecca. In 1998, its name was changed to the Custodian of Holy Shrines Institute for Hajj Research. Record 39661, No. 127, Ministerial Committee for Administrative Organization, July 10, 1982, and Record 55409, Council for Higher Education, April 22, 1998, both at the IPA Archives.

18. Hajj Research Center, *Mecca: Policy Framework and Future Development, 1976* (Mecca: Umm al-Qura University, 1976), 7. Archives of the Custodian of the Two Holy Mosques Institute for Hajj Research, Umm al-Qura University, Mecca.

19. Hajj Research Center, 11, 16.

20. Hajj Research Center.

21. Royal Decree No. 8723, 1937, IPA Archives.

22. Hajj Research Center, *Mecca*, 6.

23. Rosie Bsheer, "A Counter-Revolutionary State: Popular Movements and the Making of Saudi Arabia," *Past and Present* 238, no. 1 (February 1, 2018): 233–77.

24. In the 1950s, when newspapers in Saudi Arabia were independently owned and enjoyed limited freedoms, authors regularly critiqued Binladin's construction work and the lack of governmental oversight over infrastructural development and urban planning. For one example, see "Roma wa Binladin" [Rome and Binladin], *al-Adwa'*, January 6, 1959, Prince Salman Library at the King Saud University, Riyadh.

25. "Hal ta'rif man sammama w-ashrafa 'ala tawsi'at al-haramayn al-sharifayn? Muqabala ma' Muhammad Kamal Ismail" [Do you know who designed and supervised the expansion of the two holy mosques? An interview with Muhammad Kamal Ismail], *Waraqat*, December 5, 2009, http://www.waraqat.net/10713/; and Omar Tahir, "Muhammad Kamal Ismail.. Sanayi'i mujamma' al-tahrir" [Muhammad Kamal Ismail: Artisan of the Tahrir Compound], *al-Ahram*, December 18, 2015.

26. The expansion increased prayer areas in Mecca's Grand Mosque from 150,000 square meters with a capacity of three hundred thousand worshippers to 356,000 square meters, big enough for seven hundred thousand worshippers. Binladin also expanded the surrounding piazzas to fit four hundred thousand worshippers, up from forty-five thousand.

27. On family-company relationships, see Michael B. Miller, *The Bon Marche: Bourgeois Culture and the Department Store, 1869–1920* (Princeton, NJ: Princeton University Press, 1981).

28. Author interviews with engineers, architects, consultants, and project managers at some of Saudi Arabia's largest contracting companies: the Saudi Binladin Group, Omrania, and Diyar, Riyadh and Jeddah, 2010–2012.

29. Muhammad Kamal Ismail, *The Architecture of the Prophet's Holy Mosque: Al Madinah* (London: Hazar, 1998); and Muhammad Kamal Ismail, *The Architecture of the Prophet's Holy Mosque: Makkah* (London: Hazar, 1998).

30. Wizarat al-shu'un al-baladiyya wa-l-qarawiyya (Ministry of Municipal and Rural Affairs), Dar al-Handasa li-l-tasmim wa-l-istisharat al-Fanniyya (Dar Al-Handasah Consultants), and Saudi Consulting Group, *Makkah Region Comprehensive Development Plans: Cultural Area Plans,* Project No. 208, Report No. 6 (Riyadh: Dar Al-Handasah Consultants and Saudi Consulting Group, 1986). Like its predecessor, this plan also recommended the building of tunnels inside Mecca's mountains, a technique criticized by many urban planners and architects at the time.

31. Ismail, *Makkah*, 74–75.

32. Saleh al-Hathloul, interview with author, Riyadh, March 10, 2010.

33. Author interviews with SBG employees involved in these maneuvers, Jeddah, March 2010, and Beirut, June 2010.

34. On rare occasions, when a workaround was impossible, residents negotiated with workers to try to salvage some of the targeted spaces. Some were even able to take possession of parts of columns or other artifacts. Author interviews, Mecca, 2011.

35. Isam al-Khafaji, *Tormented Births: Passages to Modernity in Europe and the Middle East* (London: I. B. Tauris, 2004). It is important to note that this was a major shift from the 1970s, which saw the recycling of domestic petrocapital in, and through, foreign cities like New York and London that was so central to the emergence of neoliberalism. See David Harvey, *A Brief History of Neoliberalism* (Oxford: Oxford University Press, 2007).

36. Author interviews with people involved in these transactions, Riyadh and Jeddah, 2010–2012.

37. David Harvey, *The Urbanization of Capital: Studies in the History and Theory of Capitalist Urbanization* (Baltimore: Johns Hopkins University Press, 1985).

38. Urban planner and architect who has worked for the Saudi Binladin Group for over two decades, interview with author, Jeddah, June 2011.

39. F. E. Peters, *Mecca: A Literary History of the Muslim Holy Land* (Princeton, NJ: Princeton University Press, 1994).

40. The concept of Sadd al-dhara'i', or the prohibition of what may lead to committing sins, is usually used to justify these actions. See Abdulhakim Darqawi, "Sadd al-dhara'i' fi al-shari'a al-Islamiyya" [The prohibition of what may lead to committing sins in Islamic sharia], *Aluka*, August 9, 2009, https://www.alukah.net/sharia/0/6987/.

41. In addition to the discussion under "Heritage in Context" in Chapter 4, see Daniel Howden, "The Destruction of Mecca: Saudi Hardliners Are Wiping Out Their Own Heritage," *Independent*, August 6, 2005, https://www.independent.co.uk/news/world/middle-east/the-destruction-of-mecca-saudi-hardliners-are-wiping-out-their-own-heritage-304029.html.

42. There is ample evidence of corruption and the diversion of massive funds for personal enrichment through the Mecca and Medina expansion projects and the surrounding commercial megaprojects. For instance, according to experts in 2010, the project was billed as costing $550 million. Actual costs and payments, however, far exceeded $15 billion, as a result of regime and corporate corruption, overspending, and initial underreporting in order to avoid raising suspicion. ADA planners and SBG project managers, interviews with author; and "Revealed: The World's 20 Most Expensive Buildings," *Telegraph*, July 27, 2016, http://www.telegraph.co.uk/travel/lists/the-worlds-most-expensive-buildings/masjid-al-haram-mecca-saudi-arabia/.

43. Author interviews with those in charge of the construction of DOKAAE, Mecca, 2010–2012.

44. Khamis al-Sa'di, "Ta'widat 'iqariyya mu'attala fi Makkah bi 5 milyarat" [Suspended real estate compensation in Mecca worth 5 billion riyals], *al-Iqtisadiyya*, December 24, 2012, http://www.aleqt.com/2012/12/24/article_719361.html.

45. For more on the politics of endowment ownership, see Nada Moumtaz, "Modernizing Charity, Remaking Islamic Law" (PhD diss., City University of New York, 2012).

46. "Al-Saʻudiyya: Izalat qalʻat ajyad 'sha'n yakhuss siyadat al-mamlaka'" [Saudi Arabia: The demolition of Ajyad Fortress "is a matter of Saudi sovereignty"], *Elaph*, January 9, 2002, http://elaph.com/ElaphWeb/Archive/1010571450748883800.htm.

47. Hassan Dabbusi (SBG employee and DOKAAE project manager), written interview with author, February 17, 2011.

48. Ajyad, sometimes referred to as Jiyad, was an old neighborhood that housed many bureaucratic institutions in the Hamidiyya building where Dar al-Hukuma al-Saʻudiyya (Saudi Arabian House of Government) was located. Dar al-Hukuma included the offices of the General Security, the Expedited Court, Notary Public, Criminal Investigations, the Shura Council, Department of Awqaf, and the Census Bureau. Parts of Ajyad neighborhood were destroyed in the King Saud Expansion Project in 1955, but most were actually demolished in the past two decades. This included the Ajyad Hospital, Central Mecca's only hospital in 2010. Another medical center was slated for construction farther east of the former location in a commercial complex. ʻAdil Nur al-Ghabbashi, "Ajyad Fortress," *Maccawi*, January 13, 2013, http://forum.makkawi.com/showthread.php?t=99917.

49. Author interviews with employees at the Mecca Development Authority and Saudi Binladin Group, Riyadh and Jeddah, 2010–2012. Abdulmajid was the governor of Medina Province (1986–1999) when that city's central region, including the Prophet's Mosque, was overhauled. Abdulmajid then became governor of Mecca Province (2000–2007) and was appointed chairman of the Mecca Development Authority at a time when the city was undergoing the biggest redevelopment in its history.

50. DOKAAE alone had 12,500 employees on its payroll, according to its project manager, Hassan Dabbusi. Interview with author.

51. Meccan historian, interview with author, Riyadh, November 3, 2011.

52. Lamya Khalidi, "The Destruction of Yemen and Its Cultural Heritage," in "Forced Displacement and Refugees, special issue, *International Journal of Middle East Studies* 49, no. 4 (October 2017): 735–38.

53. Dabbusi, interview.

54. For a regime perspective, see "Ajyad qalʻa Islamiyya wa laysat (Ataturkiyya)" [Ajyad is an Islamic fortress, not "Ataturkist"], *Kalimat al-Riyadh*, January 11, 2002, http://www.alriyadh.com/2002/01/11/article29769.html. *Kalimat al-Riyadh* is a section of *al-Riyadh* newspaper, the mouthpiece of ruling members of Al Saud.

55. "Saudi Arabia: The Demolition of Ajyad Fortress."

56. Bureaucrats in Mecca, interview with author, Mecca, November 2011.

57. "SBG Dynamites Ajyad Mountain," unpublished documentary footage owned by a Saudi architect.

58. The clock tower was designed by Dar al-Handasah Group (Shair and Partners). For images of the clock tower in relation to the rest of Central Mecca, see "Mecca Clock Tower," Dar Group website, https://www.dar.com/work/project/makkah-clock-tower.

59. Dabbusi, interview. See "Ajyad al-tarikh awwal Majlis Shura.. w dar al-hukuma al-Sa'udiyya" [Historic Ajyad was the site of the first Shura Council, and Saudi Arabian House of Government], *Makkawi*, February 2, 2012, https://makkawi.azurewebsites.net/Article/766/أجياد-التاريخ-أول-مجلس-شورى-ودار-الحكومة-السعودية. On Barak has written about technology and temporality in *On Time: Technology and Temporality in Modern Egypt* (Berkeley: University of California Press, 2013).

60. Former MOMRA minister, author interview, February 8, 2011.

61. Adam T. Smith, "Archaeologies of Sovereignty," *Annual Review of Anthropology* 40 (2011): 420. For the ways in which landscapes can be monuments of power and sovereignty, see Christopher Tilley and Wayne Bennett, *The Materiality of Stone* (New York: Bloomsbury Academic, 2004).

62. Mark Crinson, ed., *Urban Memory: History and Amnesia in the Modern City* (New York: Routledge, 2005), xviii.

63. Two independent sources close to King Abdullah who attended the cited meeting, one of whom is a nephew of the king himself.

64. Several studies on the expansion of the Grand Mosque recommended making it mandatory for all residential projects surrounding the mosque to build prayer halls that "extend naturally" from the mosque's piazza. See Abdullah Muhammad Fuda and Samir ibn Abd al-Hamdi 'Ashi, "Al-Bada'il al-mukhtalifa li-ziyadat al-taqa al-isti'abiyya li-l-Masjid al-Haram: Amakin al-salat" [Alternatives to increase the capacity of the mosque's land: Places of prayer], preliminary report (Mecca: Institute of the Custodian of the Two Holy Mosques for Hajj Research, 2002), 41.

65. The website of Shaykh Abdulaziz ibn Abdullah ibn Baz, http://www.binbaz.org.sa/. *Jama'a* prayer is supposed to unite Muslims—though usually men and not women—behind an imam as a practical way to cultivate a disregard of differences and identity markers (socioeconomic class, nationality, race, and so on) and to inculcate discipline and humility. This sense of equality is even more important during Ramadan and the pilgrimage. It can be argued that the increasing privatization of prayer represents a contradiction of one of the basic precepts of the faith.

66. For some debates on the boundaries of the Grand Mosque (hudud al-haram), see Abdulaziz ibn Baz, "Ma hiya hudud al-haram" [What are the boundaries of the haram], Imam Ibn Baz official website, https://binbaz.org.sa/fatwas/4789/%D9%85%D8%A7%D9%87%D9%8A-%D8%AD%D8%AF%D9%88%D8%AF-%D8%A7%D9%84%D8%AD%D8%B1%D9%85; and his "Hel Kul Makkah tu'tabar haraman?" [Is all Mecca considered a sanctuary?], Imam Ibn Baz official website, https://binbaz.org.sa/fatwas/4438/%D9%87%D9%84-%D9%83%D9%84-%D9%85%D9%83%D8%A9-%D8%AA%D8%B9%D8%AA%D8%A8%D8%B1-%D8%AD%D8%B1%D9%85%D8%A7. See also Shaykh Muhammad Al Uthaymeen (known as ibn Uthaymeen), "Hel yashmol ajar al-sala fi al-masjid al-haram jami' masajid Makkah?" [Does praying anywhere in Mecca count as praying inside the Grand Mosque?], YouTube video, 3:27, https://www.youtube.com/watch?v=c3JU83NGxqE.

67. See, e.g., Roger Harrison, "Space-Share Concept in Land Use Introduced," *Arab News*, June 22, 2004, https://www.arabnews.com/node/250913; and "Zam Zam Tower Mecca," time-share marketing campaign, YouTube video, 10:47, posted October 23, 2007, http://www.youtube.com/watch?v=gvSzzBWXyIQ.

68. See the introduction for a detailed explanation of the post–Gulf War economic crisis and its effects in Saudi Arabia.

69. "Which City Has the Most Expensive Real Estate in the World? Mecca," *Al Arabiya*, July 28, 2011, https://www.alarabiya.net/articles/2011/07/28/159691.html.

70. These schools contradict official Saudi Arabian history, which claims that King Faisal ibn Abdulaziz and his wife 'Iffat established the first girls' school in 1964. Revisionist official Saudi history now attributes that accomplishment to King Saud.

71. Al-Ma'had al-'Ilmi al-Sa'udi [Saudi Scientific Institute], *Tizkar al-wala' wa-l-ikhlas* [Token of loyalty and allegiance] (Mecca: Umm al-Qura Publications, 1930). The institute issued this pamphlet on the occasion of Prince Faisal's visit in 1930. As for the preparatory school, it was opened by Mecca notable Muhammad Tahir al-Dabbagh and was the first of its kind in the country. It allowed the first wave of Saudi students to pursue college abroad in the 1940s. It was initially located in al-Misfala neighborhood before it moved to the fortress on Jabal Hindi.

72. Karl Marx, *Capital: A Critique of Political Economy*, vol. 1 (London: Penguin Classics, 1992).

73. The Extended Umrah Tourist Visa was approved by the Council of Ministers and the Shura Council in 2004 but did not come into effect until December 2013.

74. Matthew Martin, "Jabal Omar to Replace Saudi Binladin: Change in Contract Terms May Result in Saudi Arabian Contractor Exiting the Project," *Middle East Economic Digest* 54, no. 45 (November 5, 2010).

75. Nabil Raza, "Muslim Hush over Destruction of Prophet Home Shocking," *Jafariya News*, September 2, 2005, http://www.jafariyanews.com/2k5_news/sep/5prophethome_destruction.htm. For a breakdown of the different phases of construction, see the website of the Jabal Omar Development Company, at https://jabalomar.com.sa/project-update/.

76. Daylong tour of Central Mecca with a former Mecca Development Authority employee and tour operator for the Saudi Commission for Tourism and Antiquities, June 3, 2010.

77. Mecca Development Authority employee, interview with author, Mecca, May 10, 2010.

78. For more on the legalities of land expropriation, see Chapter 4.

79. "Muwatin: Hay'at Tatwir Makkah tasababat fi hadm manazilina allati ta'wina" [Saudi citizen: Mecca Development Authority caused the destruction of our homes], and reader responses to the article, in *Al-Weeam*, March 19, 2012, http://bit.ly/2olJuhE.

80. Property owners were offered between $1,000 and $3,000 per square meter, as opposed to the actual market price of $75,000 per square meter.

81. Record 58067, No. 1202/m, Royal Decree, Presidency of the Council of Ministers, December 20, 2000, IPA Archives.

82. "Sumuw wali al-'ahd yudashin mashru' tatwir mantiqat al-Shamiyya" [Crown prince inaugurates beginning of al-Shamiyya Development Project], *Al-Jazira*, November 9, 2004, http://www.al-jazirah.com/2004/20041109/ln4.htm.

83. Author interviews with property owners and lawyers, Riyadh and Jeddah, 2010–2012.

84. Ali Shuaibi and Saleh al-Hathloul, "The Justice Palace District, Riyadh," in *Continuity and Change: Design Strategies for Large-Scale Urban Development*, ed. Margaret Bentley Sevcenko (Cambridge, MA: Aga Khan Program for Islamic Architecture at Harvard University and the Massachusetts Institute of Technology, 1984), 37–48.

85. Nearly one million people live in slums in Mecca, Jeddah, and Taif, combined, and about seventy slums in Mecca make up 25 percent of the city's urban space. See Lynne Nahhas, "Mecca's Slum-Dwellers Fear Eviction as High Rises Multiply," AFP, November 12, 2012, http://now.mmedia.me/lb/en/archive/meccas_slum-dwellers_fear_eviction_as_high_rises_multiply.

86. Author interviews with Saudi Arabian bureaucrats and lawyers, Riyadh and Jeddah, 2010–2012.

87. The Hijaz, by virtue of including Mecca and Medina, but also because of its long economic history, was for centuries a global and cosmopolitan space. Its people have looked down on those who hailed from Najd. They viewed them as Bedouins who were uneducated, uncivilized, and backward, especially with the rise of Al Saud to power. These stereotypes and the sense of righteousness are not uncommon to this day.

88. Immanuel Wallerstein, "Bourgeois(ie) as Concept and Reality," *New Left Review* 1, no. 167 (January–February 1988): 100.

89. Author interviews with several individuals who have financially benefited from these transactions as well as with subcontractors who were on the payroll of the Holy Mosque Expansion Project when, in reality, they were in charge of building the private mansions. Beirut, Cairo, Jeddah, 2010–2014.

90. Author interviews with urban planners and architects who participated in drawing alternative designs for Mecca's postwar redevelopment, Jeddah and Riyadh, 2010–2014.

91. Ed Atwood, "Makkah Land Prices Hit $133,000 per Sq Metre," *Arabian Business*, February 18, 2010, https://www.arabianbusiness.com/makkah-land-prices-hit-133-000-per-sq-metre-report-40490.html; "Which City Has the Most Expensive Real Estate in the World? Mecca"; "A Square Meter of Land in Makkah Now Costs SR 1.5 million," *Arab News*, February 13, 2013, http://www.arabnews.com/saudi-arabia/square-meter-land-makkah-now-costs-sr-15-million; and Abdullah al-Dahhas, "'Markaziyyat Makkah' al-aghla 'alamiyyan.. wa-la tuwjad fiha aradhi li-l-bay'" ["Central Mecca" is the most expensive in the world: And there are no properties there for sale], *Okaz*, December 3, 2016, http://okaz.com.sa/article/1512451/قتصاد/مركزية-مكة-الأغلى-عالميا-و-توجد-فيها-أراض-للبيع.

92. Sami Angawi, interview with author, Jeddah, February 16, 2010.

93. Meccan historian, interview with author, Riyadh, February 5, 2010.

94. Sami Angawi, interview with author, Jeddah, February 16, 2010; and author interviews with notable families and ulama in Mecca between 2006 and 2014.

95. Irfan al-Alawi, director of London's Islamic Heritage Research Foundation, and Meccan architect Sami Angawi are two of the most vocal critics of the destruction of cultural heritage in the Hijaz and proponents of this view.

96. Howden's "The Destruction of Mecca" is an example of some of the journalistic articles published before the late 2010s. For examples of later coverage, see Irfan al-

Alawi, "Turning Mecca into Las Vegas," Center for Islamic Pluralism, December 12, 2010, http://www.islamicpluralism.org/2159/turning-mecca-into-las-vegas; Jerome Taylor, "The Photos Saudi Arabia Doesn't Want Seen—and Proof Islam's Most Holy Relics Are Being Demolished in Mecca," *Independent*, March 15, 2013, https://www.independent.co.uk/news/world/middle-east/the-photos-saudi-arabia-doesnt-want-seen-and-proof-islams-most-holy-relics-are-being-demolished-in-8536968.html; Oliver Wainwright, "As the Hajj Begins, the Destruction of Mecca's Heritage Continues," *Guardian*, October 13, 2013, https://www.theguardian.com/artanddesign/2013/oct/14/as-the-hajj-begins-the-destruction-of-meccas-heritage-continues; Carla Power, "Saudi Arabia Bulldozes over Its Heritage," *Time*, November 14, 2014, https://time.com/3584585/saudi-arabia-bulldozes-over-its-heritage/; and Oliver Wainwright, "City in the Sky: World's Biggest Hotel to Open in Mecca," *Guardian*, May 22, 2015, https://www.theguardian.com/artanddesign/architecture-design-blog/2015/may/22/worlds-biggest-hotel-to-open-in-mecca. For an example of a cultural and rights-based critique that also blames Wahhabism for the destruction of heritage in Mecca, see Office of the United Nations High Commissioner for Human Rights, "Mandates of the Special Rapporteur in the Field of Cultural Rights and the Special Rapporteur on Freedom of Religion or Belief," SAU 7/2015, October 14, 2015, https://spcommreports.ohchr.org/TMResultsBase/DownLoadPublicCommunicationFile?gId=21880.

97. For an example, see Ziauddin Sardar, *Mecca: The Sacred City* (London: Bloomsbury, 2014).

98. Raya Jalabi, "After the Hajj: Mecca Residents Grow Hostile to Changes in the Holy City," *Guardian*, September 14, 2016, https://www.theguardian.com/cities/2016/sep/14/mecca-hajj-pilgrims-tourism.

99. Historian of Mecca, author interview, Jeddah, 2014.

100. For an example of the destruction of historical sites, the failures of urban development, and the unfair treatment of Mecca's residents, see Hani al-Lihyani, "Muwajaha sakhina bayn amin Hay'at Tatwir Makkah al-Mukarrama wa a'da' al-Majlis al-Baladi" [Heated debate between Mecca Development Authority chair and members of the Municipality Council], *al-Riyadh*, March 19, 2012, http://www.alriyadh.com/2012/02/08/article708145.html.

101. In 2013, the Mecca Development Authority claimed to revise the Central District's master plan in response to complaints about the height of buildings around the Grand Mosque. Although such announcements gave the impression of succumbing to popular will, a review of the pre- and post-2013 plans does not indicate that

much, if at all, was revised in the area ringing the mosque. For the MDA's claims, see Amina L., "Hay'at tatwir Makkah tu'lin 'an tandhim 'imrani jadeed hawl al-haram al-Makki" [Mecca Development Authority announced new urban plan around the Grand Mosque], *Al-Nahar*, June 15, 2013. There are other examples. Until 2014, Jabal al-Noor (Mountain of Light), also known as Jabal Hira' (Hira' Mountain), which contains the small Hira' cave where the Prophet Muhammad allegedly received his first revelation in AD 610, was slated for destruction. In its stead, planners proposed building a multiuse complex with international hotels, apartments, and a mega-arcade. While the plan was abandoned after it proved economically unfeasible, the regime claimed it did so because people in Mecca and elsewhere were against it. Author interview with an MDA executive, Mecca, June 2014. Also see "Saudis to Demolish Prophet's House in Makkah," *Crescent International*, February 22, 2014, https://crescent.icit-digital.org/articles/saudis-to-demolish-prophet-s-house-in-makkah.

102. Shaykh Salih ibn Abdulrahman Hussayin was a prominent intellectual and Saudi government official who became president of the Affairs of the Holy Mosques Masjid al-Haram (Grand Mosque) in Mecca and al-Masjid al-Nabawi (Prophet's Mosque) in Medina in February 2002. For a detailed biography, see "Salih al-Hussayin.. al-'alim al-zahid" [Salih al-Hussayin: The ascetic scholar], *al-Riyadh*, December 15, 2017, http://www.alriyadh.com/1646590.

103. As a matter of fact, the majority of employees of the Mecca Development Authority were summarily laid off in December 2012. "Mafsulu Hay'at Tatwir Makkah wa-l-masha'ir yalja'un li jam'iyyat huquq al-insan bi Jidda" [Those laid off from the Mecca Development Authority resort to human rights organization in Jeddah], *al-Madina*, December 19, 2012, http://www.al-madina.com/node/279038.

104. "Hay'at al-Siyaha tahsur 384 mawqi'an athariyan fi Makkah wa-l-Madina" [Tourism Authority confines 384 historical sites in Mecca and Medina], *Makkawi*, March 14, 2013, http://www.makkawi.com/News/show.aspx?Id=2683.

105. King Abdulaziz built the library in the late 1930s on the site where historians think the Prophet Muhammad was born.

106. Wainwright, "As the Hajj Begins, the Destruction of Mecca's Heritage Continues."

107. The Saudi regime, the religious establishment, and developers have managed, for the most part, to maintain a high level of secrecy regarding the construction and redevelopment work that has occurred in Mecca since the mid-1990s. On rare occasions, the regime has made certain controversial plans public in order to gauge

the public's reaction. At times, however, it is the religious establishments—as was the case here—or the developers who leaked news of projects they opposed in order to engender public opposition. For the most part, however, the regime has allowed journalists to write about development only once the majority of historical sites and artifacts had already been destroyed.

108. Taylor, "The Photos Saudi Arabia Doesn't Want Seen"; "Mecca's Removal of Muslim History," *Al Jazeera English*, February 25, 2013, http://stream.aljazeera.com/story/201302252140-0022568; "What Have They Done to My Hajj?," *Guardian*, October 28, 2012, http://www.guardian.co.uk/commentisfree/belief/2012/oct/28/hajj-mecca-islam-skyscrapers-litter.

109. Mecca Development Authority employee, interview with author, Mecca, June 6, 2011.

110. "Tahdid al-malik li-sharikat Binladin waqta 'ardhuhum li-mashru' al-tawsi'a" [The king's threat to Binladin while watching presentation of proposal for the expansion projects], YouTube video, 4:04, August 29, 2011, http://www.youtube.com/watch?v=HhCcpSoEggA.

111. Hajj Research Center, *Mecca*, 11.

112. This announcement came over five years after a master plan had, supposedly, been approved. The previous plan was one that would address the concerns of residents and planners. "Master Plan for Mecca Development Approved," *al-Bawaba Business*, December 28, 2005, http://www.albawaba.com/business/master-plan-mecca-development-approved.

113. David Usborne, "Redevelopment of Mecca: Bulldozers Bear Down on Site of Mohamed's Birth," *Independent*, February 20, 2014.

114. Habib Shaikh, "Makkah Museum Is a Haven for Holy Artifacts," *Arab News*, July 14, 2013, https://www.arabnews.com/news/457960.

115. "A Strategic Vision of Makkah," *worldfolio*, June 2012, http://www.worldfolio.co.uk/region/middle-east/saudi-arabia/prince-khaled-al-faisal-saudi-arabia-makkah-n1295; and "Al-Amir Khalid al-Faisal: Mashru' al-Malik Abdullah li-i'mar Makkah sayaj'aluha madina mutatawira" [Prince Khalid al-Faisal: The King Abdullah project to develop Mecca will turn it into an advanced city], *al-Arabiyya*, August 21, 2011, http://www.alarabiya.net/articles/2011/08/21/163379.html.

116. Governor of Mecca Prince Khalid ibn Faisal ibn Abdulaziz Al Saud, "'Ashwa'iyyat Makkah . . . ghabat bada'il al-mashru'at al-tatwiriyya fa hadar hawamir al-ta'addiyyat" [Mecca's slums . . . alternative development projects disappeared . . .

bringing instead the big merchants of land infringement], *al-Madina*, May 21, 2011, http://www.al-madina.com/node/304772; and Majid al-Mufaddali, "Makkah warshat 'amal la tahda'" [Mecca is construction site that does not stop], *Makkawi*, August 22, 2010, http://www.makkawi.com/Articles/Show.aspx?ID=567.

117. Muhammad Said al-Zahrani, "Ta'rib al-asma' ta'kid li-irtibat al-insan bith-aqafatihi wa-l-hifadh 'ala hawiyyatih," *Okaz*, October 10, 2010, https://www.okaz.com.sa/article/358104.

118. Abdulrahman al-Rashid, "Hel yumkin tatwir Makkah?"

119. "Vision 2030: Saudi Arabia," https://vision2030.gov.sa/en/vision/themes, 21.

120. Basma Atassi, "The Man Who Dreams of Old Mecca," *Al Jazeera*, 2015, http://interactive.aljazeera.com/aje/2015/man_who_dreams_of_old_mecca/index.html.

121. Mark Crinson and Paul Tyrer, "Clocking Off in Ancoats: Time and Remembrance in the Post-Industrial City," in Crinson, *Urban Memory*, 50.

122. Tariq al-Thaqafi, "Hajj Revenues Poised to Exceed $150bn by 2020: Experts," *Arab News*, August 28, 2017, http://www.arabnews.com/node/1151751/saudi-arabia.

123. Neera Chandoke, "The Post-Colonial City," *Economic and Political Weekly* 26 (1991): 2868.

CONCLUSION

1. Abdulaziz, not his real name, is one of several religious clerics who agreed to meet with me during several years of fieldwork in Saudi Arabia. This particular interview took place in Riyadh on October 20, 2014.

2. Author interview with members of the Saudi Arabian delegation, Riyadh, March 2, 2011.

3. Rosie Bsheer, "Dissent and Its Discontents: Protesting the Saudi State," in *The Dawn of the Arab Uprisings: End of An Old Order?*, ed. Bassam Haddad, Rosie Bsheer, and Ziad Abu-Rish (New York: Pluto Press, 2012), 248–59.

4. The National Dialogue aimed to strengthen Saudi Arabian national belonging with a focus on diversity. This was in line with Abdullah's previous views of nation building and what the Saudi national idea should be based on, such as the Janadriyya Heritage Festival that he endorsed in the 1980s. For the vision of the National Dialogue, see "Vision—Message—Goals—Values," https://www.kacnd.org/OurVision.

5. "Bayan lihay'at kibar al-'ulama' hawl al-ahdath" [A statement by senior ulama on latest developments], *Al Sakina*, March 6, 2011, http://www.assakina.com/fatwa/6834.html; and Issam Saliba, "Saudi Arabia: The Regime Invokes Sharia Law to Pre-

vent Public Protest," *Global Legal Monitor*, Library of Congress, March 10, 2011, http://www.loc.gov/law/foreign-news/article/saudi-arabia-the-regime-invokes-sharia-law-to-prevent-public-protest/.

6. Prince Mit'ib ibn Abdullah ibn Abdulaziz, on behalf of his ailing father King Abdullah at the reception of dignitaries for the 2013 Janadriyya Festival, the annual two-week-long national festival for heritage and culture that takes place on the outskirts of Riyadh: 'Alyan al-'Alyan, "Al-Amir Mit'ib ibn Abdullah: 'al-malik haris 'ala an yakun ma'akum wa yublighukum al-salam fardan fardan'" [Prince Mit'ib ibn Abdullah: "The king was eager to be with you and send his individual regards"], *Al-Riyadh*, July 4, 2013, http://www.alriyadh.com/2013/04/07/article823956.html, my translation.

7. Talal Asad, *Genealogies of Religion: Discipline and Reasons of Power in Christianity and Islam* (Baltimore: Johns Hopkins University Press, 1993): 212–23.

8. Nermeen Shaikh, *The Present as History: Critical Perspectives on Global Power* (New York: Columbia University Press, 2007): 208 (interview with Talal Asad).

9. "Crown Prince Salman Tells Darah to Promote Study of History," *Arab News*, November 8, 2013, http://www.arabnews.com/news/474206.

10. Lara Aryani, "Saudi Arabia and the War of Legitimacy in Yemen," *Jadaliyya*, May 2, 2015, http://www.jadaliyya.com/pages/index/21538/saudi-arabia-and-the-war-of-legitimacy-in-yemen.

11. "Al-Imarat wa-l-Saudiyya tafrudan al-sijn w-al-gharama li-l-muta'atif ma' Qatar 'ibra mawaqi' al-tawasol" [The United Arab Emirates and Saudi Arabia impose prison terms and fines for those who sympathize with Qatar on social media!], *Al Bilad*, June 7, 2017, http://www.elbilad.net/flash/detail?id=42771; and "5-Year Jail, 3 Million Fine for Rumormongers," *Saudi Gazette*, October 13, 2018, http://saudigazette.com.sa/article/545523.

12. Samia Nakhoul, Angus McDowall, and Stephen Kalin, "A House Divided: How Saudi Crown Prince Purged Royal Family Rivals," Reuters, November 10, 2017, https://www.reuters.com/article/us-saudi-arrests-crownprince-insight/a-house-divided-how-saudi-crown-prince-purged-royal-family-rivals-idUSKBN1DA23M.

13. Andrew Torchia, "The Mysterious (and Continuing) Fall in Saudi Foreign Reserves," Reuters, June 27, 2017, https://uk.reuters.com/article/uk-saudi-economy-reserves-analysis/the-mysterious-fall-in-saudi-foreign-reserves-idUKKBN19I17R.

14. "Saudi Suspends Saudi Binladin Group over Mecca Crane Disaster," Reuters, September 15, 2015, https://www.reuters.com/article/us-saudi-haj-binladen-idUSKCN0RF20C20150915.

15. Jon Gambrell, "Over 2,400 Killed in Saudi Hajj Stampede, Crush," Associated Press, December 10, 2015, https://apnews.com/3a42a7733a8b476889bb4b7b3be3560e.

16. Timothy Mitchell, *Rule of Experts: Egypt, Techno-Politics, Modernity* (Berkeley: University of California Press, 2002).

17. See the official website of Vision 2030, at https://vision2030.gov.sa/en/node.

18. "Vision 2030: Kingdom of Saudi Arabia," https://vision2030.gov.sa/en/vision/themes, 25. It also aimed to "raise the share of non-oil exports in non-oil GDP from 16% to 50%" and "to increase non-oil government revenue from SAR 163 billion to SAR 1 trillion." Vision 2030, 61 and 67.

19. Salem Saif, "When Consultants Reign," *Jacobin*, May 9, 2016, https://www.jacobinmag.com/2016/05/saudi-arabia-aramco-salman-mckinsey-privatization/.

20. "Saudi Arabia to Push Back Balanced Budget Goal to 2023, Sources Say," Reuters, November 2, 2017, https://www.reuters.com/article/saudi-finances/update-1-saudi-arabia-to-push-back-balanced-budget-goal-to-2023-sources-say-idUSL8N1N84M7.

21. The Saudi regime also executed three other Saudi Arabian Shi'i activists along with forty-three Sunnis accused of participating in al-Qaeda terrorist attacks in the kingdom. Facing a humiliating defeat in Yemen, the Saudi regime used the executions to project a semblance of power while seeking to terrorize the Shi'a of Saudi Arabia's Eastern Province into submission. For the most part, however, the regime's belligerence was aimed at Iran. See "Shia Cleric Among 47 Executed by Saudi Arabia in a Single Day," *Amnesty International*, January 2, 2016, https://www.amnesty.org/en/latest/news/2016/01/shia-cleric-among-47-executed-by-saudi-arabia-in-a-single-day/.

22. Rosie Bsheer, "Political Imaginaries in Saudi Arabia: Revolutionaries Without a Revolution," *Jadaliyya*, April 2, 2012, http://www.jadaliyya.com/pages/index/4896/political-imaginaries-in-saudi-arabia_revolutionar.

23. Bethan McKernan, "Satellite Images Show Scale of Devastation Inside Saudi Town Under Siege from Its Own Government," *Independent*, August 9, 2017, https://www.independent.co.uk/news/world/middle-east/saudi-arabia-siege-town-awamiyah-qatif-shia-nimr-al-nimr-al-musawara-a7882266.html.

24. See the Future Investment Initiative website, at http://futureinvestmentinitiative.com/en/home.

25. See Neom's website, at https://www.neom.com/; and Justin Scheck, Rory Jones, and Summer Said, "A Prince's $500 Billion Desert Dream: Flying Cars, Robot Dinosaurs and a Giant Artificial Moon," *Wall Street Journal*, July 25, 2019, https://www.wsj.com

/articles/a-princes-500-billion-desert-dream-flying-cars-robot-dinosaurs-and-a-giant-artificial-moon-11564097568.

26. Ronen Bergman, "The Officer Who Saw Behind the Top-Secret Curtain," *Ynetnews*, June 21, 2015, https://www.ynetnews.com/articles/0,7340,L-4671127,00.html.

27. "Why They Died: Civilian Casualties in Lebanon During the 2006 War," *Human Rights Watch*, September 5, 2007, https://www.hrw.org/report/2007/09/05/why-they-died/civilian-casualties-lebanon-during-2006-war.

28. See the statistics on fatalities resulting from these wars on the website of B'tselem, the Israeli Information Center for Human Rights in the Occupied Territories, https://www.btselem.org/statistics.

29. These include Saudi writer and novelist Turki al-Hamad, Saudi writer and TV host Ahmad al-ʿArfaj, Saudi activist Suad al-Shammari, and Saudi activist and writer Ahmad ibn Saad al-Qarni, among many others.

30. "Harakat al-muqataʿa fi al-khalij tastankir al-tatbiʿ al-Saʿudi maʿ Israʾeel" [BDS Gulf condemns Saudi normalization with Israel], pacbi.com, http://www.pacbi.org/atemplate.php?id=584; "Gulf Activists Reject Saudi-Israeli 'Flirtation' at Davos," bdsmovement.com, January 23, 2017, https://bdsmovement.net/news/gulf-activists-reject-saudi-israeli-"flirtation"-davos; and "BDS Gulf Holds Its First Regional Anti-Normalisation Conference," bdsmovement.net, November 24, 2017, https://bdsmovement.net/news/bds-gulf-holds-its-first-regional-anti-normalisation-conference.

31. "Saudi Arabia's Economic Cities," Economic Cities Agency, Saudi Arabian General Investment Authority (SAGIA), n.d., https://www.oecd.org/mena/competitiveness/38906206.pdf.

32. Author interviews with urban planners in Riyadh and Jeddah between January 2010 and June 2014.

33. "Vision 2030: Kingdom of Saudi Arabia," https://vision2030.gov.sa/en/vision/themes, 50.

34. "Saudi Arabia: Thousands Held Arbitrarily," *Human Rights Watch*, May 6, 2018, https://www.hrw.org/news/2018/05/06/saudi-arabia-thousands-held-arbitrarily.

35. Muhammad ibn Salman first released his cousin, Mitʿeb, the son of the late King Abdullah, in late November 2017 in return for $1 billion of his personal wealth. Other detainees followed suit to secure their freedom. Saeed Azhar, "Senior Saudi Prince Freed in $1 Billion Settlement Agreement: Official," Reuters, November 28, 2017, https://www.reuters.com/article/us-saudi-arrests-miteb/senior-saudi-prince-freed-in-1-billion-settlement-agreement-official-idUSKBN1DS23O.

36. Lee Fang, "Inside Saudi Arabia's Campaign to Charm American Policymakers and Journalists," *Intercept*, December 1, 2015, https://theintercept.com/2015/12/01/inside-saudi-charm-campaign/; and Lee Fang, "Saudi Arabia Continues Hiring Spree of Lobbyists, Retains Former Washington Post Reporter," *Intercept*, March 21, 2016, https://theintercept.com/2016/03/21/saudi-arabia-continues-hiring-spree-of-lobbyists-retains-former-washington-post-reporter/.

37. "Prominent Saudi Women Activists Arrested," *Human Rights Watch*, August 1, 2018, https://www.hrw.org/news/2018/08/01/prominent-saudi-women-activists-arrested.

38. The women's rights activists still in detention at the time of writing include Loujain al-Hathloul, Eman al-Nafjan, Nouf Abdulaziz, Mayaa al-Zahrani, Samar Badawi, Nassima al-Saada, Ibrahim al-Modaimeegh, Abdulaziz Meshaal, and Mohammed Rabea. See "Saudi Arabia: Allow Access to Detained Women Activists," *Human Rights Watch*, December 6, 2018, https://www.hrw.org/news/2018/12/06/saudi-arabia-allow-access-detained-women-activists.

39. "Amam al-taghyirat bi al-bilad.. 'Ulama' al-Sa'udiyya: 'A'mil nafsak mayyit'" [In the face of transformations in the country, Saudi Arabia's clerics: "Pretend you are dead"], *al-Khalij* online, March 7, 2018, https://alkhaleejonline.net/%D9%85%D8%AC%D8%AA%D9%85%D8%B9/%D8%A3%D9%85%D8%A7%D9%85-%D8%A7%D9%84%D8%AA%D8%BA%D9%8A%D9%8A%D8%B1%D8%A7%D8%AA-%D8%A8%D8%A7%D9%84%D8%A8%D9%84%D8%A7%D8%AF-%D8%B9%D9%84%D9%85%D8%A7%D8%A1-%D8%A7%D9%84%D8%B3%D8%B9%D9%88%D8%AF%D9%8A%D8%A9-%D8%A7%D8%B9%D9%85%D9%84-%D9%86%D9%81%D8%B3%D9%83-%D9%85%D9%8A%D8%AA.

40. Raihan Ismail, "How Is MBS's Consolidation of Power Affecting Saudi Clerics in the Opposition?" *Washington Post*, June 4, 2019, https://www.washingtonpost.com/politics/2019/06/04/how-is-mohammads-consolidation-power-affecting-oppositional-saudi-clerics/?noredirect=on&utm_term=.b135d9f32eb9.

41. Hadi Fathallah, "Challenges of Public Policymaking in Saudi Arabia," Carnegie Middle East Center, May 22, 2019, https://carnegie-mec.org/sada/79188.

42. Article 2 of Royal Decree No. M/55, September 5, 1988, Institute of Public Administration Archives, Riyadh.

43. The author has copies of all the regulations of the National Center for Documents and Archives, which were hosted on its website at http://www.ncda.gov.sa/detail.asp?InServiceID=1&intemplatekey=MainPage. However, since the name and location change, its URL address also changed to http://ncar.gov.sa/Home/Index.

44. Under Salman's reign, Ibn Junayd, who had worked closely with the then prince to collect historical documents, was also promoted to the head of another new organization, the Center for Research and Intercommunication Knowledge.

45. "Al-Saʿudiyya.. Tawjihat biʿadam itlaf al-wathaʾiq al-hukumiyya" [Saudi Arabia: Orders to not destroy government records], *al-khalij al-jadid*, June 3, 2016, https://bit.ly/2OmGPTG.

46. "'Al-wathaʾiq wa-l-mahfuzat' yaftatih bawabatahu al-elektroniyya limutalaʿat andhimat al-dawla" ["Archives and Records" opens its e-portal to access government regulations], *al-Hayat*, October 7, 2017, https://www.sauress.com/alhayat/24535927.

47. "'Al-Semmari': Al-muʾarrikhun muqassirun fi taqdim al-maʿrifa al-tarikhiyya bi al tariqa al-haditha" ["Al-Semmari": Historians have failed to present history in modern ways], *Sabq*, May 5, 2019, https://mobile.sabq.org/yGd3g9. For opinion editorials authored by Fahd al-Semmari, most of which are about the making of history or praising the political leadership, see his page on the *al-Riyadh* newspaper site, at http://www.alriyadh.com/file/298.

48. Fahd al-Semmari, "Damʿat malik" [Tears of a king], *al-Riyadh*, December 20, 2018, http://www.alriyadh.com/1726309#.

49. For the transfer of KAFD to the PIF, see Marwa Rashad, "Saudi State Finalized Ownership Transfer of $10 Billion Financial District," Reuters, May 3, 2018, https://www.reuters.com/article/us-saudi-economy-finance-exclusive/exclusive-saudi-state-finalized-ownership-transfer-of-10-billion-financial-district-idUSKBN1I41YK; and for plans to repurpose KAFD, see "A Restructured King Abdullah Financial District," in *Vision 2030: Kingdom of Saudi Arabia*, 55, https://vision2030.gov.sa/en/vision/themes. For more on Qiddiya, see its official website, at https://qiddiya.com.

50. Muna al-Manjumi, "Al-mamlaka tuʾakidd bi 'hayʾat tatwir Mecca wal-Mashaʿir': Khidmat duyuf al-rahman al-hadaf al-asma" [The kingdom confirms that with "Mecca and Holy Cities Development Authority": Serving pilgrims is the most noble goal], *al-Hayat*, June 2, 2018, http://www.alhayat.com/article/4584443.

51. "Vision 2030: Kingdom of Saudi Arabia," https://vision2030.gov.sa/en/vision/themes, 42.

52. Stephen Kalin, "Saudi Sovereign Fund to Develop Holy Sites in Mecca, Medina," Reuters, October 2, 2017, https://www.reuters.com/article/us-saudi-fund-realestate/saudi-sovereign-fund-to-develop-holy-sites-in-mecca-medina-idUSKCN1C71DZ.

53. Shaykh Abdulrahman al-Sudais, Friday Sermon, Grand Mosque, Mecca, October 19, 2018, https://www.youtube.com/watch?v=7aco8b3_M_E, accessed June 20, 2019; and Khaled M. Abou El Fadl, "Saudi Arabia Is Misusing Mecca," *New York Times*,

November 12, 2018, https://www.nytimes.com/2018/11/12/opinion/saudi-arabia-mbs-grandmosque-mecca-politics.html.

54. Prince Badr is said to have bought Leonardo da Vinci's *Salvator Mundi* on behalf of Crown Prince Muhammad, who then donated it to the Louvre Abu Dhabi.

55. Saleh al-Zayed, "Saudi Arabia Spends Record $32 Bln on Tourism," *Asharq al-Awsat*, April 9, 2019.

56. "An Incredible Saudi-Indian Tale," *Saudi Gazette*, April 17, 2019, http://live.saudigazette.com.sa/article/563635/SAUDI-ARABIA/An-incredible-Saudi-Indian-tale-Eminent-Saudis-of-Indian-origin-evoke-nostalgic-memories; Mansur al-Assaf, "Mahmud Suroor al-Sabban.. Ra'id al-udaba' fi Makkah wa 'rajul dawla' 'amila bi-samt" [Literary pioneer in Mecca and "statesman" Mahmud Suroor al-Sabban, who worked quietly], *al-Riyadh*, October 10, 2014, http://www.alriyadh.com/983686; and 'Akl al-'Akl, "Abdullah al-Tariqi.. al-Mummahid 'li-sa'wadat' Aramco" [Abdullah al-Tariqi: Paved the way for the nationalization of Aramco], *Al-Arabiyya*, December 27, 2016, https://www.alarabiya.net/ar/saudi-today/2016/12/27/عبدالله-الطريقي-الممهد-لـ-سعودة-أرامكو-.

Bibliography

PRIMARY SOURCES
Archives
American University of Beirut Archives and Special Collections
Arriyadh Development Authority, Riyadh
Custodian of the Two Holy Mosques Institute for Hajj Research, Mecca
Institute of Public Administration Archive Center (IPA), Riyadh
King Abdulaziz Foundation for Research and Archives (KAFRA or the Darah), Riyadh
King Abdulaziz Public Library Archives, Riyadh
King Fahd National Library Archives (KFNL), Riyadh
King Faisal Center for Research and Islamic Studies, Riyadh
Library of Congress, Washington, DC
Mecca Development Authority, Mecca
Ministry of Education, Riyadh
Ministry of Municipality and Urban Planning, Riyadh
National Archives and Records Administration, United States
National Center for Documents and Archives, Riyadh
National Museum Archives, Riyadh
Prince Salman Library Archives at the King Saud University, Riyadh
Private Archives, Medina
Private Archives, Riyadh

Private Archives, Safwa, Qatif, Eastern Province
Qatar Digital Library
Saudi Aramco, Dhahran
Saudi Binladin Group Company Archives, Jeddah
Saudi Commission for Tourism and Antiquities (SCTA), Riyadh

Selected Newspapers and Magazines

Al-Adwa' (1956–1959)
Al-Ahram (2015)
Al-Arabi al-Jadid (2016)
Al-Arab Magazine (1970)
Al-Faisal Magazine (2016)
Al-Hayat (1992–2018)
Al-Jaridah (1960)
Al-Jazirah (2004)
Al-Khalij (2018)
Al-Madina (1946–1958)
Al-Musawwir (1954)
Al-Nahar (1988–1993, 2013)
Al-Riyadh (2002, 2005–2014, 2017, 2018)
Al-Safir (1964)
Al-Sharq al-Awsat (2012, 2014, 2016, 2018, 2019)
Al-Usbu' al-'Arabi (1964 and 1990–1991)
Al-Waha (2010)
Al-Watan (2012)
Arabian Business (2010)
Arab News (2010–2013, 2017, 2019)
Elaph (2002)
Okaz (1963, 2004, 2010)
Qafilat al-zayt (1953–1964)
Rasid (2003–2012)
Sabq (2015)
Sahifat Makkah (2016)
Saudi Aramco World (1978–1983)
Saudi Gazette (2011, 2018, 2019)

Sawt Al-Hijaz (1932–1964)
Sawt al-Tali'a (1980)
Shu'un Al-Awsat (1992–1998)
Umm al-Qura (1926–1960)
Watha'iq al-Khalij (2006–2009)

Reports and Proceedings

Agency for City Planning at the Ministry of Municipal and Rural Affairs. *Al-Turath al-'umrani fi al-Mamlaka al-'Arabiyya al-Sa'udiyya* [The architectural heritage in the Kingdom of Saudi Arabia]. Riyadh: Ministry of Municipal and Rural Affairs, 2002.

Al-'Askar, Fahd ibn Ibrahim. *Al-Tawthiq al-idari fi al-Mamlaka al-'Arabiyya al-Sa'udiyya* [Administrative documentation in the Kingdom of Saudi Arabia]. Riyadh: Program Management at the Institute of Public Administration, 1997.

———. *Al-Tawthiq al-idari fi al-Mamlaka al-'Arabiyya al-Sa'udiyya* [Administrative documentation in the Kingdom of Saudi Arabia]. Riyadh: Matbu'at Maktabat al-Malik Fahd al-Wataniyya, 2006.

———. "Idarat al-watha'iq al-tarikhiyya wa tatbiqatiha fi al-Mamlaka al-Sa'udiyya al-'Arabiyya" [The management of historical documents and their application in Saudi Arabia]. In *Buhuth nadwat al-watha'iq al-tarikhiyya fi al-Mamlaka al-'Arabiyya al-Sa'udiyya* [Symposium on historical documents in the Kingdom of Saudi Arabia], November 24–26, 1996, 45–90. Riyadh: Darat al-Malik Abdulaziz, 1997.

Al-Harbi, Fa'iz ibn Musa. "Turuk kashf al-tazwir fi al-watha'iq al-mahaliyya" [Authenticating local documents]. In *Sijjil dawrat al-watha'iq al-mahaliyya, 3 April 2009* [Proceedings of training course on local documents], edited by Abdullah ibn Abdulrahman al-Abduljabbar, Sa'id ibn Ali al-Gaylani, 'Owayda ibn Mutayrik al-Jihinni, and Muhammad Ali al-Abdullatif, 213–31. Riyadh: King Saud University, 2010.

Al-Semmari, Fahd. "Al-watha'iq al-tarikhiyya al-wataniyya wa-l-ihtimam al-matlub" [National historical documents and the required attention]. In *Buhuth nadwat al-watha'iq al-tarikhiyya* [Symposium on historical documents in the Kingdom of Saudi Arabia], November 24–26, 1996. Riyadh: Darat al-Malik Abdulaziz, 1997.

———. "Kalimat al-mushrif 'ala darat al-malik Abdulaziz" [The address of the Darah's supervisor]. In *Buhuth nadwat al-watha'iq al-tarikhiyya* [Symposium on historical documents in the Kingdom of Saudi Arabia], November 24–26, 1996. Riyadh: Darat al-Malik Abdulaziz, 1997.

Arriyadh Development Authority. *Comprehensive Strategic Report for the City of Riyadh* (2003). 20 vols. Metropolitan Development Strategy for Arriyadh (MEDSTAR).

———. "Executive Summary: At-Turaif District in Ad-Dirʿiyah: Nomination Document for the Inscription on the UNESCO World Heritage List." PDF. Arriyadh Development Authority, Riyadh, January 2009.

———. "Historical Addirʿiyah Development Program." Arriyadh Development Authority website, October 9, 2011. http://www.arriyadh.com/Eng/ADA/Left/Dev Proj/getdocument.aspx?f=/openshare/Eng/ADA/Left/DevProj/AddiriyaEn093 .doc_cvt.htm.

———. "Historical Precinct of Addiriyyah: Development Manual." PDF. High Commission for the Development of Arriyadh, Riyadh, May 6, 2004.

———. "Qasr al Hukm District." Arriyadh Development Authority website, October 9, 2011. http://www.arriyadh.com/Eng/Tourism/Left/Musems/getdocument.aspx ?f=/openshare/Eng/Tourism/Left/Musems/Qasr-Al-Hokm-District.doc_cvt.htm.

Attiya, Abd al-Qadir Muhammad, and Sami Yasin Brahmin. "Ruʾya mustaqbaliyya li-l-tanmiyya al-ʿiqtisadiyya wa-l-ʿumraniyya li-Makkah al-mukarramah hatta ʿam 1470h" [Future vision for the economic and urban development of Mecca until 2048]. Institute of the Custodian of the Two Holy Mosques for Hajj Research, Mecca, August 11, 2001.

Boddy, Trevor. "History's New Home in Riyadh." *Saudi Aramco World* 50, no. 5, September–October 1999.

Clark, Arthur P. "A Kingdom Revealed: The Making of the King Abdulaziz Historical Centre." Final draft submitted to the Arriyadh Development Authority, December 30, 2002. Arriyadh Development Authority Archives, Riyadh.

Darat al-Malik Abdulaziz. *Annual Financial Report 1997–1998*. Institute of Public Administration Central Library, Riyadh.

———. *Buhuth nadwat al-wathaʾiq al-tarikhiyya fi al-Mamlaka al-ʿArabiyya al-Saʿudiyya*. [Symposium on historical documents in the Kingdom of Saudi Arabia], November 24–26, 1996. Riyadh: Darat al-Malik Abdulaziz, 1997.

———. "Tajrubat al-Markaz al-Watani li-l-Wathaʾiq wa-l-Mahfuzat bi al-Darah" [The experience of the National Center for Documents and Archives at the Darah]. In *Nadwat tawthiq al-maʿlumat al-idariyya* [Symposium on archiving administrative information]. Riyadh: Institute of Public Administration, 1989.

Fuda, Abdullah Muhammad, and Samir ibn Abd al-Hamdi ʿAshi. "Al-Badaʾil al-mukhtalifa li-ziyadat al-taqa al-istiʿabiyya li-l-Masjid al-Haram: Amakin al-salat"

[Alternatives to increase the capacity of the mosque's land: Places of prayer]. Preliminary report. Mecca: Institute of the Custodian of the Two Holy Mosques for Hajj Research, 2002.

Hajj Research Center. *Mecca: Policy Framework and Future Development, 1976*. Mecca: Umm al-Qura University, 1976. Located in the archives of the Custodian of the Two Holy Mosques Institute for Hajj Research, Umm al-Qura University, Mecca.

Sadiq, Muhammad. *Tatawwur al-hukm wa-l-idara fi al-Mamlaka al-'Arabiyya al-Sa'udiyya* [The development of government and administration in the Kingdom of Saudi Arabia]. Riyadh: Ma'had al-Idara al-'Amma, 1965.

Salloom, Hamad I. *Education in Saudi Arabia*. 2nd ed. Washington, DC: Saudi Arabian Cultural Mission to the United States of America, 1995.

Salman ibn Abdulaziz, "Kalimat ṣaḥib al sumuw al-malaki al-Amir Salman ibn Abdulaziz" [Keynote speech of His Royal Highness Prince Salman ibn Abdulaziz]. In *Buhuth nadwat al-watha'iq al-tarikhiyya* [Symposium on historical documents in the Kingdom of Saudi Arabia], November 24–26, 1996. Riyadh: Darat al-Malik Abdulaziz, 1997.

Supreme Commission for Tourism. "Executive Summary: Al-Hijr Archeological Site (Madain Salih): Nomination Document for the Inscription on the UNESCO World Heritage List." January 2007. https://whc.unesco.org/en/documents/168942.

———. "National Tourism Development Project in the Kingdom of Saudi Arabia, Phase 1: General Strategy." Arriyadh Development Authority Archives, Riyadh, 2000–2002.

UNESCO World Heritage Committee. "At-Turaif District in ad-Dir'iyah (Saudi Arabia) No. 1329." In *2010 Evaluations of Cultural Properties* (report for the 34th Ordinary Session of the World Heritage Convention, July 25–August 3, 2010, Brasília, Brazil). Paris: ICOMOS International Secretariat, 2009.

———. "Cultural Properties—At-Turaif District in ad-Dir'iyah (Saudi Arabia)." In *Report of the Decisions Adopted by the World Heritage Committee at Its 34th Session (Brasilia, 2010)*. Convention Concerning the Protection of the World Cultural and Natural Heritage, Paris, September 2010.

Walls, Archie, with Rasem Badran Associates and Omrania & Associates. "Restoration of Qasr al-Murabba, Darat al-Malik Abdulaziz, Saudi National Museum." Report for Arriyadh Development Authority, November 1996. PDF, Ref. 1030/AWD. Arriyadh Development Authority Archives, Riyadh.

Wizarat al-shu'un al-baladiyyah wa-l-qarawiyya (Ministry of Municipal and Rural Affairs), Dar al-Handasa li-l-tasmim wa-l-istisharat al-Fanniyya (Dar Al-Handasah Consultants), and Saudi Consulting Group. *Makkah Region Comprehensive Development Plans: Cultural Area Plans.* Project No. 208, Report No. 6. Riyadh: Dar Al-Handasah Consultants and Saudi Consulting Group, 1986.

Textbooks

Ministry of Education, Kingdom of Saudi Arabia. *Tarikh al-Mamlaka al-'Arabiyya al-Sa'udiyya (li-l-saf al-sadis al-ibtida'i)* [History of the Kingdom of Saudi Arabia, sixth grade]. Ministry of Education, Riyadh, 2005–2006.

———. *Tarikh al-Mamlaka al-'Arabiyya al-Sa'udiyya (li-l-saf al-thalith al-mutawassit)* [History of the Kingdom of Saudi Arabia, ninth grade]. Ministry of Education, Riyadh, 2005–2006.

———. *Tarikh al-Mamlaka al-'Arabiyya al-Sa'udiyya (li-l-saf al-thalith al-thanawi, banin)* [History of the Kingdom of Saudi Arabia, twelfth grade, boys]. Ministry of Education, Riyadh, 2005–2006.

Government Publications

Al-Dir'iyya: Asalat al-madhi wa ishraqat al-hadhir [Dir'iyya: Authenticity of the past and radiance of the present], Barnamij tatwir al-Dir'iyya al-tarikhiyya [Historical *Dir'iyya* Development Program]. Riyadh: Al-hay'a al-'ulya li-tatwir madinat al-Riyadh, 2001.

Al-hay'a al-'amma li-al-siyaha wa-l-athar [Saudi Commission for Tourism and Antiquities, Kingdom of Saudi Arabia]. *Al-'abath fi al-athar* [Tampering with antiquities]. Riyadh: Saudi Commission for Tourism and Antiquities, 2009.

———. "The Role of Saudi Commission for Tourism and Antiquities in the Preservation and Development of Urban Heritage." First International Conference for Urban Heritage in the Islamic Countries. Riyadh: Saudi Commission for Tourism and Antiquities, May 23–28, 2010.

Al-hay'a al-'ulya li-tatwir madinat al-Riyadh [Arriyadh Development Authority]. *Markaz al-malik Abdulaziz al-tarikhi* [King Abdulaziz Historical Center], 1999.

Al-Mamlaka fi qalb al-tarikh: "Al-Dir'iyya" fi qa'imat al-turath al-'alami [The Kingdom in the heart of history: "Dir'iyya" in the World Heritage List]. *Ahwal al-Ma'rifa* 61, January 2011.

Isdarat darat al-malik Abdulaziz 1975–2007 [Publications of King Abdulaziz Foundation for Research and Archives, 1975–2007]. Riyadh: Darat al-Malik Abdulaziz, 2007.

King Saud. Riyadh: Darat al-Malik Abdulaziz, 2006.

Markaz al-tarmim wa-l-muhafazha 'ala al-mawwad al-tarikhiyya [Documents and Manuscripts Conservation Center]. Riyadh: Darat al-Malik Abdulaziz, 2005.

Mashru' masih al-masadir al-tarikhiyya al-wataniyya: al-marhala al-uwla, 1996–1997 [The project of surveying national historical sources: Phase 1, 1996–1997]. Riyadh: Darat al-Malik Abdulaziz, 1999.

Oral History Interviews

I conducted over sixty-eight oral history interviews between 2005 and 2011 and hundreds of regular interviews between 2006 and 2014.

Memoirs and First-Person Accounts

Abu Mudin, Abdulfattah. *Watilka al-ayyam* [Those were the days]. Jeddah: Dar Kunuz al-Ma'rifa, 1985.

Al-Huzaymi, Nassir. *Ayyam ma' Juhayman: Kuntu ma' "al-jama'a al-salafiyya al-muhtasiba"* [Days with Juhayman: I was with the "Society of Salafis" that commands right and forbids wrong]. Beirut: Al-Shabaka al-'Arabiyya li-l-abhath wa-l-nashr, 2011.

Hafiz, Uthman. *Tatawur al-sahafa fi al-Mamlaka al-Arabiyya al-Saudiyya* [The development of the press in the Kingdom of Saudi Arabia]. Jeddah: Sharikat al-Madina li-l-Tiba'a wa-l-Nashr, 1989.

Ismail, Muhammad Kamal. *The Architecture of the Prophet's Holy Mosque: Al Madinah*. London: Hazar, 1998.

———. *The Architecture of the Prophet's Holy Mosque: Makkah*. London: Hazar, 1998.

Published Primary Source Collections

Al-Issa, Abdulaziz ibn Muhammad al-Fahd. *Arshif Mamlakat al-Hijaz wa saltanat Najd wa Mulhaqatiha: min 1343h until 1346h* [The archive of the Kingdom of Hijaz and Sultanate of Najd and Its Dependencies: From 1924 until 1928]. Beirut: Jadawil, 2013.

Al-Rashid, Ibrahim, ed. *Documents on the History of Saudi Arabia*. 8 vols. Salisbury, NC: Documentary Publications, 1976–1985.

Childs, J. Rives. "Irregular Assumption by ARAMCO of Diplomatic Functions." February 13, 1947. In *Saudi Arabia Enters the Modern World: Secret U.S. Documents on* the Emergence of the Kingdom of Saudi Arabia as a World Power, 1936–1949. Vol. 1 of *Documents on the History of Saudi Arabia*, edited by Ibrahim Rashid. Salisbury, NC: Documentary Publications, 1980.

BOOKS AND ARTICLES

Aarts, Paul, and Gerd Nonneman, eds. *Saudi Arabia in the Balance: Political Economy, Society, Foreign Affairs*. New York: New York University Press, 2005.

Aba-Namay, Rahshe. "Constitutional Reforms: A Systemization of Saudi Politics." *Journal of South Asian and Middle Eastern Studies* 16, no. 3 (Spring 1993): 43–88.

Abdella-Doumato, Eleanor. "Manning the Barricades: Islam According to Saudi Arabia's School Texts." *Middle East Journal* 57, no. 2 (Spring 2003): 230–47.

Abdella-Doumato, Eleanor, and Gregory Starrett, eds. *Teaching Islam: Textbooks and Religion in the Middle East*. Boulder, CO: Lynne Rienner, 2007.

Abdulrazzaq, Mu'tasim Billah. "Al-qadaya fi qusas Muhammad Abdullah al-Malibari" [Issues in Muhammad Abdullah al-Malibari's stories], *Majalla al-Aasima* (Arabic University College) (n.d.): 1–10.

Abrams, Philip. "Notes on the Difficulty of Studying the State." *Journal of Historical Sociology* 1, no. 1 (March 1988): 58–89.

Abu El-Haj, Nadia. *Facts on the Ground: Archeological Practice and Territorial Self-Fashioning in Israeli Society*. Chicago: University of Chicago Press, 2001.

———. "Translating Truths: Nationalism, the Practice of Archaeology, and the Remaking of Past and Present in Contemporary Jerusalem." *American Ethnologist* 25, no. 2 (May 1998): 166–88.

Abu-Hamad, Aziz. *Empty Reforms: Saudi Arabia's New Basic Laws*. New York: Human Rights Watch, 1992.

Abu-Rish, Ziad. "Conflict and Institution Building in Lebanon, 1946–1955." PhD diss., University of California, Los Angeles, 2014.

Abu Sulayman, Abdulwahhab Ibrahim. *Al-amakin al-ma'thura al-mutawatira fi Makkah al-Mukarramah* [Islamic historical places in the Holy City of Makkah Al-Mukarramah]. London: Mu'asasat al-Firqan li-l-Turath al-Islami, 2010.

Abu Talib, Hasan. *Man yahkum fi al-Sa'udiyya* [Who rules in Saudi Arabia]. Riyadh: al-Matba'a al-Fanniyya, 1990.

Adnan, Ahmad. *Al-Sajin 32: Ahlam Muhammad Sa'id Tayyib wa haza'imoh* [Prisoner 32: The dreams of Muhammad Sa'id Tayyib and his defeats]. 2nd ed. Al-Dar al-Bayda', Morocco: al-Markaz al-Thaqafi al-'Arabi, 2011.

Al-Abd al-Ali, Huda. "Al-watha'iq al-tarikhiyya fi al-Mamlaka al-'Arabiyya al-Sa'udiyya: Dirasa mashiyya taqyimiyya" [Historical documents in the Kingdom of Saudi Arabia: An evaluative assessment]. PhD diss., Riyadh Women's University, 2007.

Al-Ahmari, Abdulrahman Abdullah, "Dawr Sharikat al-Zayt al-'Arabiyya al-Amrikiyya fi tanmiyat al-Mantaqa al-Sharqiyya min al-Mamlaka al-'Arabiyya al-Sa'udiyya" [The role of the Arabian American Oil Company in developing the Eastern Province of Saudi Arabia]. PhD diss., King Saud University, 2007.

Alamer, Sultan. "Beyond Sectarianism and Ideology: Regionalism and Collective Political Action in Saudi Arabia." In *Salman's Legacy,* edited by Madawi Al-Rasheed, 97–116. London: Hurst, 2018.

———, ed. *Fi tarikh al-'uruba: qira'at naqdiyya fi hawamish al-zaman wa al-makan* [On the history of Arab nationalism: Critical readings on the margins of time and space]. Beirut: Jusur li-l-Tarjama wa-al-Nashr, 2016.

Alangari, Abdulrahman ibn Mohammed. "Mantiqat Qasr Alhukm: A Twentieth-Century Development." In *Al-Mamlaka al-'Arabiyya al-Sa'udiyya fi mi'at 'am: buhouth wa dirasat* [The Kingdom of Saudi Arabia in one hundred years: Research and studies], vol. 5. Riyadh: Darat al-Malik Abdulaziz, 2007.

Alavi, Seema. *Muslim Cosmopolitanism in the Age of Empire.* Cambridge, MA: Harvard University Press, 2015.

Al-'Awwami, Ali Baqir. "Al-Haraka al-wataniyya sharq al-Sa'udiyya, 1953–1973" [The nationalist movement in eastern Saudi Arabia, 1953–1973]. 2 vols. Unpublished manuscript, al-Qatif, 2011. PDF.

Al Bassam, Abdullah ibn Abdulrahman ibn Salih. *Ulama Najd khilal thamaniyat qurun* [Religious scholars of Najd over eight centuries]. Riyadh: Dar al-'Asima, 1999.

Al-Buluwi, Mutlaq. *Al-wujud al-uthmani fi shamal al-jazira al-'Arabiyya, 1908–1923* [The Ottoman presence in the northern parts of the Arabian Peninsula, 1908–1923]. Beirut: Jadawel, 2011.

Aldakhil, Khalid. *Al-Wahhabiyya bayn al-shirk wa tasaddu' al-qabila* [Wahhabism between idolatry and fragmentation of the tribe]. Beirut: Al-Shabaka al-Arabiyya li-l-Abhath wa-l-Nashr, 2013.

Al-Dakhil, Turki. *Salman al-'Odah min al sijn ila al-tanwir* [Salman al-'Odah from prison to enlightenment]. Dubai: Madarik, 2011.

Al-Dumayni, Ali. *Zaman li-l-sijn . . . azmina li-l-hurriyya* [A time for prison . . . times for freedom]. Beirut: Dar al-Kunuz, 2004.

Al-Enazy, Askar H. *The Creation of Saudi Arabia: Ibn Saud and British Imperial Policy, 1914–1927.* New York: Routledge, 2010.

Al-Ghazali, Sayyid Hasaballah Muhammad. *Al-mahfuzat fi al-ajhiza al-hukumiyya, dirasa maydaniyya 'an al-mahfuzat fi al-Mamlaka al-'Arabiyya al-Sa'udiyya* [Archives in government institutions: A practical survey on archives in the Kingdom of Saudi Arabia]. Riyadh: n.p., 1982.

Al-Ghunaym, Ya'qub Y., ed. *Tarikh al-ta'lim fi dawlat al-Kuwayt: Dirasa tawthiqiyya* [The history of education in the State of Kuwait: A survey]. 6 vols. Kuwait: Markaz al-Buhuth wa-l-Dirasat al-Kuwaitiyya, 2002.

Al-Hamad, Turki. *Al-Karadib* [The prison cells]. Beirut: Dar al-Saqi, 1998.

Al-Hasan, Hamza. *Al-Shi'a fi al-Mamlaka al-'Arabiyya al-Sa'udiyya* [The Shi'a in the Kingdom of Saudi Arabia]. Riyadh: Mu'assasat al-Baqi' li Ihya' al-Turath, 1993.

Al-Hathloul, Saleh. "Riyadh Architecture in One Hundred Years: An Essay on a Public Lecture Presented at Darat al-Funun, Amman on April 21, 2002." Amman: Center for the Study of the Built Environment, 2003.

———. "Riyadh Development Plans in the Past Fifty Years (1967–2016)." *Current Urban Studies* 5 (2017): 97–120.

Al-Hathloul, Saleh, and Mohamed Abdul Rahman al-Sayyed. "New Towns in Saudi Arabia: Concentration or Dispersal of Urban Development." *Architecture and Planning*, 13 (2001): 1–37.

Ali, Ahmad. *Al Saud*. Beirut: Dar al-Sayyad li-l-Taba' wa-l-Nashr, 1957.

Al-Juhayni, Uwaydh. *Najd*. Riyadh, 2000.

———. *Tarikh Najd* [The history of Najd]. Riyadh: n.p., 1983.

Al-Khafaji, Isam. *Tormented Births: Passages to Modernity in Europe and the Middle East*. London: I. B. Tauris, 2004.

Al-Khidr, Abdulaziz. *Al-Sa'udiyya: Sirat dawla wamujtama', qira'a fi tajrubat thilth qarn min al-tahawulat al-fikriyya wa-l-siyasiyya wa-l-tanmawiyya* [Saudi Arabia: Biography of a state and society, a reading in a quarter-century experience of intellectual, political and developmental transformations]. 2nd ed. Beirut: Arab Network for Research and Publications, 2011.

Al-Ma'had al-'Ilmi al-Sa'udi [Saudi Scientific Institute]. *Tizkar al-wala' wa-l-ikhlas* [Token of loyalty and allegiance]. Mecca: Umm al-Qura Publications, 1930.

Al-Malik Saud ibn Abdulaziz Al Saud: Buhuth wa dirasat [King Saud ibn Abdulaziz Al Saud: Research and Studies]. 5 vols. Riyadh: Darat al-Malik Abdulaziz, 2006.

Al-Mubarak, Faisal A. "Urban Growth Boundary Policy and Residential Suburbanization: Riyadh, Saudi Arabia." *Habitat International* 28 (2004): 567–91.

———. "Urban Policy and City Form: Urban Development in Saudi Arabia." PhD diss., University of Washington, 1992.

Al-Munajjed, Mona. *Women in Saudi Arabia Today.* New York: St. Martin's Press, 1997.

Al-Muslim, Muhammad Saʿid. *Sahil al-dahab al-aswad: Dirasa tarikhiyya insaniyya li-mantiqat al-Khalij al-ʿArabi* [Black Gold Coast: Historical study of the Arab Gulf region]. 2nd ed. Beirut: Dar Maktabat al-Hayat, 1960.

Al-Naqeeb, Khaldun. *Society and State in the Gulf and Arab Peninsula: A Different Perspective.* New York: Routledge, 1990.

Al-Nqaydan, Mansur. *Al-Muluk al-muhtasibun: al-Amr bi-l-maʿruf wa-l-nahi ʿan al-munkar fi al-Saʿudiyya, 1927–2007.* Dubai: al-Mesbar, 2010.

Al-Qinaʿi, Yusuf ibn Isa. *Safahat min tarikh al-Kuwait* [Pages from the history of Kuwait]. 4th ed. Kuwait: Matbaʿat Hukumat al-Kuwait, 1968.

Al-Rasheed, Madawi. "The Capture of Riyadh Revisited: Shaping Historical Imagination in Saudi Arabia." In *Counter-Narratives: History, Contemporary Society and Politics in Saudi Arabia and Yemen,* edited by Madawi Al-Rasheed and Robert Vitalis. New York: Palgrave, 2004.

———. *Contesting the Saudi State: Islamic Voices from a New Generation.* New York: Cambridge University Press, 2007.

———. "God, King and the Nation: The Rhetoric of Politics in Saudi Arabia in the 1990s." *Middle East Journal* 50, no. 3 (1996): 359–72.

———. *A History of Saudi Arabia.* London: Cambridge University Press, 2010.

———, ed. *Kingdom without Borders: Saudi Political, Religious and Media Frontiers.* London: Hurst, 2008.

———. *A Most Masculine State: Gender, Politics, Religion in Saudi Arabia.* Cambridge: Cambridge University Press, 2013.

———. "Political Legitimacy and the Production of History: The Case of Saudi Arabia." In *New Frontiers in Middle East Security,* edited by Lenore G. Martin, 25–46. New York: St. Martin's Press, 1999.

———. *Politics in an Arabian Oasis: The Rashidi Tribal Dynasty.* London: I. B. Tauris, 1991.

———. Review of George Rentz's *The Birth of the Islamic Reform Movement in Saudi Arabia: Muhammad Ibn Abd al-Wahhab (1703–1792) and the Beginnings of Unitarian*

Empire in Arabia. Professor Madawi Al Rasheed's former website, accessed September 12, 2009.

———. *Transnational Connections and the Arab Gulf*. London: Routledge, 2005.

Al-Rasheed, Madawi, and Robert Vitalis, eds. *Counter-Narratives: History, Contemporary Society and Politics in Saudi Arabia and Yemen*. New York: Palgrave, 2004.

Al-Rashid, Saad A. "A Brief Report on the First Archeological Excavation at Al-Rabadhah." In *Proceedings of the Seminar for Arabian Studies* 10:81–84. Oxford, UK: Archaeopress, 1990.

———. "The Development of Archeology in Saudi Arabia." In *Papers from the Thirty-Eighth Meeting of the Seminar for Arabian Studies Held in London, 22–24 July 2004*, vol. 35 of *Proceedings of the Seminar for Arabian Studies*, 207–14. Oxford, UK: Archaeopress, 2005.

Alrawaibah, Alaa. "Archeological Site Management in the Kingdom of Saudi Arabia: Protection or Isolation." In *Cultural Heritage in the Arabian Peninsula*, edited by Karen Exell and Trinidad Rico, 143–56. New York: Routledge, 2016.

Al-Rimali, Suhaila. *Al-ittijahat al-fikriyya li-l-thawra al-'Arabiyya al kubra: min khilal jaridat al-Qibla* [Ideological directions of the Great Arab Revolt: Through al-Qibla newspaper]. Amman: Lajnat Tarikh al-Urdun, 1992.

Al-Rushayd, Abdulaziz. *Tarikh al-Kuwait* [History of Kuwait]. Rev. ed. Beirut: Dar Maktabat al-Hayat, 1978.

Al-Sa'id, Nasir. *Tarikh al-Sa'ud* [History of Al Saud]. Mecca: Manshurat Dar Makkah al-Mukaramah, 1984.

Al Saud, Fahda bint Saud ibn Abdulaziz. "Al-Malik Saud wa dawrahu fi ta'sis al-mamlaka" [King Saud and his role in developing the kingdom]. Paper presented at the King Saud historical workshop at the King Abdulaziz Historical Center, Riyadh, 1999.

Al Saud, Salman ibn Saud. *Tarikh al-Malik Saud ibn Abdulaziz, 1319–1389 H/1902–1969M* [The History of King Saud ibn Abdulaziz, 1319–1389 AH/1902–1969 AD. 3 vols. Beirut: Dar al-Saqi, 2005.

Al-Semmari, Fahd, ed. *A History of the Arabian Peninsula*. London: I. B. Tauris, 2010.

———. "King Abdulaziz Foundation for Research and Archives." *Middle East Studies Association Bulletin* 35, no. 1 (Summer 2001): 45–46.

AlShehabi, Omar. "Political Movements in Bahrain: Past, Present and Future." *Jadaliyya*, February 14, 2012.

Al-Shuwayʿer, Khawla bint Muhammad ibn Saad. *Marakiz hafdh al-wathaʾiq fi al-Riyadh: dirasa li-ʿadad minha* [Archives in Riyadh: A selective study]. Riyadh: King Fahd National Library, 2004.

Al-Sibaʿi, Ahmad. *Taʾrikh Makkah: Dirasat fi al-siyasa wa-l-ʿilm wa-l-ijtimaʿ wa-l-ʿumran* [Historicizing Mecca: Studies in politics, knowledge, society and architecture]. Mecca: Al-Safa Press, 1999.

Al-Surayhi, Saad. *Idiologia al-sahraʾ: afaq al-tajdid wa suʾal al-hawiiya al-muʿalaqqa* [Desert ideology: Horizons of renewal and the question of suspended identity]. Beirut: Dar Jadawil, 2015.

Althusser, Louis. "Ideology and Ideological State Apparatus (Notes Towards an Investigation)." In *Lenin and Philosophy and Other Essays*, 85–126. New York: Monthly Review Press, 1971.

Altorki, Soraya, and Donald P. Cole. *Arabian Oasis City: The Transformation of ʿUnayzah*. Austin: University of Texas Press, 1989.

Al-ʿUthaymin, Abdullah, "Najd from the Tenth/Sixteenth Century until the Rise of Sheikh Mohammad ibn Abd al-Wahhab." In *A History of the Arabian Peninsula*, edited by Fahd al-Semmari, 57–90. London: I. B. Tauris.

Al-Wardi, Ali. *Qissat al-Ashraf wa Ibn Saud* [The story of the Ashraf and Ibn Saud]. London: Alwarrak, 2007.

Al-Zayd, Abdullah Muhammad. *Al-Taʿlim fi al-Mamlaka al-ʿArabiyya al-Saʿudiyya: Namuzaj mukhtalif* [Education in the Kingdom of Saudi Arabia: A different model]. Riyadh, 1982.

Al-zayt yusahhil subul al-raqi [Oil facilitates progress]. Dhahran: Daʾirat al-ʿalakat al-ʿamma fi al-Sharq al-Awsat, sharikat al-zayt al-ʿArabiyya al-Amrikiyya. Beirut: n.p., 195.

Al-Zirikli, Khayr al-Din. *Shibh al-Jazira fi ʿAhd Abdulaziz* [The Arabian Peninsula in the era of King Abdulaziz]. Beirut, 1970.

Amar, Paul. *The Security Archipelago: Human-Security States, Sexuality Politics, and the End of Neoliberalism*. Durham, NC: Duke University Press, 2013.

Anand, Nikhil. "PRESSURE: The PoliTechnics of Water Supply." *Cultural Anthropology* 26, no. 4 (2011): 542–64.

Anderson, Benedict. *Imagined Communities: Reflections on the Origin and Spread of Nationalism*. New York: Verso, 1983.

Anscombe, Frederick F. *The Ottoman Gulf: The Creation of Kuwait, Saudi Arabia and Qatar*. New York: Columbia University Press, 1997.

Anziska, Seth. *Preventing Palestine: A Political History from Camp David to Oslo.* Princeton, NJ: Princeton University Press, 2018.

Appadurai, Arjun. "Archive and Aspiration." In *Information Is Alive*, edited by Joke Brouwer and Arjen Mulder, 14–25. Baltimore: Johns Hopkins University Press, 2003.

———. *Formations of the Secular: Christianity, Islam, Modernity.* Stanford, CA: Stanford University Press, 2003.

———. *Modernity at Large.* Minneapolis: University of Minnesota Press, 1996.

Apter, Andrew. *The Pan-African Nation: Oil and the Spectacle of Culture in Nigeria.* Chicago: University of Chicago Press, 2005.

Asad, Talal. "Conscripts of Western Civilization." In *Dialectical Anthropology: Essays in Honor of Stanley Diamond.* Vol. 1 of *Civilization in Crisis*, edited by Christine Gailey, 333–51. Gainesville: University Press of Florida, 1992.

———. *Genealogies of Religion: Discipline and Reasons of Power in Christianity and Islam.* Baltimore: Johns Hopkins University Press, 1993.

Ashworth, G. J., and J. E. Tunbridge. "Old Cities, New Pasts: Heritage Planning in Selected Cities of Central Europe." In "Post-Socialist Urban Transition in Eastern and Central Europe." Special issue, *GeoJournal* 49, no. 1 (1999): 105–16.

'Awwad, Muhammad Hassan. *Khawatir musarraha* [Authorized reflections]. Cairo: Arab Press, 1926.

Ayubi, Nazih. *Overstating the Arab State: Politics and Society in the Middle East.* New York: I. B. Tauris, 1995.

Baker, Randall. *King Hussein and the Kingdom of Hejaz.* New York: Oleander Press, 1979.

Bang, Anne K. *Sufis and Scholars of the Sea: Family Networks in East Africa, 1860–1925.* London: Routledge Curzon, 2014.

Barak, On. *On Time: Technology and Temporality in Modern Egypt.* Berkeley: University of California Press, 2013.

Bashkin, Orit. *The Other Iraq: Pluralism, Intellectuals and Culture in Hashemite Iraq, 1921–1958.* Stanford, CA: Stanford University Press, 2009.

Beasley, Betsy. "Service Learning: Oil, International Education, and Texas's Corporate Cold War." *Diplomatic History* 42, no. 2 (2018): 177–203.

Beblawi, Hazem, and Giacomo Luciano. *The Rentier State.* New York: Croom Helm, 1990.

Beinin, Joel, and Joe Stork, eds. *Political Islam: Essays from Middle East Report.* Berkeley: University of California Press, 1997.

Bellin, Eva. "The Robustness of Authoritarianism in the Middle East: A Comparative Perspective." Paper presented at the Middle East Studies Association annual conference, Washington, DC, 2002.

Berkey, Jonathan. *The Formation of Islam: Religion and Society in the Near East, 600–1800*. Cambridge: Cambridge University Press, 2003.

Bhaba, Homi. *Nation and Narration*. New York: Routledge, 1990.

Bloom, Saul, et al., eds. *Hidden Casualties: Environmental, Health, and Political Consequences of the Persian Gulf War*. Berkeley, CA: North Atlantic Books: ARC/Arms Control Research Center, 1994.

Blouin, Francis X., Jr., and William G. Rosenberg, eds. *Archives, Documentation, and Institutions of Social Memory: Essays from the Sawyer Seminar*. Ann Arbor: University of Michigan Press, 2007.

Bogdanor, Vernon. "The Monarchy and the Constitution." *Parliamentary Affairs* 49, no. 3 (July 1, 1996): 407–22.

Bonnenfant, Paul. "Real Estate and Political Power in 1970s Riyadh." Translated by Diantha Guessous and Pascal Menoret. *City* 18, no. 6 (1982): 708–22.

Bourdieu, Pierre. *The Logic of Practice*. Stanford, CA: Stanford University Press, 1992.

———. *Outline of a Theory of Practice*. Cambridge: Cambridge University Press, 1977.

———. "Rethinking the State: Genesis and Structure of the Bureaucratic Field." *Sociological Theory* 12, no. 1 (March 1994): 1–18.

Brachman, Jarret. *Global Jihadism: Theory and Practice*. New York: Routledge, 2009.

Bradley, Francis R. "Islamic Reform, the Family, and Knowledge Networks Linking Mecca to Southeast Asia in the Nineteenth Century." *Journal of Asian Studies* 73, no. 1 (February 2014): 89–111.

Breit, Suzanne. *What Is Documentation? English Translation of the Classic French Text*. Toronto: Scarecrow Press, 2006.

Bromley, Simon. *Rethinking Middle East Politics*. Austin: University of Texas Press, 1993.

Brown, Wendy. *States of Injury: Power and Freedom in Late Modernity*. Princeton, NJ: Princeton University Press, 1995.

Brubaker, Rogers. *Nationalism Reframed: Nationhood and the National Question in the New Europe*. Cambridge: University of Cambridge, 1996.

Bsheer, Rosie. "A Counter-Revolutionary State: Popular Movements and the Making of Saudi Arabia." *Past and Present* 238, no. 1 (February 1, 2018): 233–77.

———. "Dissent and Its Discontents: Protesting the Saudi State." In *The Dawn of the Arab Uprisings: End of an Old Order?*, edited by Bassam Haddad, Rosie Bsheer, and Ziad Abu-Rish, 248–59. New York: Pluto Press, 2012.

———. "Heritage as War." In "Forced Displacement and Refugees." Special issue, *International Journal of Middle East Studies* 49, no. 4 (November 2017): 729–34.

———. "Making History, Remaking Space: Textbooks, Archives and Commemorative Spaces in Saudi Arabia." PhD diss., Columbia University, 2014.

———. Review of *Politics and Society in Saudi Arabia: The Crucial Years of Development, 1960–1982*, by Sarah Yizraeli. *International Journal of Middle East Studies* 46, no. 2 (May 2014): 412–14.

———. "Teaching the Nation: State and Citizen in Saudi Arabian History Textbooks." Master's thesis, Columbia University, 2006.

———. "W(h)ither Arabian Peninsula Studies?" In *Handbook of Contemporary Middle East and North African History*, edited by Jens Hansen and Amal Ghazal. Oxford: Oxford University Press, 2017.

Bsheer, Rosie, and John Warner, eds. "Theorizing the Arabian Peninsula." *Jadmag*, 1, no. 1 (Fall 2013): 1–51.

Buckley, Michelle, and Adam Hanieh. "Diversification by Urbanization: Tracing the Property-Finance Nexus in Dubai and the Gulf." *International Journal of Urban and Regional Research* 18, no. 1 (2013): 155–75.

Budeiri, Musa. "Controlling the Archive: Captured Jordanian Security Files in the Israeli State Archives." *Jerusalem Quarterly* 66 (2016): 87–98.

Burckhardt, John Lewis. *Travels in Arabia*. London: Henry Colburn, 1829.

Burton, Antoinette, ed. *Archive Stories: Facts, Fictions, and the Writing of History*. Durham, NC: Duke University Press, 2005.

Can, Lâle. *Spiritual Subjects: Central Asian Pilgrims and the Ottoman Hajj at the End of Empire*. Stanford, CA: Stanford University Press, 2020.

Carapico, Sheila. 2000. "Arabia Incognita: An Invitation to Arabian Peninsula Studies." In *Counter-Narratives: History, Contemporary Society, and Politics in Saudi Arabia and Yemen*, edited by Madawi Al-Rasheed and Robert Vitalis, 11–33. New York: Palgrave Macmillan, 2004.

Chakrabarty, Dipesh. *Provincializing Europe: Postcolonial Thought and Historical Difference*. Princeton, NJ: Princeton University Press, 2000.

Chandoke, Neera. "The Post-Colonial City." *Economic and Political Weekly* 26 (1991): 2868–73.

Chanfi, Ahmed. *West African Ulama and Salafism in Mecca and Medina: Jawab al-Ifriqi—The Response of the African*. Leiden, Netherlands: Brill Academic, 2015.

Chatterjee, Partha. *The Nation and Its Fragments: Colonial and Postcolonial Histories*. Princeton, NJ: Princeton University Press, 1993.

Chaudhry, Kiren Aziz. *The Price of Wealth: Economics and Institutions in the Middle East*. Ithaca, NY: Cornell University Press, 1997.

Citino, Nathan J. *From Arab Nationalism to OPEC: Eisenhower, King Saud, and the Making of U.S.-Saudi Relations*. Bloomington: Indiana University Press, 2003.

Clausewitz, Carl von. *On War*. Princeton, NJ: Princeton University Press, 1989.

Cohn, Bernard S. *Colonialism and Its Forms of Knowledge: The British in India*. Princeton, NJ: Princeton University Press, 1996.

Cole, Juan. "Rival Empires of Trade and Imami Shiism in Eastern Arabia, 1300–1800." *International Journal of Middle East Studies* 19, no. 2 (May 1987): 177–203.

Coll, Steve. *The Bin Ladens: An Arabian Family in the American Century*. London: Penguin Books, 2008.

Collins, John. *Revolt of the Saints: Memory and Redemption in the Twilight of Brazilian Racial Democracy*. Durham, NC: Duke University Press, 2015.

Comaroff, John, and Jean Comaroff. *Ethnography and the Historical Imagination*. Boulder, CO: Westview Press, 1992.

Commins, David. *The Wahhabi Mission and Saudi Arabia*. New York: I. B. Tauris, 2006.

Cook, Michael. *Commanding Right and Forbidding Wrong in Islamic Thought*. Oxford: Oxford University Press, 2000.

Corancez, Louis Alexandre de. *Histoire des Wahabis depuis leur origine jusqu'a la fin de 1809*. Paris: Prapart, 1809.

Coronil, Fernando. *The Magical State: Nature, Money and Modernity in Venezuela*. Chicago: University of Chicago Press, 1997.

Coşgel, Metin M., Thomas J. Miceli, and Jared Rubin. "The Political Economy of Mass Printing: Legitimacy, Revolt, and Technological Change in the Ottoman Empire." *Journal of Comparative Economics* 40, no. 3 (August 2012): 357–71.

Crinson, Mark, ed. *Urban Memory: History and Amnesia in the Modern City*. New York: Routledge, 2005.

Crinson, Mark, and Paul Tyrer. "Clocking Off in Ancoats: Time and Remembrance in the Post-Industrial City." In *Urban Memory: History and Amnesia in the Modern City*, edited by Mark Crinson. New York: Routledge, 2005.

Dahlan, Malik. *The Hijaz: The First Islamic State*. London: Hurst, 2017.

Dakhlia, Jocelyne. *L'oubli de la cité: La mémoire collective à l'épreuve du lignage dans le Jérid Tunisien.* Paris: Découverte, 1990.

Darat al-Malik Abdulaziz: Wa masirat 'ishrin 'aman, 1972–1992 [King Abdulaziz Research Center: A twenty-year-journey, 1972–1992]. Riyadh: Darat al-Malik Abdulaziz, 1992.

Das, Veena, and Deborah Poole, eds. *Anthropology in the Margins of the State.* Santa Fe, NM: SAR Press, 2004.

Davis, Eric. *Statecraft in the Middle East: Oil, Historical Memory, and Popular Culture.* Miami: Florida International University Press, 1991.

De Certeau, Michel. *The Writing of History.* New York: Columbia University Press, 1975.

De Cesari, Chiara. "Heritage Between Resistance and Government in Palestine." In "Forced Displacement and Refugees." Special issue, *International Journal of Middle East Studies* 49, no. 4 (November 2017): 747–51.

Delong-Bas, Natana J. *Wahhabi Islam: From Revival and Reform to Global Jihad.* Oxford: Oxford University Press, 2008.

Deringil, Selim. *The Well-Protected Domains: Ideology and Legitimacy in the Late Ottoman Empire, 1876–1909.* I. B. Tauris, 1998.

Derrida, Jacques. *Archive Fever: A Freudian Impression.* Chicago: University of Chicago Press, 1996.

Determann, Jörg Matthias. *Historiography in Saudi Arabia: Globalization and the State in the Middle East.* London: I. B. Tauris, 2014.

Di-Capua, Yoav. *Gatekeepers of the Arab Past: Historians and History Writing in Twentieth-Century Egypt.* Berkeley: University of California Press, 2009.

Dirks, Nicholas. *Castes of Mind: Colonialism and the Making of Modern India.* Princeton, NJ: Princeton University Press, 2001.

———. *Colonialism and Culture.* Ann Arbor: University of Michigan Press, 1992.

Dobe, Michael Edward. "A Long Slow Tutelage in Western Ways of Work: Industrial Education and the Containment of Nationalism in Anglo-Iranian and Aramco, 1923–1963." PhD diss., Rutgers University, 2008.

Du Gay, Paul, ed. *Production of Culture/Cultures of Production.* London: Sage Publications, 1997.

Echevarria, Roberto González. *Myth and the Archive: A Theory of Latin American Narrative.* 2nd ed. Durham, NC: Duke University Press, 1998.

Eickelman, Dale F. *Muslim Travelers: Pilgrimage, Migration, and the Religious Imagination.* Berkeley: University of California Press, 1990.

El-Ariss, Tarek, ed. *The Arab Renaissance: A Bilingual Anthology of the Nahda*. New York: Modern Language Association of America, 2018.

Elkins, Caroline. *Imperial Reckoning: The Untold Story of Britain's Gulag in Kenya*. New York: Holt Paperbacks, 2005.

El Shakry, Omnia. "'History Without Documents': The Vexed Archives of Decolonization in the Middle East." *American Historical Review* 120, no. 3 (June 1, 2015): 920–34.

Esposito, John. *Islam and Politics*. Syracuse, NY: Syracuse University Press, 1998.

Evered, Emine Ö. "Rereading Ottoman Accounts of Wahhabism as Alternative Narratives: Ahmed Cevdet Paşa's Historical Survey of the Movement." *Comparative Studies of South Asia, Africa and the Middle East* 32, no. 3 (2012): 622–32.

Exell, Karen, and Trinidad Rico, eds. *Cultural Heritage in the Arabian Peninsula*. New York: Routledge, 2016.

Facey, William. *Back to Earth: Adobe Building in Saudi Arabia*. Riyadh: Al-Turath, 2015.

Fahmy, Khaled. *All the Pasha's Men: Mehmed Ali, His Army and the Making of Modern Egypt*. Cairo: American University in Cairo Press, 2002.

Fanon, Frantz. *The Wretched of the Earth*. New York: Grove Press, 1963.

Farquhar, Michael. *Circuits of Faith: Migration, Education, and the Wahhabi Mission*. Stanford, CA: Stanford University Press, 2017.

Fattah, Hala. *The Politics of Regional Trade in Iraq, Arabia and the Gulf 1745–1900*. Albany: State University of New York Press, 1997.

Fentiman, Alicia. "The Anthropology of Oil: The Impact of the Oil Industry on a Fishing Community in the Niger Delta." *Social Justice* 23 (1996): 87–99.

Flood, Finbar. "Between Cult and Culture: Bamiyan, Islamic Iconoclasm and the Museum." *Art Bulletin* 84, no. 4 (2002): 641–59.

———. "Signs of Violence: Colonial Ethnographies and Indo-Islamic Monuments." In "Art and Terror." Special issue, *Australian and New Zealand Journal of Art* 5, no. 2 (2004): 20–51.

Forty, Adrian, and Susanne Küchler, eds. *The Art of Forgetting*. Oxford, UK: Berg, 1999.

Foucault, Michel. *The Archeology of Knowledge: And the Discourse of Language*. New York: Pantheon Books, 1972.

———. *The Birth of Biopolitics: Lectures at the Collège de France, 1978–1979*. New York: Picador, 2010.

———. *Discipline and Punish: The Birth of the Prison*. New York: Vintage Books, 1977.

Frank, Andre Gunder. "Third World War: A Political Economy of the Gulf War and the New World Order." *Third World Quarterly* 13, no. 2 (1992): 267–82.

Freitag, Ulrike, Malte Fuhrmann, Nora Lafi, and Florian Riedler. *The City in the Ottoman Empire: Migration and the Making of Urban Modernity*. New York: Routledge, 2011.

Fusfeld, Daniel R. "The Rise of the Corporate State in America." *Journal of Economic Issues* 6, no. 1 (March 1972): 1–22.

Gabra, Shafeeq N. *Palestinians in Kuwait: The Family and the Politics of Survival*. Boulder, CO: Westview Press, 1987.

Galison, Peter. "Removing Knowledge." *Critical Inquiry* 31, no. 1 (Autumn 2004): 229–43.

Garba, Shaibu Bala. "Managing Urban Growth and Development in the Riyadh Metropolitan Area, Saudi Arabia." *Habitat International* 28, no. 4 (December 2004): 593–608.

Gause, Gregory. "Oil and Political Mobilizations in Saudi Arabia." In *Saudi Arabia in Transition*, edited by Bernard Haykel, Thomas Hegghammer, and Stéphane Lacroix, 13–30. New York: Cambridge University Press, 2016.

Gellner, Ernest. *Nations and Nationalism*. Ithaca, NY: Cornell University Press, 1983.

Gendzier, Irene L. "Oil, Politics and US Intervention." In *A Revolutionary Year: The Middle East in 1958*, edited by Wm. Roger Louis and Roger Owen, 101–42. New York: I. B. Tauris, 2002.

Goldberg, Jake. "Saudi Arabia's Desert Storm and Winter Sandstorm." In *The Gulf Crisis and Its Global Aftermath*, edited by Gad Barzilai, Aharon Klieman, and Gil Shidlo, 67–86. London: Routledge, 1993.

Gorman, Anthony. *Historians, State and Politics in Twentieth Century Egypt: Contesting the Nation*. London: Routledge Curzon, 2003.

Goswami, Manu. *Producing India: From Colonial Economy to National Space*. Chicago: University of Chicago Press, 2004.

———. "Rethinking the Modular Nation Form: Toward a Sociohistorical Conception of Nationalism." *Comparative Studies in Society and History* 44, no. 4 (2002): 770–99.

Gramsci, Antonio. *Selections from the Prison Notebooks*. New York: International Publishers, 1971.

Guillory, John. "The Memo and Modernity." *Critical Inquiry* 31, no. 1 (Autumn 2004): 108–32.

Habib, John S. *Ibn Saud's Warriors of Islam: The Ikhwan of Najd and Their Role in the Creation of the Saudi Kingdom, 1910–1930*. Leiden, Netherlands: E. J. Brill, 1978.

Hacking, Ian. "Between Michel Foucault and Erving Goffman: Between Discourse in the Abstract and Face-to-Face Interaction." *Economy and Society* 33, no. 3 (2004): 277–302.

———. "How Should We Do the History of Statistics?" In *The Foucault Effect: Studies in Governmentality*, edited by Graham Burchell, 181–96. Chicago: Chicago University Press, 1991.

Haddad, Bassam, Rosie Bsheer, and Ziad Abu-Rish, eds. *The Dawn of the Arab Uprisings: End of an Old Order?* New York: Pluto Press, 2012.

Hafız, Othman. *Tatawur al-sahafa fi al-Mamlaka al-'Arabiyya al-Sa'udiyya* [The development of the press in the Kingdom of Saudi Arabia]. Jeddah: Sharikat al-Madina li-l-Tiba'a wa-l-Nashr, 1989.

Hakim, Abdulhamid Abdulmajid. *Nizam al-ta'lim wa siyasatah* [The educational system and its policies]. Cairo: Itrak Press, 2012.

Hall, John A., ed. *States in History*. Oxford, UK: Basil Blackwell, 1986.

Hamid, Abbas. *Qissat al-tawsi'a al-kubra* [The story of the great expansion]. Jeddah: Majmu'at Binladin al-Sa'udiyya, 1994.

Hamouda, Houda ben. "L'accès aux fonds contemporains des archives nationales de Tunisie: Un état des lieux" [Access to contemporary holdings of the National Archives of Tunisia: An inventory]. In "Besoins d'histoire: Historiographies et régimes d'historicité au Maghreb à l'aune des révolutions arabes." *L'Année du Maghreb* 10 (2014): 41–48.

Hamza, Fuad. *Al-Bilad al-'Arabiyya al-Sa'udiyya* [Saudi Arabia]. Makkah: Matba'at Umm al- Qura, 1937.

Hamzah, Dyala, ed. *The Making of the Arab Intellectual: Empire, Public Sphere and the Colonial Coordinates of Selfhood*. New York: Routledge, 2013.

Hanieh, Adam. *Capitalism and Class in the Gulf Arab States*. New York: Palgrave Macmillan, 2011.

———. *Money, Markets, and Monarchies: The Gulf Cooperation Council and the Political Economy of the Contemporary Middle East*. Cambridge: Cambridge University Press, 2018.

Hanioğlu, M. Şükrü. *A Brief History of the Late Ottoman Empire*. Princeton, NJ: Princeton University Press, 2008.

Hanssen, Jens, and Max Weiss. *Arabic Thought against the Authoritarian Age: Towards an Intellectual History of the Present*. Cambridge: Cambridge University Press, 2018.

———. *Arabic Thought beyond the Liberal Age: Towards an Intellectual History of the Nahda*. Cambridge: Cambridge University Press, 2016.

Harvey, David. *A Brief History of Neoliberalism*. Oxford: Oxford University Press, 2007.

———. *The Limits to Capital*. Chicago: University of Chicago Press, 1982.

———. *The New Imperialism*. Oxford: Oxford University Press, 2003.

———. *Social Justice and the City*. Baltimore: Johns Hopkins University Press, 1973.

———. *The Urbanization of Capital: Studies in the History and Theory of Capitalist Urbanization*. Baltimore: Johns Hopkins University Press, 1985.

Haykal, Muhammad Hassanayn. *Al-Isti'mar li'batah al-malik* [The king is colonialism's toy]. Cairo: Dar al-'Asr al-Hadith, 1967.

———. *Harb al-khalij: awham al-quwwa wa-l-nasr* [The Gulf War: Illusions of power and triumph]. Cairo: Markaz al-Ahram li-l-Tarjama wa-l-Nashr, 1992.

———. *Sanawat al-ghalayan* [Boiling years]. Cairo: Dar al-'Asr al-Hadith, 1988.

Haykel, Bernard. "The Wahhabis and Radical Islamic Networks." Lecture in the series "Dimensions of Contemporary Islam." Hattiesburg, University of Southern Mississippi, February 5, 2007.

Haykel, Bernard, Thomas Hegghammer, and Stéphane Lacroix, eds. *Saudi Arabia in Transition*. New York: Cambridge University Press, 2016.

Hecht, Gabrielle, ed. *Entangled Geographies: Empire and Technopolitics in the Global Cold War*. Cambridge, MA: MIT Press, 2011.

Hegel, Georg W. F. *Introduction to the Philosophy of History*. Indianapolis, IN: Hackett, 1988.

Hegghamer, Thommas, and Stéphane Lacroix. *The Meccan Rebellion: The Story of Juhayman al-'Utaybi Revisited*. Bristol, UK: Amal Press, 2011.

Held, David. *Political Theory and the Modern State: Essays on State, Power and Democracy*. Stanford, CA: Stanford University Press, 1989.

Helms, Christine Moss. *The Cohesion of Saudi Arabia: Evolution of Political Identity*. London: Croom Helm, 1981.

Hertog, Steffen. *Princes, Brokers, and Bureaucrats: Oil and the State in Saudi Arabia*. Ithaca, NY: Cornell University Press, 2010.

Herzfeld, Michael. *The Social Production of Indifference: Exploring the Symbolic Roots of Western Bureaucracy*. Chicago: University of Chicago Press, 1992.

Hirschkind, Charles, and David Scott, eds. *Powers of the Secular Modern: Talal Asad and His Interlocutors*. Stanford, CA: Stanford University Press, 2006.

Ho, Enseng. *The Graves of Tarim: Genealogy and Mobility Across the Indian Ocean*. Berkeley: University of California Press, 2006.

Hobsbawm, Eric. *Nations and Nationalism Since 1780*. Cambridge: Cambridge University Press, 1990.

Hopkins, A. G., ed. *Globalization in World History*. New York: W. W. Norton, 2002.

Houtsma, M. Th., T. W. Arnold, R. Basset, and R. Hartmann, eds. *First Encyclopedia of Islam, 1913–1936*. Leiden, Netherlands: E. J. Brill, 1993.

Howarth, David. *A Desert King: Ibn Saud and His Arabia*. New York: McGraw-Hill, 1964.
Hull, Matthew. "Documents and Bureaucracy." *Annual Review of Anthropology* 41 (2012): 251–67.
———. *Government of Paper: The Materiality of Bureaucracy in Urban Pakistan*. Berkeley: University of California Press, 2012.
Ibrahim, Ahmad Abubakr. *Al-Adab al-Hijazi fi al-nahda al-haditha* [Hijazi literature in the modern *nahda*]. Cairo: Matba'at Nahdat Masr, 1948.
Izady, Mehrdad R. "The Gulf's Ethnic Diversity: An Evolutionary History." In *Security in the Persian Gulf: Origins, Obstacles, and the Search for Consensus*, edited by Gary Sick and Lawrence Potter, 33–90. New York: Palgrave Macmillan, 2002.
James, Laura M. "Whose Voice? Nasser, the Arabs, and 'Sawt al-Arab' Radio." *Transnational Broadcasting Studies* 16 (2006). http://www.tbsjournal.com/James.html.
Jones, Toby C. "Crude Ecology: Technology and the Politics of Dissent in Saudi Arabia." In *Entangled Geographies: Empire and Technopolitics in the Global Cold War*, edited by Gabrielle Hecht, 209–30. Cambridge, MA: MIT Press, 2011.
———. *Desert Kingdom: How Oil and Water Forged Modern Saudi Arabia*. Cambridge, MA: Harvard University Press, 2010.
———. "The Dogma of Development: Technopolitics and the Making of Saudi Arabia, 1950–1980." PhD diss., Stanford University, 2006.
———. "Rebellion on the Saudi Periphery: Modernity, Marginalization, and the Shi'a Uprising of 1979." *International Journal of Middle East Studies* 38 (2006): 213–33.
Karl, Terry L. *The Paradox of Plenty: Oil Booms and Petro-States*. Berkeley: University of California Press, 1997.
Karpat, Kemal. "The Transformation of the Ottoman State, 1789–1908." *International Journal of Middle East Studies* 3 (1972): 243–81.
Kassab, Elizabeth Suzanne. *Contemporary Arab Thought: Cultural Critique in Comparative Perspective*. New York: Columbia University Press, 2010.
Kayalı, Hasan. *Arabs and Young Turks: Ottomanism, Arabism, and Islamism in the Ottoman, 1908–1918*. Los Angeles: University of California Press, 1997.
Kerr, Malcolm H. *The Arab Cold War: Gamal 'Abd al-Nasir and His Rivals, 1958–1970*. Oxford: Oxford University Press, 1965.
Khadduri, Walid, ed. *Abdullah al-Tariqi: al-A'mal al-kamila* [Abdullah al-Tariqi: Complete works]. 2nd ed. Beirut: Markaz Dirasat al-Wihda al-'Arabiyya, 2005.
Khalidi, Lamya. "The Destruction of Yemen and Its Cultural Heritage." In "Forced Displacement and Refugees." Special issue, *International Journal of Middle East Studies* 49, no. 4 (November 2017): 735–38.

Khalidi, Rashid. *Sowing Crisis: The Cold War and American Dominance in the Middle East.* Boston: Beacon Press, 2009.

Khalili, Laleh. *Heroes and Martyrs of Palestine: The Politics of National Commemoration.* Cambridge: Cambridge University Press, 2007.

Khatib, Lina. *Image Politics in the Middle East: The Role of the Visual in Political Struggle.* New York: I. B. Tauris, 2012.

Khoury, Dina Rizk. *State and Provincial Society in the Ottoman Empire: Mosul, 1540–1834.* Cambridge: Cambridge University Press, 1997.

Khuri-Makdisi, Ilham. *The Eastern Mediterranean and the Making of Global Radicalism, 1860–1914.* Berkeley: University of California Press, 2010.

Kingston, Ralph. "The French Revolution and the Materiality of the Modern Archive." *Libraries and the Cultural Record* 46, no. 1 (2011): 1–25.

Kirshenblatt-Gimblett, Barbara. *Destination Culture: Tourism, Museums, and Heritage.* Berkeley: University of California Press, 1998.

Kohn, Hans. *The Idea of Nationalism: A Study in Its Origins and Background.* New Brunswick, NJ: Transaction Publishers, 2005.

———. "Nationalism." In *International Encyclopedia of the Social Sciences*, vol. 11, 63–70. Chicago: International Encyclopedia of the Social Sciences, 1976.

Koselleck, Reinhart. *Futures Past: On the Semantics of Historical Time.* Cambridge, MA: MIT Press, 1990.

———. *The Practice of Conceptual History: Timing History, Spacing Concepts.* Stanford, CA: Stanford University Press, 2002.

Kostiner, Joseph. *The Making of Saudi Arabia 1916–1936.* Oxford: Oxford University Press, 1993.

Kostiner, Joseph, and Phillip Khoury, eds. *Tribes and State Formation in the Middle East.* Berkeley: University of California Press, 1990.

LaCapra, Dominick. *History and Reading: Tocqueville, Foucault, French Studies.* Toronto: University of Toronto Press, 2000.

———. *History in Transit: Experience, Identity, Critical Theory.* Ithaca, NY: Cornell University Press, 2004.

Lacroix, Stéphane. *Awakening Islam: The Politics of Religious Dissent in Saudi Arabia.* Cambridge, MA: Harvard University Press, 2011.

Ladki, Said M., and Rayan A. Mazeh. "Comparative Pricing Analysis of Mecca's Religious Tourism." *International Journal of Religious Tourism and Pilgrimage*, 5, no. 1 (2017): 20–28.

Laffan, Michael. *The Makings of Indonesian Islam: Orientalism and the Narration of a Sufi Past*. Princeton, NJ: Princeton University Press, 2011.

Landau, Jacob M. *The Hejaz Railway and the Muslim Pilgrimage: A Case of Ottoman Political Propaganda*. Detroit: Wayne State University Press, 1971.

Laoust, Henri. *Le traite de droit public d'Ibn Taymiyah*. Beirut, 1928.

Larkin, Brian. "The Politics and Poetics of Infrastructure." *Annual Review of Anthropology* 42 (October 2013): 327–43.

Latif, Abdul. "Al-'alaqat al-adabiyya wa-l-thaqafiyya bayn Malibar wa-l-bilad al-'Arabiyya" [Literary and cultural relations between Malibar and Arab states]. *Majalla al-Aasima* (Arabic University College) 9 (2017): 233–37.

Latour, Bruno. *Pandora's Hope: Essays on the Reality of Science Studies*. Cambridge, MA: Harvard University Press, 1999.

———. *The Pasteurization of France*. Cambridge, MA: Harvard University Press, 1993.

———. *Reassembling the Social: An Introduction to Actor-Network-Theory*. New York: Oxford University Press, 2007.

———. "What Is Iconoclash: Or Is There a World beyond the Image Wars?" In *Iconoclash: Beyond the Image Wars in Science, Religion and Art*, edited by Bruno Latour and Peter Weibel, 14–37. Cambridge, MA: MIT Press, 2002.

Lefebvre, Henri. *The Production of Space*. Oxford: Wiley-Blackwell, 1991.

Le Renard, Amelie. *A Society of Young Women: Opportunities of Place, Power, and Reform in Saudi Arabia*. Stanford, CA: Stanford University, 2014.

Limbert, Mandana. *In the Time of Oil: Piety, Memory, and Social Life in an Omani Town*. Stanford, CA: Stanford University Press, 2010.

Lipsky, George A. *Saudi Arabia, Its People, Its Society, Its Culture*. New Haven, CT: HRAF Press, 1959.

Little, Douglas. "Pipeline Politics: America, TAPLINE and the Arabs." *Business History Review* 64, no. 2 (Summer 1990): 255–85.

Louër, Laurence. "The Political Impact of Labor Migration in Bahrain." *City and Society* 20, no. 1 (2008): 40–57.

Louis, Wm. Roger, and Roger Owen. *A Revolutionary Year: The Middle East in 1958*. New York: I. B. Tauris, 2002.

Luciani, Giacomo. "From Private Sector to National Bourgeoisie: Saudi Arabian Business." In *Saudi Arabia in the Balance: Political Economy, Society, Foreign Affairs*, edited by Paul Aarts and Gerd Nonneman, 144–84. New York: New York University Press, 2005.

———. "The Oil Rent, the Fiscal Crisis of the State and Democratization." In *Democracy Without Democrats: The Renewal of Politics in the Muslim World*, edited by Ghassan Salame, 130–55. London: I. B. Tauris, 2001.

Mahdavi, Hossein. "Patterns and Problems of Economic Development in Rentier States: The Case of Iran." In *Studies in the Economic History of the Middle East*, edited by M. A. Cook, 428–67. Oxford: Oxford University Press, 1970.

Mahmood, Saba. *Politics of Piety: The Islamic Revival and the Feminist Subject*. Princeton, NJ: Princeton University Press, 2005.

Makdisi, Ussama. *The Culture of Sectarianism: Community, History, and Violence in Nineteenth-Century Ottoman Lebanon*. Berkeley: University of California Press, 2000.

Marx, Anthony. *Faith in Nation: Exclusionary Origins of Nationalism*. Oxford: Oxford University Press, 2005.

Marx, Karl. *Capital: A Critique of Political Economy*. Vol. 1. London: Penguin Classics, 1992.

———. *Grundrisse: Foundations of the Critique of Political Economy*. London: Penguin, 1939.

Massad, Joseph. *Colonial Effects: The Making of National Identity in Jordan*. New York: Columbia University Press, 2001.

Masters, Bruce. *The Arabs of the Ottoman Empire, 1516–1918: A Social and Cultural History*, Cambridge: Cambridge University Press, 2013.

Matthiesen, Toby. *The Other Saudis: Shiism, Dissent and Sectarianism*. Cambridge: Cambridge University Press, 2015.

Mbembe, Achille. "The Power of the Archive and Its Limits." In *Refiguring the Archive*, edited by Carolyn Hamilton, Verne Harris, Jane Taylor, Michele Pickover, Graeme Reid, and Razia Saleh, 19–27. Dordrecht, Netherlands: Kluwer, 2002.

McCartney, Laton. *Friends in High Places: The Bechtel Story: The Most Secret Corporation and How It Engineered the World*. New York: Ballantine Books, 1988.

McLoughlin, Leslie J. *Ibn Saud: Founder of a Kingdom*. Basingstoke, UK: Macmillan, 1993.

Menoret, Pascal. *Joyriding in Riyadh: Oil, Urbanism, and Road Revolt*. Cambridge: Cambridge University Press, 2014.

Messick, Brinkley. *The Calligraphic State: Textual Domination and History in a Muslim Society*. Berkeley: University of California Press, 1993.

Middleton, Deborah Antoinette. "Growth and Expansion in Post-War Urban Design Strategies: C. A. Doxiadis and the First Strategic Plan for Riyadh Saudi Arabia (1968–1972)." PhD diss., Georgia Institute of Technology, December 2009.

Miller, Daniel, ed. *Materiality*. Durham, NC: Duke University Press, 2005.

Miller, Michael B. *The Bon Marche: Bourgeois Culture and the Department Store, 1869–1920*. Princeton, NJ: Princeton University Press, 1981.

Minawi, Mostafa. *The Ottoman Scramble for Africa: Empire and Diplomacy in the Sahara and the Hijaz*. Stanford, CA: Stanford University Press, 2016.

Mitchell, Timothy. *Carbon Democracy: Political Power in the Age of Oil*. London: Verso, 2011.

———. *Colonizing Egypt*. Berkeley: University of California Press, 1991.

———. "The Limits of the State: Beyond Statist Approaches and Their Critics." *American Political Science Review* 85, no. 1 (March 1991): 75–96.

———. *Rule of Experts: Egypt, Techno-Politics, Modernity*. Berkeley: University of California Press, 2002.

———. "Society, Economy, and the State Effect." In *The Anthropology of the State*, edited by Aradhana Sharma. Malden, MA: Blackwell, 2006.

———. "The World as Exhibition." *Comparative Studies in Society and History* 3, no. 2 (1989): 217–36.

Mouline, Nabil. *The Clerics of Islam: Religious Authority and Political Power in Saudi Arabia*. Translated by Ethan S. Rundell. New Haven, CT: Yale University Press, 2014.

Mulligan, Jennifer. "'What Is an Archive?' in the History of Modern France." In *Archive Stories: Facts, Fictions, and the Writing of History*, edited by Antoinette Burton (Durham, NC: Duke University Press, 2005).

Mundy, Martha, ed. *Law, Anthropology, and the Constitution of the Social: Making Persons and Things*. Cambridge: Cambridge University Press, 2004.

Nafi, Basheer M. "A Teacher of Ibn Abd al-Wahhab: Muhammad Hayat al-Sindi and the Revival of Ashab al-Hadith's Methodology." *Islamic Law and Society* 13, no. 2 (2006): 208–41.

Nagy, Sharon. "'This Time I Think I'll Try a Filipina': Global and Local Influences on Relations Between Foreign Household Workers and Their Employers in Doha, Qatar." *City and Society* 10 (1998): 83–103.

Nasif, Husayn Muhammad. *Madi al-Hijaz wa hadiruh* [Hijaz's past and its present]. Cairo: Maktabat wa-Matba'at Khudayr, 1930.

Nora, Pierre. "Between Memory and History: Les *lieux de memoires*." In "Memory and Counter-Memory." Special issue, *Representations* 26 (1989): 7–24.

———. *Realms of Memory: The Construction of the French Past*. New York: Columbia University Press, 1992.

Novetzke, Christian Lee. "The Theographic and the Historiographic in an Indian Sacred Life Story." In *Time, History and the Religious Imaginary in South Asia*, edited by Anne Murphy, 115–32. London: Routledge, 2011.

Ochsenwald, William L. "Arab Nationalism in the Hijaz." In *The Origins of Arab Nationalism*, edited by Rashid Khalidi, Lisa Anderson, Muhammad Muslih, and Reeva Simon, 189–203. New York: Columbia University Press, 1991.

———. "Ottoman Arabia and the Holy Hejaz, 1516–1918." In "Understanding Transformations in the Arabian Peninsula." Special issue, *Journal of Global Initiatives: Policy, Pedagogy, Perspectives* 10, no. 1 (2016): 23–34.

———. "Ottoman Subsidies to the Hijaz, 1877–1886." *International Journal of Middle East Studies* 6, no. 3 (July 1975): 300–307.

———. *Religion, Society, and the State in Arabia: The Hijaz Under Ottoman Control, 1840–1908*. Columbus: Ohio State University Press, 1984.

O'Donnell, Guillermo A. *Counterpoints: Selected Essays on Authoritarianism and Democratization*. Notre Dame, IN: University of Notre Dame Press, 1999.

Ogborn, Miles. *Indian Ink: Script and Print in the Making of the English East India Company*. Chicago: University of Chicago Press, 2007.

Okruhlik, Gwenn. "Networks of Dissent: Islamism and Reform in Saudi Arabia." *Current History* 101, no. 651 (January 2002): 22.

———. "Rentier Wealth, Unruly Law, and the Rise of the Opposition: The Political Economy of Oil States." *Comparative Politics* 31, no. 3 (April 1999): 295–315.

———. "Struggles over History and Identity: 'Opening the Gates' of the Kingdom to Tourism." In *Counter-Narratives: History, Contemporary Society and Politics in Saudi Arabia and Yemen*, edited by Madawi Al-Rasheed, and Robert Vitalis, 201–28. New York: Palgrave, 2004.

Onley, James. *The Arabian Frontier of the British Raj: Merchants, Rulers, and the British in the Nineteenth-Century Gulf*. Oxford: Oxford University Press, 2007.

Ossman, Susan. *Picturing Casablanca: Portraits of Power in a Modern City*. Berkeley: University of California Press, 1994.

Ozyuksel, Murat. *The Hejaz Railway and the Ottoman Empire: Modernity, Industrialization and Ottoman Decline*. London: I. B. Tauris, 2014.

Painter, David S. "Oil and the American Century." In "Oil in American History." Special issue, *Journal of American History* 99, no. 1 (2012): 24–39.

Papailias, Penelope. *Genres of Recollection: Archival Poetics in Modern Greece*. New York: Palgrave Macmillan, 2005.

Peters, F. E. *Mecca: A Literary History of the Muslim Holy Land*. Princeton, NJ: Princeton University Press, 1994.

Peters, John E. *Out of Area or Out of Reach? European Military Support for Operations in Southwest Asia*. Santa Monica, CA: RAND, 1995.

Peterson, J. E. "The Arabian Peninsula in Modern Times: A Historiographical Survey." *American Historical Review* 96, no. 5 (December 1991): 1435–49.

Peutz, Nathalie. *Islands of Heritage: Conservation and Transformation in Yemen*. Stanford, CA: Stanford University Press, 2018.

———. "Perspectives from the Margins of Arabia." In "Theorizing the Arabian Peninsula," edited by Rosie Bsheer and John Warner. Special issue, *Jadmag* 1, no. 1 (Fall 2013): 25–29.

Philby, Harry Saint John. *Arabia*. London: Ernest Benn, 1930.

———. *Arabia of the Wahhabis*. London: Constable, 1928.

———. *Saudi Arabia*. Beirut: Librarie du Liban, 1955.

Povinelli, Elizabeth. *The Cunning of Recognition: Indigenous Alterities and the Making of Australian Multiculturalism*. Durham, NC: Duke University Press, 2002.

Powell, Avril Ann. "Maulana Rahmat Allah Kairanawi and Muslim-Christian Controversy in India in the Mid-19th Century." *Journal of the Royal Asiatic Society of Great Britain and Ireland* 108, no. 1 (1976): 42–63.

Pyla, Panayiota. "Back to the Future: Doxiadis's Plans for Baghdad." *Journal of Planning History* 7, no. 1 (2008): 3–19.

Rao, Anupama. *The Caste Question: Dalits and the Politics of Modern India*. Berkeley: University of California Press, 2009.

Rentz, George S. *The Birth of the Islamic Reform Movement in Saudi Arabia: Muhammad Ibn Abd al-Wahhab (1703/4–1792) and the Beginnings of Unitarian Empire in Arabia*. London: Arabian Publishing, 2004.

Richards, Alan, and John Waterbury. *A Political Economy of the Middle East*. Boulder, CO: Westview Press, 1996.

Rihani, Ameen. *Ibn Saʿoud of Arabia*. London: Constable, 1928; London: Routledge, 2011.

———. *Muluk al-ʿArab: Rihla fi bilad al-ʿArab* [Kings of the Arabs: A journey in Arab lands]. Beirut: Scientific Printing Press, 1924.

———. *Tarikh Najd al-hadith* [The modern history of Najd]. Beirut: Scientific Printing Press, 1928.

Rogan, Eugene. *The Fall of the Ottomans: The Great War in the Middle East*. New York: Basic Books, 2015.

Ross, Michael. "Does Oil Hinder Democracy?" *World Politics* 53, no. 3 (April 2001): 325–61.

Roy, Srirupa. *Beyond Belief: India and the Politics of Postcolonial Nationalism*. Durham, NC: Duke University Press, 2007.

Said, Edward. *Culture and Imperialism*. New York: Random House, 1994.

———. *Orientalism*. 2nd ed. New York: Vintage, 1994.

———. *The World, the Text, the Critic*. Cambridge, MA: Harvard University Press, 1983.

Salibi, Kamal. *A History of Arabia*. New York: Caravan Books, 1980.

Samin, Nadav. *Of Sand or Soil: Genealogy and Tribal Belonging in Saudi Arabia*. Princeton, NJ: Princeton University Press, 2015.

Sardar, Ziauddin. *Mecca: The Sacred City*. London: Bloomsbury, 2014.

Sarkis, Hashim. *Circa 1958: Lebanon in the Pictures and Plans of Constantinos Doxiadis*. Beirut: Éditions Dar An-Nahar, 2003.

Satia, Priya. *Spies in Arabia: The Great War and the Cultural Foundations of Britain's Covert Empire in the Middle East*. Oxford: Oxford University Press, 2008.

Scott, David. "Colonial Governmentality." *Social Text* 43 (1995): 21–49.

———. *Conscripts of Modernity: The Tragedy of Colonial Enlightenment*. Durham, NC: Duke University Press, 2004.

Scott, James C. *Seeing like a State: How Certain Schemes to Improve the Human Condition Have Failed*. New Haven, CT: Yale University Press, 1998.

Seigel, Micol. *Violence Work: State Power and the Limits of Police*. Durham, NC: Duke University Press, 2018.

Seikaly, Sherene. *Men of Capital: Scarcity and Economy in Mandate Palestine*. Stanford, CA: Stanford University Press, 2015.

Shaikh, Nermeen. *The Present as History: Critical Perspectives on Global Power*. New York: Columbia University Press, 2007.

Shamikh, Muhammad. *Al-Sahafa fi al-Hijaz: Dirasa wa nusus* [The press in the Hijaz, 1908–1941: Study and texts]. Beirut: Dar al-Amana, 1971.

Shapin, Steven. *The Scientific Revolution*. Chicago: Chicago University Press, 1996.

Shapin, Steven, and Simon Schaffer. *Leviathan and the Air-Pump: Hobbes, Boyle, and the Experimental Life*. Princeton, NJ: Princeton University Press, 1985.

Sharma, Aradhana, and Akhil Gupta, eds. *The Anthropology of the State: A Reader*. Oxford: Blackwell, 2006.

Sharp, Deen. "The Urbanization of Power and the Struggle for the City." *MERIP* 287 (Summer 2018).

Sheehi, Stephen. *Foundations of Modern Arab Identity*. Gainesville: University Press of Florida, 2004.

Shobaili, Abdulrahman Saleh. "An Historical and Analytical Study of Broadcasting and Press in Saudi Arabia." PhD diss., Ohio State University, 1971.

Shuaibi, Ali, and Saleh al-Hathloul. "The Justice Palace District, Riyadh." In *Continuity and Change: Design Strategies for Large-Scale Urban Development*, edited by Margaret Bentley Sevcenko, 37–48. Cambridge, MA: Aga Khan Program for Islamic Architecture at Harvard University and the Massachusetts Institute of Technology, 1984.

Sick, Gary, and Lawrence Potter. *Security in the Persian Gulf: Origins, Obstacles, and the Search for Consensus*. New York: Palgrave, 2002.

Slight, John. *The British Empire and the Hajj, 1856–1956*. Cambridge, MA: Harvard University Press, 2015.

Smith, Adam T. "Archaeologies of Sovereignty." *Annual Review of Anthropology* 40 (2011): 415–32.

Smith, Anthony. *National Identity*. London: Penguin Books, 1991.

Smith, Neil. *The New Urban Frontier: Gentrification and the Revanchist City*. London: Routledge, 1996.

Spiro, David E. *The Hidden Hand of American Hegemony: Petrodollar Recycling and International Markets*. Ithaca, NY: Cornell University Press, 1999.

Steedman, Caroline. *Dust: The Archive and Cultural History*. Newark, NJ: Rutgers University Press, 2002.

Steinberg, Guido. "Ecology, Knowledge, and Trade in Central Arabia." In *Counter-Narratives: History, Contemporary Society and Politics in Saudi Arabia and Yemen*, edited by Madawi Al-Rasheed and Robert Vitalis, 77–102. New York: Palgrave, 2004.

———. *Religion und Staat in Saudi Arabien: Die wahhabitischen Gelehrten (1902–1953)*. Würzburg, Germany: Ergon, 2002.

———. "The Wahhabi Ulama and the Saudi State." In *Saudi Arabia in the Balance: Political Economy, Society, Foreign Affairs*, edited by Paul Aarts and Gerd Nonneman, 11–34. New York: New York University Press, 2005.

Stoler, Ann Laura. *Along the Archival Grain: Epistemic Anxieties and Colonial Common Sense*. Princeton, NJ: Princeton University Press, 2009.

———. *Carnal Knowledge and Imperial Power: Race and the Intimate in Colonial Rule.* Berkeley: University of California Press, 2002.

———. "Colonial Archives and the Arts of Governance." *Archival Science* 2, no. 1–2 (2002): 87–109.

Takriti, Abdel Razzaq. *Monsoon Revolution: Republicans, Sultans, and Empires in Oman, 1965–1976.* Oxford: Oxford University Press, 2016.

Taylor, Charles. *A Secular Age.* Cambridge, MA: Harvard University Press, 2007.

Tell, Tariq Moraiwed. *The Social and Economic Origins of Monarchy in Jordan.* New York: Palgrave Macmillan, 2013.

Terlouw, Kees. "Iconic Site Development and Legitimating Policies: The Changing Role of Water in Dutch Identity Discourses." *Geoforum* 57 (2014): 30–39.

Tilley, Christopher, and Wayne Bennett. *The Materiality of Stone.* New York: Bloomsbury Academic, 2004.

Tinker Salas, Miguel. *The Enduring Legacy: Oil, Culture, and Society in Venezuela.* Durham, NC: Duke University Press, 2009.

Tinkle, Lon. *Mr. De: A Biography of Everette Lee DeGolyer.* Boston: Little, Brown, 1970.

Traboulsi, Fawwaz. *A History of Modern Lebanon.* New York: Pluto Press, 2007.

Trofimov, Yaroslav. *Siege of Mecca: The Forgotten Uprising in Islam's Holiest Shrine.* New York: Penguin Books, 2008.

Trouillot, Michel-Rolph. *Silencing the Past: Power and the Production of History.* Boston: Beacon Press, 1995.

'Ujayl, Muhsin Giyadh. *Sulaiman bin Salih al-Dakhil al-Najdi: al-sahafi, al-siyasi, al-mu'arrikh* [Sulaiman bin Salih al-Dakhil al-Najdi: The journalist, the politician, and the historian]. Beirut: Al-Dar al-Arabiyya li-l-Mawsu'at, 2002.

Vitalis, Robert. *America's Kingdom: Mythmaking on the Saudi Oil Frontier.* Stanford, CA: Stanford University Press, 2007.

Wahbah, Hafiz. *Jazirat al-'Arab fi al-qarn al-'ishrin: tabi'at Jazirat al-'Arab wa-halatuha al-ijtima'iyya al-hadira* [The Arabian Peninsula in the twentieth century: The nature of the Arabian Peninsula and its present social state]. Cairo: Lajnat al-Ta'lif wa-l-Tarjama wa-l-Nashr, 1935.

Wakim, Salim. *Al-Malik Saud: Mu'assis al-dawla al-Sa'udiyya al-haditha* [King Saud: Founder of the modern Saudi state]. 2nd ed. Beirut: Dar al-Saqi, 2011.

Wallerstein, Immanuel. "The Bourgeois(ie) as Concept and Reality." *New Left Review* 1, no. 167 (January–February 1988): 91–106.

Watts, Michael. "Petro-Violence: Community, Extraction, and Political Ecology of a Mythic Commodity." In *Violent Environments*, edited by Nancy Lee Peluso and Michael Watts, 189–212. Ithaca, NY: Cornell University Press, 2001.

———. "Petro-Violence: Some Thoughts on Community, Extraction, and Political Ecology." Paper prepared for the eScholarship Repository, University of California, 1999.

———. "Violent Geographies: Speaking the Unspeakable and the Politics of Space." *City and Society* 13, no. 1 (2001): 85–117.

Wedeen, Lisa. *Ambiguities of Domination: Politics, Rhetoric, and Symbols in Contemporary Syria*. Chicago: University of Chicago Press, 1999.

———. *Peripheral Visions: Publics, Power, and Performance in Yemen*. Chicago: University of Chicago Press, 2008.

Weld, Kirsten. *Paper Cadavers: The Archives of Dictatorship in Guatemala*. Durham, NC: Duke University Press, 2014.

Westing, Arthur H. *Pioneer on the Environmental Impact of War*. London: Springer, 2013.

White, Hayden. *Metahistory: The Historical Imagination in Nineteenth-Century Europe*. Baltimore: Johns Hopkins University Press, 1973.

Wilder, Gary. "Untimely Vision: Aimé Césaire, Decolonization, Utopia." *Public Culture* 21, no. 1 (2009): 101–40.

Wilford, Hugh. *America's Great Game: The CIA's Secret Arabists and the Shaping of the Modern Middle East*. New York: Basic Books, 2013.

Willis, John. "Burying Muhammad Ali Jauhar: The Life and Death of the Meccan Republic." Unpublished manuscript, 2019. PDF.

———. "Debating the Caliphate: Islam and Nation in the Work of Rashid Rida and Abul Kalam Azad." *International History Review* 32, no. 4 (2010): 711–32.

———. "Making Yemen Indian: Rewriting the Boundaries of Imperial Arabia." *International Journal of Middle East Studies* 41, no. 1 (2009): 23–38.

———. *Unmaking North and South: Cartographies of the Yemeni Past*. London: Hurst, 2012.

Wilson, Mary C. "The Hashemites, the Arab Revolt, and Arab Nationalism." In In *The Origins of Arab Nationalism*, edited by Rashid Khalidi, Lisa Anderson, Muhammad Muslih, and Reeva Simon, 204–24. New York: Columbia University Press, 1991.

Yamani, Mai. *Cradle of Islam: The Hejaz and the Quest of an Arabian Identity*. London: I. B. Tauris, 2004.

———."Evading the Habits of a Lifetime: The Adaptation of Hijazi Dress to the New Social Order." In *Languages of Dress in the Middle East*, edited by Nancy Lindisfarne-Tapper and Bruce Ingham, 55–66. London: Curzon, 1997.

Yaqub, Salim. *Containing Arab Nationalism: The Eisenhower Doctrine and the Middle East*. Chapel Hill: University of North Carolina Press, 2004.

Yergin, D. *The Prize*. New York: Touchstone, 1991.

Yizraeli, Sarah. *Politics and Society in Saudi Arabia: The Crucial Years of Development, 1960–1982*. New York: Columbia University Press, 2012.

Young, James Edward. *The Texture of Memory: Holocaust Memorials and Meaning*. New Haven, CT: Yale University Press, 1994.

Zirikli, Khayr al-Din. *Ma ra'ayt wa ma sami't min Dimashq ila Makkah, 1929* [What I saw and what I heard from Damascus to Mecca, 1929]. Beirut: al-Mu'assassa al-'Arabiyya li-l-Dirasat wa-l-Nashr, 2009.

Index

Page numbers in italic indicate material in figures. Names beginning with "al-" are alphabetized on the major portion of the name; for instance, al-Tariqi, Abdullah, will be found under T. Names beginning with "Ibn" are alphabetized under Ibn. Political rulers can be found under their first names; for instance, Abdullah ibn Abdulaziz Al Saud will be found under A.

Abdulaziz I (Sultan), 36, 255n28

Abdulaziz ibn Saud (King), 100; and Aramco, 10, 107; Binladin's building projects for, 170–71, 175; as British ally, 47, 49, 134, 249n110, 264–65nn106–107, 294n35; as conqueror of Mecca, Medina, 134, 294n43; as conqueror of Riyadh, 20, 45–46, 97, 99, 134–36, 247n90, 298n75; crushing Ikhwan rebellion, 49; Darah and, 74, 100–102, 111, 286n64; death of, 99; DOKAAE endowment for descendants, 184; as founding father of Saudi Arabia, 10, 55, 165; and Governance Palace District, 147–48; and Hafiz Wahba, 260n73; hagiographies of, 239n34; hiring of foreigners, 35; and Historic Riyadh complex, 99; invasion of Hijaz by, 43–44; investigating 'Awwad, 44; King Salman on, 142, 213; land annexations by, 60, 264n103; Mecca library, 314n105; market for documents of, 115; and Ministry of Finance, 68; and Muhammad Hassan 'Awwad, 44; and Murabba' Palace, 99; promoted as founding father, 10, 74; and Red Palace, 301n106; scholarship on, 58; socializing nomadic tribes, 50; succession following, 10, 55, 71, 171, 213,

358 INDEX

Abdulaziz ibn Saud (*continued*)
301n106; as US ally in World War II,
53; value of documents on, 115; Wahhabi ideology of, 50–51; war against
Hijaz, 43–44, 257n55. *See also* Darah;
DOKAAE; Governance Palace;
KFNL; King Abdulaziz Historical
Center; Al Saud
Abdulhamid (Sultan), 39
Abdullah ibn Abdulaziz Al Saud (King):
and Binladin family, 195; as Crown
Prince, 18, 93, 108, 122, 129, 151,
178, 208; death of, 204; expansion
projects under, *166*, 169, 200–201, 223,
227–28; Financial District (KAFD),
227, 290n13; Historical Center, 121; as
King, 3, 25, 122–24, 128–29, *166*, 187;
destruction of heritage in Mecca,
204; National Dialogue program,
210; orders to stop destruction
ignored, 201; pretending to threaten
Bakr Binladin, 203; on religion
and politics, 212; response to Arab
uprisings, 210–11; and Salman, 122,
129; Saudi-Israeli relations under, 221;
and Saudi Binladin Group, 203–4;
supporting Darah in archive wars,
122–24; and University of Science
and Technology, 157
Abdulmajid ibn Abdulaziz Al Saud, 184
Abdulmuhsin ibn Abdulaziz Al Saud,
140, 297n65
Abraj al-Bayt Towers, 188, 192, *193*
Abu Dhabi, 274n26
Abu Madi, Iliya, 41

Administration for Saudi Government
Documents (Idarat al-Watha'iq
al-Hukumiyya al-Sa'udiyya), 82
administrative records, 124; in al-
Wajh fortress, 61; in Darah, 73, 75,
125; definition of, 124; in deserted
buildings, 69, 84; early archiving
attempts, 76–77; *versus* historical
records, 73; IPA archiving of, 81; need
for archiving of, 62, 70, 76; Salman's
centralization of, 125
Afghanistan, 14–15, 162, 263n101
age of ignorance (*jahiliyya*), 50, 68, 167,
239n34
Ajyad fortress, 167, *183*, 184–87
Al-Abd al-Ali, Huda, 123
al-Ahmadiyya School, 42
al-Ahmari, Abd al-Rahman, 269n140
Al al-Shaykh (House of al-Shaykh), 123
Al al-Shaykh, Abdullah, 115–16
Al al-Shaykh, Abdullatif ibn Abdulmalik, 296n57
Al al-Shaykh, Abdulaziz ibn Abdullah
(Grand Mufti), 10, 118
Al al-Shaykh, Hassan ibn Abdullah,
73–74, 275–76n37
Al al-Shaykh, Muhammad ibn Ibrahim
(grand mufti), 10, 240n37, 276n37
Albert Speer & Partners, 99
Albini, Franco, 146
Al-Faisal: Shahid wa shahid exhibition,
105
Al-Hijr (Mada'in Salih) site, 131, 145,
247n95
Ali Haydar, 257n47

Ali ibn Husayn (Amir), 43
Alireza, Hajj Muhammad Ali Zaynal, 38–39
Angawi, Sami, 172, 197, 312n95
al-Ansari, Abdulrahman, 137
Anti-Forgery Law (1960), 115
antipreservation, 132
Arab Cold War, 275n32
Arab League, 244n74
Arab Revolt (1916), 37, 39–41
Arab uprisings (2011), 209, xvii
Aramco (Arabian American Oil Company/Saudi Arabian Oil Company), 267n127; archives of, 64, 68, 107–8; building Saudi infrastructure, industries, 54–55; Childs warnings regarding, 268–68n137; CIA involvement with, 54; cities built by, 170; gated communities for non-Arabs, 277n51; hindering modernization to maintain control, 57; labor activism at, 55; monopoly on development, 170; oil imperialism and environmental damage by, 56; and oil nationalization, 140; preparing for Riyadh takeover celebration, 97; producing Wahhabi-centered history, 9–10; public relations films, 271n158; as Saudi Arabian Oil Company, 64, 216, 229; Saudi dependence on, 53–54, 273n13; supporting Al Saud, 9–10, 170; urban planning, development, 54–55, 170; World War II, 53, 268n136
Arafat religious site, 202
archeological sites: demolition of, 195–96; neglect of, 131; outside of Riyadh, 145; vandalism at, 13, 109, 241n48. *See also* Mecca
archives, 77, 78–80, 86, 120–21; 1966 law under Faisal, 12, 67–72, 82, 121, 125, 137; absence of single national archive, 68, 87, 100; accidental, 80–88; Aramco's, 64, 107–8; arbitrariness of, 63; and "archival thinking," 28; Archives and Documents Protocols, 124; as authoring, authorizing future, 27; bidding wars, 115; black market sales to, 1; built environment as archive, 4; Central Archives collection, 275n31; centralization of, 96, 123, 177; competition among, 79, 106; consolidation attempts, 70–71; difficulties in accessing, 87–88, 114–15, xvii; digitizing of, 80, 82, 86, *112*, 114, 119, 226, xv–xvii; *versus* "documents," 70; fear of exposure in, 80; forgeries, 115; formation of as violent act, 26, 62–63; as form of power, 62–65, 68, 72; improper storage conditions in, 71, 113; inadvertent successes, 80–85; intentional concealment of, 62–64, 68, 107–8, 124; IPA, 77, 80–82, 85; national archive in Finance Ministry, 64, 68–70; need for oversight, 120; obstacles to centralization, 79–80; in private homes, 86, 108–9, 119, iv; and production of history, 4–5, 68; records as capital, 72–73; redefining of, 4–7, 96; and regime of silencing, 92; in Riyadh, 69–70, 129; secret

archeological sites (*continued*)
confiscation of documents, 89, 92; women lacking access to, 87. *See also* Darah; King Fahd National Archive; al-Semmari, Fahd

archive wars, 5–6, 20–22, 26; Abdullah's goals in, 122–24; around centennial celebration, 114–19; changing "facts on the ground," 27; ended by King Salman, 125–26, 213–16; goals of, 122–23; impeding centralization, 78; as making of history, 231; as paradoxical, 117–18; and religion, 72, 109; in Riyadh, 107, 114; sabotage to prevent reframing history, 21–22; "state secrets" not uncovered in, 123–24

archiving law (1966), 12, 67–72, 82, 121, 125, 137

Arriyadh Development Authority (ADA), 248n96, 281n16; as arm of HCDA, 140; building King Abdulaziz Historical Center, 99, 142, 149, 153–55; building national museum, 151–52; building Red Palace, 152–53; concerns about master plan errors, 141; dealing with harrassment, intruders, 131, 144; developing al-Turaif District, 161, 302n119; establishment of, 138; ignoring MOMRA, 145; and Muhammad ibn Abdulaziz Al-Shaykh, 290n15; not preserving Bujairi buildings, 159; overseeing centennial planning, 99, 127, 133, 142, 151–52; redeveloping Dir'iyya, 22, 133, 148, 151; redeveloping Governance Palace District, 147–49; redeveloping Riyadh, 22–23, 99, 132–33, 148, 151, 156; rejecting experimental software, 157; Salman and, 93, 99, 132, 143–44, 213–14; sidelining of, 227; statement on Riyadh plans, 99–100

Asad, Talal, 212–13

Ashiyya School, 36

Ashraf, 110n249; Ajyad Fortress, 186; *al-Qibla* newspaper, 40; British competition with, 47; Jabal Hindi Fortress, 189; popular revolt against, 257n47; as previous rulers of Hijaz/Mecca, 24, 38–40, 43, 169, 249–50n110; private endowment lands of, 181; records finds of, 61

Ashshi, Abdulwahhab, 39

'Ashura celebration crackdown, 13–14

Asian pilgrims to Iraq, 264n104

'Asir region, 51, 249n110

'Awwad, Muhammad Hassan, 39, 41, 44

al-Badr, Hasan Ali (Imam), 42, 260n72

Badr ibn Farhan Al-Saud, 229

Badran, Rasem, 99, 147

Bafaqih, Husayn, 41

Bahrain, 210, 260n72, xix

al-Banat al-Ahliyya School, 189

Barid al-Hijaz/Sawt al-Hijaz newspaper, 39, 43, 256n41, 261n81

Bartholomew, Harland, 127, 289n2

Basic Law of Government (1992), 17

Bechtel Corporation, 54

Benjamin, Walter, 187

Berman v. Parker (US Supreme Court), 144
Best, Martyn, 99
Binladin, Bakr, 200–201, 203, 205, 218, 223
Binladin, Muhammad, 170–72, 174–76, 304n10. *See also* Muhammad Binladin Organization (MBO); Saudi Binladin Group
black market in historical documents, 1–3, 96, 107, 235n12
Boedeker, Wagenfeld & Partners, 99
Britain: aiding Arab Revolt (1916), 41; bombarding Jeddah, 31; encouraging Abdulaziz conquests, 47; and the Great Game, 263n101; losing out to US-Saudi ties, 53; on Mecca as rebel haven, 30; national repository for documents, 79; Qatif and Jeddah treaties, 264n107; redevelopment proposal for Dirʿiyya, 156; and Saudi oil economy, 80
Bujairi District (Dirʿiyya), 159, *160*, 162
Buro Happold, 99, 147, 151

capitalism: Abdulaziz and, 35, 58; capital accumulation, 20; "capitalist clock," 187; declining property rights under, 194–95; destroy and rebuild strategy, 179; effects of on property market, 15; as global, 31; in Mecca, 169, 174, 178; petrocapitalism, 34, 164; Salman and, 93; in urban development, 291n22; Wallerstein on, 194; Walter Benjamin on, 187

centennial celebration (1999), *98*, 130; ADA and, 133, 142–46, 149; budget freeze following, 121; building of cultural center, 99–100; commemorating capture of Riyadh, 97; and national museum, 151; presenting secular history, 122; Princess Fahda's presentation at, 104; research for, 100–103; sparking search for historical source material, 114; semicentennial of Riyadh conquest, 20, 97, *98*
Center for Documents and Archives. *See* IPA
Central Archives, 69–70, 75, 275n31
Chandoke, Neera, 207
Chaudhry, Kiren Aziz, 79
Childs, J. Rives, 268–69n137
Clark, Arthur P., 99, 294n40
Clausewitz, Carl von, 129
Cold War, 17, 53, 56, 64–65, 71, 137, 171, 275n32
colonialism, 8, 56, 64, 222
Committee of Union and Progress (CUP), 39–40, 53, 257n47
communism, 41, 259n67
constitutionalism, 32, 37–39, 220, 256n39, 257n47
corporations, Saudi dependence on, 52–55, 59. *See also* Muhammad Binladin Organization
Council of Ministers: and ADA, 140; approving Doxiadis Plan, 137; approving MEDSTAR, 128; calling for maintaining historical sites, 293n28; committees to regulate archives,

Council of Ministers (*continued*)
76–77; and Darah, 73, 75, 121, 123; edicts regarding document owners, 106; and IPA, 81; and KFNL, 279n71; Manuscripts Law (2002), 117; and MOMRA, 296n56; moved to Riyadh by Saud, 295n43; national archives in compound of, 87, 277n50; NCDA and, 77–79, 226, 277n49; Salman and, 125, 139–40, 285n52; Sultan requesting permission to destroy documents, 76

Council of Senior Scholars, 118, 292nn25–26

Cox, Percy, 264n107

cultural production, 128, 163; Al Saud and, 66; Darah and, 102; King Fahd limiting religion's role in, 18; of Middle East, 33, 41; of Riyadh, 23

Dahlan, Ahmad ibn Zayni, 36, 255n26, 256n36

Al-Dahu, 153–55, *154*

Dallah Albarakah, 25, 192

Dammam, 54, 105, 170, 297n66

al-Damuk, Khudran, 120

Darah (King Abdulaziz Foundation for Research and Archives), *113*, xv; Abdullah's interest in, 122–23; accused of hoarding documents, 119, 122; accused of pandering, 118; accused of rewriting history, 2, 21, 105–6, 109–10, 118–19; on Al Saud collaboration with British, US, 285n53; Aramco donations of records to, 273n13; attempts to enlarge mandate, 110; budget cuts, 121; building of, 99; categorization of, 73; centralizing historical, nongovernmental records, 2, 12, 101, 123–24; collecting abandoned historical records, *91*; conferences on history, 103; digitizing documents, *112*; documents from other countries, 111; engaging in knowledge production, 21–22; focusing on King Abdulaziz, postwar narrative, 101, 114; funds frozen for conservation, computerization, 121; ignoring, destroying documents, 119; improper storage of documents, 111, 113–14, 119; lack of initial funding, space for, 100–102; in Ma'zar, 100, 102; mobile labs for sterilization, restoration, 89, *90*, 92; move to King Abdulaziz Historical Center, 102; national survey of historical documents, 89, 127; as people's archive, 73–74; Prince Salman's support of, 6, 101–4, 111, 113, 285n52; prioritization in document preservation, 113; promoting history of Al Saud, 74, 116–17, 118; purchasing documents, 1, 111; *Rare Manuscript Exhibition on Saudi Arabia*, 2, 116, 133; resistance against, 109, 118–19; secret copying, confiscation of documents, 92; al-Semmari support for, 101–2; translations of Ottoman documents, 283n28; wanting power to control all documents, 106; and war over ownership of history, 106. *See also* al-Semmari, Fahd

Dar al-Handasah, 176

"day of rage" (2011), 210–11
De Cesari, Chiara, 5
Department of Antiquities, 23, 156
Derrida, Jacques, 27, 121
Development of King Abdulaziz Endowment Project (DOKAAE), 181, *182*, 184–89, *185*, *193*, 204, 206, 308n50
Dhahran, 53, 107, 170, 269n140
Dirʿiyya, 146, 234n4; Abdulaziz and, 208; al-Turaif District renovation, 155–61, *160*; destruction of, exile from, 46, 134–35, 147; as first Saudi state, 155, 159; Formula E racing championship in, 162; redevelopment plans for, 22, 130, 135, 142–43; harassment of workers at, 131; Salman personal funding for, 143; UNESCO World Heritage Site status, 161; Vision 2030 and, 227
disciplinary historiography, 9–14
documents: accidental finds, 84; collecting but not processing, 123; Darah seeking power over all, 106; dispersal of, 119, 123; "documents" (*wathaʾiq*) versus "archives" (*mahfuzat*), 70, 276–77n49; international market for, 115; lack of conservation expertise, 71; overaccumulation of, 71; traders in, 1–2, 115; forged, 1, 107, 111, 115. *See also* archives
Doughty, Charles, 258n59
Doxiadis Plan, 137, 139, 141, 146

education: under colonialism, 253n12; Faisal's centralization of, 11; al-Kairanawi school in Mecca, 32

Egypt: conflict with Saudi regime in Yemen, 56, 96; document finds regarding, 61–62; document protocol with Anwar al-Sadat, 209–10; documents on pilgrimage caravans to Mecca, 2; Gamal Abdel Nasser, 10, 56, 64–67, 72, 152, 221, 274n19; and military zone at Neom site, 220–21; Muhammad Kamal Ismail, 175–78, 184, 186, 196, 240n45; Muslim Brotherhood, 10, 16; proposal to develop Dirʿiyya, 156; Saudi information war with, 67; Saudi middle class interest in, 41; and Suez Canal, 61; troops sent against Al Saud, 46, 133–34. *See also* Nasser, Gamal Abdel
1857 Rebellion, 30
eminent domain, 144, 192
endowments (*waqf*), 144, 181. *See also* Development of King Abdulaziz Endowment Project
erasure of history, 32–34; as "act of chronophagy," 34; by Al Saud, 119; and erasure *as* history, 5; Hijazi participation in, 45; justification for, 24; in Mecca, 165, 168, 197, 205–7; remaking Saudi Arabia's cities through, 24; in Riyadh, 207; through destruction of records, objects, spaces, 4–5, 20, 23–24, 33, 163; through silencing of voices, 229
expropriation of private property: denied, 144, 146; of Dirʿiyya, 156; in Mecca, 190, 192; MOMRA control over, 139; in Riyadh, 221; ruling family and, 25; by Salman, 224

364 INDEX

Facey, William, 99
Fahda bint Saud ibn Abdulaziz Al Saud, 104–6, 152
Fahd ibn Abdulaziz Al Saud (King), 128–29, 216; and 1991 Gulf War, 14–16; as custodian of Mecca, Medina, 169, 204, 245n80; establishing Supreme Council of Islamic Affairs, 245n80; father of Faisal, 241n46; health issues, 83, 93; King Fahd Expansion Project in Mecca, 3, 175, 178, 195, 201; limiting religious influence, 18; promoting secularism, 95–96; purchase, redevelopment of Dirʻiyya, 156; reforms to counter protests (1992), 17–18; reign of (1982–2005), 175, 216; Sahwa protesting US troops on Saudi soil, 16–17; and Salman, 19, 93, 213, 280–81n8; on sharia, 245n76. *See also* King Fahd National Library (KFNL)
Faisal ibn Abdulaziz Al Saud (Prince/King), 175, 241n46; archiving project, 12, 67–68, 70–72, 125; centralizing education, economy, 11–12, 66–67; as crown prince, 55, 103–4; death of, 73, 75; and Egypt, 209; familial fiefdoms under, 72; ideology of, 240n37; incorporating religious institutions under state, 10; investigating ʻAwwad, 44; as king, 66, 71, 137, 171; King Faisal Center for Research and Islamic Studies, 1, 114, 286–87n68; media law constraining press, 67; and Ministry of Foreign Affairs, 71; and narrative of Saudi exceptionalism, 57–58; Nasser opposition to, 65–66; official history, 66, 241n46; overthrowing and discrediting Saud (1964), 10–12, 55–56, 65–67, 80, 103–5, 284n39; repression of dissidents by, 65; and Riyadh, 12, 69, 137; self-proclaimed protector of Muslim faith, 66; supporting Darah, 73; Ten-Point Program, 105; US backing for, 56, 66
Fakih, Adel, 223
al-Fakhriyya School, 37
al-Falah School, 38–39, 41
Farooqui, Imdadullah, 30
al-Fatat al-Ahliyya School, 189
al-Fawzan, Salih ibn Fawzan, 292n26
Formula E racing championship, 162
Foucault, Michel, 251n128
Free Princes, 284n45

General Administration for Central Archives, 69–70
General Auditing Bureau, 76–77
George Rentz collection, 278n63
Ghalib ibn Masaʻid (r. 1880–1882), 189
Gibran, Gibran Khalil, 41
global recession, 17, 178
Goffman, Erving, 251n128
Governance Palace (Qasr al-Hukm), 128, 130, 135, 146–48, 152, 291n18
Grand Mosque (Mecca), *182*, *193*; Binladin contracts for expansion, 171–72; documents found underneath, 1, 125; dynamiting fortress near mosque, 3, 167, *183*, 184–85; Holy Mosque Expansion Project, *166*, 167, 195, 312n89; Is-

mail's plans disregarded by Binladin, 176–77; lack of media coverage of destruction, 3–4; planned demolition and expansion, 1–3, 204; takeover by religious insurgents, 13–14. *See also* Mecca

grand mufti (*shaykh al-Islam*), 10, 18, 36, 118, 188, 242n53, 244n69

Great Depression, 52

Great Game, 263n101

Gulf War (1991), 92, 145; activism following, 108; aftermath of, 4–6, 14–16, 129, 168, 179, 204; effects of on Abdulaziz, 208; effects of on Saudi Arabia, 92, 94–95, 129; popular protests against, 15–16, 132; revisionism in response to, 19–20, 24–26, 64, 80, 96, 99, 122, 142; Al Saud and, 92–93, 95, 130, 132, 145, 163

Hacking, Ian, 251n128

Hadrami merchants, 171, 304n10

hajj/pilgrimage to Mecca. *See* pilgrims/pilgrimage

Hajj Research Center, 172–73, 196, 305n17

Hamidian clock, 187

Harland Bartholomew and Associates, 127, 289n2

Hasa, 47, *48*, 51

Hashemites. *See* Ashraf

al-Hathloul, Saleh, 137, 147, 151, 155

al-Hawali, Safar, 17

High Commission for the Development of Arriyadh/Riyadh (HCDA), 127–28, 138–40, 146–47

heritage: Abdullah Al al-Shaykh on, 115–16; as an industry in Riyadh, xiii, 23, 128–30, 137, 141, 146, 168, 205; construction of, 24, 129–30, 142; financialization and commodification of, 25, 106; global approval of destruction in name of, 162–63; and Governance Palace District, 147; Janadriyya Festival, 122; Jubba Heritage Town, 25; loss of in Mecca, 29, 168, 189, 197–98, 204–5; Muhammad ibn Salman and, 228–29; Salman ibn Abdulaziz and, 60–61, 92–93, 108–9, 129, 144, 205, 227–28; Al Saud's revision of, 19–24, 95–96, 123, 141–43, 159, 198; sites considered security issue, 137; and Sultan ibn Salman, 23, 145, 205, 228–29; tourist replicas, souvenirs presented as, 155–56; and use of eminent domain, 144; World Heritage Sites, 145, 157–58, 161, 247n95; in Yemen, 186. *See also* ADA; Dir'iyya; erasure of history

Hijaz/Hijazis, 47, 61, 71; Ashraf in, 24, 61; building of Ajyad Fortress, 186; and constitutionalism, 38; geopolitical influences on, 31–34, 41, 51; and Hajj Research Center, 172; Hijaz National Party (al-Hizb al-Watani al-Hijazi), 43, 45; *al-Hijaz* newspaper, 40, 260n76; and House of Saud, 43–45, 50, 189; intellectualism and politics, 40–44; landowners in Mecca, 192, 194; middle class in, 41; railway, 39–40; and rights of women, 44; and Riyadh

Hijaz/Hijazis (*continued*)
    construction, 136; road system in, 171–72; Salman rewriting of history, 229–30; Saudi occupation of, 43–44
hikr, 144
al-Hindi. *See* al-Kairanawi, Muhammad Rahmatullah
historical sites: construction workers trade in found documents, 1–2; High Commission for Antiquities, 293n28; historical tourism, 128; leaders' visits after destruction of, 293n32; loss of to vandals, 13; religious disagreements, vandalism, 131–32; selective development of, 25. *See also* Mecca, demolition/destruction of; Riyadh
historiography: and "archive fever," 22; Darah attempts to control, 105–6, 108–9, 118; in Egypt, 274n19; Egyptian/Saudi negotiations on, 209–10; lack of historical site preservation, 132; in Mecca, 181; political importance of, 10, 213; and "religious time," 9; revisionism compromising, 35, 44–45, 55–56, 59, 66; and Wahhabism, 11
history, 263n97; Al Saud as having none, xiii–xv; concept of progress in, 9; connected to violence, 126, xiii; Faisal's rewriting of, 67–68; flattening of, 197; importance of materiality to, xv; and memory, 12, xiv; as politics, 95; private family archives of, xiv; production of, 5, xv; as sacrosanct in Saudi Arabia, xi–xiii; as told by Aramco, 9–10
Al-Hofuf Historical City Center, 25

Hopkins, Harry L., 268n131
Husayn ibn Ali (Sharif), 37, 39–41, 43, 53, 189, 249n110, 257n47, 264n104
al-Hussayin, Salih ibn Abdulrahman (Shaykh), 200–201, 314n102
Hussein, Saddam, 15, 94

Ibn Abd al-Wahhab, Muhammad (Shaykh), 2–3; Abdulaziz's comments regarding, 208; alliance with Al Saud (1744), 2, 8, 96, 128, 133, 234n4, 247n90; and Al Saud, 9–11, 62, 123, 132–34, 161–62, 247n90; birth and early years, 234n4; and concept of the state, 2, 263n102; Darah exhibition excluding documents on, 2; grandson first chair of Darah, 73–74; Hijri centennial not marking, 20; historical sites connected to, 159–62, *160*; ideology of, 19–20, 45; Ikhwan and, 47; Mosque of, 161; move to Dir'iyya, 234n4; and Riyadh, 69, 133; Sheikh Mohammad bin Abdulwahhab Cultural Foundation, 161; shrine visitation forbidden by, 45–46. *See also* Wahhabi/Al Saud alliance
Ibn Baz, Abdulaziz (Shaykh), 18, 188, 242n53, 244n69, 292n25, 309n65, 310n66
Ibn Fahd, Abdulaziz, 120, 122
Ibn Ghalib, Abdulmuttalib (Amir), 38
Ibn Junayd, Yahya, 12, 287n72, 321n44; document find in al-Wajh fortress, 61; document find in Qasr Ibrahim, 60–61; earning library science degrees,

84; as head of KFNL, 60, 83–86; on lack of proper national archive, 87, 119–20, 283n35; on national "memory loss," 89
Ibn Muammar, Abdulaziz, 55
Ibn Saud, Abdulaziz. *See* Abdulaziz Ibn Saud (King)
Ibrahim Pasha, 133–34
Idarat al-Watha'iq al-Hukumiyya al-Saʿudiyya (Administration for Saudi Government Documents), 82
Idhhar al-Haqq (The Truth Revealed), 36, 57
Ikhwan, 47–49, 239n35, 242n53, 264n106
Imam Muhammad ibn Saud Islamic University, 84
infitah (liberal period), 210, xvi
Institute of Public Administration (IPA): classifying, cataloging administrative records, 81–82; and Darah, 111; digitizing of records, 82; lack of awareness of, 79, 83, 103; renaming of, 82; second National Center for Documents and Archives, 77; standardization by, 85; as threat to national archive, 86
International Council on Monuments and Sites (ICOMOS), 158–59, 162
Iraq, 94–95, 153, 264n106; Ikhwan raids on, 48–49; Iran-Iraq War, 15, 17, 244n74; Iraqi Revolt (1920), 42; US troops in, 17, 94. *See also* Gulf War
Islamic Awakening (al-Sahwa al-Islamiyya), 16–17
Ismail, Muhammad Kamal, 175–78, 184, 186, 196, 240n45

Jabal Hindi Fortress, 189–91
jahiliyya (age of ignorance), 50, 68, 167, 239n34
Jeddah, 25, 180, 259n67, 264n107
Jones, Toby C., 242n58
journalists: banned from covering destruction, 200, 204, 315n107; murder of Jamal Khashoggi, 225; and new press law, 67; pushed for active support, xvii–xviii; working within the system, 108
Jubba Heritage Town, 25
judicial branch, 13, 18
Justice Palace, 128, 130, 135, 146–48, 152, 291n18
Justice Square (Sahat al-ʿAdl), 130, 148

Kaaba: dictating direction of prayer, 29; Muhammad ibn Salman walking on, 228; as priceless, 30, 32
KAHC. *See* King Abdulaziz Historical Center
al-Kairanawi, Muhammad Rahmatullah: fighting British colonization, 30, 32; escape to Mecca, 30–31, 36; establishing school, 32, 36–38, 165, 189; death of, 39; and archive wars, 181; as esteemed scholar, 251–52n1; rebranded as national hero, 229; *The Truth Revealed*, 57; and Wahhabism, 34
Karbala, 49, 264n104
Khalid al-Faisal ibn Abdulaziz Al Saud, 205, 254n18

368   INDEX

Khalid ibn Abdulaziz Al Saud (King), 243n60; documents handling under, 12, 75–76; Prince Salman on, 213; putting down uprising, 14; requested to increase security in Mecca, 242–43n59; reversing university name change, 284n39; succeeded by Fahd, 83
Khashoggi, Jamal, 225
al-Khatib, Ahmad Aqil, 229
al-Khatib, Muhibb al-Din, 40
Khobar, 170
King Abdulaziz. *See* Abdulaziz ibn Saud
King Abdulaziz Center for Knowledge and Culture (Dhahran), 107
King Abdulaziz Center for World Culture (Ithra), 285n56
King Abdulaziz Historical Center (KAHC), 148–49; ADA development of, 99; before and after centennial, 121; Al-Dahu's adobe homes, shops, 153–55, *154*; before/after photos, *149–50*; Darah in, 102; financing of, 146; National Museum, 121, 142–43, 149; obtaining land from owners, 144–45; public use of outdoor spaces, 152
King Abdulaziz Public Library, 99, 114, 149, 278n63
King Abdullah. *See* Abdullah ibn Abdulaziz Al Saud
King Fahd. *See* Fahd ibn Abdulaziz Al Saud
King Fahd National Library (KFNL), 278n63, xvi; as accidental archive, 80, 85–86; archiving system of, 85; contents of, 60–61, 83–85, 111; declared Saudi Arabia's National Library, 83; Prince Salman and, 86, 103, 111, 117; purchasing documents, 1; relationship with Darah, 60, 103, 114, 116–17; Yahya Ibn Junayd as head, 60–61, 84, 119
King Faisal. *See* Faisal ibn Abdulaziz Al Saud
King Khalid. *See* Khalid ibn Abdulaziz Al Saud
King Saud. *See* Saud ibn Abdulaziz Al Saud
knowledge production, 4–5, 230–31, 242n57; Aramco and, 56; under Faisal, 67, 70, 73; *lieux de mémoire* as, 129; and mass printing technology, 255n36; materiality and, 28; in Mecca redevelopment, 169; mobile exhibits as, 105; regime control of, 21–22; "secondary Orientalism," 8
Kuwait, 42, 46–49, 94–95, 153, 235n8

land marketization/speculation, 27, 132, 206
land reclamation/land grabbing, 139, 194. *See also* Mecca; Riyadh
Law of the Consultative Council (1992), 17
Law of the Provinces (1992), 17
Lefebvre, Henri, 164
Lend-Lease Act (US 1942), 53
Lind, Nils E., 169–70

Mada'in Salih, 145, 247n95
Madrasat Tahdir al-Bi'that, 189

INDEX 369

Majid ibn Abdulaziz Al Saud, 296n57, 297n65
Majlis al-Shura (Consultative Council), 17
al-Malaz development, 136
al-Malibari, Abdullah ibn Muhyi Aldin, 30
al-Manar magazine, 41, 260n76
Manuscripts Law (Saudi Arabia), 117
Masha'ir religious site, 202
mashru' nizam al-mahfuzat (regulation system for archives), 77
Masmak Fortress, 99, 142, 146–48, 298n75
Masri, Abdullah, 13
materiality, 4, 21, 28, 164, 235n12, xv
Mbembe, Achille, 72
Mecca, 254n22; Abdulaziz takeover of (1924), 134; Amir of, 37, 39–41, 43, 53, 189, 249n110, 257nn47, 258n63; Arab Revolt (1916), 41; becoming a neoliberal city, 168; building of more museums, 206; commercialization of, 209; competing visions for, 39; current state of, 195–96; documents stolen from, 119, 288n79; governors beholden to king, 180; hajj-related deaths in, 173; middle class in, 41; Muslim pilgrims to, 205; Muslims in, 3, 7, 29, 30, 32; new development, 166, 167, 196; newspapers in, 40; as nineteenth-century rebel haven, 30–31; Ottoman influence on, 32, 37; pilgrimage/hajj to, 111, 133, 172–73, 180, 190, 205, 267n126; pre–Al Saud history of, 168; private endowment lands (*waqf dhirri*) in, 181, 184; private-public initiatives in, 194; protests in, 200; railroad bringing safety to, 39–40; real-estate market in, 178–79, 181, 189, 197; records of, 33–34; rental properties in, 179–80; Saudi king as official guardian over, 175–76; Saudi-Wahhabi attack on (1803), 133; schools in, 36; sedition charges in, 38; as tourist destination, 190, 205; traffic, parking, noise issues in, 172–73
Mecca, demolition/destruction of: Arabization of street/building names, 205; dehistoricizing of, 24–25, 33–34, 169; displacement of residents, 192, 193, xii–xiv; government disregard for ownership rights, 184; Ismail's expansion plan, 176–78; local opposition to construction, 197–99; Master Plan competition after demolition, 204; memorialization through destruction, 165, 179; no master plan for development, 202; plans to demolish library (Maktabat Makkah al-Mukarramah), 201, 204; razing of poor neighborhoods, 178; redevelopment of, 172–77, 194–96, 201, 293n32; residents' attempts to protect, 177–78, 199–200; seat of government moved from (1956), 69, 294–95n43; Wahhabis targeting monumentalization, 180–81, 199; work done in secret, 180. *See also* pilgrims/pilgrimage

Mecca Development Authority (MDA), 176–77, 184, 190, 196, 201–3, 303n4, 313–14n101

Medina: Abdulaziz takeover of (1924), 134; historical sites destroyed, 140, 202; Muslims in, 3, 7, 29, 30, 32; newspapers based in, 257n54; property owners in, 180; Saudi king as official guardian over, 175–76; Saudi-Wahhabi attack on (1803), 133

MEDSTAR (Metropolitan Development Strategy for the Arriyadh Region), 22, 127–28, 130, 214, 218, 291n21

Mehmet Ali Pasha, 133–34

memorialization: for 1996 centennial, 130; as historical, not religious, 6, 19–21, 121, 131–32; in Mecca, 168, 179; post-Gulf War, 6, 19–21, 130; religious objections to, 129–34, 168; in Riyadh, 134, 142, 165; technocratic nature of, 163; by victors, 126

Mina religious site, 202, 217

ministers. *See* Council of Ministers

Ministry of Agriculture, 69

Ministry of Culture, 229

Ministry of Defense, 71

Ministry of Defense and Aviation, 77

Ministry of Economy, 69

Ministry of Economy and Planning, 278n65

Ministry of Education, 69; Department of Antiquities under, 23; and Egyptian Muslim Brotherhood, 16; under king's jurisdiction, 11; permission for Salman/KNFL to house documents, 60–61; previously Ministry of Knowledge, 272n2; under religious control, 14, 62; and textbook content, xii

Ministry of Finance and National Economy: under Abdullah, 124, 128–29; Aramco records in, 107; archives as General Administration for Central Archives, 69; committee to regulate (1976), 76; creation of, 69; declared national archive, 68; under Fahd, 128–29; Faisal commission for, 70; freezing funding for Darah document conservation, computerization, 121; funding Dir'iyya redevelopment, 156; funding national museum, 151; funding Riyadh redevelopment, 129, 143, 247n95; HCDA control of, 128; and IPA, 77; under Prince Salman, 143; restructured of (2003), 278n65; Salman moving sovereign wealth fund to PIF, 227

Ministry of Foreign Affairs, 71, 77

Ministry of Health, 69

Ministry of Higher Education, 201

Ministry of Information, 67

Ministry of Interior, 61, 69, 71–72, 172

Ministry of Islamic Affairs, 211

Ministry of Justice, 10, 71–72, 242n59

Ministry of Knowledge, 272n2

Ministry of Municipal and Rural Affairs (MOMRA): ADA going around, 133, 145; and Doxiadis plan, 137, 139, 141; establishment of, 296n56–58; increasing power of, 139–40; Jeddah flooding due to corruption, 296–

97n60; muting evidence contradicting official history, 25; plans for Mecca development ignored, 173–77, 187, 198; and Riyadh development, 127
Ministry of Petroleum and Mineral Resources, 107
Ministry of Planning, 278n65
Ministry of Transportation, 69
Mit'ib ibn Abdullah ibn Abdulaziz Al Saud, 212, 223, 296n57, 317n6, 319n35
mobile exhibits, 105
monumentalization: by Darah, 121; as forbidden under Wahhabism, 180, 241; in Mecca, 197; as mediated form of worship, 13; as practiced by Al Saud, 93, 97, 130, 132, 197, 207, 230, xv; as twenty-first century phenomenon, 131
Moriyama & Teshima architects, 99, 151
Mount Bulbul, 181, 184
al-Mubarak, Faisal, 136, 140
al-Mubarakiyya school, 42
al-Mufid newspaper, 40
Al-Mughannam, Ali, 12, 143, 157
Muhammad Binladin Organization (MBO), 152, 171–72, 175, 177. *See also* Saudi Binladin Group (SBG)
Muhammad ibn Salman ibn Abdulaziz Al Saud, 71; crackdown on Sahwa, 220; HCDA under, 127–28, 138–40; private-public projects under, 219; promising fewer restrictions, 222; public dissatisfaction with, 218; and SBG contracts transferred to, 217; and Supreme Council of the Saudi Arabian Oil Company, 229; Vision 2030, 218, 229; walking atop Kaaba, 228; and 'Awamiyya protests, 219

Muhammad ibn Abd al-Wahhab Mosque, 161–62, 247n90
Muhammad ibn Nayif ibn Abdulaziz Al Saud, 223
Muhammad ibn Saud (died 1765), 45–46, 71, 133, 148, 159, *160*
Mumford, Lewis, 127
Murabba' Palace (Qasr al-Murabba'), 99, 130, 135, 149
Muscat, 274n26
Museum of Archeology and Ethnography, 12, 134–35
museums: in Mecca, 206; National Museum, 3, 99, 121, 131, 142–43, 149–52, 156, 240n43; neighborhood museums, archives, 12
Muslim Brotherhood, 10, 16, 220, 244n72
Mustafa IV (Sultan), 133
mutawwa'a, 47–48
Muzdalifa religious site, 202

Nahda, 32, 38–45, 253n10, 259n65
Najaf, 49, 264n104
Najd, 258n59, 264n103; Abdulaziz threat against, 49; adobe architecture in, 161; Al Saud history in, 23, 45–47, 50–51, 69; annexation of al-Ahsa, 60; British and, 264n107; Guido Steinberg on, 260n71; and Hijaz, 194, 312n87; official narrative of, 62, 118, 122; state-building project in, 167–68; tourist attractions in, 155; Wahhabis in, 48–50, 62, 240n37
nasiha, 209, 212, 225

372 INDEX

Nasser, Gamal Abdel, 10, 56, 64–67, 72, 152, 221, 274n19
National Center for Documents and Archives (NCDA): Abdulaziz ibn Fahd overseeing, 122; budget for, 78; and Darah, 74–75, 100–101, 103, 114, 125; Fahd al-Semmari overseeing, 125, 281n12; failure of, 94, 107; IPA archive by same name, 77; number of employees at, 283n35; relocated to and renamed NCAR, 226, 277n49; Salman sidelining, 125; supervision of, 77–78. *See also* Darah; NCAR
National Museum, 3, 99, 131, 142–43, 149–52, 156, 240n43
Nayif ibn Abdulaziz Al Saud, 71–72, 139, 210, 216
National Center for Archives and Records (NCAR), 74, 125, 226, 277n49
neoliberalism, 168, 195, 306n35
Neom, 220–21, 223
al-Nisa', Sawlat, 36
Nora, Pierre, 22
Nu'aimi, Mikhail, 41

al-Odah, Salman (Shaykh), 17
oil: 1938 Saudi discovery of, 52; 1973 boycott, 172; 1980s oil glut, 178; Aramco-built cities, 170; as blessing on Al Saud, 7, xii; diversification from, 178–79; impact of petrowealth, 131, 170; impact of price of, 15–16, 167; and Mecca real estate, 190; and "petromodernity," 11; Saudi Arabia as "swing producer," 7; steering away from, 25

Okruhlik, Gwenn, 249n104
Orientalism, 7–8, 30, 103, 231
Osman Nuri Pasha, 37–38, 189
Ottomans/Ottoman Empire: in 1800s, 31; Arab Revolt against (1916), 37, 39–41, 61; constitutional revolution (1908), 39; fall of, 134; influence in Mecca, 34, 36–37; and mass printing, 255–56n36; vilified by Al Saud, 19, 50, 62. *See also* al-Kairanawi, Muhammad Rahmatullah
Al Oula, 192

pearl trade, 42, 52
Pfander, D. Karl Gottlieb, 30, 36, 255n28
pilgrims/pilgrimage: Al Saud controlling, 29, 46, 168; and al-Wajh fortress, 61; competing with tourism, 205–6; construction during, 166–67; construction of/around Grand Mosque, 167, 188; documents regarding, 2, 61, 92, 111; Hajj Research Center regarding, 173–74; MBO mosques expansions, 175–76; MOMRA and, 296n56; no emergency planning for, 196; numbers of, 175, 205, 267n126, 303n5; post World War I, 40; privatization of prayer space, 194, 309n65; property speculators superseding, 174; as revenue source, 167, 170, 178–81, 190, 206, 264n104; safety of as demolition justification, 186; stampede after road closure, 217; transportation, parking for, 166, 172; VIP accommodations for, 188, 217; Wahhabi disruption of, 133; dur-

ing World War II, 52. *See also* Mecca, demolition/destruction of
political prisoners, 162, xiv
politics: competing zones of authority, 6; politico-religious socialization, 13, 18, 34, 133, 244n72, 247n90; as struggle over history, 96
polytheism, accusations of, 13, 46
press, suppression of, 66–67, 200
printing press, 38, 256n36, 257n54
private archives, 108–9
private endowment lands, 181, 184
property owners: displacement of, xiii–xiv; eminent domain, forcible eviction of, 192
Prophet Muhammad: home of, 180, 190; library on birth site of, 167, 200–201, 202; presidential palace planned for birth site, 204
provincial councils, 17

Qadriyya, 36
Qari, Abd al-Haqq, 37
al-Qarni, 'Aidh, 225
Qasr Alhukm Area Development Office, 147
Qasr Ibrahim, 60–61, 84
Qatif, 12, 42, 51, 170, 242n58, 264n107
qibla (direction of Muslim prayer), 29
al-Qibla gazette, 40–41, 43, 260n76

Al-Rajhi Holding Group, 25
Rare Manuscript Exhibition on Saudi Arabia, 2, 116–17, 133, 288n78
Rasch, Achmed, 206
Rasch, Bodo, 206

Al-Rasheed, Madawi, 247n90
Al Rasheed clan, 46, 97, 134
Red Palace (Al-Qasr al-Ahmar), 130, 146, 152–53
Reich & Petch designers, 99
religion: becoming a threat to regime, 17–18; distancing of from politics, 69, 97, 108, 129, 208, 212–13; instrumentalization of, 6; international pressure for reform, xi; legitimizing destruction, 167–68; limited under King Fahd regime, 18; religious innovation (*bid'a*) accusations, 131; "religious time," 9, 19; Saudi textbook reforms, xi–xii. *See also* Wahhabism
rentierism, 194, 222, 231
revisionism, 26, 35, 58–59, 95, 179, xviii
Rida, Rashid, 41–42
Rihani, Ameen, 265n109
Riyadh, 69–70, 136; Al Saud control of, 46, 97, 98, 134, 140–42; archive wars within, 77, 114, 116; celebration of conquest of, 20, 97, 98; Darah/ADA renovation of "old city" within, 22, 24, 135, 142–43; development near al-Futah, 135; Faisal and, 12, 137; false narrative regarding, 22, 105; General Administration for Central Archives in, 69–70; heritage industry in, 23, xiii; Hijri centennial/semicentennial of conquest of, 20, 97, 98; "historic district" (Al-Mantiqa al-Tarikhiyya), 99, 128, 136, 143–44, 152, 277; internal migration to, 139; master plans, deviations from, 140; MEDSTAR development

Riyadh (*continued*)
  plan, 22, 127–28, 291n21; modernization/redevelopment of, 99, 135–37; neglect, destruction of sites in, 135; price of land in, 141; Prince Salman's redevelopment of, 22, 92–93, 127–29, 144; rejecting adobe homes, 136; seat of government moved to (1956), 69; traffic issues, 148; urban development of in 1950s, 134; urban sprawl in, 128, 141; as Wahhabi birthplace, 69; water tower, 99. *See also* Darah; King Abdulaziz Historical Center
RMJM (Robert Matthew Johnson Marshall), 172
al-Rukban, Abdullah, 156
Rushdiye school, 37

Sabban, Muhammad Surur, 44, 230
al-Sadat, Anwar, 72, 209
Al Sagheer, 192
al-Sahwa al-Islamiyya (Islamic Awakening), 244n72, 245n77; mass support for, 16–17, 19; objecting to US troop presence, 17; opposing Al Saud, 95, 211; religious objections to Al Saud, 149, 151; suppression of, 125, 220, 225
Salih, Ahmad, 39
Salman ibn Abdulaziz Al Saud (Prince/King): and archive wars, 108–9, 116–17, 124–25; becoming king (2015), xvii; centralizing of archives, 94, 125–26, 229; as chairman of national library, 83–84, 86; claiming Al Saud's inheritance of the land, 142; in comparison to Abdullah, 129; as defense minister, 71; and Darah, 2, 6, 21, 93–94, 117, 125, 285n52, 286n65; favoring secularism, 19, 92, 205; as "gatekeeper of Al Saud's history," 20, 205; as governor of Riyadh, 19, 71, 92–93, 140–41, 143, 168–69; heritage industry, 205; housing documents at KFNL, Darah, 60–61, 113; KFNL, 60–61, 84, 86; as "leader of historians," 94; and Mecca, 169; and National Museum, 151; opposing women's movement, 19; overturning censorship of King Saud history, 103–4, 153; politics of urban planning, 146, 161–62; post–Gulf War redevelopment, 93, 168–69; private-public projects under, 219; and Salman's centralization of power, 161–62; statement on Darah, 103; and strategic plan for Riyadh, 127, 133; undermined by Abdullah, 122. *See also* HCDA
Salwa Palace, 159–61, *160*
al-Saniʻ, Sulayman ibn Abdulrahman, 84
al-Sasi, Abdulsalam ibn Tahir, 39
al-Sasi, Al-Tayyib Tahir, 40
Al Saud (House of Saud), 125, 138; Aramco narrative of, 9–10; archive battles by, 96, 106; armed struggle against (1913–24), 9–10, 43; and Bin-ladin, 170–71, 175; British, US covert support for, 123, 278n62; challenges to historical view of, 12–13; claiming

modernity, 11; conquest of cities, capitals (1902–1934), *48*; consolidation, socialization under, 50–52; controlling government ministries, 71–72; controlling official history, sites, 24–25, 29, 34–35, 60–62, 106, 118, 142, 179; Darah promoting history of, 74, 118; Dir'iyya history and redevelopment, 130, 133–35; elite support for, 25; erasing pre-Al Saud history, 21, 34, 51–52, 58, 62, 66–68, 74; Grand Mosque and Eastern Province protests against (1979), 13–14; and Gulf War (1991), 92–93, 95, 130, 132, 145, 163; as having "no history," xiii–xv; heritage project, 19–24, 95–96; and Hijaz, 43–45, 50, 189; hiring of foreigners, 35; and Ikhwan, 47; Islam as threat to, 95; labeling Ottomans polytheists, 46; Mecca, Medina occupation by (1803), 46; Mecca as threat to, 197–98, 207; MEDSTAR project legitimating, 128, 130; memorialized in urban planning, 128; and monumentalization, 197, xv; *mutawwa'a*, 47–48; Nasser public opposition to, 56, 65–67; patrilineal genealogy of, 19; prisoners forced to praise, xiv; promoting modernization, secularization, 20, 74, 122, 129, 136, 167; and Red Palace issues, 130, 146, 152–53; rehabilitating historical sites, 2–3; reliance on Aramco, 53, 55–56, 58; religious nationalism of, 52; rivalries within, 143; Sahwa religious objections to, 16–17, 149, 151; Salman on, 20, 142; secularization by, 20, 132, 142, 162, 207, 212; self-declared anti-imperial saviors, 62; shifting treatment of religion, 9–10, 132; ties with United States, 16, 58–59, 61–62; Turki ibn Abdullah ibn Muhammad, 147; unflattering "state secrets" suppressed, 123–24. *See also* Abdulaziz ibn Saud; Faisal ibn Abdulaziz Al Saud; King Abdulaziz Historical Center; Mecca; Riyadh; Salman Ibn Abdulaziz Al Saud.

Saudi Arabia, Kingdom of, 47; accusations of backwardness of, 121; border disputes, 62; British imperial support for, 169; combining nation and capital, 27; as country without history, 7–9, 62, 282n26, xiii; diffused power within, 6, 62; discovery of oil in, 52; first decade of, 52; foundation myth, 57–58, 62; founding of (1932), 49, 134–35; landscape as revenue-generator, 207; legitimacy disputes, 62; Manuscripts Law, 117; map, xxviii; merger of private and public sectors, 184; no freedom of speech in, 198; outside views of, 7–8; reliance on United States, 15, 34, 170; Al-Saud narrative of, 19, 62; self-declared "custodians" of holy mosques, 62; "severe memory loss" in, 120; sons of Abdulaziz running ministries, 71–72; state-sponsored narrative of, 8–9, 95, 165; still no national archive, 62–65; strength and weakness of, 28; as "swing producer," 7

Saudi Arabian national day, xii
Saudi Arabian Oil Company. *See* Aramco
Saudi Binladin Group (SBG): awareness of "red lines," 174–75; blamed for Mecca destruction, 205; crane collapse with fatalities, 216–17; dynamiting Ajyad fortress near Grand Mosque, 167, *183*, 184–87, 200; as Muhammad Binladin Organization (MBO), 171, 175, 177; ordered closed, 217, 227; overseeing Mecca redevelopment, 3, 169, 171, 176, 179–81, 192, 201–2, 207, 290n13; overwhelming critics, 199; paying construction costs, 181; petrochemical investments by, 305n15; Prince Muhammad ibn Salman appropriation of contracts, 205; priority in contract bidding, 25; private contacts with kings Fahd, Abdullah, 195; revenues from pilgrimage, 181; in western Saudi Arabia, 140
Saud ibn Abdulaziz Al Saud (King Saud): commissioning concrete palace, 135; as crown prince (1933), 51; and Darah, 287n68; and demolition of Riyadh palace, 148; Fahda's push to rehabilitate image of, 104–6; family "hijacking history," 104; in historical narrative, 287n68; modernization under, 69; moving administrative seat to Riyadh (1956), 69, 295n43; and Muhammad Binladin, 171; and National Museum, 149, 151; overthrown by Faisal (1964), 10–12, 55–56, 65–67, 80; relative press freedom under, 67; Salman and, 103; son of Abdulaziz ibn Saud, 10; sons running ministries, 71–72; US supporting Faisal over, 55–56
Saudi Commission for Tourism and Antiquities (SCTA), 25, 131, 201, 248n100, 293n32
Saudi Commission for Tourism and National Heritage (SCTH), 145, 248n100
Saudi Oger, 25
Saudi Scientific Institute (al-Maʿhad al-ʿIlmi al-Saʿudi), 189
Saudi-Wahhabi alliance, 133–34
al-Sawlatiyya School, 32, 36–39, 189
Sawt al-Arab radio, 66, 273n16
Sawt al-Hijaz newspaper, 39, 43, 256n41, 261n81
SBG. See Saudi Binladin Group
SCET International, 141, 146
school curricula: al-Kairanawi book in, 57; al Saud narrative in, 62; at al-Sawlatiyya, 37–38; colonial attempts to control, 253n12; early 1900s, 42; unification of under Faisal, 11; Wahhabi religious control over, 2, 9, 198
Scott, David, 6, 59
secularization: by Abdullah, 122, 129, 212–13; by Al Saud, 20, 95, 132, 142, 162–63, 207, 212; and archive wars, 213; and Darah, 107, 118; and destruction of Mecca's past, 168, 174, 180, 195, 204; and historical time, progress, 20; by King Fahd, 95; and liberal notions of progress, 9; and

Mecca, 69; opposition to, 10, 21, 72, 97, 211; replacing political religion, 19–20, 95; and Riyadh, 92, 107, 145, 165, 168; Salman and, 213–14, 229; al-Sawlatiyya school, 37; secular left in Saudi Arabia, 65

al-Semmari, Fahd: accused of pandering, 118; and archive wars, 226; on archiving industry, 106, 281n12; on Darah's goals and successes, 101–2, 110, 286n62; fears of sabotage, 22, 131; heading National Center for Archives and Records, 125; on oral history interviews, 286n62; Salman and, 213, 226–27

Al-Senai', Sulaiman, 117

September 11, 2001 attacks, xi, 27, 122, 208–9, 230

al-Sh'aifan, Tariq, 108

Al Shamiyya Development Project, 184, 189, 191–92

Shams al-Haqiqa newspaper, 40

shaykh al-Islam, grand mufti, 10, 18, 36, 118, 188, 242n53, 244n69

Al-Shaykh, Muhammad ibn Abdulaziz, 123, 290n15

Al-Shaykh, Turki, 162

Shehata, Hamzah, 39

Sheikh Mohammad bin Abdulwahhab Cultural Foundation, 161

Shuaibi, Ali, 99, 147

Shura Council, 17, 115

Siraj, Abdullah ibn Abd al-Rahman (Shaykh), 37, 39

socialism, 38, 67

space: as battlegrounds, 20, 133, 163; commemoration/monumentalization of, 131; dehistoricizing, 181–90; politics of, 77–80, 87, 129; for prayer, 194–95

Standard Oil Company of California (SOCAL), 267n127

state: archiving as essential to formation of, 64; corporatizing of, 27; modern system of, 47, 165; records as forms of capital, 72–73; *versus* "regime," 28; Saudi concepts of, 8, 58, 102, 165, 263–64nn100; urban planning as formation of, 5; as work in progress, 28

Steinberg, Guido, 258n59, 260n71

al-Sudais, Abdulrahman, 228

Suez Canal, 31, 61

al-Suleiman, Abdullah, 68

Sultan ibn Salman ibn Abdulaziz Al Saud, 131, 145, 156, 201, 205

Sultan ibn Abdulaziz Al Saud, 210; on archiving of records, 76; as Defense Minister, 15, 71; disagreements with Abdullah, 18, 129; and historical memorialization, 131, xi–xii

Supreme Commission for Tourism (SCT), 22–23, 145, 156–57, 293n32

Surur ibn Msa'id, 186

Syria, 40–41, 62

Talal ibn Abdulaziz Al Saud, 55

Tanzimat reforms, 31, 253n9

al-Tariqi, Abdullah (minister of oil), 56, 230, 267n128

tashbik (land grabbing), 139

378 INDEX

Ten-Point Program, 104–5, 284n41
Texaco, 267n127
textbooks: history textbooks as institutional struggle, 11, 86, 108; Palestine in, 244–45n74; portrayal of Ottomans, Al Saud in, 50, 62; Prince Sultan statement on, xi; recent alterations to, 9, xi–xii
Thunayyan, Abdulaziz ibn Salman ibn, 146
al-Trabulsi, Abdulkarim (Shaykh), 37
Transjordan, 48, 264n106
Trouillot, Michel-Rolph, 129
al-Turaif District (Dir'iyya), 155–61, *160*, 227
Turki al-Faisal ibn Abdulaziz Al Saud, 105, 286–87n68
Turki ibn Abdullah ibn Muhammad (r. 1823–1834), 147

Umrah tourist visas, 190
UNESCO World Heritage Sites, 157–58, 161
United States: arms sales to Saudi Arabia, 15–16; attacks on troops in Saudi Arabia, 19–20; eminent domain case law, 144; Harland Bartholomew and Associates, 127, 289n2; presence during Gulf War, 15–16; protecting ruling family, 59; pushing petrodollar recycling, 15; redevelopment proposal for Dir'iyya, 156; and Saudi oil economy, 80; World War II alliance with Saudi Arabia, 53–54
al-'Utaybi, Juhayman, 242n53

vernacular architecture, 144, 147
Vision 2030, 125, 162, 206, 218, 220, 226–29
Vitalis, Robert, 79

Wahba, Hafiz, 260n73
Wahhabi/Al Saud alliance, 45–46; as divine mandate, 8, 9; and formation of Saudi Arabia, 2, 10–11, 123; Ikhwan influence on, 47–49; occupying Mecca, Medina, 46, 133–34; recent deemphasis of Wahhabism, 19–20, 95, 132; Wahhabi alliance with (1744), 2, 234n4, 247n90; and Wahhabism, 95–96, 128
Wahhabism: attacks on shrines, 49, 180, 186; as convenient for Mecca developers, 197; disciplinary historiography of, 9–11; divine mandate of, 8–9; Faisal and, 10–11; forbidding intermediation (*tawassul*), 45; Ikhwan influence on, 48–49; monumentalization forbidden by, 168, 180–81, 186, 241; Nahda influence on, 45; obedience to rulers as to God, 11; as political, 198; politics and profit, 197; regarding US troops on Saudi soil, 17; religious awakening of, 50, 62, 132; Riyadh as birthplace of, 69; in Saudi Arabia, 49–51, 198; secular nationalism sidelining, 19; and Sunni Islam, 14; and takeover of Grand Mosque, 13–14; Unitarianism, 10, 45. *See also* Ibn Abd al-Wahhab, Muhammad
al-Wajh fortress (Qal'at al-Wajh), 61, 84

Wallerstein, Immanuel, 194
war on terror, xi
Wilder, Gary, 35
Willis, John, 254n22
women: 'Awwad promoting advancement of, 44; Hijazis and rights of, 44; lacking access to archives, 87; Salman opposing 1990s movement, 19
World Heritage Sites, 145, 157–58, 161, 247n95
World War II, 52–53

Yamani, Ahmad Zaki, 180, 192
Yanbu', 84
Yemen: loss of pro-Saudi president in, 209; Muhammad ibn Salman and, 224; Saudi border disputes with, 274n26; Saudi-Emirati War, 186, 215; Saudi source documents on, 96; Yemen revolution and proxy war (1962–1970), 56, 65, 71–72, 171, 221

al-Zirikli, Khayr al-Din, 40

Stanford Studies in Middle Eastern
and Islamic Societies and Cultures

>Joel Beinin and Laleh Khalili, editors

>EDITORIAL BOARD
>Asef Bayat, Marilyn Booth, Laurie Brand, Timothy Mitchell,
>Jillian Schwedler, Rebecca L. Stein, Max Weiss

Graveyard of Clerics: Everyday Activism in Saudi Arabia   2020
   PASCAL MENORET

Cleft Capitalism: The Social Origins of Failed Market Making in Egypt   2020
   AMR ADLY

The Universal Enemy: Jihad, Empire, and the Challenge of Solidarity   2019
   DARRYL LI

Waste Siege: The Life of Infrastructure in Palestine   2019
   SOPHIA STAMATOPOULOU-ROBBINS

Heritage and the Cultural Struggle for Palestine   2019
   CHIARA DE CESARI

Iran Reframed: Anxieties of Power in the Islamic Republic   2019
   NARGES BAJOGHLI

Banking on the State: The Financial Foundations of Lebanon   2019
   HICHAM SAFIEDDINE

Familiar Futures: Time, Selfhood, and Sovereignty in Iraq   2019
   SARA PURSLEY

Hamas Contained: The Rise and Pacification of Palestinian Resistance   2018
TAREQ BACONI

Hotels and Highways: The Construction of Modernization Theory in Cold War Turkey   2018
BEGÜM ADALET

Bureaucratic Intimacies: Translating Human Rights in Turkey   2017
ELIF M. BABÜL

Impossible Exodus: Iraqi Jews in Israel   2017
ORIT BASHKIN

Brothers Apart: Palestinian Citizens of Israel and the Arab World   2017
MAHA NASSAR

Revolution without Revolutionaries: Making Sense of the Arab Spring   2017
ASEF BAYAT

Soundtrack of the Revolution: The Politics of Music in Iran   2017
NAHID SIAMDOUST

Copts and the Security State: Violence, Coercion, and Sectarianism in Contemporary Egypt   2016
LAURE GUIRGUIS

Circuits of Faith: Migration, Education, and the Wahhabi Mission   2016
MICHAEL FARQUHAR

Morbid Symptoms: Relapse in the Arab Uprising   2016
GILBERT ACHCAR

Imaginative Geographies of Algerian Violence: Conflict Science, Conflict Management, Antipolitics   2015
JACOB MUNDY

Police Encounters: Security and Surveillance in Gaza under Egyptian Rule   2015
ILANA FELDMAN

Palestinian Commemoration in Israel: Calendars, Monuments, and Martyrs   2015
TAMIR SOREK

The authorized representative in the EU for product safety and compliance is:
Mare Nostrum Group
B.V Doelen 72
4831 GR Breda
The Netherlands

www.ingramcontent.com/pod-product-compliance
Lightning Source LLC
Chambersburg PA
CBHW031844220426
43663CB00006B/493